The Meadows of Gold

The Meadows of Gold

The Abbasids

by

Mas'udi

Translated and Edited by
Paul Lunde and Caroline Stone

LONDON AND NEW YORK

First published in 1989 by
Kegan Paul International

This edition first published in 2010 by
Routledge
2 Park Square, Milton Park, Abingdon, Oxfordshire OX14 4RN

Simultaneously published in the USA and Canada
by Routledge
711 Third Avenue, New York, NY 10017, USA

First issued in paperback 2015

Routledge is an imprint of the Taylor & Francis Group, an informa business

© 1979 and 1986 by Besin Selim Hakim

All rights reserved. No part of this book may be reprinted or reproduced or utilised in any form or by any electronic, mechanical, or other means, now known or hereafter invented, including photocopying and recording, or in any information storage or retrieval system, without permission in writing from the publishers.

British Library Cataloguing in Publication Data
A catalogue record for this book is available from the British Library

ISBN 13: 978-1-138-98061-7 (pbk)
ISBN 13: 978-0-7103-0246-5 (hbk)

Publisher's Note
The publisher has gone to great lengths to ensure the quality of this reprint but points out that some imperfections in the original copies may be apparent. The publisher has made every effort to contact original copyright holders and would welcome correspondence from those they have been unable to trace.

CONTENTS

Introduction	11
Abu Ja'far Mansur	21
A Conversation with the King of Nubia	24
Loyalty to Hisham	26
In the Audience Hall	28
The Death of Mansur	32
The Character of Mansur	33
The Caliphate of Mahdi	34
Mahdi and the Qadi	35
Mahdi and the Peasant	36
Mahdi and the Bedouin	37
Mahdi and the Treasurer	39
The Wheel of Fortune	40
Unrequited Love	43
An Amusing Story about the King of Hira	46
The Last Days of Mahdi	49
The Character of Hadi	51
Isa ibn Da'b	53
Revenge	54
The Death of the Great-great-great Grandson of the Prophet	55
The Fall of Khaizuran	57
Blood Feuds	58
The Climate of Egypt	59
Basra versus Kufa	61
Harun al-Rashid and the Death of Hadi	62
The Dream of Mahdi	64
The Sword Samsama	66
The Accession of Harun al-Rashid	67
Sheep's Head	68
A Qadi's Interpretation	70
The Last Pilgrimage of Harun al-Rashid	71
Doctor Jabra'il and a Fish	72
The Dream of Harun al-Rashid	74
A Black and a Song	76

The Meadows of Gold

Poem on a Dove	78
Ma'n ibn Za'ida	79
Amin and Ma'mun as Children	80
The Education of Amin	82
Amin and Ma'mun	83
The Succession	84
Zubaida's Opinion	86
Rashid's Pilgrimage with his Sons	87
The Devil's Song	89
A Hard-Won Song	91
Horse-Racing at Raqqa	94
Fish Tongues	95
The Name Ibrahim	96
Bamboo and Reed	97
The Death of Harun al-Rashid	98
Khalid ibn Barmak and His Sons	101
The Barmakids	102
The Advice of Yahya	103
Harun al-Rashid and the Singing Girl	105
The Avarice of Asma'i	107
A Poet on Rashid and Ja'far ibn Yahya	108
On Love	109
The Fall of the Barmakids	115
The Murder of Ja'far al-Barmaki	118
Elegies on the Barmakids	121
The Mother of Ja'far	126
The Wealth of the Barmakids	127
Fadl in Prison	128
Miscellaneous on Rashid and the Barmakids	131
The Caliphate of Amin	132
The Dreams of Zubaida	133
Trouble Between Amin and Ma'mun	135
The Jealousy of Zubaida	137
Ill-Omens for Amin	138
Amin's Beloved	140
The Frivolity of Amin	141
Amin and the Lion	142
The Birth of Musa al-Hadi	143
Miscellaneous Anecdotes	144
The Palace of Manbij	145
Musa Declared Heir Apparent	146
Rebellion	147
Amin in Retreat	149
Baghdad Besieged	151

Contents

The Naked Army	154
Baghdad in Flames	156
Resistance	160
Famine	162
Amin at Bay	163
The Death of Amin	168
An Eye-Witness Account	170
Amin's Head	172
The Laments of the Women	173
The Caliphate of Ma'mun	175
Sayings of Ma'mun	176
Ma'mun's Wedding Speech	177
Ma'mun and the Sponger	178
The Caliph and the Poet	185
Kulthum al-Attabi	187
Professionally Unlucky	189
Abu al-Atahiya	190
The Caliph's Cooking	191
Ma'mun Embarrassed	193
Ma'mun Justifies Himself to the Sufis	195
The Death of Shafi'i	198
Ma'mun and the False Prophets	200
The Rise and Death of Imam Rida	202
The Capture of Ibrahim ibn al-Mahdi	204
The Marriage of Buran	205
An Adventure of Ibrahim ibn al-Mahdi	207
The Poverty of Waqidi	210
Mansur and the Cadger	212
The Death of Ibn A'isha	214
The Death of Abu al-Atahiya	216
Ma'mun's Campaigns against the Byzantines and His Death	218
The Caliphate of Mu'tasim	222
Mu'tasim on Agriculture	223
Mu'tasim and His Doctor	224
The Kind Heart of Mu'tasim	226
The New Capital of Samarra	228
Mu'tasim	231
The Caliphate of Wathiq	232
Wathiq Discusses Medicine	233
An Aphorism on the Death of Alexander	236
The Caliphate of Mutawakkil	238
Mutawakkil	239
Mutawakkil's Palace of the Two Wings	240
A Donkey in Love	241

vii

The Meadows of Gold

A Vigorous Old Scholar	242
Saved from Rape	243
At the Caliph's Table	245
The Sailor's Stew	248
Love's Despair – Jahiz	249
The Slapping of a Secretary	253
The Death of Ahmad ibn Hanbal	254
The Testing of an Assassin	255
The Indian Sword	258
The Assassination of Mutawakkil	260
Court Factions	261
Mutawakkil's Last Day	262
The Reign of Mutawakkil	263
Mahbuba	264
The Caliphate of Muntasir	267
The Carpet of Annihilation	268
Vicious Viziers	270
On the Death of Muntasir	271
The Generosity of Muntasir	273
An Old Love Regained	275
Love at First Sight	277
Meccan Morals	279
The Caliphate of Musta'in	281
The Aftermath	282
Things That Give Pleasure	283
Afra and Urwa	285
Bugha the Elder	288
Mu'tazz Acclaimed Caliph	290
The Assassination of Musta'in	293
The Caliphate of Mu'tazz	294
A Remarkable Ring	295
The Death of Muhammad, the Grandson of Tahir	296
The Imprisonment of Mu'ayyad	297
The Murder of Bugha the Younger	298
The Caliphate of Muhtadi	299
The Death of Mu'tazz	300
The Death of Muhtadi	301
The Adventure of a Gate-crasher	303
The Austerity of Muhtadi	306
A Tradition Concerning Ali	308
The Death of Jahiz	309
The Caliphate of Mu'tamid	312
The Discipline of Saffar's Army	313
The Horrors of the Zanj Rebellion	317

Contents

Wily Muslims Admired by the Byzantines	319
Muʻawiya Takes Revenge on a Byzantine	320
The Night Conversations of Muʻtamid	325
Muʻtamid Dies by Poison	327
The Caliphate of Muʻtadid	329
The Splendid Dowry of Qatr al-Nada	331
The Wit of Abu al-Ayna	332
An Idol Comes to Baghdad	335
A Delegation from Basra	337
The Clucking of a Grammarian	339
Umm Sharif, the Aunt of the Rebel	341
On Eunuchs	345
The Funeral of Khumarawaih	347
Muʻtadid Takes a Thief	348
The Mimic and the Eunuch	352
A Master Thief	355
Alchemical Texts	358
Muʻtadid's Ghosts	360
The Death of Ibrahim al-Harbi the Jurist	361
Two Students Enamoured	362
The Qadi Ibn Jabir	364
The Eunuch Wasif	365
Why Muʻtadid Preferred the Alids	366
The Death of Muʻtadid	367
The Caliphate of Muktafi	368
Qasim's Hatred of Badr	370
The Ransoming of Treachery	373
The Avarice of Muktafi	374
Nougat and Fritters	375
Dushab and Harisa	378
The Death of Muktafi	380
The Caliphate of Muqtadir	381
Hospitality	382
The Death of Muqtadir	384
Cyprus Seized	385
The Caliphate of Qahir	386
Qahir Demands a True History	387
The Caliphate of Radi	393
The Caliph Radi's Accomplishments	394
Chess and Backgammon	395
The Qualities of a General	399
The Breeches of the Tallest Man	401
The Marvels of Creation	403
Arabic Words for Lavatory	405

The Meadows of Gold

Black and Green	408
The Garden of Qahir	409
The Generosity of Radi	411
Bajkam the Turk Coins His Own Money	412
The Caliphate of Muttaqi	414
The Blinding of Muttaqi	415
Summing Up	416
The Caliphate of Mustakfi	417
The Unwanted Page Boy	419
The Battle of the Flowers	421
The Buwaihids Come to Power	423
The Caliphate of Muti'	424
The Rising of Utrush	425
Mas'udi's Address to the Reader	426
Mas'udi's Final Words	428
Glossary	431
Bibliography	437
Notes	439
Index	451

INTRODUCTION

Mas'udi was born in Baghdad about 896 AD, during the Caliphate of Mu'tadid and died in Egypt some time around the year 956, eleven years after the Buwaihids, a Shi'a dynasty of Iranian origin, had occupied Baghdad and taken control of the Caliphate. His full name was Abu al-Hasan Ali ibn al-Husain ibn Ali ibn Abd Allah al-Mas'udi, which we have simplified to Mas'udi.

Almost everything known about this most readable of Muslim historians is gleaned from the pages of his two extant works, *The Meadows of Gold* (*Muruj al-Dhahab*) and the *Book of Notification* (*Kitab al-Tanbih*). Later entries in the Arabic biographical dictionaries are meagre, and add almost nothing to what Mas'udi himself tells us.

Aside from mentioning that he was born in Baghdad and therefore peculiarly fitted to write the history of the Abbasid dynasty, Mas'udi scarcely refers to his early life and education. We know more about his travels, which were extensive.

When he was nineteen, Mas'udi travelled widely in Persia, visiting the Zoroastrian fire temples of Nishapur and Istakhr and examining Pahlavi books still in possession of the Zoroastrian community. He went on to India, via Sind, getting as far as the Western Deccan and making first-hand observations of flora, fauna and religious beliefs and ceremonies – this last a subject that interested him very much. He returned to Iraq by sea in 917, after an absence of two years, stopping in Yemen and Oman on the way. During this first long trip out of his native land, Mas'udi met Abu Zaid al-Sirafi, a learned merchant from Siraf on the coast of the Persian Gulf, who gave him a long and interesting account of China and the way thither which he incorporated in his *Meadows of Gold*. The year of his return to Iraq was at least partly spent in Basra studying under Abu Khalifa al-Jumahi, a noted philologist of the day, whose name occurs occasionally in the pages that follow.

In 921 Mas'udi went to Syria, visiting the frontier towns between Islam and Byzantium. He talked to soldiers, merchants, priests and government officials. He met Leo of Tripoli, a Byzantine admiral who had converted to Islam, who was able to tell him a good deal about naval warfare, and Abu Umair, from Adana, who had taken part in a number of diplomatic missions to Constantinople. Much of the information about Byzantium in the *Meadows of Gold* was gathered

The Meadows of Gold

during this trip. Mas'udi's interest in Islam's hereditary enemy was unusual; he is one of the few Muslim historians, whose work has survived, who deals with Byzantium in any detail.

Five years later, in 926, Mas'udi was in Palestine, spending some time in Tiberias in the company of the Jewish scholar Abu Kathir Yahya ibn Zakariya, an authority on the Torah which he was at the time engaged in translating. (Abu Kathir was not the only Jewish scholar consulted by Mas'udi; later in Egypt he befriended the famous Sa'adia Gaon.) In Palestine Mas'udi visited Jerusalem and Nazareth, examining the Church of the Holy Sepulchre in the first and the house where Christ was born in the second. He also went out of his way to collect information about the Samaritans, whose scripture and beliefs he describes.

The next year found Mas'udi in Damascus, examining Hellenistic and early Islamic monuments, then in Palmyra, whose ruins he describes. He talked with members of the Jewish community of Raqqa; and in Harran, two day's march from Raqqa, in what is now Turkey, he was able to interview the elders of a community of pagan star-worshippers, the Sabians, still surviving in a sea of monotheism. This ancient town, said to be the birthplace of Abraham, still maintained a tradition of Greek scholarship and supplied Baghdad with a number of translators of Greek scientific works during the reign of Ma'mun. It is said that the last teachers from the medical school at Alexandria were transferred there by the Umayyad Caliph Umar II.

Mas'udi returned to Baghdad by sailing down the Euphrates, and was present at the siege of Hit by the Qarmatians. He profited from the ocasion by gathering information about this militant equalitarian sect from the lips of its leaders.

Sometime in the 930s, Mas'udi travelled in the Caspian area, collecting information about the Caucasus and the peoples who lived beyond them – Khazars, Slavs and Bulgars. He made a number of original observations in these regions and was able to correct certain false geographical notions inherited from antiquity.

The last years of his life were spent in Egypt, with occasional visits to Syria. This exile – perhaps self-imposed – may have been the result of the political upheavals in Iraq that accompanied the coming to power of the Buwaihids. The first certain year of his stay in Egypt is 942. In 944 he visited Antioch in Syria and once again went to towns along the frontier with Byzantium, talking with men who had fought on both sides. Information gathered on this trip appears in the *Meadows of Gold*, the first version of which was completed shortly after his return to Egypt.

At the very beginning of the *Meadows of Gold*, Mas'udi makes the point that a man who stays at home and relies on information that happens to come his way cannot pretend to the same authority as the man who has travelled widely and seen things with his own eyes. Unlike most of his contemporaries, Mas'udi tried to visit the places and countries about which he wrote, and this points to the most original feature of the *Meadows of Gold* – the placing of historical events in a geographical context. This is most noticeable in the early chapters of the book,

Introduction

which contain long excursuses on the geographical features of the known world, both within and without the borders of Islam.

This interest in the non-Islamic world is another characteristic that distinguishes Mas'udi from other Muslim historians. One of the major motives of his travels seems to have been to gather as much information as possible about the peoples who lived beyond the borders of Islam, in particular about their religious beliefs, which he recounts with a notable lack of distortion. He was curious, for example, about the history of the Franks, only vaguely known to his contemporaries, and he gives a list of their kings from Clovis to Louis IV, based on a Latin king-list drawn up by a bishop in Andalusia. He found a copy in Egypt in 947.

At the other end of the world, he gives a list of Chinese emperors and describes the Huang Ch'ao rebellion that brought down the T'ang dynasty. Here he is speaking not from first-hand knowledge, but from interviews with travellers, merchants and some written sources. Nevertheless, he was the first Muslim historian to treat the history of China at any length and it was not until the time of Rashid al-Din in the thirteenth century that another historian took up the subject.

His account of India is based on his own observations, however, and is precious for being written just before Mahmud of Ghazna's destructive invasion.

It is maddening not to know more about Mas'udi's background and motives. There is no evidence that he ever occupied a government post, either under the Abbasids in Baghdad or the Ikhshidids in Egypt. Although it is obvious, especially in the early portions of the *Meadows of Gold*, that Mas'udi was a Twelver Shi'a, there is no evidence that his travels had anything to do with spreading the tenets of that sect, as has been suggested. There seems to be no valid reason for supposing that he travelled for any other reason than to satisfy his curiosity and to collect first-hand information for his books. How he financed his travels is a mystery; perhaps, like other travellers of the time, by trading.

Besides the *Meadows of Gold* and the *Tanbih*, Mas'udi wrote some thirty-four works of varying length on a wide variety of subjects – jurisprudence, comparative religion, polemics, philosophy, political theory, astronomy, medicine and history. This range of interests was not untypical of the time; Mas'udi's contemporary, al-Farabi, wrote more than one hundred works on just as bewildering a number of subjects. All but the *Meadows of Gold* and the *Tanbih* have perished. The most regrettable losses are two of his previous historical works, the *Historical Annals* (*Akhbar al-Zaman*) and the *Intermediate History* (*Kitab al-Awsat*). Both are frequently referred to in the pages of the *Meadows of Gold*, often with the intention of titillating the reader's interest so that he will rush out and buy them.

The *Historical Annals* was Mas'udi's longest work, which may explain why it has not survived. It dealt with history and geography. From the many references to it in the *Meadows of Gold*, we know that it was divided into thirty chapters, many of them dealing with non-Islamic peoples. It contained detailed descriptions of peoples and places that in the *Meadows of Gold* are mentioned only in passing.

The Meadows of Gold

The *Intermediate History* was shorter than the *Historical Annals* but longer than the *Meadows of Gold*. It contained material not found in either.

The *Tanbih* (*Book of Notification*) is different again. It is a concise historical handbook about a fifth of the length of the *Meadows of Gold* and carefully organized. Digressions are kept to a minimum and although the result is drier the material is presented more fully and logically in many cases – for example in the treatment of the Byzantines – than in the *Meadows of Gold*. The *Tanbih* contains information not found in Mas'udi's previous works and corrects previous errors, showing that Mas'udi was continually revising.

This constant revision of his previous works is relevant to the *Meadows of Gold*. All the surviving manuscripts of the text are of a first, unrevised version completed in 947, nine years before the completion of the final version of the *Tanbih*, which also went through a number of revisions. We know from the *Tanbih* that Mas'udi subsequently revised this first version of the *Meadows of Gold*, added much new material and increased the number of chapters from 132 to 365. This final revised version has not survived. Readers must bear in mind that the book before them is a draft, and that many of its faults in organization were probably corrected in the final edition.

At the beginning of the *Meadows of Gold* Mas'udi gives a list of eighty-five books which he consulted. The list is only partial, for in the course of the book he directly or indirectly refers to many more. He lived at a time when books were readily available and relatively cheap. Aside from large public libraries in major towns like Baghdad, many individuals, like Mas'udi's friend al-Suli, had private libraries, often containing thousands of volumes. The prevalence of books and their low price was the result of the introduction of paper to the Islamic world by Chinese papermakers captured at the Battle of Talas in 751. Very soon afterwards there were papermills in most large towns and cities. The introduction of paper coincided with the coming to power of the Abbasid dynasty, and there is no doubt that the availability of cheap writing material contributed to the growth of the Abbasid bureaucracy, postal system and lively intellectual life. Mas'udi's constant exhortations to his readers to consult his other works presumes a world where these were available, in libraries if not in bookshops. Ibn al-Nadim, who wrote an annotated bibliography of all the books that passed through his hands, which he 'published' in 987, lists thousands of titles. Amusingly, all the information he supplies about Mas'udi and his works is wrong.

One has only to think of a European contemporary of Mas'udi – say the compiler of the *Anglo-Saxon Chronicle* – to guage the immense advantages the Muslim historian enjoyed. Not only did he have access to books by previous writers – even Greek and Persian in translation – but he was able to travel freely and even at times gain access to official archives. It was not until the Renaissance that European historians were able to work under the sort of conditions Mas'udi took for granted.

He also had the advantage of working within a recognized tradition that already enjoyed a wide audience. The sophisticated reading public of Baghdad

Introduction

and Cairo could appreciate Mas'udi's lively blend of dynastic history, anecdote, and general encyclopedia. Although the Golden Age of Abbasid literature was over, the spirit of Jahiz and the scholars associated with the translation of Greek science into Arabic lives on in Mas'udi. He is intellectually part of that world; the pages of the *Meadows of Gold* are pervaded with the tolerance, humour and intellectual curiosity of early Abbasid times. At the same time, in this volume, Mas'udi chronicles the slow decline of the dynasty under which Baghdad had become the intellectual capital of the world. The Caliphs become increasingly shadowy, pawns in the hand of ambitious viziers and the Turkish guard and finally, with the coming of the Buwaihids, they lose whatever fragments of personal power they had. It is a sad and moving tale, but the decline in the political power of the Abbasids did not as yet coincide with a decline in cultural life. It rather led to a shift away from Iraq towards Syria, Egypt, North Africa and Spain, where other dynasties attracted ambitious scholars and writers.

Historical writing among the Arabs had reached a high level in the generation just before Mas'udi's own. The traditional form of Arabic historical writing had grown out of a concern to record the sayings and doings of the Prophet and his companions. The technique employed was to transcribe, usually without comment, a number of varying traditions (*hadith*) about the same event, giving a careful list of the transmitters of the tradition as a guarantee of its accuracy: A told me that he heard from B that he heard from C that one day the Prophet, may blessings and peace be upon him, said . . . Criticism was confined to the names in the chain of authorities. Could B really have heard C recite this tradition? Was he old enough to remember it accurately? Was his memory good, bad or indifferent? The most famous exponent of this type of history is Tabari, who died in 923, when Mas'udi was twenty-seven years old. Tabari's history, published last century, fills fifteen large volumes and extends from the pre-Islamic period down to the year 910. Variant versions of the same event follow one another and allow the reader to form his own judgement, with little or no guidance from the author. It is in a sense a collection of source material, rather than a conventional history. Although a mine of information, the total effect is stupefying and Tabari can scarcely be read for pleasure.

Mas'udi expresses great admiration for Tabari and makes liberal use of his work, but chooses to follow the 'modernist' rather than the traditional school of historiography. Two men, both of whom died at just about the time Mas'udi was born, exemplify this school. They were Dinawari and Ya'qubi, both of whom, probably influenced by Persian models, chose but one version of an event from the often bewildering number of variants, arranged the events in chronological order and produced narrative histories. They made little attempt to stick to the original wording of the sources they used (the reproduction of the exact words of the *hadith* was of paramount importance for the traditionalists) and aimed at succinct readability. Dinawari's *Extended Histories* (*Akhbar al-Tiwal*), despite its title, fills only a single volume although it covers almost as long a period as Tabari. Dinawari's choice of what version of an event to follow is primarily literary rather than historical; he chooses the most dramatic or affecting. Like Mas'udi, he uses non-Islamic sources, in his case principally Persian, and is influenced by Greek ideas.

Ya'qubi, who died in 897 when Mas'udi was one year old, was a geographer as well as an historian and heavily indebted to Hellenistic thought, of which he provides a summary in the first volume of his two-volume history. But unlike Mas'udi, Ya'qubi made no effort to combine history and geography in a single work, but treated them separately. His history however is narrative, like that of Dinawari, and also includes the history of some non-Islamic peoples.

Mas'udi was more ambitious than his predecessors. He combines a number of previously independent genres of Arabic literature – chronicle, biography, geographical handbook, literary anthology, encyclopedia – into a single work. He is writing for the same audience addressed by Dinawari and Ya'qubi – the educated urban reading public – rather than the narrow audience of scholars addressed by Tabari. He had learned from Jahiz that this sort of reader quickly wearied of a dry recital of events, and so breaks up his narrative with all sorts of digressions, anecdotes, jokes and poems. Serious historians have often regarded these as intrusions in the text, and Charles Pellat, in his revision of Barbier de Meynard's nineteenth-century edition, goes so far in both the French and the Arabic editions as to set these 'digressions' apart from the purely historical narrative by printing them in a smaller typeface. But they are an integral part of the work. They almost always reveal something interesting about the people in the historical narrative – their character, taste, sense of humour or even the way they dressed. They give something of the social and material background against which these men and women lived their lives. The digressions form a kind of counterpoint to the main text. The cumulative effect is a clear and remarkably detailed picture of Abbasid court society, often illuminated by glimpses of the lives of ordinary people – the black cook with a passion for music who hides Ibrahim ibn al-Mahdi, the woodcutter whose donkey is helped out of a ditch by Mu'tasim. Without Mas'udi's digressions, how would we know that one of the amusements of Abbasid Caliphs was holding cooking contests?

These digressions should therefore not be looked upon as intrusions into the text but as an integral part of it; they are what give the book much of its flavour. They have also been chosen with considerable art. Mas'udi's gifts as a story-teller will be immediately apparent to the reader. The events that led the Abbasid dynasty to power and the feelings of the supporters of the old regime are brilliantly alluded to in the opening pages of the book, where Mansur himself recounts his meeting with the blind poet who had served the Umayyads. The misdeeds of the Umayyads, rather than being merely listed, are put in the mouth of the King of Nubia, reproaching a survivor of the dynasty. This technique is extremely effective and even when Mas'udi has lifted his anecdote from a predecessor he almost invariably improves it in the telling. Anyone familiar with the vast ocean of similar anecdotes in Arabic literature can only admire Mas'udi's sure eye for the dramatic and the effects he obtains by juxtaposition. He is

Introduction

particularly effective in his account of the civil war between Amin and Ma'mun, where the long confused series of *hadith* in Tabari are pruned to an unforgettably tragic tale, with the blind poet of Baghdad's comments on the action and how it affects ordinary people as fateful as anything in Greek tragedy.

Most Arabic historical writing is impersonal. It is impossible to get any sense of Tabari the man – aside from a sense of his enormous industry – from reading his history. Mas'udi's use of the first person is unusual and as one reads one gradually forms an idea of the sort of man he was – curious, warm-hearted, tolerant, vain, a man who disliked lawyers. He writes fluent, unmannered Arabic and uses a wide vocabulary. Although he was interested in the sciences of his day, he was no pedant. Much has been made of his credulity – he was criticized for this by no less than Ibn Khaldun. It is true that Mas'udi liked a tall tale but naive to suppose that he himself believed everything he related.

The Arabic text of Mas'udi's *Meadows of Gold* was first published in full, together with a French translation, by Barbier de Meynard and Pavet de Courteille. This edition was published in nine volumes by the Société Asiatique in Paris between 1861 and 1877. The French translation is printed below the Arabic on each page, which allows the reader to compare the translation with the original. This edition and its accompanying translation have been the standard text for almost a hundred years. In our translation, the Roman numeral at the bottom of the page stands for the volume number of this edition; the Arabic numeral for the page. Between 1966 and 1974 the French Arabist Charles Pellat revised the Arabic text of Barbier de Meynard's edition, in the light of the scholarship of the past hundred years, and this was published in Beirut by the Université Libanaise in five volumes. In this edition, the text is divided into 3,661 numbered paragraphs for ease of reference. These are the numbers following the paragraph sign (§) at the bottom of the pages. Thus readers who have one or the other edition can quickly find the Arabic original. It should be noted that both Barbier de Meynard's edition and the revision of it by Pellat are not easily found outside the major libraries. Beginning in 1967, Pellat began the publication of his revision of Barbier de Meynard's *French* translation. So far three volumes of this have appeared, published by the Société Asiatique, covering the period up to the end of the Umayyad dynasty. This, like his edition of the Arabic text, follows the division of the text into numbered paragraphs. It should be noted that Pellat's revision is not based on a fresh examination of the manuscripts, of which a large number survive. On the other hand, it seems that variants in these manuscripts are few.

Barbier de Meynard's translation is superb. The French is elegant, readable and generally accurate, given the state of Arabic studies at the time it was done. Pellat's corrections are overwhelmingly to personal and geographical names, which are often distorted or just plain wrong in Barbier de Meynard. In our translation we have followed Pellat's readings, so when the names in our text conflict with those in Barbier de Meynard, readers may assume that those in Barbier de Meynard are incorrect.

The Meadows of Gold

As a supplement to his edition of the Arabic text, Pellat also published two volumes of comprehensive indices. These contain a wealth of biographical and historical information, and in them even the minor figures in Mas'udi's text are identified and bibliographical references given. Unfortunately these two invaluable volumes exist so far only in Arabic.

The volume before the reader contains the history of the Abbasids, from Mansur, the second Abbasid Caliph, to Mut'i. It thus covers the classical period of the Islamic state, and many of the names will be familiar to readers of *The 1,001 Nights*. After much thought we decided to begin with the Abbasids, and to deal with the pre-Islamic period and the Umayyads in two subsequent volumes. This is not as eccentric as it sounds. Pellat has not yet published his revision of Barbier de Meynard's translation of this portion; only the revised Arabic text has yet appeared. We thought readers interested in the classical period of Islamic civilization who do not know Arabic should have this volume first, rather than continuing to rely on Barbier de Meynard's French translation which contains so many incorrect personal and place names. Unfortunately, it has not been possible to translate the entire text. Our selection represents about three-quarters the original. The reader may form some idea of the omitted portions from the summaries at the end of each chapter. The selection has been guided entirely by our own taste: we have translated the bits that interested us, although the choice was often difficult. The interminable quarrels of the Turkish guard have thus received rather short shrift; on the other hand we have tried to include something from each reign, although of course Mas'udi's treatment of the Caliphs ranges from almost a hundred pages down to only a few. We hope we have not distorted his intentions.

We have simplified the spelling of Arabic names in order not to disfigure the page with diacritical points. We have not been entirely consistent in this, however. The definite article *al-* has been omitted from the throne names of Caliphs (thus Mutawakkil, not al-Mutawakkil) and from some other names that occur frequently. Initial *hamza* and '*ain* have been omitted, although retained in the middle of a word, and '*ain* at the end (al-Rabi', not al-Rabi). We hope that those who know Arabic will forgive these liberties, and after their initial revulsion, find the loss of accuracy compensated by the gain in aesthetic pleasure.

We have taken another small liberty with the text. Where possible we have chosen a single version of a name and tried to stick to it, unless the point of a story or its effect turns on the use of a nickname. It is customary in Arabic to use a variety of names when addressing someone, depending on occasion, relative status and so on. People from Caliph to peasant are typically known as the father or mother of their eldest son, or sometimes their favourite child, but may also be called by a nickname, or by an adjective deriving from their place of origin – quite apart from their 'real' names. Thus the Caliph Mansur was called Abu Ja'far – Father of Ja'far – although his given name was Abd Allah. We have tried to spare the reader the exasperation that can result from suddenly realizing that when he thought he was reading about three different people he was in fact reading about one.

Introduction

When referring to himself in the *Meadows of Gold*, Mas'udi uses the editorial 'we'. This we have rendered as 'I' in almost all cases.

Although we have had to leave out some of Mas'udi's text we have only once, by omitting a description of a particularly disgusting torture, made any abridgements in the episodes we have chosen. We hope Mas'udi, who ritually curses any who curtail his text, would have forgiven us in return for reaching an audience he could never have imagined.

An asterisk (*) within the text refers to the editors' notes, pp. 439–50.

ABU JA'FAR MANSUR

Abu Ja'far Abd Allah ibn Muhammad ibn Ali ibn Abd Allah ibn al-Abbas ibn Abd al-Muttalib, known as Mansur, was proclaimed Caliph while he was on the way to Mecca. His uncle, Isa ibn Ali, received the oath of allegiance first in the name of Mansur and then in the name of Isa ibn Musa, who was to be his successor, on Sunday*, 12 Dhu al-Hijja, 136 AH/754 AD. Mansur was then forty-one years old, since he was born in the month of Dhu al-Hijja in 95 AH/713 AD. His mother was a Berber slave girl called Sallama. He died on Saturday, 6 Dhu al-Hijja, 158 AH/775 AD, having ruled twenty-two years less nine days. He was on the pilgrimage and had nearly reached Mecca, when death surprised him at a place called 'The Garden of the Bani Amir', on the high road to Iraq. He was then sixty-three years old. They buried him at Mecca, his face uncovered because he was wearing the *ihram*.

According to another version, however, he died at al-Batha', near the Well of Maimun, in which case he would have been buried at al-Hajun, in the sixty-fifth year of his age.

They say that his mother Sallama said:

'When I was pregnant with Mansur, I saw in my dreams a lion which emerged from my side and crouched, roaring, his tail beating the ground, while from all around lions appeared and, gathering about him, bowed their heads to the ground.'

According to Mada'ini, Mansur himself told the following story:

'On my way to Syria, I had as travelling companion a blind man* who was going to offer Marwan ibn Muhammad a poem he had composed in his honour. I expressed a wish to hear it, and he recited:

Would that I knew where the scent of musk had gone!
The happiness we knew at al-Khaif has vanished
Since the passing of the Banu Umayya
And the chiefs of the Abd Shams.
They preached from the *minbars* like champions,
Never were their voices stilled.
Their words were beyond criticism;
They went straight to the heart,

The Meadows of Gold

> Without ambiguity. They were full
> Of forbearance, and even when
> Restraint was despised, their
> Faces shone like freshly minted gold.

'This poet,' continued Mansur, 'had hardly finished when, by God, I felt as if someone had struck me. Nevertheless his conversation was pleasant and he was an experienced travelling companion.

'Later, in the year 141 AH/758 AD, I was performing the pilgrimage. In fulfilment of a vow, I had dismounted at al-Hamara, between the two hills of Zarud, and was walking on foot across the sands when once again I came across my blind man. I signed to my escort to stay behind, went up to him, took his hand and greeted him.

"Who are you?" he asked. "And may God take my life in place of yours! I am not quite sure I know you."

"It is I," I said, "your companion on the road to Syria in the days of the Umayyads, when you were on your way to Marwan."

'At once he greeted me and, sighing, recited the following lines:

> The women of the House of Umayya lament,
> For their daughters are orphaned.
> Their good fortune slept, their stars set,
> For fortune does sleep and stars do set.
> Their high *minbars* are vacant;
> May peace be upon them until I die.

"How much did Marwan give you?" I asked the poet.

"He made me rich. Having entreated him, I will never have to entreat another."

"But how much?" I insisted.

"Four thousand dinars, a gala robe and two riding camels."

"Where was this?" I asked.

"At Basra," he answered.

"Do you recognize me now?" I asked.

"As my travelling companion, yes, but by my life, I know nothing of your family."

"I am Abu Ja'far Mansur, the Commander of the Faithful."

"O Commander of the Faithful," he replied, trembling, "forgive me, for your cousin Muhammad, may the prayers and peace of God be upon him, has said: 'Hearts are steeped in love for those who do them good, in hate for those who bring them ill.'"

Abu Ja'far Mansur ended his story as follows:

'My first thought was to punish him and then I thought of the fact that he was sacrosanct because of his status as pilgrim and travelling companion. I ordered

Musayyab to free him and it was done. Later, in the evening, I wanted to enjoy his conversation and had him sought. But the desert had swallowed him up.'

A CONVERSATION WITH THE KING OF NUBIA

Fadl ibn al-Rabi' tells us:

At a gathering before Mansur, at which Isa ibn Ali, Isa ibn Musa ibn Muhammad ibn Ali, Salih ibn Ali, Qutham ibn al-Abbas, Muhammad ibn Ja'far and Muhammad ibn Ibrahim were present, the conversation turned to the Umayyad Caliphs, their conduct, the policies they followed and the reason their power was stripped from them. Mansur said:

'Abd al-Malik was an arrogant tyrant who did not care what he did. Sulaiman's only ambition lay in his belly and his balls. Umar ibn Abd al-Aziz was like a one-eyed man among the blind. The only great man of the dynasty was Hisham. As long as their standards remained high and their conduct not base, the Umayyads held the government which had been given to them with a firm hand, protecting, preserving and guarding the gift granted them by God. But then their power passed to their effeminate sons, whose only ambition was the satisfaction of their desires and who chased after pleasures forbidden by Almighty God. They knew not that God works slowly and believed themselves safe from His snares, although they had renounced their right to the Caliphate and had made light of God's truths and the duties of good government. Then God stripped them of their power, covered them with shame and deprived them of their worldly goods.'

Salih ibn Ali then said:

'O Commander of the Faithful, when Abd Allah, the son of Marwan fled to the land of the Nubians with a small number of followers, the king of that country asked them about their position and state, and what had befallen them, and how they had comported themselves. When he had collected this information, he rode to see Abd Allah, and questioned him on various events involving him and his family, including the causes of their disgrace. He said things which I can no longer remember, after which he expelled him from his country. The Commander of the Faithful could summon Abd Allah and have him tell his adventures himself.'

As a result of this, Mansur had Abd Allah brought from prison and when he stood before him, he said:

'Abd Allah, tell me your story and the story of the King of Nubia.'

Abd Allah replied as follows:

'O Commander of the Faithful, I had been in Nubia three days when the king

A Conversation with the King of Nubia

came to see me. Although I had had a valuable carpet spread out for him, he sat on the ground. I asked him why he refused to sit on our carpet and he replied:

'Because I am a king and the duty of a king is to humble himself before the power of God, who has made him great.'

Then he said to me:

'Why do you drink wine when your Book forbids it?'

I answered.

'Our slaves and our followers have the audacity to do so.'

'Why,' he went on, 'do you allow your cavalry to trample the fields when your Book has forbidden you destruction?'

'These are again our slaves and our followers, who have behaved thus in their ignorance.'

'Why,' proceeded the king, 'do you wear brocade and silk and gold, in spite of the prohibitions of your Book and your religion?'

I retorted:

'As power fled from us, we called upon the support of alien races who have entered our faith and we have adopted these clothes from them.'

The King bowed his head in silence, sometimes fidgeting, at others scratching in the sand, while he murmured:

'Our slaves . . . our followers . . . foreigners who have embraced our faith!'

Then he lifted his head and said:

'It is not the way you tell it! No! Your people permitted themselves what God forbade. You broke God's commandments and oppressed those you ruled. Then God stripped you of your power and dressed you in the ignominy of your crimes. The limit of God's vengeance cannot be known. I fear that his punishment may fall upon you while you are in my country, and strike me along with you. The rights of the guest last for three days. Take the provisions you need and ride out of my country.'

I obeyed his order.

This story made a great impression on Mansur. He reflected a while in silence and took pity on his prisoner and decided to free him, but Isa ibn Ali reminded him that the man had already received the oath of allegiance as Marwan's heir and he had him led back to prison.

VI:161-165
§§ 2374-2376

LOYALTY TO HISHAM

In the tenth year of the Caliphate of Mansur, 148 AH/765 AD, Abu Abd Allah Ja'far ibn Muhammad ibn Ali ibn Husain ibn Ali ibn Abi Talib died. He was buried at the cemetery of al-Baqi', with his father and grandfather. He was sixty-five years old and it is said that he was poisoned. Their tomb in the cemetery of al-Baqi' is sealed by a slab bearing this inscription:

'In the name of God, the Merciful, the Compassionate. Glory be to God who shall raise up the nations and make dry bones live! Here is the tomb of Fatima, the daughter of the Messenger of God, may the prayers and peace of God be upon him, the Queen of all the women of the world; the tomb of Hasan ibn Ali ibn Abi Talib; the tomb of Ali ibn al-Husain ibn Ali; the tomb of Muhammad ibn Ali, and that of Ja'far ibn Muhammad, may God be content with them all!'

After having first employed Ibn Atiyya al-Bahili as vizier, the Caliph Abu Ja'far Mansur gave these duties to Abu Ayyub al-Muriyani, who came from Khuzistan. He had decided in Abu Ayyub's favour for several reasons, among them that he had served as secretary to Sulaiman ibn Habib ibn al-Muhallab, who had condemned Mansur to be whipped. He wanted to flog Mansur to pieces, but his secretary, Abu Ayyub, managed to rescue him. This was the origin of the close relationship between the two. Nevertheless, after appointing him vizier, Mansur suspected him of various crimes, above all extortion and treachery. For a long time he meditated his ruin. Every time the vizier entered the Caliph's presence, he thought his time had come, yet every time he withdrew safe and sound. It was this which led people to say that he carried with him a magic ointment with which he took care to anoint his eyebrows before appearing before Mansur – and hence the popular expression, 'the ointment of Abu Ayyub'. Nevertheless, he perished in the end, and Aban ibn Sadaqa acted as secretary to the Caliph until he died.

The military tactics employed by Hisham in one of the campaigns which he had waged were mentioned in the presence of Mansur, who thereupon sent for a certain person living in the town of Rusafa, founded by Hisham, in order to question him about them. When the man was brought before him, the Caliph asked:

'You were one of Hisham's officers?'

'Yes, O Commander of the Faithful,' the man replied.

'Well then,' continued Mansur, 'explain to me his manoeuvres, undertaken in the war of such-and-such a year.'

Loyalty to Hisham

The officer replied:

'He did such and such, may God be pleased with him! He manoeuvred in such and such a way, may God have mercy upon him!'

These phrases of blessing angered Mansur.

'Get out!' he cried, 'And may God's wrath fall upon you! You tread my carpets with your feet and yet you dare call down blessings on the memory of my enemy!'

The old man rose, muttering:

'Your enemy fastened about my neck a necklace of gratitude which will be torn away only by him who washes my corpse.'

Mansur ordered him back and asked:

'What did you say?'

'Hisham', answered the old man, 'gave me a place secure from want and saved my face from the shame of beggary. Since I first saw him, I have needed to knock at no door, whether of Arab or Persian. Is it not, then, my duty to bless his name and perpetuate his memory?'

'It is well!' cried the Caliph. 'Blessed be the mother who bore you! I bear witness that you are born of one who was never a slave and are the descendant of a noble house!'

And after having listened to his account, he ordered him to be given a sum payable at the treasury.

'Commander of the Faithful,' said the old officer, 'I accept, not from need but because your gifts honour and your generosity sheds lustre upon the recipient.'

He therefore accepted the gift and Mansur said to him:

'Man beloved by God, die when you like; you belong to God, and if your people had none but you, you would be the cause of their lasting renown.'

And turning to his courtiers after the man had gone, he added:

'It is towards such men that generosity is beautiful and gifts well given and liberality praiseworthy. Would that I had men like him in my army!'

IN THE AUDIENCE HALL

One day Ma'n ibn Za'ida entered the presence of Mansur, who, when he saw him, said:

'Well, Ma'n, so it was you who gave one hundred thousand dirhams to Marwan ibn Abi Hafsa for this line:

> Ma'n ibn Za'ida! Through him the Bani Shaiban
> Heaps nobility upon nobility!'

'Not at all, O Commander of the Faithful,' retorted Ma'n, 'the verses I rewarded were these:

> At the battle of Al-Hashimiya*
> You stood forth boldly with your sword
> Before the vicar of the Merciful One.
> You protected him and defended his life
> Against the attack of lances
> And sharp-bladed swords.'

'You did well, Ma'n,' said the Caliph.

It should be explained that Ma'n had been one of the companions of Yazid ibn Umar ibn Hubaira and he remained hidden until the insurrection of the Hashimiya, when a number of the people of Khurasan rioted. Ma'n, turbaned and with his face concealed, appeared at the scene of the uprising. When he saw that the crowd was about to attack Mansur, he threw himself, sword in hand, between them and the Caliph and when he had driven them off and put them to flight, Mansur said: 'Who are you?'

He uncovered his face and said:

'I am he for whom you were searching – Ma'n ibn Za'ida!'

Mansur did not let him leave until he had granted him an amnesty, a reward, and dressed him in robes of honour and conferred upon him a rank.

This same Ma'n went one day to Mansur, who said to him:

'How quick people are to envy your House!'

To which he replied:

'O Commander of the Faithful:

In the Audience Hall

Small birds envy the crane;
Who envies the low-born man?'

According to Ibn Ayyash, known as al-Mantuf, 'He Who Plucks His Beard', Mansur was sitting one day looking out over the Tigris from the audience hall above the Khurasan Gate in the new town which he had just built and which bore his name: Madinat al-Mansur, The City of Mansur – in other words, Baghdad. Each of the gates, above the vault, had an audience hall with a view over the surrounding countryside. These gates, four in number, opened onto the principal streets, which were also vaulted and arched. They remain to our day, which is 332 AH/944 AD.

The first, the Khurasan Gate, was called 'The Dynasty Gate', because the dynasty of the Abbasids had its origins in Khurasan. Next came the Damascus Gate, facing Damascus, the Kufa Gate and the Basra Gate, so called because they led to those towns. I have described elsewhere the circumstances under which Mansur built this city and why he chose this site which lies between the Tigris and the Euphrates, and the Dujail and the Sarat – two canals branching off from the Euphrates. I have told the story of the founding of Baghdad, and why it was called by his name, and what people have said about it, described the Green Dome and its collapse in my own time, and given the legend of that other green dome built by Hajjaj in the city of Wasit, where it can still be seen in this year of 332 AH-944 AD. For all this information, see my *Intermediate History*, which this volume is only intended to supplement.

Mansur was sitting, then, in the audience hall over the Khurasan Gate when an arrow shot from who knows where landed at his feet. Mansur was terrified. Then he picked it up and began to twist it around in his hands. Between two of the vanes he read these lines:

Do you expect to live till Judgement Day?
Do you imagine there will be no Final Reckoning?
You will be asked to answer for your sins –
And then questioned on the state of the Believers.

Beside one of the vanes, Mansur read these lines:

When the days are fine, you are perfectly carefree
And do not fear the evil fate will bring;
Nights reassure you, but you are deluded;
For a clear night often brings grief.

And by the other vane:

Destiny takes its course, so be patient,
For nothing lasts. One day Fortune lifts

The Meadows of Gold

> A poor wretch to the skies;
> The next, the mighty fall.

Finally, one of the arrow's sides bore the words: 'Hamadan – a man from this town is held unjustly in your prisons.'

Without a moment's delay, Mansur sent a number of his officers to search the prisons and dungeons of the town. In one of the cells of the gaol they found an old man near whom burned a lamp. A length of cloth was hung as a kind of curtain over the entrance to his cell. He was loaded with chains and facing Mecca and repeating this verse: 'Those who oppress will learn what misfortune has been prepared for them.' (Koran 26:227)

They asked him where he was from and when he said 'Hamadan', they took him at once to the Caliph. Questioned by Mansur, he answered that he came from Hamadan and that he was one of the leading men of the city.

'Your governor,' he added, 'on arriving in our country, learned that I owned a domain worth a million dirhams. He wanted to take it from me and when I would not let him, he clapped me in irons and sent me here to you on a charge of rebellion. It is for that reason that I was thrown into a dungeon.'

'How long have you been there?' asked Mansur.

'The past four years.'

The Caliph immediately had his chains struck off and ordered him to be treated with respect. He was given his liberty and allotted the best quarters. Then Mansur called him back and said:

'O Shaikh, I return your estate to you exempt of taxes for the whole of your lifetime and as long as I shall live. Furthermore, I appoint you governor of Hamadan, your homeland, and I deliver the man that was governor into your hands – he is at your mercy and I authorize you to treat him as you will.'

After thanking the Caliph and offering prayers for his long reign, the old man said:

'O Commander of the Faithful, I accept the estate, but I am not fit for the position of governor which you have offered me. As for the governor, I forgive him.'

Mansur gave him another large sum of money and splendid presents, and, when he took his leave, had him escorted to his country with due honour, after dismissing the governor and punishing him for having set aside the canons of justice and for having stepped off the high road of truth. In addition, he invited the old man to correspond with him and inform him of his state and that of his country and to shed light on the behaviour of his agents, especially as regards matters of war and taxes.

It was on this occasion that he recited these lines:

> A man cannot trust Fate for a day,
> For fate is both sweet and bitter;

In the Audience Hall

However long their good luck lasts,
All creatures are at the end cut down.

VI:168-175
§§ 2380-2386

(Omitted: VI:176-220; §§ 2387-2430. The revolt and assassination of Abu Muslim and its aftermath; Heretics; Alid revolts and their consequences; Mansur preaches; Amr ibn Ubaid; The death of Abd Allah ibn Ali with his slave girl; Of tyrants.)

THE DEATH OF MANSUR

Mansur was born in the same year that Hajjaj ibn Yusuf died, that is, 95 AH/713 AD. He often used to say:

'I was born in the month of Dhu al-Hijja, I was circumcized in that month and in that month I succeeded to the Caliphate; I believe that in that month I shall die.'

It came to pass just as he predicted.

Fadl ibn al-Rabi' tells the following story:

'I was with Mansur on the journey on which he died. When he reached one of the halting-places along the way, he sent for me. I found him sitting in a domed chamber, his face turned to the wall. He said:

"Didn't I tell you not to let the common people come into these rooms and write ill-omened things?"

"What is it, O Commander of the Faithful?" I asked.

"Don't you see what is written on the wall?:

> Abu Ja'far, you are about to die, your years are up;
> God's commandment has been revealed.
> Abu Ja'far, can a soothsayer or astrologer put off
> God's judgement? Or are you steeped in ignorance?"

"By God," I replied, "I see nothing written on the wall. Its surface is clean and white."

"Swear by God!," he said.

"I swear!"

"By God," he continued, "then my soul is warned that she may prepare for her near departure. Let us make haste to reach the sacred places of my Lord and His protection, fleeing my excesses and my sins."

We went on our way, which was very painful for the Caliph. When we reached the Well of Maimun, I said to him: "This is the Well of Maimun. You have entered consecrated ground." He uttered these words:

"God be praised!"

And he died that very day!'

THE CHARACTER OF MANSUR

Mansur's prudence, the rectitude of his judgement and the excellence of his policies are beyond all description. He did not avoid the most extravagant generosity when there was something to be had in exchange, but he would refuse the smallest favour if granting it entailed loss. Like Ziyad, he might have said:

'If I had 1,000 camels and one became leprous, I would care for it as if I had only that one alone.'

He left 600,000,000 dirhams and 14,000,000 dinars. This great fortune did not prevent him from being miserly, nor did it prevent him from going into details which even a commoner ignores. Thus, he contracted with his cook that the latter should keep the heads, feet and skins, in exchange for providing the firewood and seasonings.

VI:221-222
§ 2431

(Omitted: VI: 222-223; §§ 2432-2434. Mansur's family; His wives and children enumerated. 'The more interesting anecdotes on Mansur and . . . other figures, together with his conversation and speeches, his life and the actions of his government are told at length with all their most interesting details in our Historical Annals *and* Intermediate History. *Here we give only an outline, while calling the reader's attention to our earlier works. All help comes from God!')*

THE CALIPHATE OF MAHDI

Next, allegiance was sworn to Mahdi. His name was Muhammad ibn Abd Allah ibn Muhammad ibn Ali ibn Abd Allah ibn Abbas and he was known as Abu Abd Allah. His mother, Umm Musa, was the daughter of al-Mansur ibn Abd Allah ibn Dhi Sahm ibn Abi Sarh, a descendant of Dhu Ru'ain, one of the kings of Himyar.

The oath of allegiance was given at Mecca, at the instigation of Rabi', his freedman, on Saturday, the 6th of the month of Dhu al-Hijja, 158 AH/775 AD. Another of his freedmen, named Minara, came to tell him of the death of his father and of his accession to the caliphate. Mahdi did not appear for two days after Minara's arrival, then he went up into the *minbar* to announce the death of his father and ask the people for the oath of allegiance.

Mahdi was born in 127 AH/745 AD. In the year 169 AH/785 AD he left Baghdad, the City of Peace, to go to Qarmasin (Kermanshah) in the province of Dinawar, but having heard the climate of Masabadhan in the Sirawan and Jurjan* region praised, he headed for a place called Arzan wa l-Ran* and died in the village of Raddain* on Thursday, the seventh day before the end of Muharram, 169 AH/785 AD, after a reign of ten years, one month and fifteen days. He was forty-three years old – but there is no absolute agreement on that point. The funeral prayers were recited by his son Harun al-Rashid, in the absence of Musa al-Hadi, who was in Jurjan. According to one version of the story, which may be read in our *Intermediate History*, Mahdi died of poison while eating fritters. The young slave Hasana, and other women of his retinue, put on hair cloth and veils of black in token of mourning. It is to this occasion that the following verses of Abu al-Atahiya refer:

> Yesterday they walked in silk brocade,
> This morning they are clothed in sack-cloth!
> Every ram, no matter how long he lives
> One day meets the hour of broken horns.
> One day you will die, even if you have lived
> As long as Noah. So if you must lament
> Let it be for your own soul that your tears fall.

VI:224-226
§ 2435

MAHDI AND THE QADI

Fadl ibn al-Rabi' said:

'One day, the qadi Sharik entered the presence of Mahdi, who said to him:

"You must accept one of my three proposals."

"What are they, O Commander of the Faithful?" asked Sharik.

"You must carry out the duties of qadi, or teach the Traditions to my sons and direct their studies, or share my meal."

Sharik considered a little and said:

"The meal is the easiest of the three."

The Caliph detained him and sent orders to the cook to prepare dishes of bone-marrow preserved with rose-flavoured sugar candy, honey and other flavourings. When the meal was over, the superintendent of the kitchen said:

"O Commander of the Faithful, now that he has tasted this dish, the Shaikh will never be happy again."'

'And indeed,' went on Fadl ibn al-Rabi', 'from that day, by God, Sharik taught the children of the Caliphs the Traditions and undertook their education, as well as acting as qadi.

The Caliph having given him a draft on the court paymaster, Sharik made difficulties over the amount.

"Oh come on," said the paymaster, "you aren't haggling over a piece of cloth!"

"By God," replied Sharik, "what I have sold for this sum is more precious than cloth; I have sold my faith." '*

VI:226-227
§ 2436

MAHDI AND THE PEASANT

According to Fadl ibn al-Rabi', the Caliph Mahdi went out hunting one day with his freedman Umar ibn Bazi', who was also a poet. In the course of the hunt, he became separated from his guards and escort. Feeling very hungry, he said to Umar:

'Find me someone who can give us something to eat.'

Umar began looking around and found a peasant who had a vegetable patch beside his little hut. He went in and asked him:

'Do you have anything to eat?'

'Yes,' replied the peasant, 'loaves of barley bread, some sardines, these vegetables you see here and a few leeks.'

'If you had a little oil to go with it,' said Mahdi, 'it would be perfect.'

'I do have just a little left,' the peasant answered.

He served them what he had and they ate with hearty appetites. Indeed, Mahdi enjoyed the food so much that he ate up every scrap. Then he said to Umar:

'Compose some verses for the occasion,' and the poet improvised the following:

> 'He who serves us sardines with oil
> And barley bread with leeks
> Deserves a cuff for his bad manners
> Or two – or even three!'

'By God, what an unpleasant thing to say!' cried Mahdi. 'Better to have made it:

> Deserves a purse for his good manners
> Or two – or even three!'

At that very moment the Caliph's guards, baggage train, eunuchs and money arrived and he had three purses of dirhams given to the owner of the vegetable patch.

VI:228-229
§ 2437

36

MAHDI AND THE BEDOUIN

Another time, when Mahdi was out hunting, his horse strayed and he found himself, very hungry, near the tent of a Bedouin.

'O Bedouin,' he said, 'can you offer me a meal? I rely on your hospitality.'

The Bedouin replied:

'You seem to me to be of goodly appearance, well fed and sturdy – however, if you can make do with what there is, we will give it to you.'

'Bring what you have,' answered Mahdi.

First, the Bedouin brought him bread cooked in the ashes. The Caliph ate it and said: 'It's good; bring the next course!'

His host brought in a skin full of sour milk, which he gave him to drink.

'Delicious!' said Mahdi. Bring the next course!'

The man brought out a little wine in a leather bag. After taking a drink, he passed it to Mahdi, who drank in his turn and said:

'Do you know who I am?'

'No, by God,' replied the Bedouin.

'I am one of the court eunuchs.'

'May God bless your employment and prolong your days, whoever you may be!'

Then he drank another bowl of wine and offered one to his guest, who drank a second time and said:

'Do you know who I am?'

'Yes,' answered the Bedouin, 'you have just mentioned that you are one of the court eunuchs.'

'Well, that's not true,' pursued Mahdi.

'So, who are you?' enquired the Bedouin.

'I am one of Mahdi's generals.'

The Bedouin congratulated him, saying:

'May your halls be spacious and your resting place fragrant!'

Then the Bedouin drank another bowl and passed one to his guest, who drank a third time and said:

'O Bedouin, do you know who I am?'

'Yes, I do know,' answered the Bedouin, 'you claim to be one of Mahdi's generals.'

'No,' came the reply, 'I am the Commander of the Faithful himself!'

At these words, the Bedouin took up his wine skin and tied it shut.

The Meadows of Gold

'Pour me another drink!' said Mahdi.

'No, by God,' cried the Bedouin, 'you are not going to drink one more mouthful!'

'But why?' asked Mahdi.

'Because at the first cupful you announced that you were a court eunuch. I let that go. At the second, you gave yourself out to be one of the Caliph's generals. I put up with that, too. But now, at the third drink, you claim to be the Commander of the Faithful. By God, if I pour you a fourth, I am afraid you will say, "I am the Messenger of God!" '

Mahdi was still laughing at this outburst when his retinue rode up to the tent. At the sight of all these great men and sons of kings dismounting before his guest, the Bedouin's heart failed and he thought only of saving himself. He made off, but they brought him back to the Caliph who reassured him and had him given a large sum of money, clothes, weapons and all sorts of goods. The Bedouin then said to him:

'Now I swear that you are a truthful man. If at the fourth and fifth drinks you had made other preposterous claims*, you would probably have found some way of wriggling out of them too!'

When the Bedouin mentioned a fourth and fifth drink, Mahdi laughed so much he almost fell off his horse. He enrolled the Bedouin in his personal service and gave him a stipend.

VI:229-231
§§ 2438-2439

(Omitted: VI:231-232; § 2440. Mahdi's vizier, Abu Ubaid Allah Mu'awiya.)

MAHDI AND THE TREASURER

Mahdi won the love of both the upper classes and the people by the acts with which he began his reign. He himself righted wrongs, spared lives and granted amnesties to those who feared punishment. Lastly, he dealt out justice to the oppressed and opened his hands wide in giving gifts of money. In this way, he spent the inheritance that had come to him from Mansur and which amounted to 600 million dirhams and 14 million dinars, not counting the taxes he levied during his own reign. When the treasury was exhausted, Abu Haritha al-Nahdi, the chief treasurer of the state, came and threw the keys of the treasury down in front of him, crying:

'What good are keys when the chests are empty?'

The Caliph sent out twenty eunuchs to press for immediate payment of taxes. After a few days, money began to flow into the treasury. Abu Haritha, completely taken up with his receipts and auditing, did not appear before the Caliph for three entire days. When he again appeared before him, Mahdi asked him:

'What delayed you?'

'Work; counting the money,' replied the treasurer.

'You are nothing but a stupid Bedouin!' the Caliph told him. 'Did you really think that money wouldn't come to us if we needed it?'

Abu Haritha answered:

'Something unexpected could come up so suddenly that you had time neither to levy the taxes nor to collect them.'

They say that, in ten days, Mahdi distributed 10 million dirhams out of his capital. After this act of generosity, Shabba ibn Iqal, in an address delivered before the Caliph, spoke thus:

'Mahdi can be compared to many things, among them the shining moon, the full flower of spring, the prowling lion and the raging sea. The shining moon resembles him in its beauty and lustre; the nascent spring in its sweetness and scent; the prowling lion by its mettle and fire and the echoing sea with its waves remind us of his generosity and bounty.'

VI:232-234
§§ 2441-2442

THE WHEEL OF FORTUNE

Khaizuran, the mother of Hadi and Rashid, was sitting one day in her palace – today known as the palace of Ashnas – among the mothers of the Caliph's children and the young women of the House of Hashim. Khaizuran reclined on an Armenian carpet and the princesses on Armenian cushions. In the place of honour sat Zainab, the daughter of Sulaiman ibn Ali. An eunuch entered and said:

'At the door there is a woman of great beauty, but dressed in a tattered garment. She refuses to give her name to any but you and demands to be admitted.'

Mahdi had recommended to Khaizuran that she should be much in the company of Zainab:

'Take advantage,' he said, 'of the lessons instilled by her manners and morals, for she is a venerable matron of our House and she knew the founders of our dynasty.'

Khaizuran told the eunuch:

'Show her in!'

A woman appeared, stately and beautiful, but dressed in a torn robe. When she spoke, her turns of phrase were most graceful.

'Who are you?' the women asked.

'I am Muzna, the wife of Marwan ibn Muhammad. See to what a sad condition I have been brought by fate. By God, even this tattered robe I wear is little better than nakedness. Now that you are in power, and power has abandoned us, I am afraid that living among the common people in this wretched state I may be subjected to violence in some dishonouring form. I have therefore come to put myself under your protection in order to live somehow until the day when He who summons all creatures shall summon me.'

Khaizuran's eyes filled with tears, but Zainab turned to the stranger and said:

'Muzna, may God never relieve your misery! Do you remember the day that I stood before you at Harran? You were sitting on this very carpet, with the women of your family all about you, there, on those same cushions. I had come to beg you for the body of the Imam Ibrahim and you refused me and had me turned out, saying:

"It is not for women to meddle in the affairs of men!"

Indeed, Marwan was more considerate than you, for when I saw him he swore that he was not the murderer of Ibrahim. He was lying, of course, but neverthe-

The Wheel of Fortune

less he offered either to give me back the body or to arrange for its burial and I accepted the first of his proposals. He even offered me money, which I refused.'

Muzna answered her:

'In truth, I think fortune has placed me where I stand today solely to requite the wrong I did you then. But one would say that you approved, since you are inciting her Highness to behave like me. Rather, it should be your duty to persuade the Queen to perform a virtuous deed and turn her from cruel retaliation, for it is thus that you will ensure her happiness and strengthen her piety.'

And then she added, addressing Zainab:

'What do you think, my dear cousin, of the punishment inflicted by God for my harshness? And yet you refuse to help me in my need!'

Then she went away, weeping.

Khaizuran did not want to contradict Zainab openly and so she signed to one of her slave girls to take the stranger to some secluded room in her apartments. Unknown to Zainab, this was done and the Queen had new clothes given to Muzna and heaped kindnesses upon her.

When Mahdi arrived, after Zainab's departure – for it was his custom to join the favourites of his harem each evening – Khaizuran told him the whole story and explained how she had ordered care to be taken of the stranger. The Caliph called the slave girl who had been entrusted with conducting Muzna to her quarters and asked:

'When you took her to her room, did you hear what she said?'

'My lord,' answered the girl, 'I caught up with her in such-and-such a corridor. She was in tears and in despair at having been sent away and she was reciting this verse from the Koran: "God offers you the parable of the village which was living in peace and security, with ample food from all sides. But it did not recognize God's mercies and God has clothed it in the robes of fear and famine as a punishment for what its people did." (Koran 16:112)

The Caliph turned to Khaizuran and said to her:

'By God! If you had not acted as you did, I would never have spoken to you again in all my life!'

And he wept many tears, adding:

'Lord, preserve us from the loss of Your grace!'

He disapproved of Zainab's behaviour and said:

'If she were not the oldest of our line, I swear that I would never speak to her again.'

Then he sent a slave to the apartments which had been allotted to the widow of Marwan and gave the following instructions:

'Greet her and say from me: "My cousin, your sisters are all with me – if I were not afraid of distressing you, I would come to you myself."'

When Muzna received this message, she understood Mahdi's intention. Zainab had just arrived. Muzna appeared, trailing her robes like a queen. Mahdi greeted her kindly, invited her to sit by him and gave her a place above that of Zainab.

The Meadows of Gold

Conversation fell on men and matters of the past times and on political changes of fortune and Muzna let no one have the last word. Indeed, Mahdi ended by saying:

'My cousin, truly, if I were not so loath to associate the family to which you belong in any way with our affairs, I would marry you. As it is, your best safeguard is to remain here under my protection and to live in my palace among your sisters. All they have shall be yours, until that day when the sentence of He who commands all nature shall be executed.'

Consequently, he gave her a settlement, like his other women and assigned her a pension and privileges and servants just like theirs.

Muzna lived in the palace until the death of Mahdi, during the reign of Hadi and until the beginning of the reign of Harun al-Rashid. She died in the time of this Caliph, who made no distinction between her and the Hashimite women, nor any of his favourites, slave or free. At her death, Rashid and all the harem mourned.

VI:234-240
§§ 2443-2446

(Omitted: VI:240; § 2447. Abd Allah ibn Amr ibn Utba consoles Mahdi on the death of Mansur.)

UNREQUITED LOVE

Some historians and story-tellers say that when the poet Abu al-Atahiya fell violently in love with Utba, one of Khaizuran's slaves, the girl complained to her mistress of the unwelcome notoriety his love was causing, which she felt was bringing her into dishonour. Mahdi found her in tears at her mistress's side, questioned her and learned the cause of her grief. He summoned Abu al-Atahiya, who was brought to him. Mahdi, addressing the poet, who was standing before him, said:

'You are the author of these lines on Utba:

May God judge between me and my mistress,
Since she shows me nothing but rejection and contempt.

Did Utba ever grant you her favours and so give you the right to complain of her rejection?'

'My Lord,' answered Abu al-Atahiya, 'I didn't say that. Here are the verses I wrote:

O camel, carry me swiftly!*
Do not flag, or be tempted to rest.
Carry me to a king to whom
God has granted the gift of miracles.
When the wind rises, the king says:
"Wind, have you had your share
Of my gifts?" His head
Bears a double crown:
A crown of beauty
And a crown of humility.'

Mahdi sat for some time looking at the ground, which he kept scratching with the staff which he was holding in his hand. Then he lifted his head and continued:
'You also said:

What does my mistress think
When she flirts? Does she know
How hard it is to bear

> Her coquettishness?
> Among the slaves of kings
> Is a young girl who hides
> Beauty itself under her chemise.

And how do you know what she has got under her dress?' asked the Caliph.

Abu al-Atahiya then made the Commander of the Faithful himself the subject of his verse, seeking to change the subject:

> 'The caliphate came to him,
> Submissive, trailing her
> Skirts majestically.
> She was fit only for him,
> And he was made for her!'

But as the Caliph went on with the interrogation, Abu al-Atahiya's answers became less ready and in the end he was ordered to atone for his boldness by being beaten. He had just suffered this penalty* and was in a most pitiable state when Utba met him. The poet reproached her as follows:

'Bravo! Excellent! For your sake the Caliph has shed the blood of a dying man!'

Tears began to well up in Utba's eyes. Sobbing and crying she ran to Khaizuran, her mistress, and there met the Caliph. He asked:

'Why is Utba crying?'

She told him that she had just seen the poet whipped. The Caliph made comforting noises and then had 50,000 dirhams sent to the poet. Abu al-Atahiya immediately distributed them to everyone he met at the door of the palace. Mahdi, told of this act of generosity, sent him a message, saying:

'What led you to give away the money I gave you?'

The poet replied:

'I would not have wanted to profit from my love.'

Mahdi sent him another 50,000 dirhams, but made him swear that he would not scatter them around as largess, too. The poet took them and withdrew.

According to Mubarrad, Abu al-Atahiya gave Mahdi, either at the New Year or at Mihrijan, the festival of the autumn equinox, a jar which contained a length of cloth scented with musk. On it were written these lines:

> My soul craves one of the good things of the world;
> The fulfilment of its longing depends on God,
> And Mahdi, God's vicar on earth.
> I despair of obtaining my desire,
> But the disdain in which you hold the world
> And all that it contains
> Gives me some reason to hope.

Unrequited Love

The Caliph was thinking of giving him Utba when the girl said:

'O Commander of the Faithful, would you, in spite of my wishes and in contempt of my rights and the good service I have given you, hand me over to a pot vendor, a man who writes verses for money?'

Mahdi sent word to the poet:

'As to Utba, there is no way you can have her, but I have filled the jar you sent with money.'

Utba happened to pass by and she saw her poet arguing with the secretaries, saying:

'The money should be paid in dinars!'

They replied:

'No. Dirhams.'

'If you really loved Utba,' she said to him, 'you would not be thinking of the difference between gold and silver!'

VI:240-245
§§ 2448-2451

(Omitted: VI:246-249; §§2452-2457. More anecdotes about Abu al-Atahiya and Utba; Several poems by Abu al-Atahiya.)

AN AMUSING STORY ABOUT THE KING OF HIRA

Abu al-Qasim Ja'far ibn Muhammad ibn Hamdan al-Mawsili, the jurisconsult, tells the following anecdote, related by Ibn Ayyash and Ibn Da'b.

'When Mansur left his son Mahdi at Rayy as governor, he set at his side Sharqi ibn al-Qutami to teach him of the "Days" – or Battles – "of the Arabs", their fine traits of character, their history and their poems. One evening, Mahdi said:

"Sharqi, entertain me with some amusing story."

"I obey, O prince, may God protect you!" replied Sharqi. "They say that a certain king of Hira had two courtiers whom he loved as he loved himself. They never left him, whether at his pleasures, sleeping or waking, in his palace or on his travels. He never made a decision without consulting them. They lived thus for a long time, but, one evening, the king, while drinking and enjoying himself, yielded to the effects of the wine, which had clouded his reason, called for his sword, drew it from its sheath and, hurling himself on his two friends, killed them. Then, overcome with drowsiness, he fell asleep.

The following morning, when he asked after them, he was told what he had done. He threw himself face down on the earth, biting it in his grief, and weeping for his friends and lamenting their loss. He would eat nothing and swore that for the rest of his life he would refrain from the drink which had robbed him of his reason. Then he had them buried and erected two pillars over the two tombs, which he called *al-Gharyan* – The Two Fair Effigies. He ordered, furthermore, that no one should pass before this monument without prostrating himself.

Now, every custom established by a king of this country was handed down and kept alive in the memory of his subjects and could not be abolished, but became an invariable law and a rule rigorously obeyed and taught by fathers to their children. This king's will was long respected. None of his subjects, no matter what their condition, would ever pass before the two pillars without prostrating themselves and this usage became for them like a religious rite which they observed most strictly. The king had in any case ordained that whosoever should refuse to conform would be punished by death, after having made two wishes, which would be granted him, whatever they were.

One day, a fuller went by carrying on his back a packet of cloth and his mallet. The guardians of the tombs cried out:

'Kneel!'

He refused.

An Amusing Story about the King of Hira

'You will be put to death if you don't!' they said.

The fuller kept on refusing, so they took him before the king and told him the whole story.

'Why did you refuse to prostrate yourself?' asked the king.

'I did prostrate myself,' said the fuller, 'but your guardians have lied to you.'

'It is you who are lying,' replied the king. 'Make your two wishes. They will be granted and then you will die.'

'Then nothing can save me from being put to death on the say-so of these people?' enquired the fuller.

'Nothing.'

'Well,' said the fuller, 'here is my wish – I want to strike a great blow with this mallet on the king's neck.'

'Imbecile!' said the king, 'you would do much better to entrust me with enriching those whom you leave behind.'

'No,' said the fuller, 'the only thing I want is to hit the king on the nape of the neck.'

The king addressed his ministers:

'What do you think of this idiot's wish?' he asked.

'It was you who instituted this custom,' they answered, 'and you know better than anyone that the breaking of a custom brings shame and perdition; it is a sin which leads to damnation. In any case, after violating one law, you will break a second, then a third; your successors will do as much and all our laws will be invalidated.'

The king proceeded:

'Beseech this man to ask for whatever he likes as long as he spares me. I am willing to fulfill his every wish, even if he should go so far as to demand half my kingdom.'

In vain they beseeched the fuller to change his mind, but he declared:

'I want nothing but to hit the king on the neck.'

The king, seeing that this resolution could not be shaken, held a public audience. The fuller was brought. He took his mallet and hit the king on the neck so hard that he knocked him from his throne and felled him to the ground, where he lay unconscious. For six months the king was so desperately ill that he could only drink water a drop at a time. At last he recovered, could speak again and eat and drink. He asked for news of the fuller and was told that he was still in prison. He had him brought before him and said:

'You still have a wish. Decide, so that I can order your death at once, as the law requires.'

'Since I absolutely have to die,' said the fuller, 'I ask to hit you again, on the other side of the neck.'

At these words the king fell on his face from fear, crying out:

'Then I am a dead man!'

At last he said to the fuller:

'Wretch, give over demanding something which can do you no good. What did

The Meadows of Gold

you gain from your first wish? Ask something else, whatever you like, and I will grant it.'

'I only want my rights,' said the man, 'the right to hit you once more.'

The king consulted his viziers, who replied:

'It is best that you should die in obedience to the law.'

'Wretches!' cried the king, 'If he hits me on the other side of the neck I shall never be able to drink water again – I know what I have already suffered!'

'We can think of no alternative,' answered his ministers.

In this extremity, the king said to the fuller:

'Answer me – on the day that you were brought here by the guardians of the tomb, did I not hear you say that you *had* prostrated yourself and that they had lied?'

'I said it,' replied the fuller, 'but no one wanted to believe me.'

'Well, *did* you prostrate yourself?'

'Certainly.'

The king leapt from his throne, kissed the fuller's head, and cried:

'I swear you are more truthful than these rascals and that they lied about you and I appoint you in their stead and give you leave to teach them the lesson they deserve.' "

Mahdi laughed until he scratched the ground with his feet, and said:

"By God, you have excelled!"

And he gave him a reward.'

VI:250-256
§§ 2458-2463

THE LAST DAYS OF MAHDI

'I was in Mahdi's reception room,' relates Haitham ibn Adi, 'when the chamberlain came to him and said:
"O Commander of the Faithful, Ibn Abi Hafsa is at the door."
"Don't let him come in!" cried the Caliph. "He is a hypocrite and a liar!"
Then Hasan ibn Qahtaba spoke up on his behalf, so the Caliph finally received him and said:
"Hypocrite! Was it not you who praised Ma'n in these terms:

He is like a mountain upon which
The tribe of Nizar has taken refuge;
Difficult of access,
The slopes defended."

"Yes," replied the poet, "but I am also the one who said this about you, O Commander of the Faithful:

O son of him whom Muhammad designated his heir
In preference to his closer relatives!"

And he recited the whole poem. The Caliph calmed down and granted him free entry to the court.'

The following story is told by Qa'qa' ibn Hakim:

'I was with Mahdi when they brought in Sufyan al-Thawri. As he came in, he greeted the Commander of the Faithful after the fashion of the common people, not using the forms reserved for Caliphs. Fadl ibn al-Rabi' was standing behind the Caliph, leaning on his sword and waiting to execute his orders. Mahdi turned to Sufyan, smiling, and said:
"Sufyan, you have escaped us twice and you thought that if we wished to do you harm we would not be able to do so. Here you are, now, in my power. Are you not afraid that we will pronounce against you any sentence we may choose?"
"If you pronounce my doom," replied Sufyan, "another ruler, one more powerful, who distinguishes between truth and error, will sentence you in your turn."
"Commander of the Faithful," cried al-Rabi', "has this ignoramus the right to speak to you with such insolence? Permit me to cut off his head!"

The Meadows of Gold

"Silence!" answered Mahdi. "This man, and men like him, ask nothing better than to die at our hands, so that by making them happy, we should be plunged into misfortune. Draw up his appointment as qadi of Kufa, and let any attempt to control his decisions be absolutely forbidden."

The document was drawn up and given to Sufyan, who took it; but as he left, he threw it in the Tigris and fled. They searched for him from city to city, but he was never found.'

Ali ibn Yaqtin describes how he accompanied Mahdi into Masabadhan:

'One day,' he said, 'the Caliph said to me:

"I am hungry; bring me loaves of bread and cold meat."

This I did. After eating, Mahdi retired to the interior of the tent and fell asleep, while we remained behind the tent-divider. His sobs awoke us and we ran to him:

"Did you see what I saw?" he asked us.

We replied, "But we have seen nothing."

"A man appeared before me," he said, "whose voice and face I would recognize in a crowd of a thousand men, and he spoke these words:

> It is as if I saw this palace emptied of its inhabitants.
> Its halls and its apartments all abandoned.
> After his power and his glory, the pillar of the people
> Has gone into a grave weighted down with stones.
> Nothing of him remains but a memory, a few stories,
> A lament by the mourning women of his house."

Ali said, 'Only ten days after having seen this apparition, Mahdi died.'

VI:256-259
§§ 2464-2466

(Omitted: VI:259-260; §§ 2467-2468. Necrology and usual list of material to be found in the Intermediate History.)

THE CHARACTER OF HADI

Musa ibn Muhammad, whose throne name was Hadi, was proclaimed Caliph at the age of twenty-four years and three months on a Thursday,* the seventh day before the end of the month of Muharram, on the very morning after the night in which his father, Mahdi, died – 169AH/785 AD. Hadi died at Isabadh, a town near Baghdad, the City of Peace, in 170 AH/786 AD, twelve days before the end of the month of Rabi' I, after a reign of one year and three months. He was known as Abu Ja'far. His mother, who was also the mother of Harun al-Rashid, was Khaizuran – 'Bamboo' – daughter of Ata' of the tribe of Jurash.

At the time he was chosen, Hadi was at war in Tabaristan and Jurjan. He returned, riding the post horses; his brother Harun had received the oath of allegiance in his name. A poet,* recalling this occasion, has said:

When the Caliphate of God came to the best
Of the children of Hashim he was in Jurjan,
Tucking up his trousers for war with a purpose
That knew nothing of inexperience or hesitation.

Hadi was hard-hearted, vicious, unapproachable, but nevertheless learned, with a passion for literature. He was strong, brave, energetic, liberal and generous.

Yusuf, the son of the secretary Ibrahim and friend of Mahdi's son Ibrahim, tells the following story on the authority of the latter. He was with Hadi, who, mounted on a donkey, was taking the air in one of the gardens of Baghdad to which he had given his name, when he was told that a Kharijite had been taken prisoner. Hadi ordered them to bring him into his presence. The Kharijite, as soon as he had drawn near, snatched a sword from one of the guards and walked straight up to Hadi:

'I threw myself to one side,' related Ibrahim, 'as did all the people around me. Hadi remained on his donkey without moving a muscle, but just as the Kharijite approached, he called out – as if he were speaking to the guards:

"Cut off his head!" although there was no one behind him. He thus distracted the Kharijite, who turned and glanced around. Instantly, the Caliph, gathering himself up, leapt on him, floored him and, seizing the sword from his hands, cut off his head.

We feared the anger of the Caliph more than we had feared the Kharijite, but

The Meadows of Gold

by God, he did not blame us for our desertion or reproach us in any way; only from that day on, he gave up riding his donkey and was never separated from his sword.'

ISA IBN DA'B

One of the favourites of the Caliph was Isa ibn Da'b, who came from the Hijaz and was one of the best-read and most learned men of his age and one of those who knew best the history and battles of the Arabs. Hadi had him given a cushion, a favour which no other courtier would have dared hope for, and often said to him:

'Isa, when you are late during the day, or when in the evening you do not appear, I seem to look for none but you.'

REVENGE

The same Ibn Da'b relates that one day Hadi received the following report:

'An inhabitant of the city of Mansura in Sind, one of the noblest and most important men in the government of the town, a member of the family of Muhallab ibn Abi Sufra, had brought up an Indian – or Sindi – slave. This young man conceived a passion for the wife of his owner and attempted to seduce her; she reciprocated. The master entered and found them together. He castrated the slave and made a eunuch of him, but looked after him until his wounds healed.

The slave was patient for a long time. His master had two sons, one still a child and the other an adolescent. One day, the master left the house, and the Sindi slave took the two children up to the top of the wall that encircled the house and there awaited the owner's return. When the man came home and, looking up, saw his two sons and his slave balanced on the edge of the wall, he cried:

"Wretch! You are risking their lives!"

"Never mind that!" shouted the Sindi, "I swear that you are going to castrate yourself in front of me, now, this moment, or else I shall throw your children down!"

"O God, O God," he said, "have pity on me and upon my two sons!"

"Leave off!" answered the slave. "I have nothing to lose but my life and I would give that away for a drink of water!"

He was just preparing to carry out his threat, when his master took out a knife and castrated himself. When the slave saw that he had done it, he threw the two children off the roof and they were smashed to bits on the ground.

"Your wounds," he said, "are in expiation of mine, and the killing of your two children is something in addition."

Hadi then wrote to the governor of Sind ordering him to have this slave put to death with the most appalling tortures and, furthermore, he ordered all Sindis to be driven out of his domains, which explains why slaves from that country became cheap and glutted the markets at that period and were sold for such low prices.'

VI:264-265
§ 2472

(Omitted: VI:265-266; § 2473. Hadi's vizier Rabi'.)

THE DEATH OF THE GREAT-GREAT-GREAT GRANDSON OF THE PROPHET

It was in this same reign that the revolt of Husain ibn Ali ibn al-Hasan ibn al-Hasan ibn Ali ibn Abi Talib broke out, in which he was killed at Fakhkh, six miles outside Mecca, on the day of *tarwiya* – that is, the 8th of the month of Dhu al-Hijja, 169 AH/11 June 786 AD. At the head of the army sent out against him was a group of Hashimites, among them Sulaiman ibn Abi Ja'far, Muhammad ibn Sulaiman ibn Ali, Musa ibn Isa and Abbas ibn Muhammad ibn Ali, with 4,000 horsemen.

Husain was killed, along with most of his companions. Their bodies, left unburied for three days, were devoured by the wild beasts and the birds of prey. Among his supporters, Sulaiman ibn Abd Allah ibn al-Hasan ibn al-Hasan ibn Ali was taken prisoner and his head cut off at Mecca. Abd Allah Ibn Ishaq ibn Ibrahim ibn al-Hasan ibn al-Hasan ibn Ali died at the side of Husain. Another of his friends, al-Hasan ibn Muhammad ibn Abd Allah ibn al-Hasan, was taken and beheaded. Abd Allah ibn al-Hasan ibn Ali and Husain ibn Ali were given safe conduct, but after having been held prisoner in the house of Ja'far, the son of Yahya ibn Khalid the Barmakid, they were killed.

Hadi flew into a rage against Musa ibn Isa because he had killed Husain instead of bringing him to him so that he could decide his fate and, as a result, he confiscated Musa's possessions. The people who brought him the head of Husain presented it with a gay and cheerful air, but Hadi wept and upbraided them, saying:

'You come to me smiling, as if you were bringing me the head of a Turk or a Dailamite, and yet this is the head of a descendant of the Messenger of God, may prayers and peace be upon him. The least vengeance I can take against you on God's behalf is to deny you any reward.'

The death of Husain ibn Ali in the battle of Fakhkh has been sung in these words by a poet of the time:

> O let me weep and lament for Hasan and Husain,
> Over the son of Atika who was laid to rest without a shroud.
> They were left that morning on the plain of Fakhkh
> Far from their homes in their native place.

The Meadows of Gold

> They were noblemen. They died fearless, indifferent to death.
> They washed away their shame, as clothes are washed clean of dirt
> Their zeal guided the servants of God. Men owe them homage.

VI:266-268
§§ 2474-2475

THE FALL OF KHAIZURAN

Hadi was extremely deferential towards his mother Khaizuran and gave her everything she asked for her protégés. Innumerable queues of petitioners stood before her gates, which led Abu al-Ma'afi to say:

> Gently now, Khaizuran!
> Stop and let your sons
> Govern their subjects.

One day, however, she asked him for a favour which it was impossible to grant and, as he was searching for excuses, she cried:
'You absolutely must agree!'
'I cannot,' said Hadi.
His mother then retorted:
'But I have already guaranteed Abd Allah ibn Malik that you would do this for him!'
These words angered the Caliph.
'Curse that son of a whore!' he said. 'I knew the request came from him. By God, I am not going to grant it to you.'
'God knows then,' said Khaizuran, 'that I shall never ask you for anything again!'
'God knows,' replied Hadi, 'that I shan't be sorry for that!'
He flew into a rage and his mother, no less angry, rose to leave.
'Stay!' he said to her, 'and hear what I have to say. If I break the oath that follows, let me deny my descent from the Prophet, may the prayers and peace of God be upon him: if any one of my generals or my court or my servants goes to ask you for favours, he will have his head cut off and his goods confiscated. Let he who wants to see, try it! What are all these crowds which besiege your gates all day from early morning? Have you no spindle to amuse you? No Koran for your prayers? No room in which to stay? Take care! And God help you if you open your mouth to plead for anyone, Muslim or tributary!'
Khaizuran rose, unable to believe her ears and scarcely knowing where she was going. From that day on she no longer said a word to her son, sweet or bitter.

VI:268-270
§§ 2476-2477

BLOOD FEUDS

'The Caliph Hadi,' relates Ibn Da'b, 'summoned me one night at an unusual hour. I hastened to him and found him sitting in a small winter room, looking at a notebook.

"Isa," he said to me.

"Here I am, O Commander of the Faithful!"

He went on:

"Besieged by my thoughts and overwhelmed by preoccupations, I cannot sleep and now my mind is taken up with the cruelty with which the Umayyads, both the descendants of Harb and those of Marwan, shed our blood."

I answered him as follows:

"Commander of the Faithful, it came to pass that Abd Allah ibn Ali killed such-and-such a member of that family on the banks of the Abu Futrus river" – and I named most of those who died in that battle. "And it came to pass that Abd al-Samad ibn Ali slaughtered at one stroke, in the Hijaz, almost as many as Abd Allah ibn Ali and it was he, who, after shedding their blood, said:

> Now my heart suffers no more.
> The vengeance I have wreaked
> On the sons of Marwan
> And the race of Harb
> Has assuaged its pain.
> Alas that our Shaikh*
> Was not present when I shed
> The blood of the children of Abu Sufyan."

'My words,' went on Ibn Da'b, 'charmed Hadi and his face showed his pleasure.'

"Isa," he said to me, "it was Da'ud ibn Ali who composed those lines and exterminated our enemies in the Hijaz, but, when you reminded me of them, I felt that I was hearing those verses for the first time."

"O Commander of the Faithful," I answered, "they are also attributed to Abd Allah ibn Ali, who is said to have composed them during the battle of Abu Futrus."

"So it is said," replied Hadi.'

VI:270-271
§ 2478

THE CLIMATE OF EGYPT

Ibn Da'b said:
'Then the conversation passed from one topic to another and in the end turned to Egypt, its defects and virtues, and its river, the Nile.

Hadi declared:
"The advantages of this country override its faults."

"Commander of the Faithful," I said, "this is a claim which the Egyptians always make, but without demonstrating its truth. Now, it is up to the person putting forward a statement to provide the proof. The people of Iraq expressly deny the qualities of Egypt and maintain that it is a country whose defects outweigh its merits."

"In what, for example?" enquired the Caliph.

"O Commander of the Faithful," I went on, "one of its defects is the lack of rain and the fact that when rain does fall, the people lament and call upon God. Now God has said, 'It is He who sends the winds as harbingers of His mercy . . .' (Koran 7:57), yet when they are honoured by this mark of Divine Favour, they reject it, because for them rain is more harmful than beneficial, since it prevents the harvest from ripening and the earth from bringing forth her fruits.

Another of the ills to which this country is subject is the south wind they call Marisiya, from the word *maris*, by which they mean the upper part of the Sa'id as far as Nubia. When this south wind, or Marisiya, blows for thirteen consecutive days, they buy aromatics for embalming and winding sheets, convinced that they are about to be visited by a deadly plague that will spread death to every place.

Egypt has another defect: its variations in temperature make it necessary for the inhabitants to change clothes many times a day, sometimes putting on a light material, sometimes a cloak, or at others clothes with warm linings; such is the effect of the atmospheric changes at the different hours and the variations of the winds from season to season, to say nothing of day and night.

Since Egypt feeds other countries and receives nothing from them, when there is a drought, they perish.

As regards the Nile, it should be enough to remind you what distinguishes it from all other rivers, great and small: not the Euphrates, nor the Tigris, nor the Oxus, nor the Jaihan, nor the Saihan, have crocodiles. These beasts harm rather than help and devastate rather than produce. This has led a certain poet to say:

> I have shown nothing but aversion and disgust for the Nile

Since I was told that it was full of crocodiles.
Let others go and admire this river from its banks;
I only want to see its waters safely in *bawaqil*."

"And what on earth are these *bawaqil*, in which one can see the Nile?" asked Hadi.

"They are," I replied, "certain sorts of buckets and jugs used in Egypt."

"What did the poet have in mind when he said that?" he asked me.

"He meant," I continued, "that he only wanted to taste Nile water out of jugs, because the edges of the river are made so dangerous by the crocodiles, which attack men as well as animals."

"That's true," answered Hadi. "This sort of beast deprives the inhabitants of all the advantages of the river. I have always had a great desire to see the Nile, but your description has thoroughly put me off."

'Hadi,' adds Ibn Da'b, 'next asked me how far Dongola, the capital of Nubia, was from Aswan.'

"They say," I replied, "that it is forty days march along the Nile, at all points over cultivated land." '

BASRA VERSUS KUFA

'Then Hadi said to me:
"Now then, Ibn Da'b, let us leave the west and its tales and turn to the merits of Basra and Kufa and to the relative advantages which distinguish them from each other."

I continued as follows:
"This is a story told by Abd al-Malik ibn Umair. 'At Kufa we were visited by Ahnaf ibn Qais, when he was there with Mus'ab ibn Zubair. I have never seen an ugly old man who could not claim some kinship with Ahnaf. His head was small, his nose crooked, his ears pendulous, he was blind in one eye, his cheeks were puffy, one corner of his mouth was drawn down, his teeth grew over each other, he had a sparse beard, and one of his feet was twisted. But as soon as he spoke, he was transfigured.

One day he was praising Basra and we were praising Kufa. We were saying that the soil of Kufa was more productive, more wholesome, wider in extent and in every way better. One of our people added:

"Truly, I cannot think of a more apt comparison for Kufa than a beautiful girl of noble birth but no fortune, so that when her poverty is mentioned, her suitors withdraw. Basra I can only liken to a wealthy old lady who boasts in vain of her property and riches – still no one comes forward to claim her."

Ahnaf replied:
"Basra has reed below, woods in the middle and meadows above. We have more teak than you, more ivory and silk brocade, and likewise more sugar and more coin. Truly, it is a city I always enter with joy and leave with regret."

A young man of the tribe of Bakr ibn Wa'il rose and asked him:
"O Ahnaf, to what do you owe the rank which you occupy? You are surely no better than other men as regards looks, generosity, or courage!"

"My friend," replied Ahnaf, "it was by doing the reverse of what you are doing now."

"What do you mean?" asked the young man.

"It was," went on Ahnaf, "by ignoring those things which are not my business, while you meddle in my affairs, which should in no way concern you."' '

VI:275-276
§§ 2481-2482

(Omitted: VI:277-280; §§ 2483-2844. Discussion of the relative merits of the waters of the Tigris and Euphrates.)

HARUN AL-RASHID AND THE DEATH OF HADI

Hadi wished to strip his brother of the title of heir apparent, in order to give it to his own son, Ja'far. He had imprisoned Yahya ibn Khalid, the Barmakid, and wanted to kill him; but Yahya, who was responsible for Harun al-Rashid's interests, said to him one day:

'O Commander of the Faithful, if that thing which I ask heaven to spare us and keep far from us, by granting your majesty long life, should come to pass, do you think, I repeat, do you think that the people would recognize the authority of your son Ja'far, who has not yet reached the age of reason, to lead the prayers, the pilgrimage and the holy wars?'

'No, I don't think so,' he replied.

'Are you not afraid,' continued Yahya, 'that they will raise one of the leading men of your family to the throne, and that the power will pass from your issue to others? You yourself will have stirred up your subjects to break their oath and hold their faith cheap. If, on the other hand, you were to respect the oath of allegiance made to your brother, and if you were to have your son accepted as his heir, it would be the strongest possible position. Then, when Ja'far comes of age, you can ask your brother to yield the supreme power to him.'

'By God,' replied the Caliph, 'you are suggesting a plan that had never occurred to me.'

But later, he determined at all costs to force Harun to give up his rights, with or without his consent, and he severely restrained his movements. Yahya advised his master Harun to ask permission to go out hunting and urged him to spend as much time as possible doing so, since the horoscope cast at the moment of Hadi's birth predicted that his time would be short.

Harun asked and obtained leave to go. He followed the banks of the Euphrates into the region of Hit and Anbar, and then struck inland in the direction of Samawa. Hadi wrote to recall him and, when Harun delayed even more, cursed him roundly. It even occurred to Hadi to go in the direction of al-Haditha, but he fell ill there and turned back. His illness took so serious a turn that no one dared go into him, except the youngest eunuchs. He signed to them to bring him his mother Khaizuran and, when she was at his bedside, he said:

'I am going to die tonight, and my brother Harun will immediately succeed me, for you know the sentence pronounced against me by fate at the very moment of my birth at Rayy. I have had to refuse you what you asked and have had to

Harun al-Rashid and the Death of Hadi

impose my orders upon you, in accordance with the dictates of policy, but to do so always went against the affection which religion demands of a son. Far, however, from having been an ungrateful child, I have never ceased to protect you, nor to be dutiful and loyal.'

Then he took his mother's hand in farewell, laid it on his heart and breathed his last. Hadi, like his brother Harun, was born at Rayy. His death, the accession of Harun al-Rashid and the birth of Ma'mun, all took place on the same night.

THE DREAM OF MAHDI

It is said that one day one of the great men of the dynasty, who was guilty of many crimes, was brought before Hadi. The Caliph reminded him of them, one after another.

'O Commander of the Faithful,' the man replied, 'to make excuses for the things which you accuse me of having done, would mean contradicting you; to accept your charges would be an admission of my guilt. I prefer to say, with the poet:

> If what you hope for from punishment is satisfaction,
> Why deprive yourself of the satisfaction of forgiveness?'

Hadi set him free and gave him a present.

A number of chroniclers, learned in the history of this dynasty, relate that Hadi said to his brother Harun al-Rashid:

'It seems to me that you are ceaselessly talking to yourself about the fulfilment of the dream and that you hope for that which is still far from you – but first "you must pluck the thorns from the tragacanth".'

'O Commander of the Faithful,' replied Harun, 'those you have raised shall be laid low and those you have humbled shall be exalted, and the unjust man shall feel his shame. If power comes into my hands, I shall heal him whom you have broken and I shall give to him whom you have refused. Your children shall be set above my children and your sons shall marry my daughters, and thus will I pay my debt to the Imam Mahdi.'

These words melted Hadi's anger and his face shone with joy.* He said:

'Harun, that is just what I would have expected of you. Come here.'

Harun rose, kissed his brother's hand and was going back to his place when Hadi said to him:

'No, by the most illustrious shaikh* and glorious king, you shall sit nowhere but by me, in the place of honour.' Then he said:

'O treasurer, bring a million dinars to my brother immediately and as soon as the taxes are collected, you are to give him half.'

When Harun wished to withdraw, they led his mount right up to the edge of the carpet.

Amr al-Rumi said:

The Dream of Mahdi

'I asked Harun al-Rashid about the dream, and he quoted Mahdi's own words:

"I dreamed that I gave a branch of a tree to Hadi and another to Harun. Hadi's branch bore only a few leaves towards the top, while that of Harun, on the other hand, was covered with foliage along all its length." '

Mahdi related his dream to the physician Ibn Ishaq al-Saimari,* who interpreted it, saying:

'They will both reign, but the reign of Hadi will be short, while that of Harun will endure longer than that of any other Caliph. His days will be the best of days and his age the best of ages.'

Amr al-Rumi adds that when Harun al-Rashid came to the throne, he married his daughter Hamduna to Ja'far, and his other daughter, Fatima, to Ismail – both sons of Hadi – and that he kept all the promises which he had made to his predecessor.

THE SWORD SAMSAMA

Abd Allah ibn al-Dahhak relates the following tradition, according to al-Haitham ibn Adi:

'Mahdi had given his son Hadi a famous sword named Samsama,* which had belonged to Amr ibn Ma'dikarib. One day, after he had become Caliph, Hadi had this sword brought in and a great basket filled with dinars. Then he ordered his chamberlain:

"Let the poets enter!"

When they had come in, he asked them to choose the sword as subject for their verse. Ibn Yamin of Basra spoke first, and said:

> Hadi, the trustworthy, alone among men
> Possesses the Samsama of Amr al-Zubaidi;
> We have heard that the sword of Amr
> Was the best blade ever closed in a sheath.
> The lightning flash lit it with fire
> And death tempered it with poison, sudden and terrible.
> When you unsheath it, it shines like the sun
> So that a man can scarcely look upon it.
> The temper of its steel flashes on the blade
> Like the ripples of clear water.
> At the moment of striking, what does it matter
> Whether it cuts with the left edge or the right?

"Take the sword and the basket of dinars," said the Caliph. "I give you them both."

Ibn Yamin distributed the contents of the basket to the other poets, saying:

"You came here with me and it is because of me that you have not been rewarded; this sword will take the place of any other fee."

Hadi sent to him later and bought the sword back from him for 50,000 dinars.'*

The story of this reign, so interesting in spite of its being cut short, is told at length in the *Historical Annals* and the *Intermediate History*.

All help comes from God!

VI:285-287
§§ 2490-2492

THE ACCESSION OF HARUN AL-RASHID

Allegiance was sworn to Harun, son of Mahdi, at Baghdad, the City of Peace, on a Friday,* on the morning after the night that Hadi died. It was the twelfth day before the end of Rabi' 170 AH/786 AD. Harun died in a village called Sanabadh near Tus on a Saturday,* the 4th of Jumada II, 193 AH/809 AD. His reign had lasted twenty-three years and six months, or, according to another tradition, twenty-three years, two months and eighteen days. He was twenty-one years and two months old when he became caliph. He died at the age of forty-four years and four months.

As soon as the caliphate came to Harun al-Rashid, he summoned Yahya ibn Khalid, the Barmakid, and said to him:

'My dear little father, it was you who placed me on this throne, it was by your aid and the blessing of heaven – yes, by your happy influence and wise advice! And now I invest you with absolute power.'

And he gave him his seal. This occasion is commemorated in the following lines by Ibrahim al-Mawsili:

> Did you not see how the sun was pale and wan
> But when Harun took power it blazed with light?
> This was because of the good fortune of Harun,
> The generous, the faithful agent of God.
> He is the sun's elect, Yahya the sun's vizier.

Raita, the daughter of Abu al-Abbas al-Saffah, died a few months after the accession of Harun al-Rashid or, according to another version, at the end of the reign of Hadi. The mother of both that caliph and Rashid, Khaizuran, died in 173 AH/789 AD and Rashid walked on foot at the head of the funeral procession. The revenues of this princess amounted to 160 million dirhams.

VI:287-289
§§ 2493-2495

SHEEP'S HEAD

In the same year, Muhammad ibn Sulaiman died. Harun al-Rashid sequestered all his goods at Basra and in other towns and they proved to be worth more than 50 million dirhams, without counting his lands, houses and other income-producing properties. His revenues were 100,000 dirhams per day.

It is said that one day Muhammad ibn Sulaiman, as he was following the funeral procession of one of his female cousins on his father's side, on horseback through the streets of Basra with the qadi Sawwar at his side, was accosted by a madman, known in the town by the nickname of 'Sheep's Head'. The madman said:

'Muhammad, is it fair that you have 100,000 dirhams revenue a day and that I ask for half a dirham and can't get it?'

Then, turning to Sawwar, he added:

'If this is justice, I renounce it!'

The pages acting as escorts rushed up to him, but Muhammad restrained them and ordered that the man be given 100 dirhams. Later, as Muhammad was coming back, still accompanied by Sawwar, Sheep's Head stood in his path once again and said:

'May God bless your position! May He glorify your ancestors! May He beautify your face and raise your rank! I hope that all these favours may be granted you that you may carry out the good deeds that God desires to accomplish through you, and I wish you all joy in this world and the next!'

Then Sawwar went up to him and said:

'You revolting fool! That's not how you were talking the first time!'

'For the love of God and of the amir,' replied the madman, 'tell me from which *sura* of the Koran this verse comes: "If they receive these gifts, they are satisfied; if they do not receive them, they grow indignant" (Koran 9:58).'

'From the *sura* of "Repudiation",' replied Sawwar.

'You are right,' cried the madman, 'and may God and his Prophet repudiate you!'

This sally so amused Muhammad ibn Sulaiman that he nearly fell off his horse.

When Muhammad ibn Sulaiman had just finished building his palace on one of the river channels at Basra, Abd al-Samad ibn Shabib ibn Shaiba came to visit him. Muhammad said:

'What do you think of my new house?'

Sheep's Head

'It is a magnificent building,' came the reply, 'built in an enchanting place, on a vast estate, under the most limpid sky. It looks out over the loveliest of waters, with a view of fish and gazelles, glimpsed through porticoes!'

'Your reply', said Muhammad, 'is constructed more beautifully than my house!'

According to other people, the speaker of these words and the builder of the palace was Isa ibn Ja'far. At least, this is the tradition related by Muhammad ibn Zakariya al-Ghulabi according to Fadl ibn Abd-al-Rahman ibn Shabib ibn Shaiba. The poet Ibn Abi Uyaina has described the same palace in these lines:

> Visit Wadi al-Qasr, the River Valley of the Palace!
> What a wonderful valley! What a wonderful palace!
> You must visit it, even without an appointment.
> Visit it, for it has no equal
> In civilized or uncivilized places.

(Omitted: VI:292-294; §§ 2498-2501. Necrology with anecdotes.)

A QADI'S INTERPRETATION

In the year 182 AH/798 AD, Abu Yusuf Ya'qub ibn Ibrahim the qadi died at the age of sixty-nine. He belonged to a family of the Ansar, and was appointed qadi in 166 AH/782-3 AD, at the time of Hadi's expedition to Jurjan. He continued to exercise his profession until the day of his death – that is to say, for fifteen years.

Umm Ja'far, the wife of the Caliph Hadi, having submitted a request for a legal opinion to Abu Yusuf, and having received exactly the reply she desired – yet one which was in accordance with the letter of the Holy Law, as construed by him – sent him as a present a silver box which held two other silver boxes, each containing a different scent. She also sent him a golden cup filled with silver coins and a silver cup filled with gold coins, slaves, chests of clothing, a donkey and a mule. Someone who happened to be with Abu Yusuf just at the moment the gifts arrived, quoted the saying of the Prophet, may the prayers and peace of God be upon him:

'He who receives a gift should share it with those in whose company he happens to be.'

Abu Yusuf replied:

'You interpret these words in their superficial sense; but reason rejects such an inference, for the gifts of that time were dates and sour milk, while those of today are gold and silver and other precious things. These, therefore, are "The bounty of God, which he bestows on whom he pleases; and God is the source of great bounty" (Koran 57:21).'

VI:295-296
§ 2502

(Omitted: VI:296-300; §§ 2503-2506. A false oath of allegiance and the sudden death of Ibn Mus'ab.)

THE LAST PILGRIMAGE OF HARUN AL-RASHID

In the year 188 AH/804 AD, Harun al-Rashid went on his last pilgrimage to Mecca. They say that Abu Bakr ibn Ayyash, one of the most highly learned men of the age, said, as Harun al-Rashid was going through Kufa on his return from this pilgrimage:

'Harun al-Rashid will never travel this road again, nor will it be taken by any of the Abbasid Caliphs who come after him.'

'Does this prophecy come from your knowledge of the invisible world?' he was asked.

'Yes,' replied Abu Bakr.

'Is it a revelation from Heaven?'

'Yes.'

'Addressed directly to you?'

'No,' he replied, 'but to Muhammad – may the prayers and peace of God be upon him – and transmitted by him who was murdered in this place.' And with his hand he indicated the place in Kufa where Ali – may God be content with him – was killed.

VI:301-302
§ 2507

(Omitted: VI:302-305; §§ 2508-2510. Necrology; The speech of Abd al-Malik ibn Salih before Harun al-Rashid.)

DOCTOR JABRA'IL AND A FISH

Yusuf ibn Ibrahim, the friend of Ibrahim ibn al-Mahdi, said:

'I had the following story from Sulaiman the Eunuch from Khurasan, a freedman of Harun al-Rashid. This servant was in attendance on the Caliph, who was dining at Hira, when the governor of that town, Awn al-Ibadi, came in holding a plate on which lay a very plump fish. He set it before Rashid together with a sauce made especially for the purpose. The Caliph was about to try this dish, but his doctor, Jabra'il ibn Bakhtishu', forbade him it and signed to the steward to remove the fish from the table and put it aside for himself. Rashid noticed this. The table having been cleared and Rashid having washed his hands, the doctor went away.

"Rashid ordered me," Sulaiman relates, "to follow Jabra'il and to surprise him in his apartments at table and then to come back and tell what I had seen. I carried out this order, but I realized from the precautions that I saw Jabra'il take that he had guessed the mission with which I had been entrusted. In fact, he entered a room in the house of Awn and called for food. Among the various dishes was the fish in question.

Then he called for three bowls. In the first he placed a piece of fish over which he poured wine from Tizanabadh, which is a village lying between Kufa and Qadisiya, rich in vines, trees, palms and orchards, watered in every direction by many canals from the Euphrates, and whose wine is described as being as good as that of Qutrabbul. After having thus moistened the fish, he said:

'This is how Jabra'il eats it.'

In the second bowl, he placed another piece of fish over which he poured iced water, and said:

'This is how the Commander of the Faithful eats it, may God glorify him, if he does not mix it with other food.'

In the third bowl he placed a piece of fish and with it all kinds of meats, roasts, sweets, spiced sauces and hors d'oeuvres; that is, he took a small portion, just one or two bites, of each dish served, and poured iced water over the whole.

'That,' he said, 'is the Caliph's meal, assuming he tasted other things beside the fish.'

Then he gave the three bowls to the steward and said: 'Set them aside until the Commander of the Faithful shall wake.' After which, he attacked the fish and ate enough to choke himself, but when he was thirsty, he called for a bowl of undiluted wine. And then he took a siesta.

Doctor Jabra'il and a Fish

When Rashid woke, he asked me for news of Jabra'il and whether he had or had not tasted the famous fish. I told him what had happened and at once he had the three bowls brought. In the first, that which Jabra'il had identified as his and into which he had poured neat wine, the fish was reduced to tiny flakes and had liquified and mixed with the wine. In the second, that which Jabra'il had considered the Commander of the Faithful's and onto which he had poured iced water, the food had swollen to half again its original volume. In the third, that which according to Jabra'il was the Caliph's portion if he ate the fish with other things, the various bits of food had gone off and produced so foul a smell that when Rashid drew near he almost retched.

The Caliph then ordered me to take 5,000 dirhams to Jabra'il and he added: 'Who could blame me for loving a man who rules me with such prudence?'
As for me, I took him the money."'

THE DREAM OF HARUN AL-RASHID

Here is another story, which we owe to Abd Allah ibn Malik al-Khuza'i, who was in charge of Rashid's household and his chief of police:

'A messenger from the Caliph came to my house at an hour at which I was not accustomed to receive messages. He had me get up and led me away, without giving me the time to change my clothes, which frightened me very much. When I reached the palace, the eunuch went before me to inform the Caliph of my arrival. He gave me leave to enter and I did so. I found him sitting on his bed. I greeted him; he remained silent. I was dumbfounded and felt my fear redouble. At last he addressed me and said:

"Abd Allah, do you know why I have summoned you at such a time?"

"No, by God," I replied, "I do not."

"Just now, I dreamed that an Abyssinian appeared before me with a lance in his hand and said: 'Give Musa ibn Ja'far* his freedom at once – or I will pierce you with this lance!' Go, Abd Allah, and let him out of prison."

"O Commander of the Faithful," I asked the Caliph three times over, "is it really Musa ibn Ja'far who is to be freed?"

"Yes," he answered, "go now, this moment, and free him from his cell, give him 30,000 dirhams and tell him from me: If you wish to remain with us, your treatment will be all you could hope; if you wish to go to Medina, permission is granted."

I made my way to the prison to let him out. When he saw me enter, Musa rose abruptly, thinking that I had come to carry out some fateful order.

"Do not be afraid," I said, "the Commander of the Faithful has ordered me to free you and to give you 30,000 dirhams; furthermore, he would have you know that if you wish to stay with him, you will be well treated, but if you prefer to go and live in Medina you are perfectly free to do so."

After having made over the 30,000 dirhams to him and having opened the prison gates, I told him how much the whole business had surprised me.

"I can explain it all," said Musa. "Last night, the Prophet – may the prayers and peace of God be upon him – came to me in my sleep and spoke to me as follows:

'O Musa, your imprisonment is unjust. Say these words and tonight you will not sleep in prison.'

'O you who are dearer to me than my father and mother,' I said to the Prophet, 'what should I say?'

The Dream of Harun al-Rashid

The Prophet replied: 'Pray thus: "O Thou, Who hearest all voices and anticipates all things, Thou Who wilt clothe our dry bones with flesh and resurrect the dead, I implore You, calling upon Your glorious names, I implore You by Your greatest and most sublime titles, by that hidden and mysterious name which no man knows! Merciful God, whose patience cannot be worn away, bountiful God, Whose favours are as ceaseless as they are innumerable, come to my aid!"'

'And, you see, my prayers have been fulfilled.'

A BLACK AND A SONG

Hammad ibn Ishaq ibn Ibrahim al-Mawsili relates the following anecdote, told him by Ibrahim ibn al-Mahdi:

'I was on the pilgrimage with Rashid and as we were travelling I became separated from the rest and went on my way on horseback, far from my companions. Overwhelmed by sleep, I did not notice that my mount had left the right road and when I awoke I was off the pilgrim route. The heat was suffocating and I was burning with thirst. Soon, I saw before me a tent and a domed structure sheltering a well near a tilled field. I was between Mecca and Medina and had not seen a single living soul. On examining the hut more closely, I saw that a black was sleeping there. He became aware of my presence and opened huge eyes like two buckets of blood and sat up. He was of enormous size.

"Black," I said, "give me some water to drink!"

He repeated my words, mimicking me, and said:

"If you are thirsty, alight and drink."

I was mounted on a bad-tempered restive nag and I did not dare dismount lest it bolt. I hit the horse on the head and then made use of my skill as a singer, which had never been more useful to me than on this occasion. I raised my voice and produced the following song:

> O my companions, if I die bury me
> On the cool plain of Arwa
> And give me water to drink
> From the wells of Urwa!
>
> There is a spring encampment near Ajaj
> And a summer encampment near the castle of Quba'.
> Its water is warm in winter
> And cool in summer and shines
> Like the full moon at night.

Then the slave raised his head and said to me:

"Which would you prefer, plain water or an infusion of water and grain?"

I replied that I wanted the second. He took a wooden cup full of *sawiq*, as it is called, which he poured into a bowl and offered me, and then he began to strike his head and breast, crying:

A Black and a Song

"O my breast is burning! O! My heart is in flames! Master, sing again and I will continue to pour!"

When I had finished drinking, he went on:

"Master, you are several miles from the road; I am afraid that you may get thirsty. I want to fill this water-skin which I have here and carry it before you."

I said:

"Do so!"

He filled his water-skin and went before me, hopping and skipping and never losing the rhythm of the song. As soon as I paused to catch my breath, he came to me and asked if I were thirsty. And thus I went on, letting him hear my songs until he had put me back on the right way.

"Go," he said to me then, "and may God keep you and may He preserve in you those precious gifts with which He has endowed you!"

At least that was what he meant, for he spoke his own barbarous tongue.

I rejoined the caravan. Rashid, worried by my absence, had sent horsemen and camel patrols out into the desert to look for me. His joy was great when he saw me again. I went to him and told him my adventure, and he said:

"Bring me the black!"

Almost at once the slave was brought before him.

"Well," the Caliph said, "for what does your heart burn?"

"For Maimuna, O my lord," answered the black.

"And who is Maimuna?"

"The daughter of Hubshiya."

"And who is Hubshiya?" asked the Commander of the Faithful.

"The daughter of Bilal, O my lord."

Rashid had him questioned in his mother tongue and he learned that the man belonged to the son of Ja'far al-Tayyar and that the girl whom he loved was in the service of the descendants of Hasan ibn Ali. Rashid ordered her to be purchased, but her master refused to take any money for her and offered her to Rashid. Then he bought the black and married him to his love, after having freed them both, and furthermore gave him two orchards, belonging to his domains at Medina, and 300 dinars.

VI:311-314
§§ 2514-2516

POEM ON A DOVE

One day, Ibn al-Sammak went to see Harun al-Rashid. Before the Caliph was a dove pecking at some grain. Rashid ordered him to paint the dove in a few words.

'It seems,' said the poet, 'as if she looks through two rubies and pecks at the grain with two pearls and walks on two carnelians.'

We have also heard another poet's description of a dove:

> A hidden voice laments
> A loved-one's leaving.
> She wears a necklace curved
> Like the letter *nūn*,
> Blood-red at the ends.
> She looks at you through
> Two rubies and sings
> From between twin pearls.
> Her feet are like amaranths;
> She has twin feathers that curl
> Like love-locks. Her legs
> Are the colour of coral.
> Two black jagged lines
> Are woven on her wings,
> The tips of which are peacock
> Coloured. She hides concealed
> In a thicket's shadow.
> She misses her lover and coos
> In pain at separation.
> Her eyelids frozen,
> She weeps without tears.
> She has no need to make up her eyes
> As women do after weeping.

VI:314-316
§§ 2517-2518

MA'N IBN ZA'IDA

Ma'n ibn Za'ida* came into the presence of Harun al-Rashid, who was angry at him. As he was walking with small steps, Harun said:

'O Ma'n, you have aged, by God!'

'Yes, O Commander of the Faithful, but in your service!' came the reply.

'You still have some strength left in you, however.'

'It is yours, O Commander of the Faithful!'

'You are a steadfast man.'

'Against your enemies, O Commander of the Faithful.'

The Caliph pardoned him and gave him the governorship of a city.

An ascetic of Basra, Abd al-Rahman ibn Zaid, to whom these words were related, cried:

'Woe to him! If he has pardoned Ma'n, he has left his Lord nothing to do!'

One day, this same Ma'n ibn Za'ida said to Rashid, who had asked him to hold himself in readiness for an important mission:

'O Commander of the Faithful, God has given me, for your service, a heart strengthened by devotion, a hand stretched out to fulfill your orders, a sword whetted against your enemies. Make known therefore your will.'

This reply is also attributed to Yazid ibn Mazyad.

AMIN AND MA'MUN AS CHILDREN

'I presented myself one day before Harun al-Rashid,' relates Kisa'i, 'and having offered my greetings and prayers for a long reign, was about to retire, when he said: "Sit down!" Almost at once, the general public retired and there remained only a handful of courtiers.

"Kisa'i," said the Caliph, "would you like to see Muhammad (Amin) and Abd Allah (Ma'mun)?"

"Commander of the Faithful," I replied, "I have no warmer desire than to see them and nothing would give me greater pleasure than to see how God has blessed you in these two children."

He ordered them to be brought.

The two young princes soon came in, shining like stars in the firmament and enchanting in their self-possession and gravity. They moved forward at a slow pace with lowered eyes, until they reached the threshold of the hall. There they addressed their father with the royal salutation, joined with the most eloquent prayers for his well-being. Rashid told them to draw near and at his orders Muhammad placed himself on his right and Abd Allah on his left. The Caliph then invited me to have them recite passages from the Koran and to ask them some questions. They replied to all of these in the most satisfactory manner and passed the test with all success. Rashid was delighted and did not hide his pleasure. Then he said to me:

"Kisa'i, what do you think of their comportment? What do you say to their answers?"

"O Commander of the Faithful," I replied, "one could say of them what the poet said:

> I see two moons of majesty
> And two sprigs of the Caliphate,
> Enhanced by a descent
> Of nobility and high lineage.

Commander of the Faithful, they are a branch from a thriving trunk, which has been well-planted, whose roots are buried in most fertile earth and are fed on sweet waters. Their father is a most powerful and effective leader, whose learning is vast and whose wisdom is immense. They will judge with the same justice, they will shine with his brilliance, they will speak with his tongue and develop under his happy influence. May God grant the Commander of the Faithful enjoyment in them! May he prolong their days and those of the Caliph, for the well-being of the Islamic community!"

After this I asked them if they could recite any poems by heart.* They both answered "yes" and Muhammad began thus:

> Poor, I have the decency of poverty;
> Rich, I share what I possess.
> I stay away from those unlike me.
> I make my wealth my honour's shield;
> I owe my pre-eminence to my own merit.

Abd Allah then proceeded to recite the following lines:

> As dawn broke she lost no time in blaming you
> But she blames without understanding.
> I am in the power of the King of all;
> He gives happiness only when He wants.
> How many rejoice in others misfortunes,
> And then are terrified when fortune changes!
> My lance will be seen on the day of battle,
> And it is a lance that does not easily break.

Among the children of Caliphs – those branches of a blessed tree – I had never seen two young princes whose replies were more to the point or whose language was more elegant, or who were more quick to display their learning, than the two sons of Rashid, and I offered up many prayers for their happiness, which their father shared in by saying "Amen". He drew them to his breast and clasped their hands together, and he had hardly let them go when I saw the tears falling on his breast. Finally, he allowed them to withdraw and when they had gone, he turned to me and said:

"I seem to see you and these two children when the final judgement is nigh and the heavens fall in upon themselves and the hour appointed in the Book shall be fulfilled, and these two brothers shall cease to be as one, their interests will divide them and their enmity will be openly shown. Their rage will cause rivers of blood to flow, death will stalk the land and the veils of women will be torn away, and many of the living will wish they were numbered among the dead."

"Commander of the Faithful," I asked Rashid, "is this the decree of the fate which attended their birth, or is it a sign that has been revealed to the Caliph?"

"Neither, by God," replied the Caliph. "It is the inexorable Tradition transmitted to the learned men by the true heirs of Ali, and to them by the Prophets."'

VI:317-321
§§ 2520-2522

THE EDUCATION OF AMIN

The grammarian Ahmar relates:

'Rashid sent for me in order to entrust me with the education of Amin. When I went in to the Caliph, he spoke to me as follows:

"Ahmar, the Commander of the Faithful entrusts to you his most precious blood, the very fruit of his heart. He gives you full authority over his son and it is his son's duty to obey you. Be worthy of the task which the Caliph has confided to you. Teach your pupil to recite the Koran and instruct him in the Traditions. Teach him to recite poetry and see that he is versed in the Sunna. See that he weighs his words and speaks to the point, and train him not to laugh out of turn. Teach him to receive the old men of the house of Hashim when they come to him with due respect and to treat the leaders who take part in his councils with consideration. Do not let one single hour of the day pass without using it for his improvement. Be neither so severe that his intelligence withers, nor so indulgent that he becomes lazy and accustomed to idleness. Correct him, as far as you are able, using friendship and gentleness, but if this has no effect, use strictness and show severity." '

AMIN AND MA'MUN

It is said that one day Umani, the poet, made a great speech before Harun al-Rashid, in which he ceaselessly praised the merits of Ma'mun and exhorted the Caliph to renew the covenant of succession in his favour. When he had finished speaking, the Caliph said:

'Rejoice, O Umani! Ma'mun is going to be my heir.'

'All thanks be to you, Commander of the Faithful,' replied the poet, 'my joy is that felt by grass for rain, the barren woman for a child, the man on his deathbed for his recovery. Ma'mun is a peerless prince, who knows how to defend his majesty, and he closely resembles his grandfather.'

The Caliph asked him:

'What do you have to say about Amin?'

'Good grazing,' replied Umani, 'but not as good as camel thorn.'

Rashid smiled and said:

'May God curse a Bedouin like you, that knows so well the place where my desire lies! I myself, by God, see in Ma'mun the energetic wisdom of Mansur, the piety of Mahdi, the pride of Hadi and, if God would permit me to make a fourth analogy,* it would not be far to seek.'

THE SUCCESSION

This is what Asma'i relates:

'I found myself near Rashid in the course of one of his evening gatherings and noticed that he was quite extraordinarily agitated. Sometimes he would sit, sometimes lie on his side, at others he would recline and murmur these lines:

> Consign the affairs of the worshippers of God
> To a trustworthy man who does not vacillate,
> One who is devoid of weakness or weariness.
> Disdain the advice of flighty minds
> Who do not understand what even
> The people themselves have understood.

When I heard these words, I guessed that the Caliph was meditating some important plan. Soon, he ordered Masrur, the eunuch:
"Fetch Yahya!"
A few minutes later, Yahya the Barmakid was with him.
"O Yahya," the Caliph said to him, "the Prophet – may the prayers and peace of God be upon him – died without making a will. Islam was then in all the vigour of its youth, the faith was new-born, unity reigned among the tribes, to whom God had given security after fear and power after humiliation. But the tribes were not slow to rebel against Abu Bakr – and you know what happened then. Abu Bakr, having handed on the succession to Umar, the Islamic community recognized him and accepted him as Caliph. But Umar entrusted the choice of his successor to the deliberations of an advisory council and you are not unaware that as a result of the ensuing civil discord, authority was taken from the hands which should have possessed it.

I myself wish to establish the succession. I wish to make certain that it passes to a man whose behaviour I approve and whose actions I respect, to a man whom I am certain will rule ably, without either weakness or fear. I am speaking of Ma'mun.

The choice of the House of Hashim, however, inclines towards Amin, despite the fact that he is a slave to his passions, his whims, which are indeed his sole rule of conduct, and despite the ease with which he dissipates his fortune and consults women – even slave girls – as to his plans.

Ma'mun, on the other hand, deserves only praise. His judgement is sound and the most important matters can be confided to him. Now, if I show my preference for Ma'mun, I unleash the anger of the House of Hashim against us; if I make Amin my sole heir, I am not confident of his acceptance by the people. Tell me how you see this matter. Give me some advice, the virtue and efficacy of which will be recognized by one and all, for you are – by God's grace – a man of inspired counsel and rare understanding."

"O Commander of the Faithful," replied Yahya, "all faults are forgiveable and all errors can be rectified, except those concerning the succession to the throne, for an error of this kind is full of dangers and such a mistake cannot be undone. But this is neither the time nor the place to talk of it."

Rashid understood that his counsellor wanted to talk with him in private and ordered me to draw aside. I rose and went to sit in a corner where I could hear what was being said. They began a long discussion and their debate lasted all night long. They only parted after having decided that the Caliphate would pass to Ma'mun, after Amin.'

ZUBAIDA'S OPINION

One day, Zubaida came to Rashid and said to him:

'You are unjust to your son Amin. You give him the government of Iraq and then strip him of supplies and officers – but you give all these things to Ma'mun.'

'And who are you,' replied Rashid, 'to discuss our actions and choose our agents? I have given your son the government of a country at peace and to Ma'mun a country at war. Now the ruler of a rebellious province has far more need of troops than the ruler of one at peace. In any case, we fear your son's intentions towards Ma'mun, but we have no fear regarding Ma'mun's intentions towards your son Amin, should he succeed to the Caliphate.'

RASHID'S PILGRIMAGE WITH HIS SONS

In the year 186 AH/802 AD, Rashid performed the prilgrimage with his two heirs apparent, Amin and Ma'mun. He wrote down the agreement between them and hung the pages inside the Ka'ba. Ibrahim al-Nakha'i tells how the document fell to the gound just as it was being hauled into place.

'I said to myself,' Ibrahim adds, 'just as this document has fallen before being raised, so will this agreement be broken before reaching its term.'

Here is the account of Sa'id ibn Amir of Basra:

'I was on the pilgrimage that year. Now, the general public was very excited by the whole business of the agreement and the oath sworn in the Ka'ba. I met a Bedouin of the tribe of Hudhail, who was leading his camel along while singing these words:

> How many an oath has been broken ,
> How many fires of rebellion have been lit!

'Woe to you!', I cried, 'what are you saying?'

'I am saying,' retorted the tribesman, 'that swords shall be unsheathed and strife and discord be loosed, and that division shall appear within the empire.'

'How do you know?' I asked him.

'Do you not see,' he said, 'the two men standing over the dead camel arguing, while two crows splash in the blood? By God, this will end in war and disaster.'

They say that Amin, having sworn the oath that Rashid demanded of him, was about to leave the Ka'ba, when Ja'far ibn Yahya the Barmakid called him back and said:

'May God forsake you if you betray your brother!'

He repeated these words three times and each time made Amin swear his oath anew.

This, they say, was the reason why Zubaida bore a grudge against Ja'far ibn Yahya. From this time on, she was ever the first to fan the Caliph's grievances and to urge him to overthrow his favourite.

In the year 187 AH/803 AD Rashid had his son Qasim recognized as Ma'mun's successor, with the provision that Ma'mun, having once assumed the Caliphate,

The Meadows of Gold

was to decide, as the ultimate authority, whether he should confirm Qasim in this position, or deprive him of it.

VI:326-329
§§ 2527-2530

(Omitted: VI:330-340; §§ 2531-2542. Necrology and verses; More poems by Abu al-Atahiya.)

THE DEVIL'S SONG

'One evening I was with Rashid,' said Ishaq ibn Ibrahim al-Mawsili, 'and I was singing him an air which seemed to enchant him. He said:
"Don't stop!"
So I continued until he fell asleep. Then I stopped, set down my lute and went to my usual place.
Suddenly I saw a handsome, well built young man appear. He was wearing a light robe of painted silk and he was very elegant. He came in, greeted me, and sat down. I was very surprised that an unknown person could simply walk in at such a time and at such a place, without having been announced. I said to myself that it was probably some son of Rashid's whom I had so far neither met nor seen.
The stranger picked up the lute from where I had left it, placed it in his lap and began to try it out with all the skill in the world. He made harmonies I could never have believed and after a prelude, more beautiful than anything I had ever heard, the youth began this song:

> Drink a few more cups with me, my friends,
> Before you go! Cupbearer, bring us some more
> Of this excellent, pure wine!
> Already the first light of morning has stripped
> Away the darkness and torn the chemise from the night.

Then he set down his lute and said:
"Son of a whore, when you sing, *that* is how you should sing!"
And he walked out.
I ran after him and asked the chamberlain:
"Who was the young man who just left?"
"No one has come in or gone out," he replied.
"No, no," I insisted, "I have just seen him walk right by me, only a minute ago, a man with such-and-such an appearance!"
But the chamberlain stated again very positively that no one had entered or left. I was more astonished than ever. As I returned to my place the Caliph awoke and asked:
"What is going on?"
I told him the story and he was extremely surprised.
"Beyond any shadow of a doubt," he said, "you have received a visit from

Satan."

Afterwards, at his request, I repeated the song I had just heard. He listened with great pleasure and then gave me a handsome present. After which I withdrew.'

A HARD-WON SONG

Ibrahim al-Mawsili tells the following story:
'One day, Rashid gathered together his singers to give a performance which was attended by all the important people of the court. I found myself among the musicians and the singer Miskin of Medina, better known under the name of Abu Sadaqa, was with us. He was a player with a particularly good sense of rhythm, with a natural genius, and was a pleasant companion and told excellent stories. Rashid, stirred by *nabidh*, demanded a certain air which had suddenly come into his mind and at his orders the Master of the Curtain invited Ibn Jami' to sing the piece. He obeyed, but did not succeed in satisfying the Caliph. Each of the singers present performed it in turn, but with no greater success. Then the Master of the Curtain, addressing Miskin, said:
"The Commander of the Faithful orders you to let him hear this air – if you can sing it skilfully."
He at once began to sing, to the great surprise of all of us. We could not understand how a man like him could dare perform in our presence a piece which we had not managed to render to the Caliph's satisfaction. When he had finished, I heard Rashid say, raising his voice:
"O Miskin, sing it again!"
Miskin began his song with a power, a spirit and a warmth unparalleled.
Rashid said:
"You have excelled, by God! Miskin, you have sung beautifully!"
Then he ordered the curtain which separated him from us to be drawn aside.
At this point Miskin said:
"O Commander of the Faithful, this song has a curious story."
"What is it?" asked the Caliph.
"I was the slave of a member of the family of Zubair and I followed the calling of tailor. My master took two dirhams from me each day, and this tax once paid I was free to attend to my own affairs. I loved singing with the greatest passion. One day, a descendant of Ali for whom I had made a tunic, paid me two dirhams, kept me for dinner and gave me plenty to drink. I was just leaving his house in a very gay mood, when I happened to meet a black woman who was carrying her water jar on her shoulder and singing the air which you have just heard. In my enchantment, forgetting all serious matters and giving no thought to my poverty, I said to the woman:
"By Him who is in this tomb* and by the *minbar*! I beseech you to teach me

The Meadows of Gold

your song!"

"By the Truth of Him who is in this tomb and by the *minbar*," she replied, "I will only teach it to you if you give me two dirhams!"

Then, O Commander of the Faithful, I pulled out of my pocket the two dirhams destined for my daily tax and gave them to her. She, putting down her jar, sat on the ground and beating the rhythm on the jar, sang her song, repeating it until it was engraved in my heart. I then went back to my master. As soon as he saw me he said:

"Give me your tax!"

I told him my story and he said:

"Son of a whore! Didn't I warn you that I would never accept any excuses, even if there were only the smallest part missing?"

So saying, he laid me on the ground and gave me fifty of the hardest possible strokes of the rod. Furthermore, he had my head and beard shaved. In truth, O Commander of the Faithful, I spent the saddest night of all God's Creation. The smart of the punishment I had just endured had made me forget my tune and nothing hurt me more than the loss of that song.

The following day, I wrapped up my head, slipped my tailor's shears into my sleeve and set out for the place where I had met the black woman. I stood there at a loss, for I knew neither her name nor her address. I was still in this perplexity, when I saw her approaching. At the sight of her, I forgot all my troubles. I went up to her and she said:

"By the Lord of the Ka'ba! You have forgotten the song!"

"It's just as you say," I answered, and told her how my head and chin had been shaved and offered her a reward if she would go through her song again.

"By the Truth of the Tomb, and He who dwells therein," the woman replied, "I shall not repeat it for you for less than two dirhams!"

I pulled my shears out of my sleeve and ran to pawn them for two dirhams, which I then gave her. She set down the jar which she was carrying on her head and began to sing as she had done the day before.

"Give me back my two dirhams!" I said to her, "I do not need you to sing any more!"

"By God," she answered, "you won't see them again! Don't hope that I will ever give them back." And she added: "I am sure that the four dirhams you have spent will be worth 4,000 dinars from the Caliph."

Then she once again took up her song, accompanying herself on her jar, nor did she cease repeating it until it was rooted in my breast. We parted and I went back to my master, but trembling and very worried. On seeing me, he said:

"Give me your tax!"

My tongue stammered out excuses.

"Son of a whore!" he said to me, "wasn't yesterday's lesson enough for you then?"

"I will tell you the truth," I said, "and without lying. Yesterday's tax money and today's went to pay for this song." And I hastened to let him hear it.

A Hard-Won Song

"What!" he cried, "you've known such a song for two days and haven't told me about it? May I divorce my wife if it isn't true that I would have freed you yesterday if you had let me hear it! Your head and your chin are shaved – there is nothing I can do about that – but I will let you off your tax, for the love of God, until your hair grows back."

Rashid laughed whole-heartedly and said to the musician:

"I don't know which I like better, your story or your song, but I do want to ensure that the black woman's promises are fulfilled!"

And indeed, before he left, Miskin was given his 4,000 dinars.'

HORSE-RACING AT RAQQA

Rashid held horse races one day at Raqqa. After the starting signal had been given, he went and took his place at the end of the hippodrome, which was the finishing line, mounted on his horse. Soon the first horses appeared. In the lead were two, neck and neck; neither seemed able to draw ahead of the other. He watched them carefully, then cried:

'By God, that's my horse!'

And then, recognizing the other, he added:

'And here is my son Ma'mun's horse, arriving second by a length!'

And indeed, outstripping all the others, his horse arrived first and that of Ma'mun second.

This double victory filled the Caliph with joy. The other horses having passed the finishing line and the race being over, he was thinking of leaving when Asma'i, who was present at the occasion and had witnessed the Caliph's pleasure, said to Fadl ibn al-Rabi':

'Fadl, this is a day of days for us! Do me the pleasure of taking me into the presence of the Commander of the Faithful.'

Fadl went to Rashid and said to him:

'O Commander of the Faithful, Asma'i is here. He wants to recite something on the victory of the two horses which, God willing, can only serve to increase the Caliph's joy.'

Rashid gave orders that he should be allowed to enter and, when he saw him, said:

'Well, Asma'i, what do you have for us?'

'O Commander of the Faithful,' replied the latter, 'you and your son, after the victory of your two horses, are in the situation described in the following lines by Khansa':

> Racing with his father, they drew neck and neck;
> They were like two falcons falling on a nest.
> His father drew ahead and flew at the finish;
> None could be worthier to contend with him
> Than a son who respects his years and his majesty.'

VI:348-349
§ 2547

FISH TONGUES

The following anecdote is related by Ibrahim ibn al-Mahdi:

'The Caliph Harun al-Rashid, while at Raqqa, was pleased to accept my invitation and come to visit me. Now Rashid was in the habit of eating hot dishes before the cold, and when the latter were served, he noticed near him a silver cup of fish slices that had been shaped into the form of a fish. Thinking that the fish had been sliced into pieces that were much too small, he asked me:

"Why did your cook chop the fish so fine?"

"O Commander of the Faithful," I replied, "those are fish tongues, not slices of fish."

"It looks as if there are at least a hundred in this cup," answered Rashid.

Muraqib, my eunuch, said:

"O Commander of the Faithful, there are more than 150 tongues there."

Rashid asked him to swear to tell the truth and say how much the dish had cost. The eunuch replied that the price was above a thousand dirhams. Rashid lifted his hand from the dish and swore that he would touch no other food until Muraqib had brought him one thousand dirhams. When this sum had been handed over to him, he gave orders that it should be distributed to the poor.

"I want it to be," he said, "some expiation for your insane wastefulness. A thousand dirhams for a cup of fish!"

And taking the plate he gave it to one of his eunuchs, saying:

"Go out of my brother's house, wait for the first beggar that comes by and give it to him." '

Ibrahim said:

'Now this dish which I had bought in the Caliph's honour had cost me 270 dinars. I signed to one of my servants to leave at the same time as the Caliph's man and to buy back the plate from whoever came to possess it. But Rashid was aware of my intention. He called his eunuch and said to him:

"My page, when you give it to the beggar, tell him that the Commander of the Faithful recommends that on no account should he sell it for less than 200 dinars and in fact it is worth more than that."

Rashid's eunuch accomplished his mission faithfully and, by God, in order to buy back this precious object from the beggar, it cost me 200 dinars.'

VI:349-351
§ 2548

THE NAME IBRAHIM

'I found myself one day,' Ibrahim ibn al-Mahdi again relates, 'on board a boat which was taking us to Mosul. We were playing chess, while the sailors were plying the oars. When the game was over, Harun al-Rashid said to me:

"Ibrahim, in your opinion, what is the most beautiful of all names?"

"The most beautiful name," I replied, "is that of the Messenger of God, may the prayers and peace of God be upon him."

"And then?"

"That of Harun, the Commander of the Faithful."

"And what, according to you," went on the Caliph, "is the most hateful name?"

"Ibrahim," I replied.

He upbraided me for this.

"What!" he cried, "was Ibrahim not the name of the Friend of God, Abraham?"

"Yes," I answered, "and thanks to that inauspicious name he was persecuted by Nimrod."

"Nonetheless," retorted Rashid, "the son of the Messenger of God, may the prayers and peace of God be upon him, was called Ibrahim!"

"That's true," I replied, "and that is why he died young."

"And the Imam Ibrahim?"

"Through the baleful influence of his name, Marwan al-Ja'di put him to death in a sack filled with quicklime. Do you want other examples? Ibrahim ibn al-Walid was driven from his throne; Ibrahim ibn Abd Allah ibn al-Hasan was killed; in a word, I see that all who have borne this name have been killed, flogged or exiled."

I was still speaking when I heard a sailor in one of the boats shout at the top of his voice:

"Hey there, Ibrahim! Row!"

And a moment later:

"Hey, Ibrahim! Suck your mother's cunt! Row!"

I turned to Rashid and added:

"Well, O Commander of the Faithful, will you believe me when I say that the most inauspicious of names is that of Ibrahim?"

Rashid began to laugh and shake with joy.'

VI:351-353
§ 2549

BAMBOO AND REED

'One day I was with Rashid,' relates this same Ibrahim, 'when a messenger from Abd Allah ibn Salih brought some bamboo trays covered with napkins and a letter which Rashid began to read.

"May God bless and reward him!" he exclaimed.

"O Commander of the Faithful," I said, "tell us on whose behalf these cordial good wishes are being offered, that we may add our thanks to yours."

"Abd Allah ibn Salih," replied Rashid.

Then he drew aside the napkins and we saw several trays stacked one on top of the other, containing pistachios, hazel nuts and several kinds of fruit.

"Commander of the Faithful," I said, "this gift does not seem to me to justify your invocation; perhaps there is something I don't know in the letter you have just received."

He gave it to me and I read these words:

"O Commander of the Faithful, I went to visit the garden next to my house, which I have been able to till thanks to your kindness. Its fruits being at the point of perfect ripeness, I have picked some of each variety and placed them in reed trays and sent them to the Commander of the Faithful, in order to obtain the blessing of his prayers, just as I have been favoured by his generous gifts."

"By God, O Commander of the Faithful," I said to Rashid, "I still don't see anything in this letter worth so many complimentary remarks."

"Dolt!" he answered. "Don't you see that out of respect for the name of our mother, may God have mercy on her soul, he used the word *qudban* (reed) instead of *khaizuran* (bamboo)?" '

VI:353-354
§ 2550

(Omitted: VI:354-356; §§ 2551-2552. A thousand dinars paid for each verse of a poem; The best kind of dates.)

THE DEATH OF HARUN AL-RASHID

Abd al-Malik ibn Salih was going to visit the Caliph, when the chamberlain warned him that in the course of the previous night the Commander of the Faithful had lost one son and that another had been born to him; thus he would have to combine condolences with congratulations. When Abd al-Malik stood before Harun, he spoke thus:

'Commander of the Faithful, God has given you great joy at the very moment in which he has inflicted on you great grief. He has balanced the one with the other, because he rewards resignation and repays gratitude.'

The illness from which Harun al-Rashid was suffering grew worse during his journey to Tus in the year 193 AH/809 AD. His doctors making light of it, he sent for a Persian reputed to have some knowledge of medicine who lived in that town. Several vials of urine were presented to him, one of which was the Caliph's. As he examined this last, not knowing where it came from, the Persian said:

'Warn the patient that there is no hope and tell him to make his will, for his sickness is incurable.'

Harun al-Rashid wept bitterly when he heard these fatal words and turning over on his bed, he repeated these lines:

> The doctor, with his medicine and his remedies
> Cannot avoid the dreadful decree of fate.
> How can it be that the doctor should die
> Of the very illness he has cured in times gone by?

Harun al-Rashid's weakness increased when he heard the diagnosis of this doctor and people began to spread the rumour that he was dead. He heard it and sent for a donkey, which he wished to mount, but when he approached it, his legs gave way and he could not stay in the saddle.

'Help me dismount,' he then said. 'These spreaders of ill-tidings have told the truth.'

He had several shrouds spread out before him and chose one for himself. He ordered his grave dug and on seeing it cried:

'What use are my riches? My majesty has been stripped from me!' (Koran 69:28-9).

Then he ordered that the brother of Rafi' ibn al-Laith* be brought before him and he said to him:

The Death of Harun al-Rashid

'See to what a state you have reduced me. It was you who forced me to undertake this expedition, although I was sick and weak.'

Rafi' ibn al-Laith's brother was among those who had taken part in the revolt against Harun al-Rashid.

'By God,' went on the Commander of the Faithful, 'I shall make you die under tortures which have never been inflicted on anyone before!'

And he gave the order that his limbs be hacked off one by one. As for Rafi', he asked Ma'mun for amnesty and his story can be found in my *Historical Annals*.

Then Harun al-Rashid gathered together all the descendants of Hashim who were in his army and said to them:

'Everything that lives must die. Everything that is young must grow old. See what fate has wrought with me. I am going to give you three pieces of advice: keep your promises religiously; heed the advice of your Imams and maintain your unity; look after Muhammad (Amin) and Abd Allah (Ma'mun). If one of the two rises against his brother, put down the revolt and censure his treachery and the violation of the pact.'

That same day he distributed many fiefs, estates and territories.

Abu Khalifa al-Fadl ibn al-Hubab al-Jumahi and Muhammad ibn al-Hasan ibn al-Duraid tell, on the authority of al-Rayyashi, the following story, which we owe to Asma'i:

'One day I entered the presence of Harun al-Rashid and found him reading, tears streaming down his cheeks. I remained standing, waiting for him to regain control of himself and notice me. At last he said "Sit down!" And when I had taken my place, he asked: "Did you witness my tears?"

"Yes, O Commander of the Faithful," I said.

"They were not flowing on account of the affairs of this world," he said, and threw me the piece of paper he was holding in his hand, which bore the following lines by Abu al-Atahiya, written in a most beautiful script:

> Will you be warned by the example of him who has left
> His palaces empty on the morning of his death?
> By him whom death has cut down and who lies
> Abandoned by kinsfolk and friends?
> By him whose thrones stand vacant,
> By him whose daises are empty?
> Where now are the kings and where
> Are the men who passed this way before you?
> O you who have chosen the world and its delights,
> You who have always listened to sycophants,
> Take what you can of the pleasures of the world
> For death comes as the end.

"By God," said Harun al-Rashid, "It is as if these words were addressed to me alone out of all men!"

The Meadows of Gold

He died not long after.

The main events and principal facts of the reign of Harun al-Rashid are to be found in my previous works and in this book. But while considering the history of this Caliph, I have so far said nothing of the Barmakids. I will therefore devote the following chapter to a rapid review of their history and the succeeding stages of their prosperity and their fall, quite independently of the details I have given elsewhere in my books on this family and the flower of their days.

KHALID IBN BARMAK AND HIS SONS

Not one of the children of Khalid ibn Barmak could match his excellent judgement, courage, knowledge and other qualities. Not even Yahya, in spite of his prudence and his great intelligence, nor Yahya's sons – Fadl, with his generosity and talents; Ja'far, with his skill as a writer and his eloquence; Muhammad, with his nobility and high-mindedness; Musa, so brave and energetic.

The poet Abu Ghul has praised their merits in the following lines:

> All four of the children of Yahya ibn Khalid
> Are princes and worthy to govern.
> If you ask about their merits, why
> They are divided among them and yet
> Conjoined in each.

THE BARMAKIDS

When the Caliphate came to Harun al-Rashid, he appointed the Barmakids his viziers and they seized all the wealth, not sharing their riches with the ruler, who could not extract from them the sums – even small – which he needed. It was in 187 AH/803 AD that Rashid overthrew them. Men differ in the reasons for their disgrace. The obvious motives were their monopoly of the wealth and their having released a descendant of Abu Talib,* whose keeping was in their hands. The real motive is not known; although many have been suggested, God alone knows what it was. We will report those which come to mind and those we have heard as we write this chapter dedicated to their history; but first let us sketch out the main events of their days of favour and the flower of their times.

THE ADVICE OF YAHYA

According to someone who is well acquainted with the history of the Barmakid family, Harun al-Rashid one day received a dispatch from the superintendent of the posts* in Khurasan, which informed him that an exclusive interest in his own pleasures and in the chase were diverting Fadl ibn Yahya from the management of the affairs of state. Yahya ibn Khalid was with Rashid at the time. Rashid, having read the letter, threw it down before Yahya and said:

'Dear father, read this letter and write to your son in a manner that will deter him from this kind of behaviour.'

Yahya stretched out his hand for Rashid's inkwell and wrote to Fadl on the back of the superintendent of the post's letter:

'My son, may God protect you and grant you enjoyment! The Commander of the Faithful has just learned that, ceaselessly engaged in the chase and in a round of pleasures, you are neglecting the affairs of those in your charge. He disapproves of your behaviour. Return to occupations which will do you more credit, for the way a man is judged by his contemporaries depends upon the habits he has formed, honourable or dishonourable. Fare well.'

Then he wrote these verses at the bottom:

> Devote your day to the pursuit of glory
> And bear with patience the absence of the beloved.
> Then, as night draws nigh and casts
> Her veil over the vices of men,
> Conspire with her to take your pleasure,
> For night is the day of the clever man.
> How many men you have thought so austere
> Greet the night in strange fashions?
> Night throws her veil over them
> And they pass it in voluptuous sport.
> The pleasures of the fool are public,
> And bring every hidden enemy into the open.

Rashid watched Yahya as he wrote, reading each line, and when the letter was finished, said:

'Dear little father, how perfect!'

The Meadows of Gold

As for Fadl, as soon as he received the letter he began to spend all his days at the mosque and this continued until he left his post.

HARUN AL-RASHID AND THE SINGING GIRL

Ishaq ibn Ibrahim al-Mawsili says:
'One day Rashid was drinking with the Barmakids. A young girl brought by Yahya ibn Khalid sang the following air:

> I have lain sleepless so long
> Insomnia is my lover.
> My body is so worn away
> It would seem created so.
> My heart is drowned in my tears.
> Who can say he has seen
> A woman aflame in water?

Rashid asked: "Who wrote this song?"
Khalid ibn Yazid, the secretary, was named and the Caliph said:
"Fetch him!"
"So I was brought in," Khalid relates, "and he said to the girl: 'Sing it again for me!' so she did. When it was over, he asked me:
'Who wrote that song?'
'I did, O Commander of the Faithful,' I replied.
We had just reached this point, when a serving girl appeared, holding an apple in her hand on which was inscribed in ink scented with musk and ambergris:

> Happiness has made you forget your promise;
> I send you this apple to remind you.

Rashid took another apple upon which he wrote:

> You command me to fulfill my promise.
> I did not forget; this apple is my excuse.

Then he said to me: 'Say something on this theme.' I recited the following verses:

The Meadows of Gold

>An apple marked by the pearls of her teeth
>Is dearer to me than the world and all that's in it;
>White marks on the red, inscribed with scented ink
>As if plucked from the cheeks of she who gave it." '

VI:364-366
§ 2562

THE AVARICE OF ASMA'I

Mubarrad owes the following story to Jahiz, who owes it to someone who had it from Anas ibn Abi Shaikh.

One day Ja'far ibn Yahya the Barmakid mounted his horse and ordered one of his eunuchs to bring the sum of one thousand dinars, adding:

'I am going to visit Asma'i. If you see me laugh at any of the stories he tells me, give him these dinars.'

Ja'far alighted at the house of Asma'i* and Asma'i set about telling him all sorts of amazing tales and witty stories to make him laugh, without managing to make him so much as smile. When Ja'far left the house of his host, Anas ibn Abi Shaikh said:

'You have just amazed me. You had planned to give Asma'i a present of one thousand dinars and yet after he had worn himself out to entertain you, you walk out of his house without even having smiled. And yet it is not your habit to return money to your treasury once you have drawn it out.'

'Now wait,' answered Ja'far. 'Asma'i has already had 100,000 dirhams from me and yet I find in his house nothing but rags and tatters. He was wearing an old torn gown. He was sitting on a filthy old cushion. Everything I saw in his house was shabby. Now I personally think the tongue of happiness is more eloquent than his tongue and the sight of my benefactions would imply praise – or satire – more powerful than anything he composes. Why should I give him the pleasure of my gifts, since nothing in his house publishes my generosity towards him and since he does not prove, by being happy, that he is grateful?'

VI:366-367
§ 2563

A POET ON RASHID AND JA'FAR IBN YAHYA

A poet has written thus of Rashid and Ja'far ibn Yahya:

> Let the caliphate of Rashid be praised,
> For he has drawn tight the reins of power.
> He added a second reign to a first,
> And this was due to Ja'far alone.
> The sons of Barmak have established his dominion
> And made the throne secure for his heir.

ON LOVE

Yahya, the son of Khalid ibn Barmak, an enlightened man, learned and fond of discussion and philosophical inquiry, gathered at his house for symposiums a number of famous controversialists chosen from among Muslim theologians, free-thinkers and divines of various sects. In the course of one of these gatherings, Yahya spoke as follows:

'You have discussed at length the theories of potentiality and actuality, pre-existence and creation, duration and stability, movement and rest, union and separation from the Divine substance, being and nothingness, bodies and accidents, acceptance and refutation of authorities, the absence or presence of God's attributes, potential and actual forces, substance, quantity, modality, connection, existence and non-existence. You have examined the question of whether the Imamate is by right of succession or elective, and you have exhausted all metaphysical questions both in their principles and their corollaries. Today, describe love. But do not begin a debate. Let each of you limit himself to giving a brief definition, saying whatever occurs to him.'

The first to speak was Ali ibn Maitham of the Imamite sect and a celebrated Shi'a theologian.

'O vizier,' said this doctor, 'love is the fruit of similarity and the index of the fusion of two souls. It issues forth from the sea of beauty, from the pure and subtle principle of its essence. Its extent is without bounds; too much of it destroys the body.'

The second speaker, Abu Malik al-Hadrami, of an extreme Kharijite sect, the Shurah, expressed himself thus:

'O vizier, love is a magic emission. It is more hidden and more glowing than a burning coal. It exists only through the union of two souls and two forms. It penetrates the heart like water from a rain cloud seeping through desert sands. It reigns over all other qualities; intelligence bows in submission to it, opinions give way to it. All novelties and all time-honoured customs are left aside in its favour and subordinated to it.'

The third to take up the subject was Abu al-Hudhail Muhammad ibn al-Hudhail, known as Allaf – 'The Fodder Merchant'. He was a Mu'tazilite and the Shaikh of the school of Basra:

'O vizier, love sets its seal upon the eyes and impresses its signet upon the heart. Its pasture is the body; it drinks from the liver, seat of passion. The lover's thoughts are thrown into disorder and the mind becomes unbalanced. For the lover, nothing remains pure, no promise binds; misfortunes hasten after him. Love is a draught from death's cup, a drink from the cisterns of bereavement. But love comes from the bounty of nature itself and from the beauty which dwells in the qualities of the beloved. The man who loves is open-handed, deaf to the appeals of prudence and indifferent to all reproach.'

Hisham ibn al-Hakam of Kufa, Shaikh of the Imamites of his age, famous in his time for his works, was the fourth to speak:

'O vizier, destiny has set love like a snare into which only hearts that are mutually sincere in their misfortunes can fall. When a lover is caught in love's net and is trapped in its toils, it is then no longer possible for him to withdraw safe and sound nor to escape his impending doom. Love is born from the beauty of form and the perfect concord of ardent souls. Love is a mortal wound in the depths of the entrails, in the innermost depths of the heart. The most eloquent tongue freezes; the slave-owner becomes a slave; the master becomes chattel and abases himself before the lowliest of his subjects.'

The fifth was Ibrahim ibn Sayyar al-Nazzam, of the Muʻtazilite sect and one of the principal dialecticians of the Basra school in those days.

'O vizier, love is more subtle than a mirage, more insidious than wine circulating in the veins. It is an aromatic clay worked in the vat of sublime power. As long as it is moderate, it is sweet, but if it passes certain limits it becomes a madness which leads to death, a mysterious sickness for which no cure can be hoped. It pours forth on the heart like a rain cloud and makes troubles sprout and grief bear fruit. A man overwhelmed by love suffers without respite. Each breath is an effort, a kind of paralysis threatens him; he is plunged in melancholy. When night covers him, he lies sleepless; he passes his days in anxiety. Grief starves him; he breakfasts on sighs.'

The sixth speaker, Ali ibn Mansur, of the Imamite sect, a Shiʻa dialectician and a disciple of Hisham ibn al-Hakam, expressed his views as follows:

'At the beginning love is but a slight ill which filters into the soul, altering it as it wills. It penetrates the thoughts and quickly possesses them. Whoever drinks from this cup does not recover from his intoxication; he does not recover from the loss of his blood. Love is born from the contiguity and homogeneity of forms and composition.'

The seventh definition was given by Muʻtamir ibn Sulaiman, one of the leading shaikhs of the Muʻtazilite school:

'O vizier, love is the result of similarity and resemblance. It creeps into the heart like an ant. Its prisoner can rarely burst his bonds. He who is in its grip rarely recovers. It is mutual recognition by different natures and the union of souls; it summons hearts and draws different natures together. But this happiness is short-lived, troubled by the fear of separation at meeting and spoiled, in its sweetest moments, by the fear of evil tongues. Thus philosophers have called it a cutting weapon, destroyer of the body.'

Bishr ibn Muʻtamir spoke eighth. This learned Muʻtazilite was a shaikh of the school of Baghdad, master of such dialecticians and theologians of that town as

Ja'far ibn Harb, Ja'far ibn Mubashshir and others:

'O vizier, love unmans and engenders abasement. A man under its sway is beneath criticism. Had he the strength of a lion, he would still smile on every slave and become himself the slave of desire. He speaks of nothing but his aspirations and is interested in nothing but his passions.'

The ninth to take up the theme was Thumama ibn Ashras of the Mu'tazilite sect:

'O vizier, love occurs when the substance of which souls are made draws in the emanations of similarity, homogeneity and fellow-feeling. It darts rays of brilliant light which illuminate the sense of understanding and touch the very sources of life with its refulgence. From this ray, or glance, emanates a pure light which strikes the soul and becomes an essential part of it: this is what we call love.'

Al-Sakkak of the Imamite school, a disciple of Hisham ibn al-Hakam, gave a tenth definition:

'O vizier, love is engendered of mutual liking and the seal is set on it by similarity. It proves the existence of the sympathetic soul and is witness to the mutual attachment of similar species. It pervades the body like wine. He who loves is illuminated by an inner flame, all his being shines, his qualities exalt him. But the agitation of his senses betrays his passion to other eyes and before love exalts someone, it first humiliates him.'

The eleventh doctor, Sabbah ibn al-Walid of the Murji'ite sect, defined love thus:

'O vizier, love's effects are swifter than words. The heart of a man which is marked with innocence and purity and who has a pleasing appearance will not reject love, for love inclines only to mutual affinity and a delicate sensibility on the part of the lover.'

Ibrahim ibn Malik, the jurisconsult of Basra, a highly skilled polemicist, who belonged to no school and was attached to no sect, spoke twelfth:

'O vizier, love is nothing but a series of thoughts which occur to a man; sometimes they incapacitate him, sometimes they comfort him; by engendering disquiet in his heart, they consume his very entrails.'

The thirteenth speaker was a *mubadh*, that is to say, a judge of the sect of the Magians, which is in fact what the term *mubadh* means in Pahlavi, the ancient form of Persian:

'O vizier, love is a fire kindled in the area around the heart and its blaze spreads between the heart and the ribs. It is inherent in the existence of beings and in the actions of the heavenly bodies. Its origin is in animal motion and depends on material causes. It is the flower of youth, the garden of generosity, the charm of the soul and its diversion. The elements engender it, the stars cause it, the action of the sublime mysteries gives it its form. Then it combines the best of the substance with the purest elements. It gives rise to the attraction of hearts, the concordance of passions, the fusion of souls, the joining of like minds, the purity of feelings in hearts and sympathy. It cannot exist without beauty, without intelligence, without delicate senses, without health, harmony and the equilibrium

The Meadows of Gold

of the various forces, for its sublime origin gives rise to movements of the celestial spheres which then harmonize with the feelings which bodies experience.'

Both ancients and moderns have argued about the nature of love and its first manifestations – is it born of the eye and of the ear? Of the will? Or of necessity? What are the causes which bring it into existence where it was not, or destroy it after its appearance? Is it an action of the rational soul? Or of the body and its nature? Here is a definition which is attributed to Hippocrates:

'This passion,' he said, 'consists of the mixing of two souls and is analogous to the mixing of two waters of the same nature, which are then difficult, even impossible, to separate by any process whatsoever. The soul being finer and more subtle in its nature even than water, the passing of time cannot obliterate love; duration cannot lessen it. Nothing can impede it. Its course is too subtle to imagine; its seat is hidden from the sight. Reason cannot tell how it establishes its sway, she knows only that its starting point and greatest power lies in the heart, whence it spreads through all the limbs. Then it shows itself in a trembling of the hands, pallor, difficulty of speech, weakening of the intellect, a heaviness on the tongue, slips and stumblings which make it seem that he who is dominated by this passion declines in intelligence. Many natural philosophers and those dedicated to medical research consider love as an appetite which is born in the heart, grows there and there draws to itself all the elements of desire. As its strength grows, the lover becomes more agitated, more irritable. He is absorbed in his thoughts, his vague aspirations, his sorrows. He draws breath with difficulty, is permanently wrapt in his reveries and loses his appetite. His intelligence withers, his brain dries up and his life becomes exhausted, for, through the ceaseless action of desire, the blood becomes heated and converted into black bile. This increases and invades the seat of thought. Fever develops and then the yellow bile becomes inflamed, turbid, decays and ends by mixing with the atrabilious humour, of which it becomes an integral part, increasing its strength. Now one of the properties of this atrabilious humour is to act on the thoughts. When thought weakens, the gastric juices mix and decompose, hence sluggishness, dwindling of the intellectual powers, desire for the impossible and at last, madness. Then the lover either commits suicide or dies of grief and despair. Sometimes a simple glance cast on his beloved makes him die of joy, love and regret, or else he gives a great cry and falls into a coma which lasts twenty-four hours. He is thought dead and is buried, although he is still alive. At other times, he gives a deep sigh, the blood flows to the heart, the heart contracts and he is only delivered from this state by death. Or, yet again, if after having passionately longed to see the beloved she appears before him suddenly, love flees at once. Everyone has seen a lover when he hears his beloved named – his blood flees and his face changes colour.'

If certain philosophers are to believed, God, in his wisdom and great goodness, gave every soul at its creation a rounded form like a sphere. Then he divided them in half and placed each half in a different body. When one of these bodies meets that which encloses the other half of its own soul, love is of necessity born between

On Love

them owing to the fact that they were once one. Afterwards, it develops with greater or less strength, depending on temperament.

The originators of this theory have developed it at length. According to them, souls, luminous, pure essence, descend from the sublime spheres to find the bodies in which they will dwell. They search each other out on a basis of their previous closeness or distance in the immaterial world.

The same doctrine has been adopted by a certain number of those who profess Islam, who defend it by means of proofs drawn from the Koran, the Sunna and by analogy, according to their own reason, from these two sources. They quote, for example, the words of God: 'O serene soul! Return to your Lord, joyful, pleasing unto Him. Enter my paradise, numbered among my worshippers!' (Koran 89:27-9).

Now, these men say that the return to a first state implies an earlier existence. They also produce the following statement of the Prophet, may the prayers and peace of God be upon him, taught by Sa'id ibn Abi Maryam, to whom it was transmitted by Yahya ibn Ayyub, according to Yahya ibn Sa'id, according to Amra, according to A'isha, who had it from the Prophet himself, may the prayers and peace of God be upon him:

'Souls are like armed battalions. Those who know each other make alliances, those who do not know each other fight.'

A similar view was current among some of the Arabs, as is proved by the verses in which Jamil ibn Abd Allah ibn Ma'mar of the tribe of Udhra, singing of his mistress Buthaina, conjures up the memory of an earlier existence and a union which would have preceded their appearance in this world:

> My soul clung to yours before we were created,
> Before we were weaned, before we were laid in the cradle.
> Our love has grown and developed with our selves;
> Death cannot break the promises of this love.
> It will survive all the trials of fate
> And visit us among the shadows of the tomb,
> In the depths of the grave.

According to Galen, sympathy is born between two intelligent beings because of the very similarity of their intelligences, but it cannot exist between two stupid people with limited minds, because of the stupidity which they share.

'Indeed,' he said, 'intelligence follows a regular path and it is possible for two beings following the same path to meet, while stupidity moves in a completely unpredictable way, which renders all encounters impossible.'

VI:368-382
§§ 2565-2582

The Meadows of Gold

(Omitted: VI:383-385; §§ 2583-2587. The debate continues – astrological aspects, the views of Ptolemy, the Sufis and others are given. The following saying of Plato is also quoted: 'I do not know what love is. I only know that it is a divine madness, a passion which is neither to be praised, nor is worthy of blame.' But this discussion of love and these quotations which we have allowed ourselves to be drawn into giving have led us far from the history of the Barmakids, who were what concerned us at the beginning of this chapter. Let us, therefore, return to this subject and see how their power and their prosperity came to grief in a most terrible catastrophe.)

THE FALL OF THE BARMAKIDS

This is what a certain person, very well versed in the history of the Barmakids, relates:

'Yahya, the son of Khalid ibn Barmak, his two sons Ja'far and Fadl and other members of this family were at the height of their power, which was without limit, and unassailable in their high offices. The days of their rule, it is said, were like a perpetual wedding feast, filled with unending happiness and joy. It was during this time that Harun al-Rashid said to Ja'far:

"Ja'far, there is no one in the world dearer or closer to me than yourself and no one whose conversation is sweeter or more desirable than yours. Now my sister Abbasa holds in my heart a place not inferior to that which I have given you. I have considered the feelings that each of you inspire in me and I have realized that I cannot easily dispense either with you or with my sister. When you are absent no pleasure or satisfaction is perfect in her company and when I am alone with you, her absence inspires the same regrets. I know of only one way to procure myself this double pleasure and to enjoy henceforth the sweetness of both your companies."

"Commander of the Faithful," answered Ja'far, "may God approve your intentions and inspire you with wise thoughts in all your actions."

Rashid continued thus:

"I wish to have you marry Abbasa and to give you the right, by this marriage, to pass your evenings with her, to see her, to be near her, whenever I am with you both. But your privileges will end there."*

Indeed, the marriage took place after Ja'far's renunciation of his conjugal rights. In the presence of the eunuchs and favourite freedmen of the Caliph, he was constrained to swear before God and bind himself with the most sacred oaths that he would never visit his wife nor remain alone with her or stay under the same roof with her unless the Caliph was present. These arrangements were made. Ja'far accepted them sincerely and considered himself as bound by his word. Whenever they all met under these conditions, he avoided looking at his wife and lowered his eyes out of respect for the Caliph and he kept his plighted troth with a fidelity which won him the approbation of Rashid. But Abbasa grew fond of him and secretly resolved to beguile him.

Abbasa wrote Ja'far letters. He sent away her messengers with every sort of curse and threat. She tried again and met the same response. In despair, she addressed herself to Ja'far's mother, an imprudent woman with little judgement,

The Meadows of Gold

and soon won her over with magnificent presents, precious jewels and much money – in short, everything a royal treasury could provide.

When Abbasa saw that the woman was as submissive to her as a slave and as devoted as a mother, she told her part of her designs and made her see the happy consequences for herself and how glorious it would be to have a son bound to the Caliph by marriage. Lastly, she persuaded her that such an event, if it took place, would assure her safety and that of Ja'far and that they would no longer have to fear any disgrace or loss of their position in the state.

Ja'far's mother welcomed these suggestions. She promised to use all her cunning to carry the matter to a successful conclusion and to devote her energy to bringing husband and wife together. She therefore went one day to Ja'far and said to him:

"My child, I have been told of a young slave girl who is living at such-and-such a place. She has had a royal education, she is lettered and learned, gracious and charming, her beauty is beyond compare, her figure perfect and she has a winning personality. In fact, she is a constellation of perfections the like of which I have never seen. I resolved to buy her for you and the matter is almost settled with her owner."

Ja'far was delighted at her words, took them to heart and thought of nothing else. But his mother kept him waiting for a while, to sharpen his desire and make his passion the more ardent. His entreaties and the eagerness with which he pressed his mother to fulfill her promise, proving to her that he was overcome with impatience and extreme restlessness, made her finally agree that on a given night she would give him the pretty slave. She sent a message to Abbasa telling her of all this.

When the time came, she made preparations fitting to her rank and went to the house of Ja'far's mother. That night Ja'far, his head still turning from wine, left the Caliph's palace to come to the tryst. Scarcely had he entered the house than he asked for the slave girl and was told that she had arrived. Abbasa, on going in to her husband, found a man sufficiently drunk not to know her face or figure. Once the marriage had been consummated and her husband's lust satisfied, Abbasa asked:

"What do you think of the ruses of the daughters of kings?"

"Whom do you mean?" he asked, convinced that he was talking to some Byzantine slave girl.

"Of myself!" she answered. "I, your mistress, Abbasa, daughter of Mahdi!"

Ja'far rose in horror, his drunkenness suddenly gone, and returned to his senses. At once he went to his mother and said to her:

"You have sold me cheap and placed me on the edge of an abyss. See what the outcome of my predicament will be!"

Abbasa, when she left her husband, was pregnant. She bore a son whom she entrusted to the care of one of her eunuchs called Riyash and from among her women she chose a wet-nurse called Birra. But she was afraid the story would get about and become widely known, so she sent her child to Mecca with the two

The Fall of the Barmakids

servants in whose care she had placed it.

Time passed, and Ja'far, his brother and his father became masters of the state. Zubaida, also known as Umm Ja'far, the wife of Rashid, had a sway over the Caliph such as none of her rivals enjoyed. Now Yahya ibn Khalid, Ja'far's father, the superintendent of Rashid's harem, had forbidden the Caliph's women to be attended by their eunuchs. Zubaida complained of this to Rashid. The Caliph said to Yahya:

"Dear father" – for so he used to address him – "what is Zubaida's grievance against you?"

"My lord," answered Yahya, "do you doubt my loyalty as superintendent of your harem and your palace?"

"Certainly not," said Rashid.

"Well then," said Yahya, "do not listen to anything she says against me."

Rashid promised that the matter should be discussed no further and Yahya enforced his prohibitions even more strictly than before. When night came, he ordered the gates of the harem to be shut and locked and he carried the keys away with him to his house. This measure gave the crowning touch to Zubaida's irritation. One day she went to the Caliph and said:

"Commander of the Faithful, why does Yahya go on depriving me of the use of my eunuchs and why does he not treat me as befits my rank?"

Rashid answered that he had no complaints to make of the way in which Yahya watched over the harem.

"If that is so," retorted Zubaida, "he would have been able to prevent his son committing a certain crime."

Rashid asked her to explain her words and she told him the whole story, revealing the intrigues of Abbasa with Ja'far. Rashid was absolutely dumbfounded.

"Have you," he asked at last, "any proof or witness?"

"What clearer proof than a child?" replied Zubaida.

"Where is he?" demanded the Caliph.

"He was here, but his mother, fearing a scandal, sent him to Mecca."

"Does anyone but you know of this affair?"

"Every slave girl in the palace knows."

Rashid kept silent and hid his resentment. Shortly afterwards he expressed his intention of visiting Mecca and set out with Ja'far. Abbasa immediately wrote to the eunuch and the wet-nurse, telling them to take the child to Yemen. When Rashid reached Mecca, he entrusted various dependable people with finding out about the child and the wet-nurse and eunuch. He learned that it was all true. His pilgrimage completed, he set off brooding over schemes for disgracing and revenging himself upon the House of Barmak.'

VI:386-394
§§ 2588-2595

THE MURDER OF
JA'FAR AL-BARMAKI

Rashid and Ja'far were staying in a quarter of Anbar called al-Umr, enjoying the best of spirits and having a most pleasant time. When Ja'far left, Rashid accompanied him until he had mounted and ridden off, then went back and sat on his throne and ordered the remains of the feast to be removed.

Returning to his house, Ja'far, who had had too much to drink, called for Abu Zakkar the singer and *tambur* player and for his secretary, Ibn Abi Shaikh. The curtain was lowered and the slave girls sat down behind it in order to accompany Abu Zakkar with their voices and their instruments. Abu Zakkar sang the following air:

> What do people want of us?
> Why are they so inquisitive?
> Their sole thought is to reveal
> What we have been careful to conceal.

Meanwhile Rashid summoned one of his servants, Yasir – known as Rikhla – and spoke to him thus:

'O Yasir, I am going to entrust you with a mission that not Amin, nor Ma'mun, nor Qasim seems to be capable of fulfilling. Only you have the independence and energy to bring it to a successful conclusion. Justify the confidence I am placing in you and beware of disobeying – disobedience would mean losing your position in my service and ruining your reputation with me, as well as laying yourself open to all the severity of which I am capable.'

'O Commander of the Faithful,' replied Yasir, 'if you order me to run my sword through my belly and out of my back in your presence, I will do it. Let me know your desire and you will find me ready to obey.'

'Do you know Ja'far ibn Yahya, the Barmakid?'

'O Commander of the Faithful, whom would I know, if not him!' retorted Yasir. 'There is no one who does not know such a man.'

'Did you notice how I bade him farewell when he left?'

'Certainly.'

'Go to him this very hour and, no matter in what situation you find him, bring me his head.'

At these words, Yashir shivered, then, trembling, remained silent.

The Murder of Ja'far al-Barmaki

'O Yasir,' went on the Caliph, 'did I not warn you of the danger awaiting you if you disobey?'

'By God,' came the answer, 'but the matter is graver still – I would rather die than take the least part in carrying out this order which the Commander of the Faithful has given me.'

'You have hesitated long enough,' cried Rashid. 'Do what I have told you to do!'

So Yasir went to the house of Ja'far, whom he found occupied with his pleasures, and he said to him:

'The Commander of the Faithful has ordered me to bring him your head.'

'The Commander of the Faithful,' said Ja'far, 'likes to tease me. This is no doubt one of his jokes.'

'By God,' replied the officer, 'I have never seen him more serious.'

'If it isn't a joke, then he was drunk.'

'No, by God, he seemed fully in possession of his reason, and from the prayers I have seen him perform, I cannot believe that he has drunk any *nabidh* today.'

Ja'far continued:

'If ever I have done you some service, there will never be any better occasion for you to recognize it than now.'

'I am completely at your service, for anything that is not against the will of the Commander of the Faithful.'

'Go back to him,' said Ja'far, 'and tell him that you have carried out his orders. If he shows regret, I shall owe you my life and you may count on new favours from me. If, on the other hand, his decision remains constant, tomorrow you will perform your duty.'

The officer answered that this was not possible.

Ja'far said:

'Then I will accompany you to the Commander of the Faithful, and I will place myself so as to hear his words and your reply. If, after you have exhausted all excuses, he will still not be satisfied with anything but my head, you will come at once and accomplish your mission.'

'I agree to that,' replied Yasir.

They went, therefore, to Rashid's camp. Yasir went in to the Caliph and said to him:

'I have brought the head, O Commander of the Faithful, and it is here.'

'Bring it at once!' cried Rashid, 'or at once yours shall fall!'

Yasir went back to Ja'far and said:

'You have heard?'

'Yes,' he replied, 'do as you have been ordered.'

Then, drawing a small kerchief from his sleeve he bandaged his eyes and stretched out his neck. Yasir cut off his head and took it in to Rashid and placed it before him. The Caliph approached it and began to ennumerate all of Ja'far's sins. Then Rashid said:

'O Yasir, bring me so-and-so.'

The Meadows of Gold

When they arrived, he said:
'Cut off Yasir's head, I cannot bear the sight of the murderer of Ja'far!'

ELEGIES ON THE BARMAKIDS

Here is Asma'i's account:

'Rashid sent for me that night. As soon as he saw me enter, he said:
"I have made some verses and I want to recite them to you."
"Speak, O Commander of the Faithful," I replied. Then he recited the following lines:

> If Ja'far had feared death,
> A swift bridled steed
> Would have saved him.
> To escape annihilation
> He could have sought shelter
> From the eagle's talons.
> But when his hour came,
> No astrologer had the skill
> To avert his destiny.

'I went home,' added Asma'i, 'and before I had even arrived, news of the murder of Ja'far was already on every tongue.'

On the morning after the night in which this murder was committed and the ruin of the Barmakids consummated, the following lines* written in a beautiful hand were found on the gate of the castle of Ali ibn Isa ibn Mahan in Khurasan:

> The unhappy sons of Barmak
> Are stricken down by fate.
> May their destiny serve as a warning
> To the one who dwells in this palace!

The authority of the Barmakids and the happy and fortunate days of their rule lasted from the accession of Rashid until the murder of Ja'far, that is to say, for seventeen years, seven months and fifteen days. Their overthrow gave rise to a great number of elegies recalling their glory.

One of the most remarkable of these elegies is by Ibn Abi Mu'adh. Here is a fragment of it, for it is very long:

The Meadows of Gold

O you seduced by Fortune,
Mutable Fortune, full of guile,
Do not put your trust in her,
Guard against her snares.
If you think she is not capricious,
Regard the crucified corpse on the bridge.
It is a terrible warning.
Profit from it, you who are wise
And possessed of discernment.
Sieze the sweet days from the world,
Flow with the current of Fate.
Ja'far was the vizier of the one
Pleasing to God. He had
Power, merit and glory.
The whole world obeyed him,
On land and at sea.
His opinions ruled the empire,
His will was respected everywhere.
On Friday evening, Ja'far,
At the pinnacle of his power,
Was at al-Umr. He flew
Above the world with his wings,
Thinking to live forever.
Fate tripped him into the abyss;
Heaven protect us from being tripped by Fate!
His sandal slipped and his body
Was broken in the fall.
Poor wretch, as dawn broke
On Saturday he was dead.
When Fadl ibn Yahya awoke,
His old father had been dragged away,
He knew not where.
They took the old man with his children,
Walking in the midst of them,
Laden with chains. The Barmakids
And their followers, throughout
All countries and cities
Seemed to have been called before
That dread Judgement Seat
To which mankind is called
On the Last Day. Their misfortunes
Have passed into legend.
Glory to Him who is All-Powerful!

Elegies on the Barmakids

Among the poets who composed elegies for them is Ashja' al-Sulami, and here is a portion of the ode that he wrote:

> Let us stop and rest our horses.
> There are no more generous men.
> There is no one to ask for help.
> Tell the camels they need no longer fear
> The vast distances through wasteland
> To reach Fadl. Tell Generosity:
> You died with Fadl. Tell Adversity:
> You are made new. See how the Barmakid
> Blade of Indian steel has been struck
> By the Indian steel of the Hashimites!

One of the poets who has shown most talent in celebrating this family is Salm al-Khasir, in the following passage:

> The stars of generosity are out;
> The hand of benevolence is closed.
> The seas of bounty have ebbed away
> Now that the Barmakids are gone.
> The stars of the sons of Barmak
> Which showed the guide the true path
> Have fallen.

Another poet among those who praised the Barmakids, Salih al-A'rabi, was no less well inspired in the following verses:

> Fate has betrayed the sons of Barmak,
> But what kings have not fallen to her treachery?
> Did Yahya not govern the whole earth?
> Yet he woke to find himself beneath it.

Among the most remarkable elegies on this theme are these lines, by Abu Hazra al-A'rabi, which others attribute to Abu Nuwas:*

> Fate did not protect the House of Barmak,
> No, it suddenly cast down their power.
> Fate, which did not recognize the rights of Yahya
> Will have no more respect for the House of Rabi'.

And there are these no less beautiful lines by another poet:

> Sons of Barmak, I lament your fate

The Meadows of Gold

> And the days of your prosperity.
> The world was your bride and now
> She stands widowed, bereft of her young!

More lines from Ashja' al-Sulami:

> The Sons of Barmak have departed this world,
> But had they continued in power, men
> Could not have profited more.
> The days of their supremacy were
> A perpetual feast for all mankind.

Another poet says, with the same theme:

> The days of their sway were like the great festivals,
> Perpetual pilgrimage, Fridays and feasts.

Lines by Mansur al-Nimri:

> Announce the death of the sons of Barmak to the world
> That every one of its dry river beds might weep.
> For a time the world was their bride;
> Today she is dressed in sackcloth.

Let us also quote these eloquent verses by Di'bil al-Khuza'i:

> Have you not seen how Fate changed for the House of Barmak
> And for Ibn Nahik, and the centuries that have passed?
> They seemed as firmly rooted in the earth as the palm,
> Yet were rooted up like a blade of grass.

And these from Ashja':

> Destiny has overthrown the sons of Barmak
> Without leaving us one. They had all the good things
> By right, but now the good things of the world are gone.

After the murder of Ja'far, Yahya and Fadl were arrested and kept in close confinement. They suffered the most cruel privations and a whole series of hardships which Fadl ibn Yahya has recalled in the following lines:

> We beseech God in our affliction,
> For the remedy of our pain and tribulation
> Lies in His hands.

Elegies on the Barmakids

> We have departed from this world,
> Yet we inhabit it still,
> Neither dead nor alive.
> When the gaoler enters our cell
> We stare at him in wonder
> And say: 'This man comes from
> The outer world!'

After the death of the Barmakids, Rashid often repeated these two lines:

> When the reversal of Fate comes,
> It is equal to the heights
> She once lifted you.
> When the ant spreads her wings to fly,
> The end is near.

VI:399-406
§§ 2600-2610

THE MOTHER OF JA'FAR

Here is a story told by Muhammad ibn Abd al-Rahman the Hashimite, the prayer leader at Kufa:

'I went to visit my mother on the Day of Immolation* and found her talking to a woman, respectable in appearance, but dressed in rags. My mother asked me:

"Do you know who this is?"

I answered that I did not.

"She is," my mother said, "Abbada, the mother of Ja'far ibn Yahya."

I turned my face to her and greeted her with respect. After a few moments' conversation, I said to her:

"Dear lady, what is the most extraordinary thing you have ever seen?"

"My child," she answered, "there was a time when this same feast saw me escorted by 400 serving-girls – and yet I thought my son showed me a lack of respect. Today the feast is here again and I desire no more than two sheep skins, one to serve me as a bed and one to clothe me."

I gave her 500 dirhams and she nearly died of joy. From then on she continued to visit us, until death parted us for ever.'

THE WEALTH OF THE BARMAKIDS

They say that one of Rashid's uncles went to visit Yahya ibn Khalid just as Rashid's feelings towards him were changing, but before the disgrace that was the consequence.

'The Commander of the Faithful,' he said to him, 'loves to amass wealth. His children are many and he wishes to endow them with estates – this is why he finds you too rich, you and your friends. If you draw up an inventory of what they possess in money and lands and make it over to the children of the Caliph, I have reason to hope this sacrifice may save your life and reinstate you in our master's good graces.'

Yahya replied:

'By God, I would rather lose all my own wealth than despoil those whose fortune has been made because of me.'

VI:407-408
§ 2612

FADL IN PRISON

Khalil ibn al-Haitham al-Sha'bi, to whom Rashid had entrusted the watch over Yahya and Fadl in their prison, tells us the story that follows:

'One day the eunuch Masrur came in to me accompanied by several slaves, one of whom was carrying a folded napkin. I thought at first that Rashid, relaxing his severity towards the two prisoners, had sent them some presents. Masrur said to me:

"Bring me Fadl ibn Yahya!"

When he was before him, he spoke to him as follows:

"The Commander of the Faithful has this to say to you: 'I call on you to reveal the whole truth regarding the riches of your family. You claim to have spoken candidly, but I am certain that you have concealed important sums. I have ordered Masrur, if you do not provide him with precise information, to give you 200 strokes of the lash.' "

"By God, Masrur, I am a dead man!"

"Fadl," replied the other, "I advise you not to value your riches above your life, for I fear that if I carry out the orders I have received, you will die."

"Masrur," continued Fadl, "I have not lied to the Commander of the Faithful. If I possessed the entire world and had to yield it all rather than receive a single stroke of the whip, I would not hesitate before this sacrifice. The Commander of the Faithful is well aware, and you know too, that we have always sacrificed fortune to honour. Do you expect us today to lose our lives in order to preserve our fortune from your power? If you have received orders, execute them."

Masrur called for the cloth and shook it and a whip with all its knots fell out. Two hundred strokes were inflicted on the prisoner. The slaves in charge of executing the punishment used so much force and so much cruelty that they left him for dead, or at least so we feared.'

Khalil ibn Haitham adds that he then addressed his second-in-command, a man named Abu Yahya, and said to him:

'There is in this prison someone who knows how to treat such wounds and injuries of this kind. Go and find him and ask him to come and look after this man.'

Abu Yahya continued the story as follows:

'I went and asked him, and the man replied:

"Doubtless it is for Fadl ibn Yahya that you are asking my help; I have heard what has happened to him."

"It is indeed for him," I replied.
"Well," he went on, "lead me to him. I will treat him."
Having examined him, he said:
"I would guess that he has had fifty lashes."
"No, indeed," I cried, "200 blows."
"That can't be," he answered, "there are only the marks of fifty cuts. This wounded man must now stretch out on a reed mat so that I can tread on his chest."

Fadl, at first frightened by this treatment, ended by submitting to it. The man set to work and after having trampled him, he took him by the hand and pulling him, forced him to get up. Great rags of flesh remained stuck to the mat. He continued visiting him and lavishing every attention on him until one day, after having examined the sick man's back, he prostrated himself before him.

"What is it?" I asked him.
"Abu Yahya," he said to me, "Fadl is healed. Come and look."
Indeed, I approached and he showed me the flesh on his back had grown back. Then he asked me:
"Do you remember what I said – that there were only the marks of fifty lashes?"
"Of course," I replied.
He went on:
"By God, if he had received a thousand cuts, his wounds could not have been worse. I only said that so that he would take courage and help me in my treatment."

When he had spoken, he went away.
Fadl then said to me:
"Abu Yahya, I need 10,000 dirhams. Go to the man named Sina'i and tell him that I must have them."

I delivered the message. The man had the money brought to Fadl, who proceeded to say to me:
"I would like you to take this money to the man who healed me. Beg him to make allowances for the modesty of the present and to accept."

I went to the man and found him sitting on a reed mat. A stringed instrument hung from the wall, and a few bottles of *nabidh* and some sticks of furniture made up the contents of his cell.

"Abu Yahya," he said, "what do you want of me?"
I presented Fadl's apologies, reminded him of the great distress in which he had been and then told him the reason for my visit. He flew into a rage and cried out so impetuously that I was afraid.
"10,000 dirhams!" he repeated furiously.
I did my best to make him accept them, but he refused, so I went back to Fadl and told him what had happened.
"By God!" he cried, "he has found my gift too mean!"
Then he added:
"I beg you to go back to Sina'i and to tell him that I need another 10,000

dirhams. As soon as he gives them to you, carry the 20,000 to our man." '

The narrator continues:

'After having collected the money from Sina'i, I went back to the man with the whole sum and told him the story. But he still refused to accept anything and said to me:

"How should I accept a fee for caring for a noble descendant of the Abna? Get out of here, by God, and be assured that if you had offered me 20,000 dinars, I would no more have accepted them."

Fadl, when I came to tell him this adventure, said:

"Abu Yahya, tell me which was the noblest of all our actions that you ever witnessed or else heard related?"

After I had cited a certain number, he broke in, saying:

"Leave all that. By God, the noble behaviour of this man surpasses our finest deeds during all the years of our power!" '

Ja'far, the son of Yahya, was killed at the age of forty-five, although others say less. His father, Yahya ibn Khalid, died at Raqqa in 189 AH/805 AD, as we have said before.

MISCELLANEOUS ON RASHID AND THE BARMAKIDS

Several interesting incidents from the life and history of Rashid are to be found in my earlier books in the sections on the Kings of Rum – Byzantium – after Islam. As regards his relations with Nicephorus, I have already discussed them in this work.

The extraordinary and remarkable history of the Barmakids, their great qualities, their benefactions, their noble actions, all in fact that makes the story of their lives so interesting, the poems composed in their honour and the elegies composed after their disgrace, all these things are to be found in my *Historical Annals* and *Intermediate History*.

Here I have merely given an outline of the facts which I have not mentioned in my previous works. In these same books may be found the origins of the family of Barmak before the coming of Islam, their functions in the temple of Nawbahar, that is, the fire temple at Balkh, as has been said earlier; the explanation of the name Barmak, Barmak the Elder's relations with the kings of the Turks, the history of this family since Islam, under the Umayyads and, in particular, under Hisham ibn Abd al-Malik, and others, and lastly, in the days of the Caliph Mansur. The small glimpses which I give here of their lives and story seem to me sufficient. God knows best the truth.

THE CALIPHATE OF AMIN

Amin, the son of Harun al-Rashid, was proclaimed Caliph on the same day that Rashid died in the city of Tus, which was on Saturday the 4th of the month of Jumada I, 193 AH/809 AD. The eunuch Rija' brought him the news of his nomination. Fadl ibn al-Rabi' presided over the ceremony of taking the oath of allegiance. The Caliph was also called Abu Musa after one of his sons. His mother was Zubaida, the daughter of Ja'far, who in turn was the son of the Caliph Mansur.

Amin was born at Rusafa and was killed at the age of thirty-three years, six months and thirteen days. His body was buried at Baghdad and his head sent into Khurasan. His reign had lasted four years and six months, or, according to others, four years and nine months, or, again, eight months and six days, for we have found a certain amount of disagreement on this point in the chronicles. It is thought that at his accession he was twenty-two years, seven months and twenty-one days old. He was six months younger than Ma'mun.

The length of the siege which he withstood at Baghdad was, from its beginning to his death, one year, six months and thirteen days, including the two days of his imprisonment.

When Rashid died, Ma'mun was living at Marv. Salih, another son of Rashid, sent the eunuch Rija', the freedman of Amin, to bring the new Caliph the news of what had happened. Rija' took only twelve days to reach Baghdad and he entered the city on Thursday, the 15th of Jumada II.

THE DREAMS OF ZUBAIDA

Some chroniclers and historians of the Abbasids, such as Mada'ini and Utbi and others, relate that Zubaida, on the very night in which she conceived Amin, dreamed that three women came into her room and sat down, two on her right and the third on her left. One of them drew near and placing her hand on the belly of Zubaida said the following words:

'A magnificent king, open-handed in his generosity, his yoke will be heavy, his life misfortune.'

The second, having imitated the gesture of the first, spoke thus:

'A weak-willed king, blunt-edged, insincere in friendship; he will rule as a despot and by fortune be betrayed.'

The third, doing as those who came before had done, said:

'A sensual king, wasteful of blood, surrounded by revolt and sparing of justice.'

Zubaida went on with the story:

'I awoke prey to the deepest horror. On the night in which I gave birth to Amin, they appeared again in my sleep just as I had seen them the first time. They sat at my bedside and stared fixedly at me. The first then said:

"A verdant tree, a fair flower, a lovely garden."

The second went on:

"A copious spring, but swift to run dry and swiftly gone."

And the third:

"Enemy of himself, weak in power and fast in rage – he will lose his throne."

I woke with a start, seized with fear. One of the women in charge of my household, to whom I told this dream, persuaded me that it was no more than an odd chance of sleep, a game played by the female demons who attend women in childbirth.

One night, when my son was weaned, I had placed the cradle in which my child slept beside me and was getting into bed, when the three women appeared once more and headed towards the cradle. The first said:

"A tyrant, a wastrel, a babbling fool, his way lost, riding for a fall."

The second added:

"His speeches contradictory, his battles lost, his desires baffled, sad and with troubles overwhelmed."

The third ended:

"Dig his grave, open his coffin, bring out his winding sheet, prepare the procession. His death is better than his life."

The Meadows of Gold

I awoke profoundly troubled and deeply disturbed at the fate of my son. In vain the astrologers and interpreters of dreams whom I consulted assured me that he would live out long years of happiness; my heart would not believe their promises. But at last I began to reproach myself for my weakness and I said to myself:

'Can love, care and forethought cheat destiny? Can anyone drive fate back from the one they love?'

VI:416-419
§§ 2621-2623

(Omitted: VI:419; § 2624. 'In 193 AH Abu Bakr ibn Ayyash of Kufa, who was known as Asadi, died. He was ninety-eight years old and died eighteen days after Rashid.')

TROUBLE BETWEEN AMIN AND MA'MUN

When Amin was meditating the overthrow of Ma'mun, he sought the advice of Abd Allah ibn Khazim, who answered him:

'O Commander of the Faithful, I beseech you! Do not be the first Caliph who has violated his promise, broken his engagements and trampled his oath of allegiance underfoot.'

'May God silence your tongue!' replied Amin. 'Abd al-Malik ibn Salih was better advised than you when he said: "Two bull camels cannot share the same herd." '

He then gathered his generals and consulted them; all approved of his plans. Only Khuzaima ibn Khazim, when his turn came, spoke as follows:

'O Commander of the Faithful! He who lies to you does not serve your interests and he who tells you the truth does not betray you. Do not encourage your officers to vote for the deposition of your brother, for it is you whom they will one day depose. Do not incite them to break their sworn oath, for later they will violate the oath they swore to you. He who deceives shall be defeated, he who perjures himself shall be betrayed.'

At this point, Ali ibn Isa ibn Mahan* came in. The Caliph said to him, smiling:

'Be the leader of our cause, the eyetooth of our dynasty, you who do not revolt against the Imam and do not violate the obedience which is due to him.'

And he gave him greater honours than any he had bestowed up to that day, to reward him for having been the first of the generals to agree to the deposition of Ma'mun. Next he appointed him to the command of a very numerous army and sent him towards Khurasan.

When Ali ibn Isa ibn Mahan approached Rayy and learned that Tahir ibn Husain was in that town, he cried, convinced that such an adversary could not resist him:

'By God! Tahir is no more than a thorn on one of my branches, a spark of my fire. A man like him is not competent to lead an army. Scarcely will he have glanced at our countless host and he will be a dead man. Can the lamb stand up to the horns of the ram? Does the fox dare face the onslaught of the lion?'

As his son was advising him to send scouts on ahead in order to find a favourable place to pitch camp, Ali replied:

'To fight such a one as Tahir there is no need for elaborate plans, precautions or prudence. He cannot escape from these alternatives: either he will entrench

The Meadows of Gold

himself at Rayy and the inhabitants, rising against him, will do our work; or else he will leave the shelter of his walls and at the mere approach of our cavalry will take flight.'

When his son replied: 'A spark can well become a blaze!' Ali cried:

'Hold your tongue! Tahir is not a rival worthy of me! Brave men are concerned only with enemies that are their equals.'

Then, continuing on his march, Ali ibn Isa ibn Mahan reached the town of Rayy with his army. Once there, he saw with what care Tahir had fortified it and prepared it for battle, and he turned off to the right and pitched camp in a nearby village. While his troops were spreading over the countryside, Tahir, at the head of 4,000 horsemen, came out to assess the strength of his enemy's troops. Convinced that he would not be able to get the better of such a numerous and well equipped army, he announced to his officers:

'We will fight like the Kharijites.'*

So he divided his cavalry into squadrons and himself marched against the main force of the enemy with 700 horsemen drawn from Khwarizm and Khurasan.

A brave horseman rode out to challenge him. It was Abbas ibn Laith, the freedman of Mahdi. Tahir swooped down upon him, holding his sword in both hands, and Abbas was overthrown. At the same moment, a certain Dawud Siyah – David the Black – threw himself on the general Ali ibn Isa ibn Mahan, who was riding a chestnut horse, and in the confusion cut him down with a single stroke of the sword. The soldiers then flung themselves on Ali, fighting over his ring and his head. A certain Tahir ibn al-Raji cut his throat. Another seized a tuft of hair from his beard and a third his ring. The blow of the sword which Tahir struck with both hands against Abbas ibn Laith was the cause of the flight of the army of Baghdad and its defeat. From that time, in memory of his way of striking, Tahir was nicknamed Dhu al-Yaminain, 'The Man with Two Right Hands'.

Here is the account of Ahmad ibn Hisham, one of the commanders of Ma'mun's army:

'I went to Tahir's quarters. He thought I had been killed in the battle. My page was carrying Ali ibn Isa's head in a nosebag, which he threw down in front of Tahir. Soon the body of this general arrived, the hands and feet tied together as one ties up a beast of burden that has just died. Tahir had these remains thrown down a well, then he wrote of his triumph to Fadl ibn Sahl, Dhu al-Riyasatain, in the following words:

'May God grant you long life and may He overthrow your enemies! As I write these lines, I have before me the head of Ali ibn Isa ibn Mahan, and his ring is on my finger. Glory to God, Lord of the Worlds!'

Ma'mun received this news with delight and it was from that day that he was addressed by the title of Caliph.

VI:419-424
§§ 2625-2628

THE JEALOUSY OF ZUBAIDA

Zubaida had not borne Harun al-Rashid any children. One day he lamented her barrenness to a learned man of the court and asked his advice in the matter. The man suggested making her jealous and cited the example of Abraham, the Friend of God. Sarah remained childless, but when Hagar, the slave she had given Abraham, became the mother of Ishmael, Sarah, spurred on by jealousy, bore Isaac. Harun al-Rashid therefore bought a girl and retired all alone with her; she conceived Ma'mun. Zubaida, jealous of this, conceived in her turn Amin.

VI:424-425
§ 2629

(Omitted: VI:425-426; § 2630. On the sacrifice of Isaac.)

ILL-OMENS FOR AMIN

Yusuf ibn Ibrahim al-Katib had the following anecdote from the lips of Abu Ishaq Ibrahim, the son of Mahdi:

'The Caliph Amin summoned me; it was during the siege of Baghdad. I went to him and found him in a kiosk of aloe and sandalwood, ten cubits by ten in size. With him, at the back of the kiosk, was Sulaiman ibn Mansur. This kiosk, where Amin was accustomed to spend much of his time, was domed and hung and decorated with silk, green brocades woven with a pattern in red gold and other kinds of silk stuffs. The Caliph had before him a crystal goblet inlaid with gems which held more than five measures of wine. I greeted him and sat down facing Sulaiman. I was brought a similar cup of the same capacity and in front of Sulaiman was set yet another like it. Amin addressed us as follows:

"I had you come here because I have learned that Tahir has reached Nahrawan. Overwhelmed by this man's constant attacks and persecution, I summoned you in order to find some relief from my troubles in your company and conversation."

Our words and reassurance somewhat lightened his sadness and he became more cheerful. He summoned one of his favourite slave girls, who was called Da'f – 'Weakness' – which seemed to me a bad omen, and ordered her to sing while we drank. She laid her lute across her lap and began thus:

> By my life, Kulaib had more allies than you
> And was more resolute, yet he lies there in his blood.

At these words, the Caliph was overwhelmed with dismal forebodings.

"Silence!" he cried. "May God curse you!" And he sank once more into his gloomy meditations. At last, our cheerful conversation succeeded in lifting his spirits. He ceased to frown and, turning towards the girl, asked for another song. She began to sing:

> They killed him to usurp his place,
> Just as Chosroe was betrayed by his satraps.

Amin silenced her menacingly and his mood grew darker still.* Our comforting words succeeded in bringing him round, however. For the third time he addressed the girl, ordering her to sing, and this is what we heard:

Ill-Omens for Amin

> It seems there is no longer
> A single friendly face
> Between al-Hajun and Safa.
> There is no more conversation
> To while away the Meccan nights.
> Once we used to live there,
> But Fate and the nights
> Turning in their course
> Have driven us from our homes.

In a different version of the story, the words are given as these:

> By the Lord of Movement and Repose,
> Destiny sets many snares!

"Get out of here and may God curse you!" shouted Amin.

As she rose, the girl caught the goblet set before the Caliph with her foot. It shattered and the wine spread. The moon was shining in all her brilliance. We were on the banks of the Tigris, in the grounds of the Khuld Palace. At that very moment, I heard someone saying:

"So hath the matter whereof you two did enquire been decreed!" (Koran 12:41).'

'I rose,' added Ibrahim, 'and saw the Caliph shudder, when suddenly a voice rang out from the far end of the castle and we heard these two verses:

> Do not stand in amazement at what has happened.
> That which is to come is more terrible by far.
> Yes, a terrible thing is about to occur
> Which will truly amaze the man of pride.

This was the last time we kept the Caliph company before the day he was killed. May God have mercy on his soul.'

VI:426-430
§§ 2631-2634

AMIN'S BELOVED

Amin was passionately in love with Nazm, the mother of his son Musa, whom he called al-Natiq bi-l-Haqq – 'He Who Proclaims the Truth'. For his sake he wished to disinherit Ma'mun, so as to leave the throne to the child. When Nazm, the mother of the young prince, died, Amin mourned deeply. As soon as Zubaida learned what had happened, she said to her attendants:
'Carry me to my son, the Commander of the Faithful!'
He came out to meet her, crying:
'Alas, my lady, Nazm is dead!'
His mother Zubaida answered him with the following lines:

> Let my soul be a ransom for yours! Do not
> Be carried away by grief, for something
> Is left you of she who has gone.
> Musa will take her place for you
> And calm all grieving. With Musa,
> She who has gone will leave no regrets.

VI:430
§ 2635

THE FRIVOLITY OF AMIN

'One day,' relates Ibrahim ibn al-Mahdi, 'I asked permission to enter Amin's presence. It was during the period when the capital was being besieged on every side. At first they refused to announce me and I had to pull rank in order to force my way in.

I found Amin engaged in staring attentively at the Tigris through the window-grill. There was a large tank in the courtyard of the palace, fed by the river through a conduit fitted with an iron mesh. I greeted him. He went on looking in the direction of the river, while his eunuchs and pages searched up and down the tank. He seemed to be beside himself. When I bowed and greeted him for the second time, he said:

"Did you hear, O my uncle? My fish with the earrings has just got out of the tank into the Tigris."

He was speaking of a fish which he had caught very young and decorated with earrings of gold embellished with two great pearls or – some say – rubies.

I went away, despairing of his safety and saying to myself:

"If ever he was going to leave off frivolity, this surely should have been the moment." '

AMIN AND THE LION

Amin was endowed with rare strength and vigour. He was daring, handsome and well built, but had poor judgement, was uncertain in his plans and incapable of constructive thought.

They say that one morning while he was drinking, the huntsmen and lancers, whom he kept to hunt lions, mounted their mules and had set out in pursuit of a lion which had been sighted in the Kutha and al-Qasr district. They caught it in a trap and brought it in a wooden cage carried by a Bactrian camel up to the gate of the palace. It was then taken in and set down in the courtyard where the Caliph was drinking.

'Pull up the door of the cage,' he said to his people, 'and set it free!'

'O Commander of the Faithful,' they said, 'it is a formidable beast, a black lion and very savage.'

'Free him!' repeated Amin.

They obeyed. The door having been opened, a black lion covered with a shaggy pelt like a bull came out, roaring and lashing the earth with his tail. At the sight of it, everyone fled, slamming the gates in its face. Only Amin remained sitting in his place, without showing the slightest trace of emotion. The animal went straight for him. As it came close, Amin snatched up an Armenian cushion and used it as a shield. At the very moment in which the animal was reaching for him with its claws, Amin grabbed it, caught it at the root of the ears, stabbed it with his dagger, shook it roughly and pushed it away. The lion fell back on its haunches and died.

Everyone hastily crowded round the Caliph. His wrist and fingers were out of joint. A bone-setter was called, who immediately set the dislocated members, after which the Caliph sat down again as if he had done nothing remarkable. And yet, when the body of the lion was opened, it was found that the gall had become detached from the liver.

VI:432-433
§ 2637

THE BIRTH OF MUSA AL-HADI

They say that the Caliph Mansur, giving an audience one day to the Hashimites and other members of his family, said to them with a smile:

'Let me announce to you that Mahdi is, since yesterday, the father of a boy, to whom we have given the name Musa.'*

When those present heard these words, they were speechless. It was as if ashes had been thrown in their faces. They remained silent, not knowing what to reply. Mansur, struck by their demeanour, said:

'This would be the time to offer your congratulations and good wishes, yet you are silent.'

After having pronounced the invocation, 'We belong to God and to God we return,' he went on:

'I see that it is the name Musa which saddens you. You are thinking, with dread, that under the reign of a Musa ibn Muhammad revolt will break out and blood flow in streams, that treasuries will be put to the sack and the kingdom overthrown, that his father will die murdered and he himself be bereft of the Caliphate. But this does not apply to this child, nor to these times. I swear that the grandfather of the child whom these misfortunes threaten is not yet born.'

By this he meant Harun al-Rashid.

The assembly then offered their compliments and good wishes to Mahdi in honour of the new-born child, who was Musa al-Hadi, the brother of Rashid.

MISCELLANEOUS ANECDOTES

The pact concluded between Amin and Ma'mun, dictated by Rashid, was deposited in the Ka'ba and it set forth that whichever of the two should betray his brother was to be considerd as having forfeited his rights and the Caliphate was to belong to the one who had been the object of the treachery.

Yasir, one of the eunuchs and confidential advisors of Zubaida, tells how she went to her son Amin in floods of tears during the siege of Baghdad. He spoke to her as follows:

'Silence! It is not with the worries and despairs of women that crowns are bound on. The affairs of the Caliphate cannot be sustained by the breasts of wet-nurses. Away! Away!'

It is also said that Tahir, who considered Amin a weak character, was walking one day in his garden when he received a letter in the hand of Amin himself, which was framed as follows:

'In the name of God, the Merciful, the Compassionate! Know, Tahir, that since our accession, whosoever has revolted against our authority has expiated his crime at the sword's edge. Tremble therefore for your life – or else give up your plan.'

He who tells the story adds:

'This letter seemed to produce a lingering impression on Tahir, for later, when he returned to Khurasan, he showed it to his intimates and said to them:

'By God! This is not the letter of a weakling, but of a man who has been led astray.'

There have not been, from the past until the present year of 332 AH/ 944 AD, any other Caliphs born of Hashimite fathers and mothers, except Ali ibn Abi Talib and Muhammad ibn Zubaida (Amin). This is why the poet Abu al-Ghul,* speaking of the latter, said:

> A king whose father and mother were both
> From the source from which burst forth
> Muhammad, the dazzling light of our Nation.
> They drank, in the protection of the valleys
> Of Mecca, the pure, unmixed waters of prophecy.

VI:435-436
§§ 2639-2642

THE PALACE OF MANBIJ

It was in the year 194 AH/810 AD that Amin began to betray his brother Ma'mun.

In 197 AH/813 AD, during the reign of Amin, there died at Raqqa Abd al-Malik ibn Salih ibn Ali, the most eloquent man of his age among the sons of Abbas.

Rashid, passing the region of Manbij in Syria, saw an imposing palace and garden filled with trees heavy with fruit. He said to Abd al-Malik:

'Who owns this palace?'

'O Commander of the Faithful,' he replied, 'first you – and then me, thanks to your generosity.'

Rashid then said:

'How was the palace constructed?'

'It yields to your palaces, but surpasses all other habitations.'

Rashid then asked:

'And how is your city?'

Abd al-Malik replied:

'The water is sweet, the temperature cool, the earth hard and firm, and diseases rare.'

'And its nights?' asked Rashid.

'A perpetual dawn,' answered Abd al-Malik.

Another time, Rashid said to him:

'O Abd al-Malik, how beautiful your country is!'

'How could it be otherwise?' the latter replied. 'The earth is red, the ears of corn yellow, the trees green, the plains rich in fragrant herbage and the mountains are covered with southernwood and artemisia.'*

Rashid then turned to Fadl ibn al-Rabi':

'The executioner's whip,' he said, 'would have made me suffer less!'

MUSA DECLARED HEIR APPARENT

When Amin named his son Musa 'al-Natiq bi-l-Haqq', 'He Who Proclaims the Truth', and his vizier Fadl ibn al-Rabi' had him recognized as heir to the throne, Musa was a child who still lisped as he spoke and could not tell good from evil. A child who still, day and night, sleeping or waking, sitting or standing, needed the care of his attendants. His education had been entrusted to Ali ibn Isa ibn Mahan. This is what a certain blind poet of Baghdad, known under the name of Ali ibn Abi Talib, says on the subject:

> The deceptions of the vizier,
> The depravity of the Imam,
> The advice of perfidious councillors,
> These have destroyed the Caliphate.
> What is this but the road of error?
> The roads of error are the worst.
> The behaviour of the Caliph is peculiar,
> That of the vizier even stranger.
> But even more amazing is the oath
> We have sworn to a tiny child,
> A poor creature which cannot yet
> Wipe its nose or leave
> The shelter of its nurse's lap.
> Observe how a tyrant and a seducer*
> Are conspiring together
> To rend the Book of Light!*
> If it were not for the whims of fortune,
> What would these two ever have amounted to?
> But destiny lifts up mountains
> Upon which stand the base and lowly
> Men she raises up from nothing.

REBELLION

Tahir, having killed Ali ibn Isa ibn Mahan, continued on his march and made camp at Hulwan, five days journey from Baghdad. The progress which he made each day, the setbacks of the supporters of Amin and their discomfiture in every encounter, excited the wonder of the people and made them certain that Tahir would gain the upper hand and Ma'mun triumph over his brother Amin. As to Fadl ibn al-Rabi' and his followers, they were put to confusion. The blind poet of whom we have already spoken, who was born and lived in Baghdad and was as devoted to Ma'mun as he was implacable against Amin, the son of Zubaida, then made the following verses:

> I am amazed at the confidence of this gang
> Who hope for the success of a cause
> Which can but come to nothing.
> How can what they have built
> And hoped for stand, when its foundations
> Are iniquity and whoredom?
> They are urged on to error by a seducer
> And a devil, whose promises are betrayals.
> They are harrassed and toyed with
> As wine makes mock of its drinker.
> They have conspired against the Truth
> And betrayed Ma'mun – but the perfidious
> Can never triumph. Ma'mun
> Is just, noble and generous to us;
> The love he inspires dwells in our hearts.
> There is no doubt that the future belongs to him;
> The Holy Law and the Psalms* bear witness to it.
> He will reign for forty years,
> Complete with new moons and months.
> Consolidate your efforts, set your snares;
> These very snares only ensure his joy.

Amin, on learning of the progress made by Tahir, gathered his generals and his most confidential advisors.

'Now lend me your aid,' he said, 'as Khurasan has given its aid to Ma'mun,

The Meadows of Gold

complying with this line of A'sha Rabi'a:

> And then they were not afraid,
> No, they drove forward
> The ram of war
> Whose horns slay all they meet.

God knows at what length I have studied the traditions of the peoples of the past, and that I have read the books of their wars and the stories of those who founded dynasties. By the memory of my father, I swear that I have not found one tale to equal that of this man Tahir, as regards his daring and his cunning. He is acting against me, I am the target of his audacious attack, it is to fight me that he has gathered a powerful army, a great number of generals and wily strategists. Today, it is your turn to show your mettle.'

His councillors answered him:

'God will preserve the life of the Commander of the Faithful. He will suffice him as He has sufficed the Caliphs who went before him. Whoever rises against him is a traitor!'

But after the army of Amin had been scattered by Tahir and rendered completely powerless, Sulaiman ibn Mansur spoke as follows:

'May the curse of God fall upon this traitor Amin! How much evil has his treachery and evil counsel caused the people! May God not admit him to the ranks of the blessed! Rather, may He soon make triumph the cause of Ma'mun, with the help of the Ram of the East*, that is, Tahir!'

Here are some verses which set forth the same thought:

> Alas for the sinner and heretic,
> Who drove him to eternal perdition!
> To treachery against the good,
> The pious, the virtuous Ma'mun –
> This leader who has never
> Strayed from the path!
> Ma'mun, the glory of the Caliphate,
> The Imamate, and of Wisdom;
> Master of generosity,
> Of unending bounty!
> If, in your folly, you conspire
> Against the Prophet's heir,
> Against him who inherits
> From so many heaven-favoured princes,
> Know: Ma'mun will have the best of helpers;
> God and that glorious warrior,
> The Ram of the East!

VI:439-443
§§ 2646-2648

AMIN IN RETREAT

Amin was surrounded by the enemy both in the eastern and western quarters of Baghdad. Harthama ibn A'yan was encamped by Nahrawan, near the Khurasan Gate and the Three Gates. Tahir encircled the western quarter of the town, including al-Yasiriya, Bab al-Muhawwal and Bab al-Kunasa. Amin then gathered his generals and addressed them in the following words:

'Glory be to God, Whose power raises and abases as He wills! Glory be to God, Who has the power to give and to withhold! Glory be to Him when His hand is closed and when it showers blessings! All things return to God! I praise Him among the reverses of fortune, the betrayals of my allies, in the eclipse of my state and the failing of my heart. May the prayers and peace of God be upon Muhammad, His Messenger, and upon his family!'

He continued with a long speech, which he ended thus:

'I leave you, my heart aching, my soul saddened and overwhelmed with regrets. I still seek a means whereby to save myself, and I ask God to grant me His aid!'

He next wrote to Tahir:

'You are a servant who has done his bidding. Your devotion has been relied on and you have proved yourself. You have fought and triumphed. The conqueror has been conquered, the victor has been brought low. I now consider it wise to advance my brother and abdicate in his favour, since he is the more deserving and the more worthy. Give me a safe conduct for myself, for my children, my mother, my grandmother, my eunuchs and my household, my supporters and my allies. I will then come to you and lay down my crown on behalf of my brother, who will ratify the amnesty you have granted or do whatever he considers fair and just.'

Tahir read this letter and cried:

'Pardon him now, when we have him by the throat! When his wings are broken and his impious soldiers on the run! No, by He Who holds my soul in His hands! No, not until he has put his hand in mine and yielded to my authority!'

Amin then wrote to Harthama, proposing to surrender on whatever terms he should dictate. The deposed Caliph had, previously, equipped a company of Abna and other supporters who had asked him for protection in return for defending him from the supporters of Ma'mun. This band headed against Harthama, who had just received reinforcements from Tahir ibn Husain. But Harthama had no need to put up a serious fight for, at the approach of the enemy troops, Bishr and Bashir, two Arabs of the tribe of Azd who were commanding the Abna, frightened by the menacing tone of the messages that Tahir sent them and alarmed at the consequences which his approaching attack would bring, deserted their post, and the troops fled.

Tahir was then encamped in the garden near Bab al-Kunasa known as the Garden of Tahir. One of the vagabonds from the Baghdad prisons composed these occasional verses:

> Tahir has given us a momentous battle, full of danger.
> He has defeated us, thanks to that dog Harthama.
> But we gave Tahir a hard time. Every cut-throat
> And thief eaten up with mange threw himself at him,
> And both his sides bear the marks of the staves
> Of the Naked Warriors. While he charged from the east,
> We attacked him from the west.

Meanwhile, Amin, gathering all his money, distributed 500 dirhams to each of his new officers, excluding the others, and gave them each a vial of perfume, without allotting anything to the veterans. Tahir, informed of this by his emissaries and spies, entered into correspondence with the disaffected. By means of promises and threats, he succeeded in rousing the lower ranks against their officers, until their anger grew so great that they revolted against Amin on Wednesday, the 6th of Dhu al-Hijja, 196 AH/812 AD.

One of those who revolted against Amin said on this subject:

> Tell Amin that his army
> Was dispersed by vials of scent.
> Tahir – may my soul be a ransom for his –
> Thanks to his messengers and measures
> Holds the reins of the kingdom
> In his hands, facing the rebels.
> Traitor! You have been undone
> By your own treachery. Your sins
> Have quickly come to light.
> Here is the lion who advances
> Threateningly against you.
> He roars among his hungry cubs.
> Flee then, but you cannot escape
> Such an enemy, other than by falling
> Into Hellfire and the Pit.

VI:443-446
§§ 2649-2653

BAGHDAD BESIEGED

Next, Tahir moved from al-Yasiriya to Bab al-Anbar and laid siege to Baghdad. The war continued towards its bitter end, night and day, until both camps showed the marks of exhaustion. Mansions were destroyed, most remarkable monuments obliterated; prices soared. This was in the year 196 AH/812 AD. Brother turned his sword against brother, son against father, as some fought for Amin, others for Ma'mun. Houses and palaces fuelled the flames; property was put to the sack. This is how the blind poet, known under the name of Ali ibn Abi Talib, describes this tragedy:

> The bonds of affection between kin have been broken;
> They have been disavowed even by the pious and wise.
> God's vengeance has been loosed upon his creatures
> To chastise them for the crimes they have committed.
> We show no sign of guilt for our sins,
> We do not seek to heal the secret corruptions of our hearts.
> Deaf to exhortations and prayers,
> Appeals and commands no longer avail.
> Now let us weep for Islam. Its millstone is broken.
> Unbelievers lead the warriors against our faith.
> Men kill each other, but both conqueror and vanquished
> Are lost. A leader raises himself to power;
> Any scoundrel can become one of their chiefs.
> The evil do not respect the sanctity of the good,
> And the good are powerless to repel the evil.
> Someone stands up and preaches the cause of ignorance;
> The first-come prescribes laws against us for his followers.
> They are like wolves who sight blood
> And make for it; nothing can stop them.
> When the enemy succeeds in destroying one house,
> They then begin the destruction of others.
> The flock wanders among the ruins, fleeing
> The sharp swords that pursue them.
> The man of violence in every tribe
> Falls on his rivals, dagger in hand.
> We weep for the death of a friend, a generous brother,

The Meadows of Gold

A kindly neighbour whose concern was our protection
A mother, streaming tears, weeps over her son
And the very birds, moved by pity, share her grief.
In vain she resigns herself with courage
To her loss; her tears betray her resolution.
She who had a husband has become a widow
And weeps for him with unrestrained tears.
'You were,' she said, 'my strength and support;
Now I am alone and unprotected.
I weep over the smoking ruins of our homes.
I weep for the dead and our wealth all pillaged.
The women of the harem are exposed to every eye,
They wander without veil or covering,
Lost, not knowing the way, trembling
Like gazelles in flight.
Is there then no honour and no faith
To prevent the ripping of the silken veil?
Was Baghdad not the loveliest of cities,
A spectacle that held the eye spell-bound?
Yes, she was all that. But now her beauty
Is worn away. The north wind of fate
Has made her a desert.
Her people have suffered as have so many before.
She has become an object of pity to nomad and settler.
O Baghdad, city of kings, goal of all desires,
Centre of all the learning of Islam,
Paradise on earth, you who sought wealth and gave
Birth to hope in every merchant's breast,
Tell us, where are they whom once we met
Along pleasure's flowery roads?
Where are the kings, shining amidst their trains
Like brilliant stars?
Where are the qadis, resolving by reason's light
The conundrums of the Law?
Where are the preachers and poets with their wisdom,
Speaking harmonious words?
Where are your gardens rich in charm, the palaces
Along the river banks, the flourishing land?
Where are the royal pavilions I once knew,
Glittering with jewels? Once
The earth was sprinkled with musk and rose,
The smoke of incense spread far and wide.
Every night the joyful guests gathered
At the home of some noble and generous host.

Baghdad Besieged

He gave his orders and the singing girls
Raised their beautiful voices and married
Them to the sound of the flute in a song.
Where have they gone, those glorious kings,
Scions of Hashim's noble house?
Where are their much-honoured followers?
They walked in royal power as friends.
The great grown weak by what has come to pass,
Are now held at the mercy of the mass.
Yet had they helped each other, I do swear,
Their victors soon were overwhelmed with fear.'

VI:447-451
§§ 2654-2655

THE NAKED ARMY

Harthama ibn A'yan sent Zuhair ibn Musayyab al-Dabbi from his camp in the eastern quarter to occupy al-Matir near Kalwadha. He levied a tithe on all boats laden with merchandise coming from Basra and Wasit. Next, he set up mangonels directed against Baghdad and made camp in the marshes at Kalwadha and al-Jazira.

As the people suffered from his assaults, gangs of vagabonds and prisoners marched against Zuhair. They went into battle almost naked, wearing only short trousers or drawers. They had made themselves a sort of helmet out of plaited palm-leaves, which they called *khūdh*. Their shields were made of these same leaves and of reed mats coated with tar and stuffed with sand and gravel.

Each band of ten men was commanded by an *'arīf*, ten *'arīf* by a *naqīb*, ten *naqīb* by a *qā'id*, and ten *qā'id* by an amir. Each of these officers had human mounts, proportionate to the number of men he commanded. Thus the *'arīf* had, as well as his soldiers, a certain number of men who served as horses. Similarly, the *naqīb*, the *qā'id* and the amir had as mounts men who were naked, with bells and pompoms of red and yellow wool round their necks. They had bridles and bits and had made themselves horse-tails out of brooms and fly-whisks. The *'arīf* went against the enemy mounted on one of these men and preceded by ten soldiers, each wearing his palm-leaf helmet and carrying a reed-mat shield. The *naqīb*, the *qā'id* and the amir marched into battle with similar equipages.

The curious gathered in large numbers to watch the battles of these men against the horsemen on the other side, who were excellently mounted and provided with breast-plates, coats of mail and armour, including arm-guards and armed with lances and leather Tibetan shields.

The struggle between the naked soldiers and the forces armed as we have described began. At first the battle turned against Zuhair, but reinforcements arrived from Harthama and the naked warriors fled. The men who were acting as horses shed their riders and, with swords at their backs, all fled behind the ramparts of the city.

A great number of dead drawn both from among the combatants and the onlookers were left on the field of battle. The following lines by the blind poet describe the attack led by Zuhair, with the help of his mangonels, and the massacre of the crowd and the naked soldiers:

The Naked Army

Do not go near the mangonels or the stones,
For you saw the corpse they are laying in the grave;
It is that of a man who came out early in the morning
To see the show. The only news he left with was his death.
He didn't want to learn the result of the battle
From hearsay; little did he know what fate had in store.
You who work the mangonels, what have you done?
It is your hands that have taken his life;
You cannot give it back to him. This
Was not the outcome he hoped for, but alas
Man's wishes are powerless against fate.

BAGHDAD IN FLAMES

Amin no longer knew how he was going to pay his troops and so he secretly had melted down his vessels of gold and silver in order to pay them. Meanwhile, al-Harbiya and the other suburbs, from Bab al-Anbar to Bab al-Harb and Bab Qutrabbul had sided with Tahir. The battle was therefore taking place in the heart of the western quarter, and the mangonels were continuing their work of destruction between the two camps. The blind poet Ali recalls these events:

> O you who work the mangonels,
> You are all without pity!
> You care no more for a friend
> Than you do for an enemy.
> Accursed ones! Do you know
> Whom you are striking down?
> Innocent passers-by!
> Many a graceful and beautiful girl,
> Slim and swaying as a fresh branch,
> Making her way home has become
> Food for crows. They have been
> Ripped from the shelter of the world
> And a pleasant, untroubled life;
> Finding no place to hide
> They lie exposed to all eyes
> On the day of fire.

Flames and destruction were great in Baghdad, Karkh and in the other quarters, on both sides. All the splendours of the capital were effaced. The situation was becoming critical. The inhabitants, driven from their quarters and streets, roamed from place to place. Everyone was gripped by terror, which steadily increased. As the poet said:

> Who has cast the evil eye upon you, O Baghdad?
> Were you not once the delight of all who beheld you?
> The dwelling place of a great multitude,
> Whose presence was one of your glories?
> Time has declared the hour of departure

Baghdad in Flames

> And they are gone. How deeply I regret
> Their going. I seek God's protection
> For the absent; when I recall them
> My tears begin to flow. They were here;
> Destiny has separated and scattered them,
> For destiny is happiest when parting friends.

The war continued thus between the supporters of Ma'mun and those of Amin for fourteen months. The population of Baghdad did not know where to take refuge. The mosques were deserted, the prayers no longer said. No such disaster had occurred there since the foundation of the city by Mansur. Later, however, at the time of the wars between Musta'in and Mu'tazz, the inhabitants had again to suffer something very similar. The 'Vagabonds' of the city then went again into battle using men as horses. They were commanded by a man called Ninawaih, by Khalawaih and other leaders, who, mounted on certain of these vagrants, led onto the field of battle 50,000 half-naked soldiers.

No war was more disastrous for Baghdad, however, than that between Ma'mun and his deposed brother Amin. In the present year, 332 AH/944 AD, the inhabitants consider the departure of Muttaqi as an unparalleled misfortune. They complain of the previous troubles which the struggle between the Baridi family, Ibn Ra'iq and Tuzun the Turk, brought upon them. They deplore as a calamity the revolt of Abu Muhammad al-Hasan ibn Abi al-Haija Abd Allah ibn Hamdan, known as Nasir al-Dawla, and that of his brother Ali ibn Abd Allah, known as Saif al-Dawla. What has happened is that time has passed since the tragedies which once overwhelmed their country and things which took place long ago have been obliterated from their memories – and indeed, the 'War of the Vagabonds' belongs to a very remote period.

The fighting between the partisans of Ma'mun and the naked warriors and other supporters of the deposed Caliph Amin became fiercer and fiercer. Amin was held in check in the Salih Palace in the western quarter. After a great battle one day, in the course of which a large number of people perished on both sides, a certain Husain, whose careless and profligate life had caused him to be nicknamed al-Khali – 'The Depraved' – composed the following verses:

> Amin, put your trust in God;
> He will grant you patience and success.
> Consign your fate to His hands:
> God the All-Powerful will protect you.
> His aid will accord us victory;
> We will charge instead of fleeing.
> He will give the renegades, your enemies
> A day of shame and humiliation.
> The cup of death is a hateful drink,
> Bitter to the tongue.

The Meadows of Gold

> They gave it to us to drink,
> And we gave it back to them.
> Such are the vicissitudes of war;
> One day we are conquered,
> The next, we are conquerors.

Every day the situation became worse for Amin and his supporters. The population of Baghdad divided into two factions. General fighting broke out between them in a quarter on the western bank known as Dar al-Raqiq. It was extremely bloody. High roads, squares, streets and alleys were strewn with corpses. The contending forces killed each other, crying: 'Take this for Ma'mun!' or 'Take this for Amin!'. Houses were plundered and put to the torch. In this extremity, there was unexpected happiness and joy for all those men, women, old people and children who could escape with some fragments of their fortune to the camp of Tahir, where they and their chattels were safe. A witness to that sad day recalls it in the following lines:

> I weep for Baghdad, I who have lost
> The sweetness of a fortunate life.
> We have exchanged our happiness
> For grief, ease for misery.
> Envy's evil eye has found us out.
> The people have perished by the mangonel.
> Some are cruelly thrown into the flames;
> Here a woman weeps over someone drowned.
> One calls to his family with loud cries,
> Another beseeches his beloved friend.
> A young girl weeps from huge eyes,
> Charming in her yellow tunic;
> She calls out to her brother.
> But she has no brother. He has fallen
> At the side of his friend.
> There a whole family is banished
> From the protection of the world.
> Their goods are on sale in the bazaars.
> A stranger from afar lies headless
> In the middle of the street.
> The massacre spreads. No one knows
> To what faction the other belongs.
> Son no longer defends father,
> Friend flees friend.

Baghdad in Flames

All we once loved has vanished.
I will not forget Dar al-Raqiq.

RESISTANCE

One of the generals from Khurasan came to find Tahir. At the sight of these men fighting half-naked and without arms, he cried contemptuously:

'What use are the endeavours of these people, who do not even have arms, against our troops, who are strong, brave, well armed and well equipped?'

Noticing that he was being observed by one of the naked warriors, he strung his bow, aimed his arrow and stepped out of the ranks. His adversary had a reed-mat shield on his arm and slung over his shoulder a nosebag full of stones and bits of brick. As fast as the leader shot his arrows, they embedded themselves in the shield or fell to one side, whereupon the naked 'vagabond' picked them up and tucked them into a corner of his shield which he had made in the form of a quiver precisely for this purpose. He continued thus until his adversary, having exhausted his arrows, fell upon him sword in hand. The 'vagabond' then drew a stone from his bag and hit him right in the eye. Another stone nearly knocked him off his horse. The general fled at full speed, dropping his helmet:

'No,' he cried, as he tore away, 'these are not men but devils!'

This is what an eye-witness, Abu Ya'qub al-Khuraimi, a supporter of Amin and fanatic enemy of Ma'mun, says on the subject in a very long ode in which he describes the revolts and battles of which Baghdad was the scene:

> The markets of Karkh are abandoned,
> 'Vagabonds' and passers-by run hurriedly through them.
> The war has raised from the rabble
> Savage lions with cruel jaws.
> Their shields are of reed matting
> And their helmets of palm leaves.

The following passage from a poem by the blind poet Ali also serves to confirm our account:

> These wars have brought men forward
> Who are not from the Arab tribes
> Of Southern or Northern descent;
> A band armed with breast-plates of wool
> Have hurled themselves into battle
> Like starving lions. A helmet

Resistance

> Of palm leaves protects their heads,
> A reed mat serves as a shield.
> They do not know what it is to flee,
> Even at that hour when the bravest
> Flees from the lances.
> A single one of them, not even
> Clad in a loin-cloth, will attack
> Two thousand men. A hero cries
> As he strikes: 'Take that!
> Compliments of the "vagabond" warrior.'

Every day the fighting became more bitter and the resistance of the two parties more obstinate. The deposed Caliph, Amin, had no other troops than these naked warriors with their helmets of palm leaves and the matting shields.

Tahir increased the pressure on the people. All the quarters of Baghdad fell into his power, one after another, and the inhabitants, as they came under his control, supported him against the enemy. The part of the town which had not yielded to him suffered more than anywhere else from his depredations. He had had trenches dug right through the middle of the houses, khans and palaces which separated his troops from those of Amin. Tahir's army increased in strength and aggressiveness and that of Amin dwindled and weakened. While Tahir's soldiers razed buildings, the supporters of the deposed Caliph were reduced to sheltering under bits of wood from the ruins of houses, pieces of cloth and other materials. It is to this that the following verses by one of the supporters of Amin, a relentless enemy of Ma'mun, refer:

> Every day another breach is opened that we cannot fill.
> The enemy advances towards its goal and our forces weaken.
> When they destroy a house, we gather the fragments of the roof
> And try to combine it with another to form a barricade.
> They have made the wide places of our land narrow,
> They have become dwellers in it and filled it up.
> They start the quarry with the beating of their drums;
> When they see the face of their prey, they strike.
> They have laid our country waste from east to west.
> We no longer know where to seek refuge.
> The people tell stories of what they have seen;
> If no disaster has befallen them, they invent one.
> Nevertheless, you see the hero distinguished in battle
> Run like a dog when confronted by one of the naked warriors.
> Even the Koran reciters have a dispensation to fight,
> And the sins of all those who fall in battle are forgiven.

VI:461-464
§§ 2667-2671

FAMINE

Tahir, angered by the constancy of the supporters of the deposed Caliph Amin in battle and in spite of the ruin, fire and slaughter caused by the mangonels, cut off their provisions from Basra, Wasit and all the other supply routes. Thus it was that when in a street of Baghdad inhabited by the supporters of Ma'mun bread cost one dirham for twenty rotls, in another, held by the partisans of Amin, a single rotl went for that price. The people, overwhelmed by want and prey to all the horrors of famine, despaired of survival. Joy reigned in the camp of Tahir and dejection in that of Amin, the deposed Caliph. The proof is to be found in these lines by Ali, the blind poet:

> The inhabitants, ruined and driven from their homes,
> Tell each other the latest rumours.
> O you who ask about their plight, look well,
> And you will have no need to question.
> Once their '*Allahu akbar!*' was addressed to the Merciful;
> Now it has become their battle cry.
> Cast your eye over their numbers,
> Wait for the last departure, count the nights.
> No one is left in Baghdad but those
> Too poor to leave, or with too many dependants,
> Or prisoners escaped from gaol
> Who are not Arabs, or even clients of the Arab tribes.
> The mother is no longer safe in her house,
> There is no uncle or protector to guard the threshhold.
> Why are we being killed for our faith?
> O Lord for Whom all is possible, may Your Name be praised!

AMIN AT BAY

One day Tahir, at the head of all his troops, made a sortie from several points at once and attacked Bab al-Kunasa. The battle was bloody. The leaders ran here and there. Sword and fire spread death.

Both sides stood fast, but nevertheless greater numbers of Amin's supporters perished in the river and the flames. There were also many victims among the naked warriors. These men carried nosebags filled with stones and bricks, wore helmets made of palm leaves and shields of reed matting. They carried cane lances. Rags of cloth served as standards and they blew into reed-pipes and ox-horns. The blind poet describes this battle, which took place on a Sunday, as follows:

> The Battle of Sunday will leave memories
> That will last forever.
> How many bodies have you seen,
> Thrown one upon another?
> This man, driven by curiosity,
> Went out to watch the battle
> And was struck down by a stray arrow
> Which tore his liver in two.
> A son cries out: 'O father!'
> A father weeps: 'O my son!'
> How many strong swimmers,
> Hard and enduring, drowned,
> And only the girls of the town
> Will miss them. Another
> Writhes in the flames
> Hotter than the July sun.
> He stands on the battle field
> Straight and unmoving as a stake
> Planted before a tent.
> 'They have killed a thousand,
> Not more,' said one. 'More,'
> Said another, 'the dead
> Are past counting.' I spoke
> To a man whose lance-wound

The Meadows of Gold

> Was past curing. 'Who are you,
> O hapless one? An unhappy
> Follower of Amin?' He answered:
> 'I have here neither country
> Nor family. I have fought
> Neither in the name of error
> Nor to defend the truth,
> But only that some of the riches
> Of this perishable world
> Should fall into my hands.'

In this critical situation, the blockade became more and more rigorous and Amin ordered one of his generals called Zuraij to search the houses of everyone, resident or stranger, who had, or was believed to have, money or precious possessions. He sent with him on this mission another person called Hirsh. These two men descended on the people and stripped them of everything they had on mere suspicion, and thus collected considerable sums. The people fled on the pretext of making the pilgrimage to Mecca, and the rich also tried to escape from Zuraij and Hirsh. The blind poet mentions this incident:

> They announced the pilgrimage,
> But that is not their real aim;
> They wish to flee from Hirsh.
> How many men woke up happy,
> Yet by nightfall were ruined?
> Each house visited by Zuraij and Hirsh
> Is given over to misery and destruction.

These lines are taken from a long poem.

When these afflictions were extended even to respectable women, the merchants gathered at Karkh in order to write to Tahir and tell him that it was impossible for them to leave Baghdad, that their persons and goods were exposed to violence of every kind and, lastly, that the naked warriors, the itinerant vendors and the rabble of the market quarters were the scourge of the city. But one of them raised an objection, saying: 'If you enter into correspondence with Tahir, you will have no protection against reprisals from Amin. Leave to God', he added, 'the task of destroying them.'

This is what one of their poets said:

> Leave the riff-raff of the streets –
> They will soon fall into the lion's claws.
> The livers of these evil men will be torn;
> The tomb awaits them.

Amin at Bay

> God will annihilate them,
> To punish their insolence and sin.

It was on one of these days that the naked warriors, 100,000 strong, armed with lances and staves and wearing paper crests on their helmets and blowing into reeds and ox-horns, joined the other defenders of Amin and rushed out from many different points to attack the followers of Ma'mun. Tahir ordered a number of his officers and generals to advance against them from several directions at once. An extremely bloody engagement then took place. It was a Monday. Until midday, the naked warriors had the best of it against the supporters of Ma'mun, but afterwards attacked, together with others of Amin's soldiers, by the whole of Ma'mun's force, they fled. About 10,000 of them drowned or died by steel or fire. The blind poet said of this day:

> By the Amir,* and by Tahir, son of Husain!
> They attacked us at dawn on Monday.
> They gathered their forces by night and cried:
> 'Today seek your revenge for Husain
> Ibn Ali ibn Isa ibn Mahan!
> At the sound of their drums,
> The warriors brandishing lances
> Rushed out to meet them.
> You who lie by the river bank,
> Victim of the naked warriors,
> Trampled by the horsemen of both sides,
> Were you a vizier? An officer?
> Alas, now you are as far
> From those dignities
> As you are from the two
> Bright stars in the Great Bear!
> How many came, curious, to feed
> On this sight and went away
> With but a single eye!
> For the enemy did not miss
> His mark – and he aimed
> Only at the eyes.

Amin, the deposed Caliph, reduced to the direst extremity, secretly sold all that was left in his treasury and gave it to his supporters. But soon he had nothing left to give them. Their demands increased. Tahir camped at Bab al-Anbar, in a garden by that gate, and pressed him sorely.

'I wish,' Amin then cried, 'that God would destroy both sides together, for I have only enemies, both those who are with me and those who are against me. One side covets my goods, the other my life.'

The Meadows of Gold

Then he added:

> O go away and leave me,
> You who are supposed to be
> My supporters. You all
> Have faces of many colours.
> Everywhere I see nothing
> But lies and delusions.
> I no longer own anything,
> So go beg from my treasurers.
> All my troubles come
> From him who is camped
> In that garden.

He was referring to Tahir.

The situation of the deposed Caliph Amin was critical and extremely dangerous. Harthama ibn A'yan was occupying the eastern part of the city while almost the whole of the western had been surrounded by Tahir. Amin now held only the City of Abi Ja'far, the old town founded by Mansur. He consulted his confidential advisors as to the chances of saving himself, and each put forward his point of view and gave his advice. One of them said to him:

'Write to Tahir and by making such pledges as are likely to inspire his confidence, promise him that you will place your kingdom and your authority in his hands. Perhaps he will accede to this request.'

'May your mother bewail your death!' Amin retorted. 'I was very wrong to consult you. Do you not know that this man is not given to treachery? Would Ma'mun, left to his own resources and to his own counsel, have gained a tenth of what he has gained without the help of Tahir? Having watched this man and studied his designs, I have understood that all he sought was glory, splendid deeds and fidelity to his promises. How then could I hope to lead him by gifts to treachery? Alas! If he but recognized my authority and joined me, in vain would the Turks and Dailamites form a league against me. I would not be troubled by their enmity, for I could then apply to myself that which Abu al-Aswad al-Du'ali said of the tribe of Azd, when Ziyad ibn Abihi placed himself under their protection:

> When he saw them first looking for his vizier
> And at last coming after him too,
> Ziyad went to the tribe of Azd,
> Seeking protection from death.
> His decision was a wise one.
> The people of Azd said to him:
> 'Welcome. You got away. Tell us
> Whom we should fight for you.'

From then on he had no need
To fear any enemy in the world,
Even if they had attacked him
With all the power of 'Ad.*

By God! I would hope that he might accept my request. My treasuries would be open to him, my power would pass into his hands and I would live willingly under his protection. But I know that even if I had a thousand lives, I could never escape him.'

'You are right, O Commander of the Faithful,' replied Sindi. 'Even if you were his own father, Husain ibn Mus'ab, he would not spare you.'

Amin added:

'How could I take refuge with Harthama, "When there is no longer time to be saved" (Koran 38:3)?'

Nevertheless, he sent messages to this general, who showed a certain sympathy for him. Harthama replied affirmatively to all his requests and promised his protection against those who were plotting his death. Tahir was told of it and showed his displeasure and anger. Harthama then undertook to move his prisoner by boat to the quay at the Khurasan Gate and to take him thence to Tahir's camp, together with anyone else he wished.

THE DEATH OF AMIN

When Amin made up his mind to flee that night, Thursday,* the 25th of Muharram, 198 AH/814 AD, those of his defenders who were known as the 'Beggars', brave soldiers chosen from among the Abna and other troops, came to him and addressed him as follows:

'O Commander of the Faithful, you no longer have men who can give you good advice, but we are 7,000 men ready for battle and you have 7,000 horses in your stables. Let each of us mount a horse, open one of the gates of the city and leave this very night. Under cover of darkness we will steal the march on the enemy. We will reach al-Jazira and Diyar Rabi'a; there you can collect the tax, recruit new troops and, crossing Syria, enter Egypt, where you can increase your army and your funds, and so acquire new power.'

'This, by God,' said Amin, 'is an idea!'

So Amin resolved upon this plan, allowed it to mature and seemed decided to carry it out. But even within the depths of his palace itself, there were pages and eunuchs sold to Tahir, who were keeping him informed hour by hour of all that happened. Almost immediately, Tahir learned the news, with no small anxiety, since he knew the plan could be successful if put into action. So he sent messages to Sulaiman ibn Mansur, to Ibn Nahik and to Sindi ibn Shahak, who were all of Amin's party, saying:

'If you do not prevent this escape, I swear to ravage your houses and lands, destroy your fortunes and see that you all die.'

That night, they entered Amin's presence and dissuaded him from his plan.

While all this was going on, Harthama arrived by boat at the Khurasan Gate. Amin had saddled a black horse with white socks on both fore and hind legs and a blaze, which he called Zuhairi. He summoned his two sons, Musa and Abd Allah, embraced them, kissing them and weeping over them, and said:

'I consign you to God's care. I do not know if I shall ever see you again.'

Then he went out, dressed in white and wearing a black hood. A torch guided his steps. When he reached the quay by the Khurasan Gate, he found the boat ready and embarked, having first hamstrung his horse. Harthama kissed his forehead in welcome.

Tahir, meanwhile, warned of the Caliph's flight, had sent down river several boats manned by troops from Herat and elsewhere and had sailors ready in small boats on the bank. Harthama had only a small number of men with him. As soon as his boat cast off, Tahir's men, naked, plunged under the boat and overturned

The Death of Amin

it on top of all those who were on board. Harthama was above all in haste to save his own life. He clung to one of the little skiffs and managed to get out of the water; then he made his way back to his troops in the eastern quarter.

Amin tore off his clothes, threw himself in the water and reached the Sarat Canal near the camp of Quraish al-Dandani, one of Tahir's pages. One of the grooms, noticing that the fugitive was scented with musk and perfumes, arrested him and led him to Quraish. This last sent to Tahir for instructions, then, acting on an order which he received as he was on his way to the general with his prisoner, he put him to death. Amin, at the very moment that his throat was cut, cried out:

'We belong to God and to God we return! I am a cousin of the Messenger of God! I am the brother of Ma'mun!'

The swordblows were redoubled until his corpse grew cold. Then the head was severed from the body. According to some this took place on the night of Sunday, the 25th of Muharram, 198 AH/814 AD.

AN EYE-WITNESS ACCOUNT

This is the story told by Ahmad ibn Sallam, who was with Amin in the boat when it was capsized. This man, having swum away, was caught by one of Tahir's soldiers, who would have killed him had he not been tempted by the reward of 10,000 dirhams which his prisoner promised to make over to him the very next morning.

'I was led,' said Ahmad, 'into an extremely dark room. Soon after, I saw a man come in, almost naked, for he was wearing only drawers, a turban which veiled his face and a rag of cloth over his shoulders. He was imprisoned with me and the people of the place were warned to keep a watch on us. As soon as he entered, he pushed aside the turban which was hiding his features and I recognized Amin. I could not restrain my tears and murmured very softly the prayer: "We belong to God and to God we return."

He began to study me and said:

"Are you one of theirs?"

"Me, O my lord?" I replied, "I am your freedman."

"What is your name?"

"Ahmad ibn Sallam."

"I've seen you somewhere else, though," he went on. "Didn't you come to me once in Raqqa?"

"Yes," I said.

"Ahmad," he cried soon after, calling me.

"Master, I am here."

"Come close to me," he said, "and hold me, for I am cold and afraid."

I obeyed and felt his heart beating violently.

He continued:

"Tell me the news of my brother Ma'mun. Is he alive?"

"If he were not alive," I answered, "who would be the author of this war?"

"May God punish them!" cried Amin. "They told me he was dead."

"Yes", I replied, "and may God punish your viziers, for it is they who have placed you in this sad predicament."

"Ahmad," he said again, "this is not the time for such reproaches. Do not speak of my viziers except with praise, for they are not at fault. I am not the first to have failed to reach his goal."

I then said: "Take my wrap and throw off those rags which cover you."

"Ahmad," he answered, "for a man in my situation, they are more than adequate."

And he added:

"I have no doubt that they will take me to my brother. Do you think that he will order my death?"

"Certainly not," said I, "the voice of kinship will plead for you."

"Alas," replied Amin, "royalty is barren; it has no kin."

I told him: "The amnesty granted you by Harthama will be ratified by your brother."

After that I had him recite the *dhikr* and *istaghfar* prayers, calling upon God and seeking His forgiveness. While we were so occupied, the door of the room opened. An armed man entered, looked Amin in the face with the most serious attention and when he was quite sure that he had recognized him, he went out, locking the door. I had recognized Muhammad ibn Humaid, a partisan of Tahir, and I no longer had any doubts that Amin was a dead man. There remained the *witr* prayer, recited in the third part of the night, for me to say. I was afraid that I would be killed before having completed it, and so was just about to begin when Amin called me again:

"Ahmad," he said, "don't go away. Pray beside me, for I am very much afraid."

I moved close to him. A few moments later we heard the sound of horses' hooves. Someone knocked at the door, which opened and a number of Persians entered, drawn swords in their hands. Amin, sensing their approach, rose and said:

"We belong to God, and to God we return! My soul is about to fly to God. Where can I flee? How can I defend myself?"

They stopped at the threshold of the room where we were, encouraging one another to enter and pushing each other forward. Amin seized a cushion and cried out to them:

"I am the cousin of the Messenger of God! I am the son of Harun! The brother of Ma'mun! God . . . God will call you to account for my blood!"

A freedman of Tahir came straight up to him and struck him a sword blow on the crown of his head. Amin struck him in the face with the cushion which he was holding in his hand and bent over him to snatch away the sword. The murderer began to cry out in Persian:

"He has killed me! He has killed me!"

His companions ran up. One of them plunged his sword into Amin's side. Then they threw him to the ground, cutting his throat from behind and, after having struck off his head, they went to offer it to Tahir.'

VI:478-482
§§ 2685-2686

AMIN'S HEAD

There are several accounts of the death of Amin other than that which I have just given and I have noted the divergencies among them in my *Intermediate History*.

Next, they arrested one of Amin's eunuchs, called Kawthar, who had been his favourite. He had with him the ring, the cloak, the sword and the staff – the insignia of the Caliphate. The following day, on Tahir's orders, Amin's head was exposed on one of the gates of Baghdad, known as the Bab al-Hadid – Iron Gate, towards Qutrabbul in the southern area of the western quarter. The body was buried in a nearby garden. When Amin's head was placed before him, Tahir recited the following verses from the Koran: 'You give power to whom You please, and You strip power from whom You please; You exalt whom You will, and You humble whom You will. In Your hand lies all that is good; You have power over all things' (Koran 3:26).

The head was next sent to Ma'mun in Khurasan. It was wrapped in a kerchief, packed in cotton and coated with a sort of varnish. Ma'mun wept and showed all the signs of violent grief, but Fadl ibn Sahl said to him:

'Commander of the Faithful, let us thank God for this single favour. You know that Amin would have been delighted to see you in the state which God now shows him to you.'

Ma'mun had the head placed on a stake in the middle of the great court of the castle. Then he distributed the pay to the army. He ordered each man, as he took his money, to curse the exposed head. All obeyed. A Persian soldier came forward to be paid. He was told: 'Curse this head!', and he uttered the following words:

'May God curse him, him and both his parents and their children! May he cause them to enter the — of their mothers!'*

'But you have just cursed the Commander of the Faithful himself,' someone pointed out to him.

Ma'mun, hearing these words, smiled and did not seem troubled by them, but nevertheless he had the head removed and forbade the pronouncing of the name of the deposed Caliph. The head was embalmed, placed in a basket and sent back to Iraq, where it was buried near the body.

And thus it was that God, taking pity on the people of Baghdad, delivered them from the horrors of famine, siege and death.

VI:482-484
§§ 2687-2689

THE LAMENTS OF THE WOMEN

Among the poems in memory of Amin is that by his mother, Zubaida Umm Ja'far. Here is a portion of it:

> He who spares no one has struck down
> Him who was dearest to you. This murder
> Has plunged your heart in never-ending despair.
> Since I saw death swoop down and strike
> Amin in the heart and in the head,
> I have passed my nights in grief,
> Watching the stars, trying to trace
> His lineaments upon the page of night.
> Death drew near him; sorrow did not
> Leave him till the hour in which
> His murderer poured out the cup of death.
> He who has died will never return.
> How can I approach him? I weep,
> Comparing other men to what he was,
> For it was upon him I had built my hopes.

His wife, Lubbada, the daughter of Ali, the son of the Caliph Mahdi, with whom his marriage at the time of his death had not been consummated, dedicated these lines to him:

> I weep for you not in the name
> Of joy and happiness but in that
> Of glory, the sword and buckler.
> I weep for the cavalier
> By whose death I have been stricken,
> Who has left me a widow
> Before the wedding night.
> O King, stretched out naked
> Upon the earth, the dregs
> Of your people have betrayed you,
> As have your guards.

The Meadows of Gold

A great number of other poets composed elegies for the death of Amin.

After the murder of Amin, one of Zubaida's eunuchs went to her and said:

'Why do you sit quietly when the Commander of the Faithful has just been killed?'

'Well, what can I do?' asked Zubaida.

'Go out,' replied the man, 'and demand vengeance for the blood which has been shed, as did A'isha for the blood of Uthman.'*

'Away, you bastard!' cried Zubaida. 'Is it fitting then that women should demand the price of blood and take the place of warriors?'

Nevertheless, she called for the robes of mourning and put on a rough hair-shirt. Then she demanded ink and paper and addressed the following verses to Ma'mun:

> To the best of Imams, scion of the noblest stock,
> To the best of those who have ascended the *minbar*!
> To the inheritor of the knowledge of the ancients,
> And of their glory, to the King Ma'mun, from Umm Ja'far:
> I write, O cousin, and tears fill my eyes.
> I am striken through him who was bound to you
> By the closest of links, he whose death has left
> A void in my heart and my fortitude exhausted.
> Tahir murdered him – may God refuse him His benediction!
> Tahir, whose name means 'Pure', can never
> Be purified of such a sin. He has exposed me
> In my grief to all eyes. He has pillaged my goods,
> He has set fire to my domains. Harun
> Would have been horrified at what this ugly
> One-eyed creature has made me suffer.
> But if my misfortunes are by your command,
> I submit to the will of an all-powerful sovereign.

Ma'mun wept as he read these lines, and cried:

'My God, I say, as the Commander of the Faithful Ali said, when he learned of the death of Uthman: "God knows I did not perform this murder; I neither ordered it nor approved it!" O God, fill the heart of Tahir with grief!'

The other details of the history and life of Amin over which I have passed in silence, are reported in detail in two of my works – the *Historical Annals* and the *Intermediate History* – which means I do not have to return to the matter in this book.

God is the master of all grace!

VI:484-487
§§ 2690-2693

THE CALIPHATE OF MA'MUN

Ma'mun, whose name was Abd Allah ibn Harun, known as Abu Ja'far – or according to others, Abu al-Abbas – was proclaimed Caliph at the age of twenty-eight years and two months. His mother was from Badghis in Afghanistan, and her name was Murajil. He died at Budandun, near Ain al-Ashira, which is the source of the Budandun river. It is said that in Greek this source is also called Raqqa.

His body was taken to Tarsus, where it was interred to the left of the mosque, in the year 218 AH/833 AD. He was forty-nine years old. He had held the Caliphate for twenty-one years. His war with his brother Amin, as we have said, lasted fourteen months, although other historians give the figure of two years and five months. Throughout that war, the people of Khurasan recognized him as Caliph and pronounced his name in the public prayers from their *minbars* in the various cities, as well as in Mecca and Medina and in the provinces and plains and mountains that Tahir had conquered and occupied on behalf of Ma'mun. Amin was recognized as Caliph only in Baghdad and nowhere else.

VII:1-2
§ 2694

(Omitted: VII:2-7; §§ 2695-2700. Ma'mun dominated by Fadl ibn Sahl whom at last he puts to death; Ma'mun's viziers; Ma'mun writes satirical verses against his uncle 'Ibrahim ibn al-Mahdi, known as Ibn Shikhla. The Caliph, who followed the Shi'a doctrines, criticized Ibrahim who was a Sunni'; Verses quoted; 'The very odd story of Ibrahim's relations with Ma'mun are to be found in a book called The Book of Ibrahim ibn al-Mahdi*'; Abu Dulaf's poems of war and love; He explains how he recognized a verse by Ma'mun: 'Commander of the Faithful, poetry is like a woollen carpet – when a finer and more beautiful wool is mixed with the ordinary thread, its excellence stands out from the cloth and shines with a greater splendour than the rest of the work.')*

SAYINGS OF MA'MUN

Ma'mun often said:

'A king can pardon everything except a slander against his person, a revelation of his secrets and an insult to his harem.'

Ma'mun also said:

'Put off war as long as possible and, when it becomes inevitable, give battle only at the end of the day.'

But this maxim is also attributed to Anushirvan.*

Again, Ma'mun used to say:

'All strategems are powerless to repel fate when she draws near and powerless to hold her when she hastens away.'

And when Ma'mun came to power and his authority was no longer contested, he said:

'This would be a prodigious thing, were it not flawed; this would be kingship, did it not end in perdition; this would be joy, did it not end in delusion; what a day, if the morrow could be trusted!'

He also said:

'Courtesy consists of a pleasing exterior, a character which warms and takes root in men's hearts, ease of access, far-reaching benevolence and a generous distribution of praise. This quality is, for people of merit, both a gift and a force to be reckoned with, for it is chief among the traits which attract, it is the beacon of power, the most praiseworthy of mental habits, the gateway to popularity and the key to understanding.'

'The kings among the men of this world,' he also used to say, 'are the generous, and among those of the world to come, the pious. A great fortune in hands that do not know how to use it, is like a feast set on the edge of a gutter. If avarice were a road, I would not follow it; if it were a tunic, I would not put it on.'

VII:7-9
§ 2701

MA'MUN'S WEDDING SPEECH

Ma'mun, attending a wedding which was being celebrated between members of his family, was asked by the assembled company to give a speech, and spoke as follows:

'Glory to God! All praise belongs to God; His chosen is the Apostle of God; the best of His works is the Sacred Book. The Most High has said: "Marry those among you who are not married; unite your honest servants and your virtuous serving maids. If they are poor, God will give them of His bounty, for God encompasses all, and all things are known to Him." (Koran 24:32). Even were there no verse with such a precise meaning and the sanction of unbroken custom and marriage had been endowed by God with the sole merit of uniting creatures, whether friends or strangers, every well intentioned and hard-working man would hasten to it, and every wise and intelligent man embrace it swiftly. So and so, whose genealogy you know well, asks you for the hand of so-and-so, your noble daughter, and brings her a bride-price of such-and-such. Accede to our intercession, sanction the union for which we seek, and speak only kind words, that you may be thanked and rewarded through God. I end by imploring God's mercy – for me and for you.'

VII:9-10
§ 2702

(Omitted: VII:10-12; §§ 2703-2704. Discussion on jurisprudence and truth between Thumama ibn Ashras and others; Eloquence of an envoy from Kufa.)

MA'MUN AND THE SPONGER

According to Thumama ibn Ashras,* ten inhabitants of Basra were denounced one day to Ma'mun for professing the doctrines of Mani and the dualist principles of Light and Dark. After he had had them named one by one, he ordered them to be brought to him. A professional sponger who saw them just at the moment when they were gathering, said to himself:

'Oh look! People gathering for a party!'

And he slipped in among them and went with them, not knowing who they were, until their escort brought them to the boat on which they were to embark. Immediately, however, chains were brought and they were all manacled together, including the intruder, who said to himself:

'My greed has finally put my feet in irons!'

Then turning to the elders of the group, he said:

'Excuse me, but who are you?'

'Rather, who are *you*? Are you to be numbered among our brothers?' they replied.

'God knows, I hardly know you,' answered the interloper. 'Quite frankly, I am a professional sponger and when I went out today I happened to come across you. Struck by your pleasant appearance, your attractive looks and your apparent prosperity, I said to myself: "Here are some elderly gentlemen, some men of mature years and some young people going out to a feast." I made my way among you and walked along next to one of your number as if I belonged to your party. When we reached this boat and I found it adorned with cushions and carpets and saw these trays and bags and well-filled baskets, I added to myself: "They are going to have a feast at some villa or pleasure garden. This is my lucky day!" I was still feeling happy and exhilarated when this guard came and chained you up and me along with you. All this is making me feel very confused, so please tell me what is going on.'

These words entertained the prisoners and made them smile. Amused, and put in a good mood, they said to him:

'Now that you have your chain, you should know that we are Manicheans who have been denounced to Ma'mun, and we are being taken to his presence. He will ask us who we are, question us on our beliefs, exhort us to repent and forswear our faith, putting us to various tests. He will, for example, show us an image of Mani and order us to spit on it and recant: he will force us to sacrifice a marsh bird called a *tadruj*.* Whoever consents to do these things will be spared, whoever

Ma'mun and the Sponger

refuses will die. When you are called and put to the test, explain who you are and declare your faith, after which, say whatever your wit suggests. But didn't you tell us you were a professional sponger? Now professional spongers always have a fine supply of stories and gossip. How about making our trip to Baghdad seem less long by telling some good tale or amusing anecdote?'

On reaching Baghdad, the prisoners were led into the presence of Ma'mun. He called each in turn by name, asked each their sect and exhorted them to embrace the Muslim faith. He invited them to abjure Mani, showing them his image and ordering them to spit on it and recant. One by one, as they refused, he handed them over to the executioner.

Thus, at last, they came to the professional sponger, but as they had already disposed of ten prisoners and there were no more names on the list, Ma'mun asked the guards:

'Who is this?'

'Quite honestly, we know nothing about him,' they answered, 'we found him in with the others and brought him along.'

'What is your story?' the Caliph asked him.

'Commander of the Faithful, I swear to divorce my wife if I understand a word of what is going on. I am only a poor sponger.'

And he told them his story from beginning to end.

The Caliph was very much amused and had him given a picture of Mani. Not satisfied with cursing and denying him, the sponger added:

'Give it to me and I'll decorate it with a fine load of shit! But, by God, I don't know whether this Mani was a Muslim or a Jew!'

Ma'mun, however, said:

'Let him be punished as he deserves for his uncontrolled sponging and his foolhardiness.'

Then Ibrahim ibn al-Mahdi, who was present, said:

'O Commander of the Faithful, grant me the favour of sparing this man and I will tell you a very strange tale of an uninvited guest, of which I was the hero.'

The Caliph said:

'Go ahead, O Ibrahim.'

'Commander of the Faithful, I had gone out one day and was wandering aimlessly round the streets of Baghdad when I found myself in front of a many-storeyed house, from the belvedere of which wafted the scent of spices and aromatics and the delicious smell of cooking food. I was very much attracted. I stopped at a tailor's shop and asked:

"Who owns that house?"

"A cloth merchant," he said.

"What is his name?"

"So-and-so, son of so-and-so."

I looked up at the belvedere and from the carved wooden lattice which protected the window I saw a hand and a wrist appear – and I had never seen anything so enchanting. The charm of this sight, O Commander of the Faithful,

179

The Meadows of Gold

made me forget the aromas of the kitchen and I stood for a while much troubled, not knowing what to do. At last I asked the tailor:

"Does the master of the house drink *nabidh*?"

"Oh yes, he does," he replied, "and in fact I think he is entertaining today. But his guests are always merchants, discrete people like himself."

We had reached this point when two noble-looking men on horseback came into view at the end of the street and headed towards us.

"Here are his two guests," said the tailor.

"What are their names and how are they familiarly known?"

He told me, and at once I urged on my mount and coming up between the two men said:

"May my life be a ransom for yours! So-and-so – may God strengthen him – is waiting for you impatiently."

I escorted them to the door, they preceded me in and I followed close behind. The master of the house saw me and since it never occurred to him that I had not been brought by his two friends, he welcomed me warmly and had me sit in the place of honour. Then, O Commander of the Faithful, they brought in the tables. The dinner was very handsomely served and we showed our appreciation of the various dishes, which tasted even better than they had smelled.

"Well," I said to myself, "I have eaten the food, but there remains the mystery of the hand and the wrist."

Once the table was removed and we had finished washing our hands, we made our way to the reception room, which was a large, elegant chamber, richly furnished. My host redoubled his attentions and turned towards me as he talked. The two guests had no doubts that I had been invited, while my host treated me thus because he believed I had been brought by his two friends.

We had already emptied a few cups when a young slave girl appeared, as slim and graceful as a willow branch, and greeted us without shyness. A cushion was offered her and a lute was brought in and laid on her lap. She tuned it with a skill which struck me and then began to sing the following air:*

>My glance suspected she was there
>And wounded her cheek
>And this single secret look
>Has left its trace.
>
>My heart drew her to me
>And when our hands touched
>Her fingers trembled
>From my heart's touch in mine.
>
>The thought of her
>Pierces my heart and now

Ma'mun and the Sponger

I in my turn hurt her.
I did not know a thought could wound.

Truly, O Commander of the Faithful, the beauty and perfection of her singing troubled and moved me. She took up her lute again and sang:

I asked her with a sign:
Do you know how much I love you?
She with a glance replied:
You have a promise.

Carefully I concealed
Her secret and she too
Made sure that no one
Came to know.

I cried out; my emotions were so aroused I was no longer master of myself. Then the girl sang once more:

Is it not terrible
That we share one room
Yet cannot be alone
To speak our love?

Only our eyes in secret tell
The passion which torments,
The fire that consumes
Our inmost souls.

We understand each other
By nothing more than the trembling
Of our lips, the movement
Of our brows,

Our half-veiled glances,
Our hearts which greet each other.

By God, O Commander of the Faithful, the skill and learning of this singing girl, the talent with which she turned the words of the song without ever losing the original theme, gave rise to a pang of jealousy, and I said:
"You still have things to learn, young lady."
These words angered her and she threw down her lute, crying:
"Since when have you had such tiresome guests in your house?"
Seeing the attitude of those present change towards me, I regretted what I had done.

The Meadows of Gold

"Is there another lute here?" I asked.

"Yes, sir," they answered.

As soon as they brought it, I tuned it to the mode I wanted and sang the following lines:

>Why are these dwelling places
>Indifferent to my grief?
>Are they deaf? Or are
>They overthrown by Time?

>Alas! Those I loved all
>Left at close of day.
>I have been told
>Of their going.

>If they must die,
>Let them die.
>If they live,
>Then so shall I.

My song was not yet ended when the beautiful slave girl threw herself at my feet and kissing them said:

"My lord, in the name of heaven forgive me. I have never heard anyone sing that song so perfectly."

Her master and all those present followed her example, and everyone rejoiced. The cups were passed from hand to hand more quickly and we drank them down, each one filled to the brim. I went on:

>Tell me, I beseech you
>How can you forget me
>When the memory of you
>Makes me weep tears of blood?

>I lament before God my love's avarice
>And my own prodigality.
>I offer her honey and she gives me back
>Colocynth of the bitter juice.
>I complain to God that she
>Is far away, and have no wish
>But to give her my love
>As long as I live.

>Spare the life of a lover
>Whose heart you have broken.

Ma'mun and the Sponger

Do not abandon him in his cups
Maddened with desire.

The rapture of my audience became so violent that I was afraid they would take leave of their senses. I fell silent for a time to allow them to recover themselves; then, taking up my lute for the third time, I sang:

Your lover is wracked
By the sharpest pains,
A stream of tears
Has flooded his parched body.

One hand is raised in supplication
Begging Heaven release
From his pains. The other
Is pressed against his heart.

Oh come and look upon
A poor lover delirious with despair
Whose eyes and hands alone
Tell of his desire.

Then, O Commander of the Faithful, the slave girl cried:
"By my salvation! That, my master, is singing, by God!"
Drunkenness, however, was beginning to make heads spin. The master of the house was less affected by the wine than his guests, and entrusting them to the care of his servants and their own, he had them taken home. I remained alone with him and, having drunk a few more cups, he said:
"Truly, sir, I consider the time before I made your acquaintance wasted. Dear friend, tell me who you are."
He was so insistent that I ended by giving my name. He immediately rose and kissed my forehead, saying:
"I should have been much surprised, my lord, by anyone of a lower rank possessing such talents. I have been in the presence of the Caliphal House all evening, and did not even know it!"
Pressed by him to relate the whole adventure and what had first attracted me, I told him the story of the meal being prepared and the appearance of the hand and wrist at the window. He called one of his slaves and said to her:
"Go and tell so-and-so to come down."
Thus he had all the slave girls brought to me one after another. After having examined the hands of each one, I cried:
"It is not her!"
"By God!" said my host at last, "there are only my mother and my sister left. I will have them brought to you."

The Meadows of Gold

Such generosity, such extraordinary kindness, amazed me. I therefore said:

"May my life be your ransom! Before calling your mother, begin with your sister. Perhaps it is she I am looking for."

"True," he said, and gave the appropriate order.

As soon as I saw her hand and wrist, I cried:

"It is she, my dear host, it is she!"

Without wasting a moment, he ordered his people to summon ten venerable men from among the persons of distinction in the neighbourhood. He next had brought in the sum of 20,000 dirhams, divided into two parts, and said:

"Here is my sister; I take you as witnesses that I am marrying her to Ibrahim ibn al-Mahdi and that I am settling on her, on behalf of her husband, a dowry of 20,000 dirhams."

We each gave our consent to the marriage, after which I gave one of the purses to my young wife and divided the other among the witnesses, saying to them:

"Forgive me, but this is all I have to hand just at the moment."

They accepted my present and withdrew.

My host then suggested preparing an apartment for me and my bride in his own house, but in truth, such generosity and kindness quite overwhelmed me and I asked him simply to find me a litter, saying I wanted to take my wife home. He agreed, saying "I will do as you wish," and had a litter prepared which carried us to my home. And I swear, my lord, that he sent a trousseau so magnificent that one of my houses was not enough to hold its splendours.'

Ma'mun marvelled at the generosity of this man. First of all he freed the sponger and gave him a handsome present. Then he ordered Ibrahim to introduce his father-in-law, who became one of the Caliph's courtiers and one of his familiars, who was invited, with the most flattering attentions, to all the private parties and other such occasions.

VII:12-25
§§ 2705-2713

THE CALIPH AND THE POET

Mubarrad and Tha'lab* relate that Kulthum al-Attabi was standing at the door of Ma'mun when Yahya ibn Aktham went by. Kulthum said to him:

'Would you tell the Caliph I am here?'

'I am not a chamberlain,' said Yahya.

'I know,' retorted the poet, 'but you are a man of merit and a man of merit is a man who helps.'

'But you are taking me out of my way.'

'God,' proceeded Kulthum, 'has given you rank and fortune. These two blessings will increase if you are grateful; if you are ungrateful, they will wane. I am today more generous to you than you are to yourself, since I am offering you an opportunity to increase your good luck and you are turning it down. Anyway, the tithe has to be paid on everything, and a powerful man works off his share by giving to those in need of assistance.'

So Yahya went in and told Ma'mun the story and he had Kulthum brought into his presence. Ishaq ibn Ibrahim al-Mawsili was present at the audience. Ma'mun invited the newcomer to sit down and asked after his health and his affairs. He replied with a felicity of expression and an elegance which charmed the Caliph. Ma'mun then began to make jokes, and the old man, feeling that he was being treated lightly, said:

'O Commander of the Faithful, you have to fondle them before they will give milk.'

Ma'mun did not understand what the poet meant and looked at Ishaq, who tipped him a wink. Then the Caliph said:

'A thousand dinars!'

They were brought and set down in front of Kulthum. Then he continued with his conversation, egging Ishaq on to make fun of their guest. Ishaq therefore began to contradict him, whatever topic of conversation came up, and never allowed him the last word. Kulthum was very surprised at this and not realizing whom he was talking to, said:

'Would you permit me, O Commander of the Faithful, to ask this man his name and lineage?'

'Go ahead!' said the Caliph.

Then Kulthum said:

'Who are you, and what is your name?'

'I belong to the human race,' answered Ishaq, 'and my name is Kul Basal –

The Meadows of Gold

"Eat Onions".'

'As to your descent,' replied Kulthum, 'that is obvious. But your name is unbelievable. No one is called "Kul Basal".'

'Oh, how unfair!' burst out Ishaq. 'Isn't Kulthum – "Eat Garlic" – a name? And onions taste better than garlic.'

'Curse you!' cried the poet. 'Here is a finely salted wit! No, I have never come across anyone more amusing to talk to. Would the Commander of the Faithful allow me to offer him the present with which he has honoured me, for truly, he has defeated me.'

'No,' said Ma'mun, 'keep your part intact. We are going to give him an equal sum.'

Ishaq then went back to his house and kept the poet with him there for the rest of the day.

KULTHUM AL-ATTABI

This Kulthum al-Attabi originally came from the military frontier region of Qinnasrin and al-Awasim, and lived in Raqqa, a town in the province of Diyar Mudar. He excelled in the study and recitation of the Koran, in belles-lettres, cultural affairs, letter-writing and rhymed prose. His memory, the aptness of his quotations, the purity of his diction, his eloquence, his exceptional gift for conversation, his talent as a writer, the charm of his speech, the excellence of his handwriting and, finally, his pleasant disposition, were all qualities which served to set him above the greater part of his contemporaries. The following sentence is a quotation from him:

'A man's tongue is his secretary, his face his chamberlain, and his bosom friend is another self.'

He versified the same sentiments:

A young man's tongue is his secretary,
The face of a young man is his chamberlain;
His best friend is another self,
And these are all things he needs.

The following saying is also attributed to him:

'When you hold the reins of government, choose your secretary with care, for those who are at a distance will judge your worth by his. Take on an intelligent chamberlain, since supplicants coming to you will judge you in accordance with their reception from him. Seek out confidants and intimates who are noble and sympathetic in character, for the merit of a man is measured by his entourage.'

A secretary, pluming himself on his superiority over a courtier, said to the latter:

'I am an aid, you are only a plaything; I am used in serious affairs, you are only for frivolities; we are sought out – I for rigours, you for pleasures, you for peace, I for war.'

The courtier retorted:

'I am fit to enjoy favours, you serve for revenge. I enjoy a high degree of consideration, while servility is your portion. You remain standing, while I sit, and you tremble while I am treated as a friend. It is to please me that you work; all your labours contribute to my well being. I am a companion, you are only an aid. I am an equal, you are an inferior, and if I am called courtier – *nadim* – it is

The Meadows of Gold

because I am always left with regret – *nadam*'.

But I cannot tell all the amusing anecdotes about Kulthum al-Attabi, nor quote from all his very fine works, without straying from the plan I have drawn up, or wandering away from the goal at which I am aiming. I have only slipped these fragments in here because I was carried along by the flow of what I was saying and the general course of my story.

PROFESSIONALLY UNLUCKY

The following story is told by Jawhari, according to Utbi, who had it from Abbas al-Dairi:

'A certain man submitted a petition to Ma'mun, requesting an audience and the favour of being allowed to plead his case. His request having been granted, he presented himself to the Caliph and greeted him. The Caliph said:

"Tell me your problem."

"You must know, O Commander of the Faithful, that the cruelties of fate and the random misfortunes of destiny have united against me, carrying off all that which fortune had granted me. I no longer have an estate which has not been ruined, a canal which has not silted up, a house which is not falling down, nor any capital which has not been dissipated. Today I am penniless and without a roof over my head. I have crippling debts and a large family, with small children, both boys and girls. I am old. I have many responsibilities and am too old to satisfy them by working. I can only hope that the generous glance of the Commander of the Faithful will light upon me."

As he was speaking, he could not restrain a loud fart.

"You see, my lord," he cried at once "this is another proof of fate's implacable persecution of me. By God, such a thing has never happened to me before, except at the appropriate time and place."

Ma'mun, turning to his courtiers, said that he had never seen such a firm, stout-hearted man, nor one with such resolution of spirit. And he ordered an advance of 50,000 dirhams to be counted out for him.'

VII:30-31
§ 2719

ABU AL-ATAHIYA

Here is a story told by Abu al-Atahiya:
'Ma'mun having sent for me, I went to him. I found him thoughtful and sad, hanging his head. In the state he was in, I did not dare go up to him. Then he lifted his head and gestured me to approach and I obeyed. He fell again into a reverie for a moment, then again raising his head addressed me:
"Abu al-Atahiya, boredom and the wish for novelty are among the natural impulses of the soul, and the soul grows accustomed to loneliness as well as to company."
"True, O Commander of the Faithful," I answered, "and I have expressed this sentiment in a line of verse."
"What is it?" asked the Caliph.
I recited:

> When the soul has gone astray
> Its only pleasure is to drift
> From one state to another.

Ma'mun said:
"You have expressed it well; go on!"
"I can add nothing to it," I said, and passed the day with him, after which he gave me a present and I withdrew.'

VII:31-32
§ 2720

THE CALIPH'S COOKING

They say that one night this Caliph ordered a eunuch, one of his confidential attendants, to go out and bring back the first passer-by he should come across in the street, noble or base, whoever he might be. The court official went off and soon came back with one of the common people. With the Caliph on this occasion were his brother Mu'tasim, Yahya ibn Aktham and Muhammad ibn Amr, the Greek, and each had cooked a dish in his own way. Muhammad ibn Ibrahim al-Tahiri said to the man:

'These men you see gathered here are intimate associates of the Commander of the Faithful. Answer their questions.'

'Where were you going at this time of night?' asked Ma'mun. 'There are still three hours of darkness left.'

The man answered:

'I was misled by the moonlight, and hearing an Imam call out "*Allahu akbar!*" I assumed without thinking that it was the call to prayer.'*

Ma'mun said to him: 'Be seated!', and they put him at his ease until he began to relax. When he was accustomed to the situation in which he found himself, the Caliph went on:

'Each of us has just cooked a different dish. You will be brought a sample of every one and you must taste them and then say which you like most and describe its merits.'

'Alright,' he said, 'bring them.'

They brought him all the plates on a big tray, covered, with nothing to distinguish them, although each cook had privately put his own mark on his work. Our man first tried the dish prepared by Ma'mun:

'Well done!' he cried, and after having swallowed three mouthfuls, went on: 'You would think it was all made of musk. The man who produced this must be a very clever cook – clean, imaginative and elegant.'

He went on to the food cooked by Mu'tasim and said:

'By God! I would have said this was produced by the same hands that produced the other and that it was put together with the same skill.'

Then he tasted that cooked by Muhammad ibn Amr, the Greek:

'This, by God, is the work of a distinguished cook – someone who succeeds in everything he attempts!'

But when he had tasted the effort of Yahya ibn Aktham, the qadi, he turned his head away and cried:

The Meadows of Gold

'Ugh! By God, whoever cooked this used shit instead of onions!'

Everyone laughed heartily, carried away by hilarity. Then he began to crack jokes and amused the gathering very much with all he had to say. At the first light of dawn, Ma'mun, who had realized that the man had understood in whose presence he was, warned him to tell no one what he had found them doing. He had him given 4,000 dirhams and ordered each of the 'cooks' to add a contribution proportionate to their rank. Then he said to the man:

'And beware if you go out again at such an hour!'

'May God not hinder us – you from your cooking, me from going out!'

They asked him his trade and took his address, and from that time on he entered the Caliph's service and became an habitué of the court.

VII:32-35
§ 2721-2722

MA'MUN EMBARRASSED

Abu Abbad, the secretary, one of Ma'mun's intimates, tells the following story:

'Ma'mun said to me one day:

"Nothing has ever left me so speechless as the answers given by three people. The first was the mother of Dhu al-Riyasatain – Fadl ibn Sahl – when I went to express my regrets on the death of her son and I said to her:

'Do not grieve and cease to weep for the loss of your son. Almighty God has replaced him by giving you, in me, a child who will be a substitute for him who is no more. Do not exchange the confidence with which you treated him in all matters for an attitude of reserve towards me.'

She wept and answered:

'Commander of the Faithful, how can I not regret the loss of my son, when such a one as you has been given me in his stead?'

The second occasion was when they brought me a man who was passing himself off as a prophet.

'Who are you?' I asked.

'Moses, son of Imran.'

'Be careful,' I went on, 'Moses had signs and manifest proofs of his mission. For example, the staff which he threw down and which swallowed up the spells of the magicians and his hand, which he drew, quite white, from his bosom.' (cf. Koran 28:31-2) I then began to enumerate the proofs which were granted to Moses to confirm his prophethood.

'So,' I continued, 'if you show me just one of the signs, just one of the miracles which he accomplished, I shall be the first to believe in your mission, otherwise you will die.'

'You are right,' the man answered, 'but I only produced the signs of my prophethood after Pharaoh said: "I am your supreme lord." (Koran 79:24) If you are willing to say as much, I am ready to show you the miracles which I performed before him.'

The third occasion was as follows. The inhabitants of Kufa had joined together to complain to me of their governor, a man whose policies and behaviour had my entire approval. I had this reply conveyed to them:

'Although I know all there is to be known about this man, I have nevertheless resolved to grant you an audience tomorrow morning. Choose, therefore, a delegate who will speak for you, for I know how prolix you are.'

They answered me as follows:

The Meadows of Gold

'The only man whom we feel is worthy to carry on a discussion in the presence of the Caliph is afflicted with deafness. However, if the Commander of the Faithful will be kind enough to tolerate this, perhaps he will do us the honour of letting us know.'

I agreed to bear patiently with their delegate and, on the very next day, the deputation arrived. I had the deaf man brought in. I invited those present to sit and then I asked him what their grievances against the governor were.

'Commander of the Faithful,' he replied, 'he is the worst governor in the world. The year you appointed him, we had to sell our clothes and furniture; the next year, our savings and land; and now, in the third year, we are forced to leave our homes in order to beseech the Commander of the Faithful, that, touched by our sufferings, he may do us the great favour of ordering his removal.'

'You are lying, you bastard!' I cried. 'He is a man whose policies and behaviour I admire, as I honour his piety and wisdom. I chose him for you on purpose, because I know well how often you revolt against those who govern you.'

'My lord,' the speaker replied, 'what you say is true and it is I who lied, but since you so admire the piety, loyalty, integrity, justice and moderation of this governor, why have you left him exclusively with us all these years, to the prejudice of so many other cities, the interests of which Almighty God has confided to your care, as he has confided ours? Set him therefore over these other lands, that he may grant them, in their turn, the treasures of moderation and justice which he has lavished on us.'

'Get out!' I said, 'and may God refuse you His protection! I agree to dismiss your governor.'

VII:35-38
§§ 2723-2725

MA'MUN JUSTIFIES HIMSELF TO THE SUFIS

According to Yahya ibn Aktham, the Caliph Ma'mun presided over a discussion on jurisprudence every Tuesday.

When the jurisconsults and other scholars presented themselves for their debate with him, they were shown into a room spread with carpets and told:

'Remove your shoes!'

Next a meal was served and it was announced:

'Partake of food and drink, then wash again, and if anyone's shoes are uncomfortable, take them off, and if anyone's *qalansuwa* – headdress – is too heavy, remove it.'

When the meal was over, braziers were brought and incense burned. They breathed in the fragrance and scented their garments. Next, they went to Ma'mun who invited them to draw near and began the most delightful and moderate discussions, quite devoid of arrogance or pedantry. This continued until sundown, when a second meal was served and, after eating their fill, they went away.

Yahya proceeded with his story as follows:

'One day, the Caliph was in such a meeting when his chamberlain, Ali ibn Salih, came in and said:

"Commander of the Faithful, a man wearing white clothes of coarse cloth, worn tucked up, is at the threshold of the palace. He asks to be allowed in so as to take part in the debate."

I understood that it was some sufi and wanted to make a sign to the Caliph not to let him in, but he forestalled me and said:

"Give him permission to enter."

A man entered whose robe was tucked up and who was holding his sandals in his hand. He stood at the edge of the carpet and said:

"Greetings! May the mercy of God and His blessings be upon you!"

Ma'mun returned his salutation and the stranger asked:

"Would you permit me to draw near?"

"Do so," said Ma'mun, "and be seated."

Once the man had taken his place, he said:

"May I speak?"

"Speak of whatever you wish," replied Ma'mun, "but in such a way as to be

The Meadows of Gold

approved by God."

The stranger proceeded thus:

"Do you owe this throne upon which you sit to the unanimous agreement and full consent of the Muslims, or do you owe it to the violence you have used against them, abusing your strength and power?"

Ma'mun answered:

"I owe it neither to their consent, nor yet to the use of violence. A ruler who, before me, had charge of the Muslims and whom they supported whether they wished to or not, handed on to me and to another the exercise of this authority after his death. He had those who were present swear to recognize it and he demanded on my behalf and on behalf of another the oath from the pilgrims assembled at the inviolable House of God in Mecca – and, willingly or unwillingly, they swore it. He who together with me had been invested with power followed the road on which he had started out and when I came to power I felt the need to be recognized by the Muslim people of both east and west with their unanimous and freely expressed approbation, but, after having reflected, I believed that if I left them to their own devices the rope of Islam would unravel, trust in oaths would vanish and the state be broken up. I realized that evil-doing and disorder would prevail in the midst of civil discord, Almighty God's laws would lose their strength, that access to the Holy House would become impossible and the war against the unbelievers would be abandoned, since my subjects would no longer be united under one authority which would direct them. Lastly, brigands would infest the roads and the weak would be handed over, defenceless, to the oppressor. I have, therefore, taken power in order to protect the Muslims, fight their enemies and ensure the safety of the highways, and so I will lead the Muslims by the hand until they choose, by their unanimous will and approbation, a leader who pleases them and I can resign my authority into his hands and become a simple subject, like any other Muslim. Be, therefore, my representative in the community of the Muslims and when they are unanimous in their choice, I will abdicate in his favour."

"May peace be upon you!" replied the unknown man, "and may God grant you His mercy and His blessings!"

And he went away.

Ma'mun told the chamberlain Ali ibn Salih to have him followed in order to find out where he would go. The chamberlain fulfilled his mission and returned and said:

"Commander of the Faithful, I sent someone to follow this man. He went to a mosque, where fifteen men like him and wearing similar clothes were assembled.

'Well, have you seen the man?' they asked him.

'Yes,' he answered.

'What did he say?'

'Nothing but good. He said that he held the government of the Muslims in his hands to assure the safety of the roads, to uphold the pilgrimage and the holy war, to protect the weak against the oppressor and to prevent the violation of the holy

Ma'mun Justifies Himself to the Sufis

laws, but, that when the people should cast their votes for a leader unanimously chosen, he would hand over the power to this last and abdicate in his favour.'

'We can see no harm in that,' replied those who were listening. Then they parted."

Ma'mun then turned to me and said:

"Yahya, we have satisfied these people using the simplest language."

I answered:

"My lord, I give thanks to God, who inspired you in the choice and honesty of your words as well as your actions." '

VII:38-43
§§ 2726-2728

(Omitted: VII:43-49; §§ 2728-2734. The misdemeanours of the qadi of Basra, Yahya, and his relations with Ma'mun.)

THE DEATH OF SHAFI'I

In the reign of Ma'mun, Shafi'i* died during the night of Friday, the last day of Rajab, in the year 204 AH/819 AD, just as day was beginning to break. He was fifty-four years old.

The funeral prayers were recited by al-Sari ibn al-Hakim, who was governor of Egypt at that time. This is the tradition related by Ikrima according to Rabi' ibn Sulaiman the muezzin, and it is also cited by Muhammad ibn Sufyan ibn Sa'id the muezzin and by other traditionalists on the authority of this same Rabi' ibn Sulaiman. Shafi'i was buried in Egypt in the quarter of the Tombs of the Martyrs, in the cemetery, among the graves of the Banu Abd al-Hakim. A great stone column was placed at his head and another column at his feet. On the larger, the one that stood above his head, was cut a cartouche in which is to be read the following inscription, engraved on the stone:

'Here is the tomb of Muhammad ibn Idris al-Shafi'i, the Confidant of God.'

That which we have just related is very well known in Egypt.

Shafi'i was related both to the Hashimites and to the Umayyads through Abd Manaf, because he was descended from Mutallib, a son of Abd Manaf. The Prophet said: 'We and the sons of Mutallib are like this,' and he held two fingers together. The Quraish besieged the Banu Mutallib and the Banu Hashim in the mountain pass.

The following tradition was handed on to us by Faqir ibn Miskin, on the authority of Muzani, whose traditions Faqir used to transmit. We heard it from Faqir at Aswan, a town in Upper Egypt:

'Muzani told me that he visited Shafi'i on the very morning of his death and said to him:

"Abu Abd Allah, how are you?"

Shafi'i answered:

"Like a man about to leave this world, who bids farewell to his brothers and drinks the cup of death. I do not know whether my soul is destined to paradise and I should congratulate it, or whether it is condemned to the eternal fire and I should weep for it."

> When my heart grew hard
> And my belief narrow
> I made a stairway
> Of my hope for Your pardon.

The Death of Shafi'i

My sins seem great to me
But are small, my Lord, compared to Your compassion.

VII:49-51
§ 2735-2736

(Omitted: VII:51; § 2737. Necrology for the year 204 AH/819 AD.)

MA'MUN AND THE FALSE PROPHETS

Umari tells us that a man who was passing himself off as a prophet in Basra in the reign of Ma'mun was chained and dragged before the prince. Ma'mun said to him:

'So you are a prophet charged with a mission?'

'For the moment charged with chains,' the man replied.

'Wretch,' went on the Caliph, 'who led you astray?'

'Is that how one speaks to prophets?' the other retorted. 'If I were not in chains, I would order Gabriel to destroy you.'

'But the prayer of a captive is not answered?'

'Particularly in the case of prophets – when they are in irons, their prayers no longer rise to heaven.'

Ma'mun began to laugh and added:

'Who chained you up?'

'He who is before you.'

The Caliph went on:

'We will have you freed, but you are to order Gabriel to carry out your threat. If he obeys, we will believe in you and in the truth of your mission.'

The prisoner cried:

'God was right to say: "So they will not believe until they see the dreadful punishment." (Koran 10:88) And now, if you will, do what you said.'

The Caliph had his bonds removed. Happy to feel himself free, the man exclaimed, raising his voice:

'Oh Gabriel! Send whom you wish and may there be nothing more between you and me – another possesses the good things of this world and I have nothing! Only a pimp would get involved in your affairs.'

He was given his freedom and furthermore received some presents.

'I was at one of Ma'mun's receptions in his palace,' relates Thumama ibn Ashras, 'when they brought in a man who gave himself out to be Abraham, the Friend of God.'

'Never,' cried Ma'mun, 'have I heard such impudence aimed against God!'

'My lord,' I said to him, 'will you let me speak to this man?'

'He is all yours.'

'You know,' I said to the would-be prophet, 'that Abraham, on whom be peace, gave proof of his mission.'

'What proof?'

'They lit a great fire and hurled him into it and he found there coolness and comfort (Koran 21:69). We will light a fire and throw you into it; if the fire treats you as it treated Abraham, we will believe in you and in your words.'

'Ask me some easier proofs.'

'Well,' I went on, 'the proofs which Moses gave.'

'What were they?'

'He threw down his staff, "and lo, it was a wriggling snake" (Koran 20:20); he struck the sea with his staff and the waves parted (Koran 26:64); lastly, his hand became quite white without his suffering from it (Koran 26:33).'

'This is still too difficult. Suggest something easy to do.'

'The miracles of Jesus?'

'What miracles were they?'

'He raised the dead.' (Koran 3:49)

Our man interrupted my recital of the miracles of Jesus and cried:

'I am heralding the "great catastrophe".' (Koran 79:34)

'No,' I replied, 'we must absolutely have proofs.'

'I have nothing like that,' he said, 'but I did say to Gabriel: "Since you are sending me among the devils, at least give me some sign that I can take with me, otherwise I shan't budge." But the angel got angry and said: "You are bearing with you a catastrophe more terrible than the hour of judgement. Go and see what these people will answer you." '

Ma'mun began to laugh and said:

'This is the kind of prophet one needs to keep one amused in one's leisure hours.'

VII:52-55
§§ 2738-2739

(Omitted: VII:55-59; §§ 2740-2744. 'In the year 198 AH/813 AD Ma'mun stripped his brother Qasim, son of Rashid, of his rights as heir.' Revolts of the Alids; The death of Ibn Tabataba; Various imams. One of these, Ibn al-Aftas, during the pilgrimage of 199 AH/814 AD, 'entered Mecca and stripped the Ka'ba of all its hangings, except for the white veils made in Egypt.')

THE RISE AND DEATH OF IMAM RIDA

In the year 200 AH/815 AD, Ma'mun detailed Rija ibn Abi al-Dahhak and the eunuch Yasir to go to Ali ibn Musa ibn Jafar ibn Muhammad ibn Ali ibn al-Husain ibn Ali, known as Rida, and bring him to him. They escorted Rida, showing him the greatest respect.

At the same time, Ma'mun ordered that a census should be taken of the descendants of Abbas, men and women, children and old people; and their number came to 33,000 souls.

Rida joined Ma'mun in the city of Marv, where this prince gave him the best of welcomes. After gathering together the most important leaders, he declared that having considered the descendants of Abbas ibn Abd Muttalib and Ali ibn Abi Talib, he had found no one among his contemporaries more distinguished or more worthy of power than Rida. He therefore recognized him as his heir, had his name stamped on the gold dinars and the silver dirhams, and married his own daughter Umm al-Fadl to Rida's son, Muhammad. He forbade the use of black on clothes and banners and replaced it with the colour green, there and everywhere else. When this news reached Iraq, the descendants of Abbas were deeply shaken, for they saw themselves thus excluded from power.

That year, on the orders of Ma'mun, the pilgrimage was led by Ibrahim, Rida's brother. All the Abbasids in Baghdad, together with their freedmen and supporters proclaimed the deposition of Ma'mun and swore the oath of allegiance to Ibrahim ibn al-Mahdi, known as Ibn Shikla, whom they elected Caliph on Thursday, the 5th of Muharram 202 AH/817 AD or, some say, 203 AH/818 AD.

In 202 AH/817 AD, Dhu al-Riyasatain Fadl ibn Sahl was murdered in his bath at Sarakhs, a town in Khurasan, in the very same palace where Ma'mun was staying, as he was on his way to Iraq. Ma'mun appeared much affected by this event. He had the murderers put to death and then went on his way.

Ali Rida ibn Musa died at Tus from indigestion brought on by eating too many grapes. They say that the fruit was poisoned. This occurred in the month of Safar 203 AH/818 AD. Ma'mun recited the funeral prayer. Rida died at the age of fifty-three, or, according to another version, forty-nine years and six months. He was born at Medina in 153 AH/770 AD. Ma'mun had given to Rida in marriage his daughter Umm Habib, so that of the two sisters, one had married Muhammad ibn Rida and the other this young man's father, that is to say, Ali Rida.

VII:59-62
§§ 2745-2747

(Omitted: VII:62-63; §§ 2748-2749. The revolt in Baghdad during the time of Ibrahim ibn al-Mahdi; Ma'mun enters the city dressed in green, but later changes back to Abbasid black; In the year 204 AH/819 AD, famine and plague; The revolt of Babak.)

THE CAPTURE OF IBRAHIM IBN AL-MAHDI

Ma'mun sent his spies to search for Ibrahim ibn al-Mahdi through the city of Baghdad, where he knew he was hiding, and they seized him during the night of Sunday, the 13th of Rabi' I, in the year 207 AH/822 AD. Disguised in female clothes and accompanied by two women, Ibrahim was arrested by a black belonging to the police force on the street called Darb Tawil – Long Street. Led before the Caliph, who said, 'Well, Ibrahim?', he answered as follows:

'Commander of the Faithful, *lex talionis* gives the right to take reprisals, but forgiveness is "closer to piety" (Koran 2:238). Man, the plaything of fortune and filled with delusions, yields himself utterly to the vicissitudes of fate. God has set you above all those that pardon, just as He has placed all that is sinful below me. If you punish me, it is your right; if you pardon me, it will be by your generosity.'

'Yes. A pardon, then, O Ibrahim!' cried Ma'mun. Then he said: 'God is Greater,' and bowed in prayer.

Nevertheless, he wanted the woman's veil with which Ibrahim was covered left draped over his chest, so that everyone could see in what garb he had been arrested. He also ordered that the prisoner should be put on view to the public in the police station. Afterwards, he was entrusted to the care of Ahmad ibn Abi Khalid. A short time later he was restored to favour.

VII:63-64
§§ 2750-2751

(Omitted: Ibrahim's four-line poem of thanks, § 2751.)

THE MARRIAGE OF BURAN

In the month of Sha'ban 209 AH/825 AD Ma'mun halted at Fam al-Silh, a canal beyond Wasit, to marry Khadija, the daughter of Hasan ibn Sahl. She was known as Buran.* On this occasion, Hasan scattered gifts such as not even a king had ever given, before or after the coming of Islam. Indeed, he distributed among the members of the family of Hashim and, similarly, to the generals, secretaries and other outstanding personages, balls of musk the size of filberts with a note hidden inside each giving the name of an estate, or a slave girl, the description of a horse, etc. Each one opened the ball which had fallen to his lot, read the note and found in it a better or less good prize, depending on whether fortune had favoured him more or less. He then showed the note to an officer entrusted with handing out the prizes and claimed an estate in such-and-such a district of such-and-such a province, or a certain slave girl named such-and-such, or else a horse described in a particular way. In addition to all this, gold and silver pieces, bladders filled with musk and eggs of ambergris were tossed to the rest of the people.

During the whole length of their stay, the expenses were met, not only of Ma'mun, his generals, his suite and accompanying guards, but also the keep of the muleteers, sailors, porters, servants, camp-followers, mercenaries and any others who accompanied the army. Not a soldier in Ma'mun's army had to buy food for himself or forage for his beasts.

While he was preparing to go back up the Tigris on the return journey to Baghdad, Ma'mun said to Hasan:

'Hasan, is there any request you would like to make of me?'

'O Commander of the Faithful,' answered the other, 'I beg you to retain for me the place in your heart which I hold now, for if I do keep it, it will be thanks to you alone.'

The Caliph granted him the revenues of Fars and Ahwaz for a year.

The poets lavished their praises and the orators their eloquence on these nuptials. Among the occasional verses, one of the most original is this couplet by Ibn Hazim al-Bahili:

> May God bless the son-in-law of Hasan, the husband of Buran!
> You have triumphed, but over whose daughter, O son of Harun?

The Meadows of Gold

When these words were reported to Ma'mun, he said 'I'm not sure quite how to take this.'

AN ADVENTURE OF IBRAHIM IBN AL-MAHDI

One day, some time after having fallen into his hands, Ibrahim ibn al-Mahdi waited upon the Caliph. Ma'mun said, indicating his brother Mu'tasim and his son Abbas:

'Here are the ones who advised me to put you to death.'

Ibrahim replied:

'That is how they should advise their sovereign, but sacrifice your fears to your hopes.' And he added these verses:

> You have given me back my possessions
> And shown your generosity towards me;
> Before returning them, you spared my life.
> You spared it without asking recompense
> And you have spared it twice;
> Once, by saving me from death,
> And then by saving me from want.
> Your generous soul made it easy
> For me to ask forgiveness
> For you have never uttered
> A single word of blame or reproach.
> Your indulgence, pleading my case
> To yourself, has served me
> As a truthful witness, beyond all suspicion.

The interesting events in the life of Ibrahim, his remarkable poetry, his adventures when he was hiding in the Suwaiqat Ghalib quarter of Baghdad, his wanderings on the night he was arrested, are all to be found in those of our works we have already mentioned and to which the present volume forms no more than a supplement. Yusuf ibn Ibrahim, the secretary, the friend of Ibrahim ibn al-Mahdi, is the author of a number of works, among them the book called *Tales of Doctors and Kings*, which deals with food, drink, clothes and so on, and a collection of anecdotes known under the title *The Book of Ibrahim ibn al-Mahdi*, as well as other works.

One of the strangest stories regarding Ibrahim is his adventure with the

The Meadows of Gold

barber, which occurred when he was wandering incognito through Baghdad. Ma'mun, on entering the town, had set his emissaries to track down Ibrahim – as we have already mentioned earlier in this chapter – and promised a rich reward to anyone who would betray his hiding place. Let us allow Ibrahim to speak:

'I went out one summer day, about noon, without knowing where I was going. I started up a dead-end street and noticed a black standing in front of the door of a house. I went straight up to him and asked whether he could lodge me in some corner of his home for a short while. He agreed and let me in. The room was furnished with straw mats and leather cushions, all very clean and elegant. Then he left me, locking the door in my face, and went away. A suspicion flitted through my mind: the man knew there was a price on my head and had gone off to denounce me. While I was sunk in these depressing thoughts, he returned accompanied by a porter who was carrying an ample supply of bread and meat, a new cooking vessel with all its accessories, a jug and some pots, all shining with cleanliness.

"May my life be a ransom for yours!" he said. "I am a barber and blood-letter, and I know how much my profession disgusts you. Use these things – my hands have not touched them."

I was very hungry. I got up and prepared myself a stew – and I cannot remember ever eating anything as good.

"How do you feel about *nabidh*?" he asked me.

"I certainly don't dislike it," I replied.

Observing the same reserve as with the food, he offered me vessels of the greatest cleanliness, which his hand had never touched. He then said:

"May my life be a ransom for yours! Would you allow me to sit by you and drink your health in the *nabidh* which I shall produce?"

I agreed. After emptying three cups, he opened a cupboard and brought out a lute.

"My lord," he said, "it is not fitting for a man of my condition to ask you to sing, but your kindness makes me feel as if I had a certain claim. If you would deign to consent, it would be a great honour for your slave."

"How do you know I am a good singer?" I asked him.

He replied with an astonished air:

"Almighty God! Your reputation is too great for me *not* to know it! You are Ibrahim ibn al-Mahdi and Ma'mun has promised 100,000 dirhams to the man who betrays you."

At these words, I took up the lute and was about to begin when he added:

"My lord, would you first sing a piece of my choosing?"

On my consenting, he chose three tunes at which he knew I was unrivalled. I then asked:

"That you recognize me, I am willing to accept, but how did you come to know of these airs?"

"I was," he answered, "in the service of Ishaq, the son of Ibrahim al-Mawsili, and I have often heard him speak of the great performers and the pieces of music

An Adventure of Ibrahim ibn al-Mahdi

in which they excelled. But who would ever have thought that I would one day hear you myself, in my own home?"

I sang and stayed with him, very taken with the distinction of his nature. Night came and I took my leave. I had brought with me a purse filled with gold coins, and I offered it to him, saying:

"Use it to defray your expenses; God willing, one day I will be able to do more for you."

"It is an odd thing," he said to me, "but I wanted to offer you all I have, begging you to do me the honour of accepting it and only respect for you prevented me."

He therefore refused to take anything from me. Then he went out with me and put me on the right road for the place where I wanted to go; after which he went away and I never saw him again.'

VII:67-72
§§ 2754-2757

(Omitted: VII:72-73; § 2758. Necrology for the year 206 AH/821 AD.)

THE POVERTY OF WAQIDI

Waqidi died in 209 AH/824 AD. His full name was Muhammad ibn Amr ibn Waqid, and he was a freedman of the family of Hashim. He was the author of biographical works and books on the early military expeditions of the Muslims. His authority as a Traditionist is weak.

Ibn Abi al-Azhar tells the following story, according to Abu Sahl al-Razi, who had it from people to whom Waqidi himself had related it in the following words:

'I had two friends, one of whom was of the family of Hashim, and we shared, so to speak, a single soul. As the festival of the end of the fast of Ramadan approached, I found myself extremely hard up, and my wife said:

"I wouldn't mind if it were just us – we can put up with poverty and hardship – but our poor children! They really break my heart, I can hardly bear it. They will see all the other children of the neighbourhood dressed up in new clothes for the holiday, while they will have to make do with their wretched old rags. Couldn't you manage to find some way of getting the wherewithal to dress them properly?"

I wrote to my friend the Hashimite and asked him to help me in the situation which had arisen. He at once let me have a sealed purse, saying that it contained a thousand dirhams. I had barely had time to collect myself, when a letter came from my other friend, exactly repeating the laments I had just addressed to the Hashimite. I therefore sent on the purse in the same state it reached me and then went on to the mosque, where I spent the night, not daring to go home to my wife. She, however, when I did go home, approved of what I had done and did not breathe a word of reproach. And that is how we were, when my friend the Hashimite came in, carrying the purse, still sealed up, and said:

"Tell me frankly what use you made of what I sent you."

I told him what had happened and he then went on:

"At the time your message reached me, I had nothing in the world but the sum I sent you. I therefore wrote to our common friend to ask him to help me and he sent me my own purse, still sealed with my ring."

We therefore divided it into three parts and shared it out among us, having first of all set aside a hundred dirhams for my wife.

Rumours of this incident, however, reached Ma'mun. He summoned me and I had to tell the story. He gave us a reward of 7,000 dinars, that is to say, 2,000 for each of us and a thousand for my wife.'

Waqidi died at the age of seventy-seven.

VII:73-75
§ 2759

(Omitted: VII:75; § 2760. Death of Yahya ibn al-Husain ibn Zaid ibn Ali ibn al-Husain.)

MANSUR AND THE CADGER

Azhar, known as Samman – 'the Butter Merchant' – also died in this year (209 AH/ 824 AD). He had been a friend of Abu Ja'far Mansur in the reign of the Umayyads and they travelled together collecting Traditions. Mansur bore him a great deal of affection and he grew old with him as his intimate.

When Mansur became Caliph, Samman left Basra for the court. The Commander of the Faithful asked him for news of his wife and daughters, whom he knew by name, received him with honour and made him a gift of 4,000 dirhams, strongly advising him, however, not to come again asking for money.

A year later, Samman reappeared.

'Didn't I warn you,' said the Caliph, 'not to come to me begging again?'

'I only came,' replied the other, 'to greet you and renew our friendship.'

'I am sure you did,' said Mansur and, after having 4,000 dirhams counted out to him, he added:

'Never come back, either to greet me or to cadge.'

A year later, Samman presented himself again before the Caliph and said to him:

'I have come for neither of the reasons which you forbade, but, having heard that the Commander of the Faithful was ill, I wished to visit him.'

'I think,' said Mansur, 'that it was really the bait of a present that drew you here.'

And he gave him the same sum of 4,000 dirhams.

Another year passed. Samman's wife and daughters kept saying to him:

'The Caliph is your friend – go back to him.'

'You wretched women,' answered Samman, 'what am I going to say to him? I have already used the excuse that I had come to beg his generosity, to greet him and to visit him when he was sick. What can I say? What reason can I give now?'

But they refused to give in.

The poor old man went back once more to Mansur and addressed him as follows:

'I have not come to beg from you, nor to greet you, nor to have news of you, but exclusively to hear from your lips a certain Tradition originating with the Prophet, which we heard together at such and such a place from such and such a scholar. It contains one of the names of Almighty God which welcomes and grants the prayers of he who pronounces it.'

'Don't bother looking for it,' cried Mansur. 'I've tried it and it doesn't work.

Mansur and the Cadger

Ever since you have been besieging me with your visits, I have been using it to ask God not to keep bringing you back to me. And yet you keep coming with your eternal words – greeting, seeking news, visiting.'

Saying which, he had him given another 4,000 dirhams and added:

'You have exhausted all my resources; from now on, come back whenever you feel like it.'

THE DEATH OF IBN A'ISHA

In 209 AH/824 AD Ma'mun rode to the dungeon during the night with a great retinue, to have Ibn A'isha put to death. He was a descendant of Abbas ibn Abd al-Muttalib and was called Ibrahim ibn Muhammad ibn Abd al-Wahhab – the son of the Imam Ibrahim, who was the brother of Saffah and Mansur. Muhammad ibn Ibrahim al-Ifriqi and others were killed at the same time. Ibn A'isha was the first descendant of Abbas to be crucified since the coming of Islam. When ordering his death, Ma'mun quoted this line of the poet's:

> Fire is hidden in the veins of the stone,
> But at the shock of steel it flashes and ignites.

In Baghdad, there was a descendant of Abbas ibn Ali ibn Abi Talib, a rich and indeed very wealthy man, who had influence and authority and was distinguished by his eloquence and wit. He was called Abbas ibn al-Hasan al-Alawi. Mu'tasim, who could not bear him on account of a difference which had arisen between them, insinuated into Ma'mun's heart the conviction that this man hated him, him and his dynasty, and that he had designs on his life. Now, that same night, Abbas met Ma'mun on the bridge.

'Well,' Ma'mun said to him, 'that [revolt] for which you have always been waiting has happened.'

'Commander of the Faithful,' replied Abbas, 'may God preserve me from such a thought! On the contrary, I was repeating these words: "What reason had the inhabitants of Medina and the Bedouin Arabs from round about to separate themselves from the Messenger and to prefer their existence to his?".' (Koran 9:120)

This reply had an excellent effect on the Caliph, who allowed his interlocutor to accompany him as far as the dungeon. After the execution of Ibn A'isha, Abbas said:

'Does the Commander of the Faithful permit me to speak?'

'Speak,' said the Caliph.

'I entreat you, in the name of God, to spare human blood. A king, if he becomes accustomed to shed it, can no longer sate his thirst for it and spares none of his subjects.'

To which Ma'mun replied:

'If you had spoken thus before I mounted my horse, I would have stayed and

The Death of Ibn A'isha

the blood would not have flowed.'

And he had him given 300,000 dirhams.

In the *Historical Annals*, I have related the story of this Ibn A'isha, the plot which he wove against Ma'mun and other facts about him.

VII:78-80
§§ 2763-2764

(Omitted: VII:80-81; § 2765. The death of Abu Ubaida Ma'mar ibn Muthanna, the Kharijite.)

THE DEATH OF ABU AL-ATAHIYA

In this same year, 211 AH/826 AD, the poet Abu al-Atahiya died. He had long lived a life of austerity and had 'donned the wool' – that is, become a sufi.

Earlier in this book I have given some entertaining anecdotes of his relationship with the Caliph Rashid. Let me add this: One day Rashid ordered the poet to be brought and forbade anyone to speak to him along the way, or to tell him why he was being called. Nevertheless, one of his companions, as they were going along a certain street, managed to write these words on the ground: 'You are being summoned only to die.' Abu al-Atahiya improvised these lines:

> It may be that your fears will not come to pass
> And that your hopes will be fulfilled.
> Perhaps that which seemed simple to you will not be so
> And the difficulties that you feared will be made easy.

He accompanied Rashid on one of his pilgrimages. The Caliph dismounted and walked for a while, then, feeling tired, he asked:
'Abu al-Atahiya, do you feel like resting in the shade of this milestone?'
After having sat down, he turned towards Abu al-Atahiya and said:
'Move us!'
So Abu al-Atahiya recited:

> The good things of the world have been given you,
> But will not death take them away?
> Oh you who seek after the good things of this world,
> Leave them to pursue your true interests.
> What will you do with things of this world,
> Since the shadow of a milestone suffices you?

The interesting events of Abu al-Atahiya's life and a good number of his poems have been quoted in my earlier works. There is also a selection of his poems taken from his *diwan*, where they are classed according to their rhymes and, further-

The Death of Abu al-Atahiya

more, I have given some fragments in this book, while recounting the history of the Abbasid Caliphs.

VII:81-83
§§ 2766-2767

(Omitted: VII:83-94; §§ 2768-2777. Poems by Abu al-Atahiya; Metres and miscellaneous notes on poetry; Ma'mun's hatred of Mu'awiya; Necrology for the years 212-15 AH/827-30 AD.)

MA'MUN'S CAMPAIGNS AGAINST THE BYZANTINES AND HIS DEATH

In 217 AH/832 AD, Ma'mun went to Egypt and there put to death Abdus, who was ruling the country like a tyrant.

In 218 AH/833 AD, he led an expedition against the Byzantines. He had undertaken to rebuild Tyana, a Greek town at the entrance to the pass that leads to Tarsus. He offered all the strongholds of the Byzantines the chance to capitulate and invited them to embrace Islam, giving the choice of Islam, poll-tax or the sword. Christianity was brought low and a large number of Greeks submitted to paying the tax.

The qadi Abu Muhammad Abd Allah ibn Ahmed ibn Zaid al-Dimashqi told us the following story at Damascus:

'When Ma'mun – may his soul be with God! – came, in the course of his expedition, to camp at Budandun, an ambassador from the King of Byzantium brought him the following message:

"The King proposes either to reimburse you for all the expenses of the war from the time you left your country until your arrival here or to return, without any ransom, not a dirham or a dinar, the Muslim prisoners who are confined in Byzantine territory; or, yet again, to restore the Muslim cities ravaged by the Christians – on condition that you put an end to the war."

Ma'mun rose, went into his tent, prayed two prostrations and, having consulted God's will, returned and said to the envoy:

"Tell your master from me that as regards your offer to pay the expenses of the war, I am reminded of the words which Almighty God, in His holy book, placed in the mouth of Bilqis, the Queen of Sheba: 'But I will send him a gift and await the return of my messengers.' When the Queen's envoy came before Solomon, the latter said to him: 'You wish, then, to increase my treasures? That which God has given me is worth more than the riches he has given you; but you base your happiness on your wealth.' (Koran 27:35-6)

As regards your offer to free all Muslim prisoners held by the Greeks, my reply is that you have in your power only two kinds of captives – those who fought for God and their salvation, and they have attained their aim, and those who fought for the wealth of this world, and they do not deserve that God should break their chains.

Regarding your offer to repair the damages caused by the Greeks in Muslim towns, know that even when I have torn down the last stone of the last of your fortresses, I shall not have taken sufficient vengeance for the poor woman who cried out, stumbling under the weight of her chains: 'Oh Muhammad, Muhammad!'

Go back to your master. Between him and me there is nothing but the sword. Page – sound the advance!"

Continuing on his march, he did not turn aside until he had taken fourteen strongholds. Then he doubled back on his tracks and camped at 'Ain Budandun, better known by the name of al-'Ashira, as we have said in earlier pages. He halted there awaiting the return of the envoys from the fortresses, and encamped on the banks and at the very source of this river. Enchanted by the cool water, pure and limpid, and by the beauty of the countryside and its green vegetation, he had long planks cut down and laid above the source, over which they built a kind of pavilion of poles and the leaves of trees, and he settled down in this rustic shelter which had been made for him and beneath which rose the spring. They threw in a beautiful silver coin and the water was so clear that he could read the inscription at the bottom of the river and so cold that no one could bathe in it.

Meanwhile, a fish appeared, a cubit long and bright as a silver ingot. A reward was promised to anyone who could catch it. An attendant hurried down, took the fish and climbed back onto the bank but, as he approached the place, or rather the pavilion, where Ma'mun was sitting, the fish wriggled, slipped through his hands and plumeted back into the depths of the spring like a stone. The water splashed on to the breast, neck and collar-bone of the Caliph and soaked his clothes. The servant hastened back down, caught the fish and placed it, quivering, in a napkin before the Caliph. Ma'mun said:

"Fry it!"

But at that instant he was suddenly overcome with a shivering fit and could not move. It proved useless wrapping him in blankets and quilts; he continued to tremble like a palm leaf and cry:

"I'm cold! I'm cold!"

They carried him to his tent, covered him and lit a big fire, but he continued to complain of the cold. When the fish was fried, they brought it to him, but he did not even want a taste – his suffering was too great to touch it.

As he grew worse, Mu'tasim – his brother – questioned Bakhtishu' and Ibn Masawaih about the condition of the sick man, who was already dying. He asked them what conclusions medical science could provide and whether it could even restore him to health. Ibn Masawaih took one of the sick man's hands and Bakhtishu' the other and they both felt his pulse at the same time; its irregularity indicated that the end was near. Their hands stuck to his skin on account of the sweat which had broken out all over his body and was flowing like syrup, or the slime of a viper. When Mu'tasim was told of this, he asked the two doctors to explain it to him, but they could not, for it was in none of their books. They did declare, however, that it presaged the swift dissolution of the body.

At this moment, Ma'mun regained consciousness and came out of his stupor.

The Meadows of Gold

He opened his eyes, ordered some Byzantines to be summoned and asked them the name of the spring and the place. Various prisoners and guides were brought and asked: "What is the meaning of the name of this spring – al-'Ashira?" "It means," they said, "Stretch out your feet"* i.e. 'Die'. The dying man was troubled by this reply and felt sad forebodings. He next wished to know the Arabic name for that place and they told him that it was called Raqqa – "Water Meadow". Now a horoscope cast at the time of Ma'mun's birth stated that he would die at a place of this name, which is why the prince always avoided living in the town of Raqqa, fearing to meet his death there. When he heard the answer given him by the Greeks, he no longer doubted that it was that same place where his horoscope predicted he would die.

According to another version, it was the word Budandun which meant "Stretch out your feet." God knows best how that might be.

Ma'mun had his doctors called, hoping that they would cure him, but, feeling worse, said:

"Carry me out that I may look at my camp and gaze once more at my men and my kingdom."

It was night. As he looked over the tents, the long lines of soldiery and the camp fires, he cried out:

"Oh You Whose reign will never end, have pity on him whose reign is ending!"

Then he was taken back to his bed.

Mu'tasim, seeing that he was growing worse, had someone whisper into his ear the Muslim profession of faith. As the man raised his voice so that Ma'mun could repeat his words, Ibn Masawaih said to him:

"There is no need to shout, for truly he can no longer distinguish between his God and Mani."

The dying man opened his eyes. They were unnaturally large and extraordinarily brilliant and shot with red; their like had never been seen. He reached out his hands to seize Ibn Masawaih, he made an effort to speak to him, but could not. His eyes turned to heaven and filled with tears. At last his tongue was loosened and he said these words:

"Oh You Who are undying, have pity on him who is about to die!"'

He died immediately. It was on Thursday, the thirteenth day before the end of Rajab 218 AH/833 AD. His body was carried to Tarsus and buried in that city, as we said at the beginning of the chapter.

All the best stories of the life and rule of Ma'mun, his conversations, his remarkable poems and his fine qualities are to be found related in detail in our earlier works and there is no need to return to them here.

The following lines by Abu Sa'id Makhzumi refer to him:

> Did you see the stars protect Ma'mun
> Whose royalty was so deeply rooted?
> No. They abandoned him
> Between the two plains of Tarsus,

Ma'mun's Campaigns against the Byzantines and His Death

As at Tus they abandoned his father.

Ma'mun often repeated these lines:

> When a man continues to tempt the fates,
> The day will come
> When they will bring him affliction.
> They may miss the first time,
> But they will not be slow
> To remedy their fault.
> And while he turns aside
> To avoid their attack,
> They will forestall him,
> Overwhelming him before he can flee.

VII:94-102
§§ 2778-2785

THE CALIPHATE OF MU'TASIM

Mu'tasim was proclaimed Caliph on the same day that Ma'mun died at the source of the Budandun river, that is, on Thursday, thirteen days before the end of Rajab 218 AH/833 AD.

His name was Muhammad ibn Harun and he was known as Abu Ishaq. A quarrel over the Caliphate arose between him and al-Abbas, the son of Ma'mun, but al-Abbas then rendered Mu'tasim allegiance.

When he came to the Caliphate, Mu'tasim was thirty-eight years and two months old. His mother was named Marida bint Shabib. Some say allegiance was sworn to him in the year 219 AH/834 AD. He died at Samarra in 227 AH/842 AD, at the age of forty-six years and ten months, after a reign of eight years and eight months. His tomb is in the Jawsaq Palace at Samarra.

VII:102-103
§ 2786

(Omitted: VII:103-104; § 2737. Mu'tasim's viziers, especially Muhammad ibn Abd al-Malik, who also served under the Caliph Wathiq, but was put to death early in the reign of Mutawakkil.)

MU'TASIM ON AGRICULTURE

Mu'tasim loved agriculture and used to say:
'This art has innumerable advantages: in the first place, the cultivation of the earth gives life to the world. The land-tax is levied on the basis of agricultural productivity, which increases the wealth of the state. Agricultural produce feeds domestic animals; it lowers the price of food; it increases the flow of commerce and produces well-being.'

He also used to say to his vizier, Muhammad ibn Abd al-Malik:
'When you find a piece of land which, by spending ten dirhams, will bring me eleven dirhams by the end of the year, there is no need to ask for orders.'

VII:104
§ 2788

MU'TASIM AND HIS DOCTOR

Mu'tasim had rare vigour and physical strength and great courage. This is what Ahmad ibn Abi Du'ad, one of his favourites, has to tell:

'At just the time when Mu'tasim had ceased to spare his health or his strength, I went to him one day and found him with Ibn Masawaih – his doctor. The Caliph went out for a moment, after saying:

"Don't go away before I return."

"Woe to you," I said to Yahya ibn Masawaih, "it seems to me that the Commander of the Faithful looks drawn, his strength is less and his liveliness dimmed. How do you find him?"

"Undoubtedly," replied the doctor, "the Caliph is as strong as an iron bar, but he holds in his hand an axe with which he strikes the bar ceaselessly."

"How so?" I asked him.

He proceeded.

"In the past, he only ate fish when it was seasoned with a sauce made of vinegar, caraway, cumin, rue, celery, mustard and walnuts, and so, by using this sauce, he avoided the undesirable effects of fish and its dangers for the nervous system. If he had heads served, he had them covered with sauces which made this kind of food lighter and harmless. In fact, in all cases, he took care of himself at meals and consulted me frequently. But today, as soon as I forbid him some dish, he disobeys me and says:

'I will eat it, even under the nose of Ibn Masawaih!'

What can I do about that?"'

The narrator adds:

'Mu'tasim, hidden behind a curtain, was listening to us.

I answered the doctor:

"Well, Ibn Masawaih, you must put your finger in his eye [i.e. force him]."

"May my life be a ransom for yours," he went on, "but I cannot contradict him and I dare not cross him."

He had scarcely finished speaking, when Mu'tasim appeared before us and said to me:

"What were you talking about with Ibn Masawaih?"

"Commander of the Faithful, I was discussing the changes in your face and your lack of appetite, which in turn destroy my limbs and cause me to decline."

"And what did he say to you?"

"He lamented that after having at one time taken his advice and followed his

Mu'tasim and His Doctor

prescriptions for your diet, you now disobey him."

"What did you reply to that?" the Caliph asked me.

I tried to change the conversation, but he added laughing:

"Yes, but is this before or after he was supposed to thrust his fingers in my eye?"

A cold sweat broke out over my body. I realized that he had heard our conversation. But he noticed my consternation and said:

"Ahmad, may God pardon you! You took lightly something which I thought you would have heard with sorrow, but I find nothing more in your words than a kind of frankness and familiarity." '

VII:104-107
§§ 2789-2790

(Omitted: VII:107-111; §§ 2791-2793. An amusing but coarse anecdote on the Caliph and one of his travelling companions.)

THE KIND HEART OF MU'TASIM

This same Ali ibn al-Junaid al-Iskafi went one day to see Mu'tasim. Having laughed and talked to him for a moment, the Caliph said:

'Well, Ali, you should be ashamed. Why don't we see you any more? You are neglecting your friends and forgetting the duties of friendship.'

Ali replied:

'You have just said to me what I was going to say to you – you must be the Devil himself!'

Mu'tasim burst out laughing and asked:

'Why don't you ever come to see me any more?'

'Alas!' said Ali, 'how many times I have come and not been allowed to see you! You are a great man now – in fact, one would think you belonged to the House of Marimma' – a family of the Sawad whose pride had become proverbial in that region.

'This is Sindan, the Turk,' said Mu'tasim, pointing out a page who was waving a flywhisk over his head and, turning to the page, he added:

'When Ali comes, let me know. If he gives you a note, bring it to me. If he entrusts you with a message, tell me of it.'

'Yes, my lord,' replied the page.

Ali went away.

A few days later, he came back and asked for Sindan. He was told:

'Sindan is sleeping.'

He tried again another day and they said:

'Sindan is in the harem; you can't see him.'

He returned yet again and this time was informed that the page was with the Commander of the Faithful. Ali managed, however, to get in to Mu'tasim another way. The Caliph joked with him and reproached him in a friendly way, then said:

'Have you some request to make of me?'

'Yes, O Commander of the Faithful,' said Ali. 'If you see Sindan the Turk, give him my regards.'

'Why, what is the matter?' asked the Caliph, laughing.

'What the matter is, is that you have placed between us a man more difficult to see than you yourself! Now, I am very impatient to meet him, so I do earnestly beg you to pass on my greetings.'

Mu'tasim laughed his fill. Then he introduced Ali to Sindan a second time,

The Kind Heart of Mu'tasim

recommending the latter to show him the greatest civility. And from then on, Ali had free access to the Caliph.

On one occasion, Mu'tasim was passing through the western quarter of Samarra. It was raining and had rained during the preceding night. The Caliph had become parted from his escort, when he saw a donkey which had slipped and let fall its load of brush – that is to say, the thorny scrub which is used in Iraq for lighting ovens. His master, a poor, weak old man, was standing there waiting for a passer-by to help him pick up the load. Mu'tasim stopped and asked him what had happened.

'Forgive me,' replied the old man, 'but my donkey has let fall its load and I am waiting for someone to help me lift it.'

Mu'tasim dismounted and was preparing to haul the donkey out of the mud, when the old man said:

'May my life be a ransom for yours! Are you going to dirty your clothes and spoil the delicious perfume they exhale for the sake of this donkey?'

'Don't worry about that,' answered the Caliph.

Dismounting, Mu'tasim pulled the animal up with one hand and dragged it out of the mud, while the old man looked on in amazement. Next, using his horse's reins to gird round his waist, he bent down to gather up the load of thorn, which was tied in two bundles, picked it up and set it on the donkey's back. Then he went to a pool, washed his hands and remounted.

The old man from the Sawad blessed him, adding these words in the Nabatean tongue: *'eshqul gharmi tahutaka'*, which means: 'May I be your ransom, oh young man!'

The mounted escort had just ridden up and so the Caliph said to one of his guards:

'Give this old man 4,000 dirhams and accompany him until he is past the sentries and back in his own village.'

VII:111-114
§§ 2794-2796

(Omitted: VII:114-118; §§ 2797-2800. Necrology for the year 219 AH/834 AD; 'In the same year, Mu'tasim condemned Ahmad ibn Hanbal to thirty-eight strokes of the whip to force him to consider the Koran as created;' Death of Muhammad, the son of Imam Rida: 'They also claim that Umm al-Fadl, Ma'mun's daughter, poisoned him when she took him from Medina to the court of Mu'tasim; she was married to his brother;' Trouble with the Alids.)

THE NEW CAPITAL OF SAMARRA

Mu'tasim sought out Turks and had them bought by his freedmen. He thus gathered together a troop of 4,000, whom he dressed in brocade with gilded belts and ornaments, distinguishing them by their costume from the rest of the army. He also formed for his service a corps made up of soldiers from the two districts of Egypt, the district of Yemen and that of Qais, and he called them the Maghribis – 'Westerners'. He also fitted out men from Khurasan and in particular Fergana and Ushrusana. These Turks soon made up a numerous army. They subjected the inhabitants of Baghdad to great annoyance, riding their horses at full gallop through the middle of the markets and doing much harm to the infirm and to children. On several occasions the people took vengeance and killed more than one horseman who had knocked over a woman, an old man, a child or someone blind.

Mu'tasim therefore decided to move the Turks away from his capital and to settle them on a great plain. He encamped first at Baradan, four parasangs from Baghdad, but finding this place neither sufficiently healthy, nor yet sufficiently large, he continued to move about, exploring different areas along the Tigris and elsewhere. In this way, he came to a place named Qatul, the climate of which pleased him. There was a village there inhabited by the Jaramiqa – a Persian tribe which had settled near Mosul during the early years of Islam – and by Nabateans. It stood on the edge of the Qatul Canal, which is one of the canals which flows out of the Tigris. He built a palace and soon the people of Baghdad, responding to his summons, emigrated there, leaving the capital almost abandoned. It is to this event that one of the 'vagabond' poets refers in the piece in which he reproaches Mu'tasim for his desertion of his subjects, saying:

> Oh you who live in Qatul in the midst of the Jaramiqa,
> You have left none in Baghdad but arrogant noblemen.

Meanwhile, the troops which had followed the Caliph were suffering cruelly from the cold of that place. The earth was hard and made construction work difficult. One of the soldiers in his suite said on this subject:

> They told us Qatul would be our winter encampment,
> But we count on the intervention of God, our master.
> Men make their plans, but each day

The New Capital of Samarra

God causes some new disaster to take place.

Discouraged by the drawbacks of the place and the difficulties of building there, Mu'tasim left it and, continuing his search, reached Samarra. At this place, there was an old Christian monastery. The Caliph asked one of the monks who lived there what the place was called. He answered:

'Samarra.'

'And what does Samarra mean?' went on the Caliph.

'We find it given,' said the monk, 'in our ancient books and in the traditions of the past, as meaning the city of Shem, the son of Noah.'

'What country is it and of which province is it a part?'

'It is of the country of al-Tirhan, to which it belongs.'

Mu'tasim examined the countryside carefully. Vast plains unfolded before his eyes. The air was healthy, the soil fertile. Struck by these advantages and the mildness of the climate, he stopped there for three days, which he spent hunting. He noticed that his appetite was stronger and that he ate more than usual, which he did not fail to attribute to the effect of the climate and the soil and water. He liked it. Then, summoning the people from the monastery, he bought their land for 4,000 dinars. He chose a site to build his palace and the foundations were laid. This is the quarter of Samarra, known as Waziriya, and hence the name 'Waziri' given to a quality of fig which is superior to any other, thanks to its sweetness, the smoothness of its flesh and the smallness of its seeds. Neither the figs of Syria, nor those of Hulwan can be compared to this kind.

The building began to rise. He had masons, workmen and craftsmen come from every country, and obtained seedlings and young trees from all around. He distributed land to the Turks in different areas and gave them as neighbours soldiers originally from Fergana, Ushrusana and the cities of Khurasan, always bearing in mind the relative geographical positions of their native lands. Ashnas, the Turk, and his companions were given a grant of the area known as Karkh Samarra and some of the men from Fergana were established in the quarters known as al-Umari and al-Jisr – the Bridge.

The plan of the city was laid out. The different estates, quarters and roads were marked. Each trade and each branch of commerce had its separate market. Everyone began to build his house. Things were going up on every side – houses and solidly built palaces. Agriculture flourished and canals leading from the Tigris and other water courses were dug. When people learned that a new capital was being built, they came crowding in, bringing with them every kind of merchandise and the vast quantities of provisions necessary for the existence of men and animals. Life became rich and easy. Equity, justice and prosperity spread through the land.

The Caliph Mu'tasim began the works we have just described in 221 AH/836 AD.

VII:118-123
§§ 2801-2805

The Meadows of Gold

(Omitted: VII:123-144; §§ 2806-2828. The revolt of Babak and his fate; An expedition against Theophilus; The revolt and death of Mazyar, the heretic: 'The gibbet on which Mazyar hung slowly leaned towards that of Babak, so that the two corpses gradually grew closer and closer and, furthermore, the body of Batis (Aetius), the patriarch of Amorium, inclined towards the other two, thanks to the angle of the upright from which he was hung'; The death of Abu Dulaf and stories of him and his son Dulaf's hatred of Ali – on account of the tradition 'to hate Ali one must be a bastard', Abu Dulaf, although by temperament jealous, was prepared to declare Dulaf a bastard because he publicly execrated Ali; Necrology for the years 223-7 AH/838-42 AD.)

MU'TASIM

The Caliph Mu'tasim died at his palace on the Tigris, called Khaqani, on Thursday 18 Rabi' I 227 AH/842 AD at, they say, the second hour of the night. He was forty-eight years old, or, according to others, forty-six, as we said at the beginning of this chapter. He was born at Khuld – the royal residence – at Baghdad in the year 180 AH/796 AD, in the eighth month. He was the eighth Abbasid Caliph, the eighth generation in descent from Abbas and at his death left eight sons and eight daughters.

Mu'tasim's interesting reign, the part he played in the conquest of Amorium, his battles before he became Caliph, the period of his expeditions into Syria, Egypt, etc, what happened to him after his accession to the throne, the fine actions and virtuous character of this prince, have been related by Ahmad ibn Abi Du'ad, the judge, and by Ya'qub ibn Ishaq al-Kindi in various passages of his work entitled *Ways of Merit*. All this information, in a word, is to be found in my *Historical Annals* and *Intermediate History*.

What I have given here is only an outline, an index of my previous works, intended to resuscitate interest in events already old, the memory of which is fading.

God is our support!

THE CALIPHATE OF WATHIQ

Wathiq, whose name was Harun ibn Muhammad ibn Harun al-Wathiq, was known as Abu Ja'far. His mother was a Greek slave named Qaratis.

Allegiance was sworn to him the same day Mu'tasim died, Thursday, 18 Rabi' I 227 AH/842 AD. He was thirty-one years and nine months old when he became Caliph. He died at Samarra at the age of thirty-seven years and six months, after a reign of five years, nine months and thirteen days. According to other accounts, he died on Wednesday, the 24th of Dhu al-Hijja 232 AH//847AD at the age of thirty-four.

His vizier was Muhammad ibn Abd al-Malik, as we have already said in the chapter devoted to Mu'tasim. The chronicles give notably different dates both for the ages and for the lengths of the reigns of the Caliphs.

VII:145–146
§ 2831

(Omitted: VII:147–171; §§ 2832–2856. Abu Tammam and a Bedouin; On the poetry and impiety of Abu Tammam; Abu Tammam and Buhtari; Verses quoted; Necrology for the years 230–31 AH/845–6 AD; Wathiq's taste in food and drink.)

WATHIQ DISCUSSES MEDICINE

Just as Wathiq loved philosophical speculation and honoured those who devoted themselves to it, so he hated those who blindly followed received authority. He enjoyed developments in the sciences and had a lively curiosity about the opinions of philosophers and specialists in the law, both ancient and modern.

One day, when a number of philosophers and medical men had gathered at his court and were discussing various questions in the natural sciences and metaphysics in his presence, Wathiq said to them:

'I would very much like to know how one acquires a knowledge of medicine and upon what principles this science is based. Is it founded on empirical observation? Or is knowledge of it obtained through analogical reasoning and experience? Is it grasped *a priori* by the intelligence, or is it learned through a course of oral instruction, as certain doctors of the religious law maintain?'

Bakhtishu', Ibn Masawaih and his son Mikha'il were present at this meeting and Hunain ibn Ishaq and Salamawaih are also said to have been there.

One of those present replied:

'O Commander of the Faithful, one school of physicians, particularly among the ancients, claimed that the only path which leads to an understanding of medicine is experience. This school defines medicine as a science born of repeated empirical observation of a single sensory object – the patient – in all its various manifestations. By observing results as well as causes, the observer endowed with a good memory becomes experienced. This school claims that experience can be classified under four basic headings, which are in fact its premises and give it the character of a scientific discipline; although composed of these four elements, experience remains an integral whole.

The first of these headings, or principles, is called "natural", that is, the normal phenomena which occur in both sickness and health, such as nosebleeds, sweating, diarrhoea, vomiting and the good or bad symptoms they reveal to the observer.

The second is called "accidental", because it involves the study of the purely fortuitous accidents which happen to all living things: for example, the more or less copious bleeding which occurs when a man is wounded or has a bad fall, or the effects of cold water or some other drink taken by the patient whether sick or well, and the salutary or harmful consequences which result.

The third principle is called "intuitive", because it results from the intuitive faculty, that is, the mind. A doctor, for example, dreams that he treats an illness which he has observed while waking, with a known remedy, and that the treatment is successful. When he wakes, the doctor recalls his dream, turns it over in his mind, and thus submits an idea which arose from the unconscious working of his mind to the process of reflection. He then tries out the treatment he imagined in his dream and the results turn out as he envisaged. Or else they do not, in which case he renews the treatment until it is successful.

Finally, there is the principle of "transference", which may be divided into three kinds, namely: a single treatment is transferred from one illness to another analagous illness, for example, from the "red tumour" to the tumour called *namla* (*formicatio*); or the transference of the treatment of one limb to another, such as that of the arm to the thigh; or, lastly, the shifting from one remedy to a similar one, such as from syrup of quinces to syrup of medlars in cases of looseness of the bowels. Doctors do all of these things based upon experience.

But there is another school, O Commander of the Faithful, which maintains that the correct strategy with which to approach the art of medicine and facilitate its comprehension is to relate pathological conditions and the organs affected by them to general principles, since there is no limit to the different forms they can take. The treatment is deduced from Nature herself and the illness observed on the spot and in its actual form, without taking into account either the causes which gave rise to it and which no longer exist, or considerations of time, habits, or age of the patient, and without studying the nature and limitations of each organ or the symptoms which are present or absent in each disease. They base their position on the following piece of reasoning: it is obvious and incontestable that two contrary principles cannot coexist; they mutually exclude each other. "Is this not like", they say, "deducing the existence of something invisible from something apparent when the apparent thing contradicts the invisible and thus invalidates the conclusions drawn from it." This, O Commander of the Faithful, is the opinion of a number of skilful physicians and men of the ancient Greek school like Namunis (Namounius?), Sasalis (Thessalus?) and other doctors known under the name of "theoretical".'

Wathiq then asked the assembled doctors:

'Now tell me to which system do the majority of doctors adhere?'

'The analogical,' they replied.

'And why is that?' asked Wathiq.

'In the view of this school', they answered, 'the method and basic principles of medical studies have as their point of departure a certain body of knowledge or first principles: for example, the knowledge of the nature of bodies, the individual limbs and their functions, how the body behaves in sickness and in health, the effects of climatic variations, a knowledge of what the actions and circumstances of a man's profession entail, his habits, food, drink, age and, finally, an understanding of the power of the illness itself.

It has been established by observation, these doctors say, that the differences of forms and temperaments which exist among animals are also evident in the animal's organs. The bodies of animals vary as a result of the environment in

Wathiq Discusses Medicine

which they live, their activity – or lack of it – the food and drink they ingest, their sleep or wakefulness, the matter which they expel or retain and, lastly, such incidentals of a non-physical nature as grief, fear, anger and anxiety. Medicine, by governing the body, aims to preserve the health which it enjoys or to recover it when it has been lost. Now the preservation of health presupposes a knowledge of the causes which are apt to lead to that result. It is, therefore, an absolute duty for the doctor who undertakes a cure to possess not only this positive basic knowledge, but also to examine the nature of the illness as well as that of the body – its nourishment, habits, present circumstances and, in a word, all contributory causes.

These, O Commander of the Faithful, are the doctrines of Hippocrates, Galen and many other doctors, ancient and modern.

It is true that these same doctors, although agreed as to the principles we have just set down, differ when it comes to diet and treatment. These differences of opinion result from their different processes of deduction. Thus, some believe that one comes to know the nature of foods and remedies by their taste, smell, colour, virtues and the effect and influence they have on the body. They maintain that the only method of deduction which can be trusted consists in analyzing the substances, since colours, tastes and everything else are under the influence of the four elements, according to the presence of which they produce effects of heat, cold, dryness, etc. Another approach claims that the surest evidence and best judgement that can be obtained as to the nature of remedies and foods lies in a knowledge of their action on the body, quite apart from their taste, smell, etc. and that beyond the observation of these influences and effects there can be no unfailing solution or opinion as to the nature of a remedy, whether a simple or a compound.'

VII:172-180
§§ 2857–2861

(Omitted: VII: 181-184; §§ 2862-2866: Hunain ibn Ishaq on Dentistry.)

AN APHORISM ON THE DEATH OF ALEXANDER

This exchange of questions and answers went on for a long time until the Caliph, whose attention was flagging, called a halt. He gave a present to each of the learned men who had been present at this debate, after which he invited them to quote from memory a few phrases on the renouncement of this world where everything passes and everything vanishes. One after another, they related what they knew on this subject, drawing examples from the lives of the ancient philosophers and the Greek sages, such as Socrates and Diogenes. Afterwards, Wathiq said to them:

'You have developed this theme and you have embroidered it with the charm of your eloquence. Now I want one of you to repeat for me the most apposite of the words spoken by the sages who surrounded the coffin of red gold in which Alexander had just been laid.'

One of the scholars answered as follows:

'All their words are worthy of admiration, but the most beautiful of all the phrases spoken by the wise men gathered for the ceremony was that of Diogenes (others attribute it to an Indian sage):

"Yesterday Alexander was less silent than today, but today he teaches us better than yesterday." '

Abu al-Atahiya translated the aphorism of this philosopher into the following verse:

'The sight of your tomb in this place
Overwhelms me with grief,
As I shake the earth
Of your grave from my hands.
Living, you gave me much wise advice,
But today you teach me even better
Than when you were alive.'

Wathiq wept copiously and sobbed loudly, and all those present mixed their tears with his. Then, suddenly, he rose and said:

'There are many slips and falls

An Aphorism on the Death of Alexander

Among the capricious evils
Meted out by fate. A man
Who was at the summit of good fortune,
Has fallen here and lies
Still in the depths of the abyss.
The pleasures of mankind last but a day
And the life of man is but a borrowed robe.'

An account of the most interesting events which took place under the reign of Wathiq and a description of the discussions held by the jurisconsults and scholastic theologians whom he gathered together at his assemblies to debate on the principles and corollaries of those sciences which are the domain of reason or of tradition and other details are given in our earlier works. Further on, in the chapter dedicated to the Caliphate of Qahir, we will give a few more of the character traits of the Abbasid Caliphs in order to illustrate something which took place during that Caliph's reign.

Wathiq having fallen ill, it was Ahmad ibn Abi Du'ad, the chief qadi, who recited the public prayer on the day of the Feast of Sacrifice. This officer mixed good wishes for Wathiq with his sermon and spoke the following words:

'Oh my God, save him from the trial You have inflicted upon him!'

As to the date of Wathiq's death, I have given it at the beginning of this chapter and it is therefore pointless to go back to it.

THE CALIPHATE OF MUTAWAKKIL

The throne name of Ja'far ibn Muhammad was originally Muntasir, but on the day after receiving the oath of allegiance, Ibn Abi Du'ad gave him a new throne name – Mutawakkil. He became Caliph on the day his brother Wathiq died, that is, Wednesday, the 24th of the month of Dhu al-Hijja 232 AH/847 AD. He was known as Abu al-Fadl.

He was twenty-seven and some months old when he was proclaimed. He was killed at the age of forty-one, after having reigned fourteen years, nine months and nine days. The date of his death was Wednesday, the 3rd of the month of Shawwal 247 AH/861 AD. His mother was a slave from Khwarizm named Shuja.

VII:189
§ 2872

MUTAWAKKIL

When the Caliphate came to Mutawakkil, he abolished free thought, philosophical disputes and the things which had preoccupied men's minds under Mu'tasim, Wathiq and Ma'mun. He re-established orthodoxy and submission to traditional religious values, and insisted that the heads of the schools of Tradition should teach that Tradition and devote themselves to the propagation of the Sunna and practices sanctioned by the community of Islam.

He appeared wearing clothes of a material called *mulhama*, which he preferred to any other cloth, and this fashion was adopted first by those in his household and then it spread among the people. Everyone wished to imitate his dress, so lengths of this material fetched high prices and the technique of producing it was perfected in response to the fashion and in order to meet the tastes of the ruler and his subjects. A few pieces of this material are still to be found in people's hands to this day; they are known as 'Mutawakkiliya', and are a kind of *mulhama* cloth, very beautiful, finely woven and of a very good colour.

The reign of Mutawakkil was one of the happiest and most flourishing, thanks to the order which obtained throughout the empire and to the people's concern for public security and justice.

This Caliph cannot be cited for his generosity and open-handedness, but, equally, he cannot be accused of parsimony or avarice. None of his predecessors among the Abbasid Caliphs had allowed within their palaces any games, horseplay and jokes, or other things of the kind which are normally forbidden. Mutawakkil was the first to adopt them and the amusements of this sort which he invented later spread to the majority of his courtiers and then to most of the public at large.

No one among his viziers, his principal secretaries, or officers, can be singled out for his generosity or nobility of character, nor could any of them rise above these habits of lightness and dissipation. His freedman, Fath ibn Khaqan, the Turk, the favourite who gained most influence over him and whom he most often invited to share his privacy, never succeeded – in spite of the credit he held with the Caliph – in making himself loved for his good deeds or feared for his severity. Nevertheless, he was an educated man and a distinguished writer, and he has left a work on the different aspects of belles-lettres and ethics called the *Book of the Orchard* (*Kitab al-Bustan*).

VII:190-192
§§ 2873-2874

MUTAWAKKIL'S PALACE OF THE TWO WINGS

During his reign, Mutawakkil constructed a building according to a plan unknown until that time, which was known as al-Hiri,* 'Of the Two Wings and the Loggias'. The idea was suggested to him by one of his courtiers, who, in the course of an evening's conversation, told him that a king of Hira, of the dynasty of Nu'man of the tribe of the Bani Nasr, had a passion for war and, wishing always to have it constantly in mind, had had constructed at his capital of Hira a building which would evoke an army drawn up in battle lines. The loggia of the palace – intended as the king's reception room – represented the centre of the army. The two wings symbolized the right and left flanks and were for the use of the most important members of the court. The right-hand wing was the royal wardrobe, while the left-hand one served as a repository for drinks. The loggia of the palace stretched over the centre and the two wings, and the three gates of the palace led to it. This is the building which is still today called 'The Two Wings' and also 'al-Hiri', in memory of the town of Hira. The people had similar houses built in imitation of the style of the palace of Mutawakkil – and it has remained famous down to our own day.

VII:192-193
§2875

(Omitted: VII:193-204; §§ 2876-2887. The heirs of Mutawakkil; Arrangements for the succession; The fate of Ibn Zayyat; The madman of the monastery of St Heraclius; The poet Buhtari.)

A DONKEY IN LOVE

Mutawakkil said to Abu al-Anbas:

'Tell me the story of your donkey and how it died and tell me the verses that he recited to you in a dream.'

'With pleasure, O Commander of the Faithful!' replied Abu al-Anbas. 'This donkey had more sense than all the qadis put together – and no shamelessness, no lapses into sin. A sudden illness came and carried him off. I saw him in a dream and said to him:

"O my donkey, was not your water always cool and your barley carefully sifted? Did I not lavish on you every care? Why this sudden death? What happened to you?"

"It was like this," he said to me. "On such-and-such a day, when you stopped at the apothecary and were chatting of this and that, a beautiful she-ass passed by. I saw her; my heart became enamoured of her; I loved her with such violent passion that I succumbed to my despair."

"Well, my donkey, did you not make some verses on this subject?"

"Indeed," he answered, "here they are:

My heart was ravished by a she-ass
Standing at the door of an apothecary.
She enslaved me with her flirtatious ways
And her two smooth cheeks
The colour of *shanqarani*.
I died for her; if I had lived
My passion would only have grown worse."

I asked, "What does *shanqarani* mean?"

"*Shanqarani* is an outré expression used in the poetical language of donkeys," he replied.'

Mutawakkil, who was much amused by this narrative, ordered his musicians and singers to set the poem to music, for that day's song. Never was he seen gayer, nor more exuberantly joyful. As for Abu al-Anbas, he was overwhelmed with honours and presents.

VII:204-206
§ 2888

(Omitted: VII:206-209; §§ 2889-2893. The piety of Abu al-Hasan Ali.)

A VIGOROUS OLD SCHOLAR

Muhammad ibn Sama'a, the qadi, a disciple of Muhammad ibn al-Hasan al-Shaibani and of Abu Hanifa, died in the reign of Mutawakkil, in the year 233 AH/848 AD. Although a hundred years old, his mind and body were vigorous. He was in full possession of his faculties, deflowered virgins, broke difficult and spirited horses and denied himself nothing. This is what his son Sama'a related:

'My father, Muhammad ibn Sama'a, told me:

"During the lifetime of Sawwar ibn Abd Allah, who was qadi under Mansur, I found a work in his hand containing these lines, which he had composed himself, or at least liked very well:

> You have stripped the flesh from my bones
> And left them naked and thin under the skin.
> You have fed on their marrow and now
> They are like glass tubes through which
> The wind blows. Take me
> In your hands and part my robes
> And see how I am wasted.
> But I hide myself from your gaze." '

This Muhammad ibn Sama'a left a number of good works on law, as well as books of Traditions collected from al-Shaibani and other learned men, among them the *Treatise on Unusual Questions*, following al-Shaibani, which runs to thousands of folios.

SAVED FROM RAPE

It was also in 235 AH/850 AD that Ishaq ibn Ibrahim ibn Mus'ab died. He governed the city* of Baghdad and was succeeded in his office by his son. In the *Historical Annals* I have given some interesting stories of his life. One such is the following curious episode, which took place while he was in Baghdad and which was gathered from his own lips by Musa ibn Salih ibn Shaikh ibn Umaira al-Asadi.

'The Prophet appeared to him in a dream and said:
"Set the murderer free!"

Ishaq was seized with terror. He examined the reports sent to him from the prisons and, finding in them no mention of any murderer, summoned Sindi and Abbas and asked them whether some person had been brought to them suspected of murder.

"Yes," replied Abbas, "and we have already questioned him and drawn up a report."

Ishaq began to search through his papers again and found the document which had slipped in between other pieces of paper. It dealt with a man who had been accused of murder by numerous witnesses and who had confessed to his crime. Ishaq sent for him and when he was brought, seeing him overwhelmed with the greatest fear, said:

"If you tell me the truth, I will free you."

The man told the following story:

He and a gang of accomplices had been in the habit of committing every sort of misdemeanor and breaking all the injunctions of the law. They gathered in a house in the City of Abu Ja'far Mansur – that is to say in Old Baghdad – where they applied themselves to all kinds of villainy. One day, an old woman who pandered to them in their debauchery brought a remarkably beautiful young girl. She gave piercing screams as she was driven through the house.

"I left my companions," continued the prisoner, "and running to her, made her enter one of the rooms. After having calmed her fears, I wanted to know her story.

'My God!' she cried, 'my God, protect me! This old woman tricked me by saying that in her cupboard she had an incomparably beautiful casket. She so aroused my curiosity to see what was in it that I followed her without the slightest suspicion – and it was thus that she lured me here. The Messenger of God is my grandfather, Fatima is my mother and Hasan ibn Ali my father. May their

243

The Meadows of Gold

memory be my protection!'

"Having decided to save the girl, I went back to my friends and told them what had happened, but apparently my words only excited them the more, for they replied:

'First you slake your own lust, then you try to keep her away from us!'

"They flung themselves on the poor girl. I stood in front of her to defend her and the quarrel became so heated that I was hurt in several places. I hurled myself at the most determined of them at the very moment he was throwing himself on her in his bestial passion – and I killed him. Then, redoubling my efforts, I at last managed to get away from them safe and sound. Having escaped from the threat of this danger, I had her leave the building and overheard her words:

'May God protect you, as you protected me! And may He be to you as you were to me!'

"Meanwhile, the neighbours, drawn by the cries, had gathered. Seeing me with a knife in my hand standing by a man weltering in his own blood, they arrested me and delivered me just as I was into the hands of justice."

Ishaq then said to the prisoner:

"I wish to recognize the protection you afforded this woman: I pardon you for the love of God and His Messenger."

"And I," answered the man, "swear by Those in Whose name you pardon me, that I will commit no further crimes and avoid all occasions of sin, until the day I stand before God's tribunal."

Ishaq then told him of his dream, adding that God did not let such a deed go unrewarded and he therefore wished to offer him a considerable sum, but the man refused to accept anything.'

AT THE CALIPH'S TABLE

In 237 AH/852 AD Mutawakkil forgave Yahya ibn Aktham, the qadi, and recalled him to Samarra to take up the position of Chief Justice. He dismissed Ahmad ibn Abi Du'ad in disgrace, together with his son, Abu al-Walid Muhammad, who had formerly held that position, and he confiscated the latter's fortune – a sum of 120,000 dinars and jewels valued at 40,000 dinars; then he exiled him to Baghdad. Abu Abd Allah Ahmad ibn Abi Du'ad had been struck with paralysis forty-seven days after the death of his enemy Ibn Zayyat in 233 AH/848 AD. He died in 240 AH/855 AD, twenty days after the death of his own son, Abu al-Walid Muhammad ibn Ahmad.

Ahmad ibn Abi Du'ad was, as is well known, one of those privileged men whom God uses to spread His blessings, a man before whom God has smoothed the way and who is inspired with a love of virtue and the performance of good works.

They say that Mu'tasim had gathered together a number of courtiers at the Jawsaq Palace to drink wine one morning and had ordered all of them to cook something, each in his own manner. He saw Sallama, the page of Ibn Abi Du'ad, approaching and said:

'Here is Ibn Abi Du'ad's page, come to ask us what we are doing. In a moment his master will make his appearance and he will make demands of me on behalf of so-and-so of the family of Hashim and of so-and-so from the Quraish and of such-and-such from among the Ansar and of such-and-such an Arab, until with his persistence he has spoiled all our fun. Bear me witness – I am not going to grant him any of his requests today.'

Scarcely had he spoken, when the chamberlain announced Ibn Abi Du'ad.

'What did I tell you?' said the Caliph to his guests.

And as they were trying to persuade him not to receive him, Mu'tasim answered:

'Oh you are all hopeless! It would be simpler to have a fever for a year!'

The qadi came in and greeted everyone. Scarcely had he sat down and begun talking, than the Caliph looked cheerful again and a flood of happiness seemed to be spreading all through him.

'Ibn Abi Du'ad,' he then said to the new arrival, 'everyone here has prepared a dish in his own manner and you shall be the judge.'

'Let the dishes be brought,' replied the qadi, 'that I may taste them and from direct experience pronounce judgement.'

The Meadows of Gold

He began to eat large amounts from the first plate offered him.

'That isn't fair,' said Mu'tasim.

'Why not?'

'It seems to me that having eaten this one dish with so much pleasure, you will give a verdict in favour of the man who prepared it.'

'Commander of the Faithful,' retorted Ibn Abi Du'ad, 'I undertake to do justice to the rest of the food, as much as to this.'

'So be it,' said Mu'tasim, smiling, 'that is up to you.'

The qadi kept his promise and proceeded to hold forth as follows:

'The great merit of the man who prepared this dish is that he was generous with the pepper, but sparing with the cumin. The virtue of this man, on the other hand, is that he used an abundance of vinegar, but spared the oil. What makes this other dish so good is that the spices are mixed in equal proportions, whereas the creator of that one showed his good taste by putting less water than stock.'

And thus he went over the merits of each sauce and stew, with praises which charmed those who had cooked them.

Then he sat down with the other guests and ate with the best grace and the best appetite, telling stories of the great eaters of the early days of Islam, such as Mu'awiya ibn Abi Sufyan, Ubaid Allah ibn Ziyad, Hajjaj ibn Yusuf and Sulaiman ibn Abd al-Malik, or of the feats of the greatest eaters of the day, such as Maisara, the date-merchant, Dawraq, the butcher, Hatim, the corn-chandler, or Ishaq, the bath-house keeper.

When the table had been cleared away, Mu'tasim asked him:

'Do you have any request you would like to make?'

'Yes, O Commander of the Faithful,' said the qadi.

'Speak, for our guests are impatient for the entertainment.'

'Well, Commander of the Faithful, a member of your family has been cast down by fortune and now finds himself in a wretched state and living in misery.'

'Who is it?' asked Mu'tasim.

'It is Sulaiman ibn Abd Allah al-Nawfali.'

'Estimate what he needs.'

'Fifty thousand dirhams.'

'They are his.'

'I have another request,' proceeded the qadi.

'What is it?'

'Will you return to Ibrahim ibn al-Mu'tamir his estates?'

'I give my consent.'

'Here is a third request.'

'Granted,' said Mu'tasim.

And thus Ibn Abi Du'ad did not leave until he had mentioned thirteen different requests and not had a single refusal. He then rose and made the following speech:

'O Commander of the Faithful, may God grant you long years, for your existence makes the gardens of your subjects flourish and makes their lives

At the Caliph's Table

pleasant and their wealth multiply! May you enjoy most perfect felicity, basking in God's favour and safe from all the vicissitudes of fortune!'

When he had gone, Mu'tasim said:

'By God, one is truly proud to know a man like him and to enjoy his company. He is worth a thousand of his peers. Did you notice how he came in, how he greeted us and how he spoke? How elegantly he tasted and praised the food, and spread himself in conversation? And, lastly, how much he added to the gaiety of our meal? One would need to be truly low and vile to refuse a request from him! By God, if he had asked me as I sat there for ten million dirhams all at once, I would not have known how to refuse them, for I am convinced that in exchange for the gift, he would have won me glory in this world and an eternal reward in the next.'

VII:214-220
§§ 2898-2904

THE SAILOR'S STEW

Tradition has preserved the following story, told by Fath ibn Khaqan:

'I was,' he said, 'with Mutawakkil one day when he had sent for his courtiers and singers, with the intention of going to spend the morning drinking wine at the Ja'fari Palace. We were walking, the Caliph leaning on me and listening to me, when we came to a point from which we could see the canal. The Commander of the Faithful called for an armchair and sat down. As he was talking to me, he caught sight of a boat moored along the bank of the canal. A sailor was cooking a beef *sikbaj* – a sweet and sour stew seasoned with vinegar and honey – in a big pot in front of him and the aroma was spreading far and wide.

"Fath," said the Caliph, "that seems to be *sikbaj*! By God, my friend, have you noticed the delicious smell? Someone bring it to me, just as it is!"

The footmen ran as quickly as they could to snatch the stew-pot from the sailor's hands – at which the men on the boat almost died from fear and shock. The pot was brought to the Caliph still bubbling and just as it was, and was set before us. Delighted with the aroma and with the appetizing colour of the stew, Mutawakkil asked for a loaf of bread, broke off a piece which he gave me, took another for himself and we each ate three mouthfuls of the dish. After us, the courtiers and singers each came and had a bite, then luncheon was brought and the tables laid. When the meal was over, Mutawakkil had the pot emptied and washed out in his presence and ordered that it should be filled with dirhams. They poured in all the contents of a purse, but as about 2,000 dirhams would not fit and were left in the bag, the Caliph said to an eunuch who was standing there:

"Take the jar and carry it to the sailors and say: 'This is the price of your stew, which we have eaten.' Then give the man who prepared it the money which is left over, to reward him for his excellent cooking."'

Fath added that the Caliph often said, when reminded of the sailor's stew:

'I have never eaten anything better than the *sikbaj* prepared that day by the sailors!'

VII:220-222
§§ 2905-2906

LOVE'S DESPAIR – JAHIZ

The jurisconsult Abu al-Qasim Ja'far ibn Muhammad ibn Hamdan al-Mawsili, who originally came from the town of Hadithat al-Mawsil, told me, in the city of Juhaina,* the following story related to Abu al-Hasan al-Salihi by Jahiz:*

'I had been recommended to the Commander of the Faithful Mutawakkil,' said Jahiz, 'as tutor to one of his sons, but when the Caliph saw me he found my physical appearance so repellent that he had me given 10,000 dirhams and sent me away. As I was leaving, I met Muhammad ibn Ibrahim, who was about to go to Baghdad, the City of Peace. He suggested that I should accompany him and sail down the Tigris in his boat. I took a place next to him and when we reached the mouth of the Qatul Canal after leaving Samarra, Muhammad lowered the curtain and summoned his singing girls. A lute player began, with the following words:

> Each day a parting, a reproach!
> Time passes, but our rage does not.
> Is this misfortune mine alone
> Or does it afflict every lover's heart?

She fell silent and on Muhammad's orders a player of the *tambur* sang these lines:

> Pity the poor lovers
> For whom there is no help!
> They are cruelly rebuffed
> And sent away; they are separated,
> Yet they bear it patiently.

The lute player said:
"Then what should they do?"
The *tambur* player replied:
"*This* is what they should do!"

And she tore down the curtain with her hand, revealing herself for a moment as brilliant as a splinter of the moon, before she plunged into the river.

At Muhammad's couch stood a young page, her rival in beauty. Seeing her despairing act, he flung down the flywhisk he was holding, ran to the place where

The Meadows of Gold

she had jumped and seeing her sinking beneath the waves, cried out:

> If you but knew, it is you
> Who have plunged me in these depths!

And he threw himself into the river after her.

The sailors turned the boat and we saw, for one moment, the two lovers, twined in each other's arms. Then they vanished and were seen no more.

This event saddened Muhammad and affected him profoundly. He said to me, therefore:

"Jahiz, tell me some story to comfort me for the loss of my two servants, otherwise I will send you to join them!" '

And this, proceeded Jahiz, is the tale I told:

'They say that one day as Yazid ibn Abd al-Malik was dispensing justice, he found among the petitions presented to him a request phrased as follows:

"May it please the Commander of the Faithful – and may God exalt him – to have his slave so-and-so appear before me to sing me three songs."

Yazid, angered, ordered them to bring him the head of the offender, but then he sent a second messenger after the first with instruccions to bring him the author of the message. When the man stood before him, Yazid asked him what had brought him to do what he had done.

"It was," he replied, "my trust in your goodness and my confidence in your forgiveness."

The Caliph had him sit down and when all the Umayyads, down to the very last one, had gone away, he had the slave girl come in with her lute in her hand. The young man asked for the following tune:

> Gently, Fatima! Don't be so coquettish!
> If you have decided to leave me,
> At least leave me kindly.

The girl sang, and afterwards, the young man, with Yazid's permission, asked for this air:

> Lightning flashes over Najd!
> I said: 'Lightning, I no longer care to watch you.'
> Another gives you satisfaction in my stead.
> An angry, vengeful foe keeps you from me,
> Holding a naked blade like a lance in his hand.

She sang that too.

"Speak!" said Yazid to the young man.

"Tell them to bring me a jug of wine!" he replied.

It was brought. He drained it and immediately rose, climbed to the top of the

250

dome under which the Caliph was sitting, threw himself down head first and died.
At this, Yazid cried:

"We belong to God and to God we return! Look at this fool, this madman, who imagined that having shown him one of my slave girls I would have kept her in my possession! Pages, take this girl away and return her to her family, if she has one; otherwise, sell her and distribute the money as alms in the name of the dead man."

They led her away at once. As they crossed the courtyard of the palace, she saw a pit which had been dug in the middle to carry off rainwater, and slipping from the hands of the guards, she spoke these words:

> Those who die of love should die thus;
> Love without death is of no worth!

Then she threw herself in head first and died.'

'This story,' Jahiz added, 'comforted Muhammad and he gave me a fine reward.'

Others say, however, that Sulaiman ibn Abd al-Malik was the protagonist of this story, instead of Yazid ibn Abd al-Malik.

Jahiz continued as follows:

'When I had told this story to Abu Abd Allah Muhammad ibn Ja'far al-Anbari in Basra, he said to me:

"I would now like to tell you a story very similar to the one you have just told me. I owe it to the eunuch Fa'iq, who was the freedman of Muhammad ibn Humaid al-Tusi. He was sitting one day with some companions and was listening to a slave girl, who, separated from the company by a curtain, was singing these words:

> O moon of the palace,
> When you rise, shining,
> I suffer because
> Another enjoys you.
>
> But if God himself
> Has ordained me to suffer,
> What can I do?

Behind Muhammad, a young page with a goblet in his hand was offering him a drink. The youth dashed the cup to the ground, ran to the window and threw himself into the Tigris, crying:

'This is what you should do!'

The Meadows of Gold

Immediately, the singer tore aside the curtain and hurled herself into the stream after him.

All the efforts of the pages to recover the two victims were in vain, and Muhammad, breaking short the party, withdrew." '

THE SLAPPING OF A SECRETARY

In 233 AH/848 AD Mutawakkil lost patience with Umar ibn Faraj al-Rukhkhaji, a secretary of unusual talent, and confiscated his goods and jewels, which represented a sum in the region of 120,000 dinars. He also took from his brother Muhammad some 150,000 dinars; Muhammad later obtained pardon and the return of his estates in exchange for the sum of 21,000,000 dirhams. The Caliph later grew angry with him a second time and sentenced him to be slapped every day – according to the calculations they made, the poor man got 6,000 slaps – and furthermore he had to wear a woollen cloak. After a brief reconciliation, he occasioned the Caliph's displeasure a third time and was exiled to Baghdad, where he lived until his death.

VII:228-229
§ 2912

(Omitted: VII:229; § 2913. Gift of scent to the Caliph from a Zoroastrian.)

THE DEATH OF AHMAD IBN HANBAL

Ahmad ibn Hanbal* died in Baghdad, the City of Peace, during the reign of Mutawakkil and was buried at the Bab al-Harb – War Gate – in the western quarter, in the month of Rabi' II 241 AH/July 855 AD. Muhammad ibn Tahir recited the prayers, and never were so many people seen gathered at a jurist's funeral. The most varied and contradictory stories were circulating among the people; for example, that one of those present kept crying out:

'Cursed be he who stands in judicial error!' – an accusation that is in direct contradiction to what tradition tells us on this point of one of the leading expositors of the Holy Law, may peace be upon him.

On the other hand, one of the great men accompanying the procession, one who took rank immediately behind the Imam of the funeral cortege, pronounced this verse in a resounding voice:

The loss of Muhammad covered the world with shadows;
The world has grown dark at the loss of Ibn Hanbal.

By this he meant that the world had already been darkened after the death of Muhammad, may peace be upon him, and that the passing of Ibn Hanbal had spread shadows over the earth as thick as those which marked the Prophet's end, may the prayers and peace of God be upon him.

This same year was distinguished by falls of stars, the like of which had never been seen before. This phenomenon took place on the night of Thursday,* the 6th of Jumada II, but it occurred again, in 323 AH/935 AD, equally frightening, on the night that the Qarmatians attacked the pilgrims of Iraq on the Kufa road in the month of Dhu al-Qa'da.

VII:229-231
§§ 2914-2915

(Omitted: VII:232-262; §§ 2916-2946. Mu'tazilite controversies; Necrology for 245 AH/859 AD; An anecdote concerning Suli; A critique of his opinions; A selection of his verse; The death of Abbas ibn al-Ahnaf; The exile of the poet Ali ibn al-Jahm to Khurasan; His death; A selection of his verses; Mutawakkil leaves Damascus for Samarra for three months in 243 AH/857 AD; The troops revolt.)

THE TESTING OF AN ASSASSIN

Sa'id ibn Nakis said:

'Bugha the Younger, having resolved that Mutawakkil should die, summoned Baghir the Turk. This man, who was Bugha's creature and whom he had cultivated and upon whom he had bestowed many gifts, was of an extreme boldness and ready to face all dangers.

"Baghir," Bugha said to him, "you know how fond I am of you and that I have set you in the first rank, preferring you to the others and heaping favours upon you. I therefore have a right to expect my orders to be carried out without question. I have an order to give you – but tell me first whether your heart is inclined to obey me."

"You know where my heart lies," Baghir replied. "Tell me your desires that I may fulfil them."

Bugha continued:

"My son Faris is spreading disorder in my government. He has sworn to kill me and longs to shed my blood. I have certain proof of it."

"Well, what do you want me to do?"

"This: tomorrow Faris will come to my house. I shall place my cap on the ground. As soon as you see me do so, kill him."

"It's all very well," replied the Turk, "but I am afraid that you will change your mind and that afterwards you will take against me."

"I take God as my witness that I will not," replied Bugha.

The following day, when Faris arrived, Baghir was present and waiting to strike, watching for the moment when his master would place his cap on the ground, but, seeing that he did nothing and attributing it to an oversight, he signed to him with his eyes that the order should be given. Bugha said "No." The signal was not given.

When Faris had gone away, Bugha said to him:

"I have reconsidered. He is very young and he is my son. I have decided to spare him this time."

Baghir replied:

"I hear and I obey. You know best and what you have decided concerning him is undoubtedly the best course."

Bugha proceeded as follows:

"It is now a matter of something more serious, more important. Tell me how you feel about it."

The Meadows of Gold

"Say what you wish and I shall do it."

"It concerns my brother Wasif," Bugha went on. "It has been proved to me that he is plotting against me and my friends and that our high position weighs heavily on him. He intends to kill us, wipe us out and remain the sole master of power."

"What do you want done to him?"

"This is what you are to do. Tomorrow my brother comes to my house. When you see me come down from the prayer dais, where he will have taken his place at my side, that will be the signal. You are to throw yourself upon him, sword in hand, and kill him."

"I will do it," answered the Turk.

And indeed, when Wasif arrived at Bugha's house, Baghir was there and ready to act; but he waited in vain for the agreed sign, until Wasif rose and left.

"Baghir," Bugha then said to him, "I have reflected that he is my brother and that I have sworn a binding oath with him. I therefore did not dare carry out what I had planned."

Bugha rewarded his servant with gifts and money and let a fairly long time pass without discussing anything with him. Then he summoned him and said:

"O Baghir, today something will arise which is more serious than that which I discussed with you before. Is your heart steadfast?"

"My heart," replied the Turk, "is as you would wish it. Tell me what you want and I will do it."

Bugha continued as follows:

"I hold the certain proof that Muntasir, the son of Mutawakkil, is preparing a plot against me and against certain other persons. He wishes our death and I wish his. Are you prepared to help me?"

Baghir remained a long time with his head bent, lost in thought, and then at last he cried:

"It will do no good!"

"Why?" asked his master.

"If you kill the son and let the father live," he went on, "your undertaking will be incomplete, for the father will avenge his son by killing all of you."

"Well, what do you advise?"

"Begin with the father. Once we have killed him, the question of the son will be easier."

"But you are mad! Is such a plan possible? Can it be carried out?"

"Certainly," answered Baghir, "and I will undertake it. I will not leave the Caliph until I have killed him."

Then, as his master seemed to hesitate, Baghir repeated:

"There is nothing else to be done."

And he added these words:

"Follow me into the Caliph's apartments. Either I shall kill him, or I shall fail. In the latter case, kill me and as you pierce my body with your sword say:

"This man wished to kill his Lord!"

The Testing of an Assassin

Bugha then understood that he was decided and entrusted to him the task of preparing for the murder of Mutawakkil.'

VII:262-266
§§ 2947-2950

THE INDIAN SWORD

In 247 AH/861 AD, Shuja', the mother of Mutawakkil, died and the funeral prayers were recited by Muntasir. This happened in the month of Rabi' II. Mutawakkil was assassinated six months after his mother's death, on Wednesday in the third hour of the night of 3 Shawwal 247 AH, or, according to others, on the 4th of that month. He was born at Fam al-Silh – a canal above Wasit.

This is what Buhtari says:

'One night we were gathered in the presence of Mutawakkil with a number of courtiers and we were talking about swords, when one of those present spoke as follows:

"Commander of the Faithful, I have been told that a certain inhabitant of Basra has an Indian sword which is beyond compare, whose like has never been seen."

Mutawakkil ordered someone to write to the governor of Basra to buy this weapon, no matter what the price. The letters were sent by the state post and soon the answer came back from the governor reporting that the sword had been sold to an inhabitant of Yemen. Mutawakkil ordered agents sent there to seek out and buy this precious sword and letters to this effect were transmitted.

At this point, Ubaid Allah ibn Yahya entered the Commander of the Faithful's presence, announcing that he had bought the sword from the Yemeni who owned it for 10,000 dirhams. Mutawakkil was enchanted with this lucky discovery and thanked God for having so quickly fulfilled his desires. Then he drew the blade from its sheath and admired its beauty. When each of us had finished saying whatever he felt was suitable, the Caliph slipped the sword under his cushion.

The next day, he said to Fath:

"Find me a page of proven strength and courage. I want to entrust this sword to him and have him stand behind me, not leaving me for a moment during the day, as long as I am in council."

He was still speaking when Baghir the Turk stepped forward.

"Commander of the Faithful," said Fath, "this is Baghir the Turk. His courage and fearlessness have been much praised to me. He is the man the Caliph needs."

Then Mutawakkil called him forward, handed over the sword and gave him his orders. He began by promoting him and doubling his allowance.'

'And I declare,' went on Buhtari, 'that the sword in question never left its sheath from the moment it was given to Baghir until the night he used it to kill the Caliph.'

VII:266-269
§ 2951-2953

(Omitted: VII:269-271; §§ 2954-2955. Premonitions of Mutawakkil's death.)

THE ASSASSINATION OF MUTAWAKKIL

Meanwhile, Mutawakkil had become very drunk. It was the custom for the eunuchs who were in attendance to sit him up again when his body slumped under the effects of drunkenness.

At this moment – it was about the third hour of the night – Baghir appeared, accompanied by ten Turks. Their faces were veiled and the swords which they were holding in their hands glittered in the light of the candles. They hurled themselves at us, making straight for the Caliph. Baghir and another Turk having climbed onto the throne, Fath cried to them:

'Wretched creatures, that is your master!'

Meanwhile, the pages, courtiers and guests had fled in all haste. Fath remained alone in the room, fighting the assassins and driving them back.

'I heard,' adds Buhtari, 'the cries given by Mutawakkil when Baghir struck him on the right side with the sword which the Caliph had given him and cut him to the hip. Then he struck him again on the left side and gave him a similar wound. Fath was still defending his master, when one of the murderers plunged his sword into his belly. The blade came out at the back. Fath neither tried to yield nor to flee their blows. I have never seen a man', said Buhtari, 'with such a steadfast heart and so noble in spirit. He threw himself on the body of the Caliph and they died together.

The two corpses, rolled in the carpet on which they had been struck down, were pushed into a corner, where they remained that night and for most of the following day. At last, when Muntasir was recognized as Caliph, he gave the order for them to be buried together.'

According to another version, Qabiha had them buried in that very cloak which the Caliph Mutawakkil tore.

VII:271-272
§ 2956

COURT FACTIONS

Bugha the Younger was furious with Mutawakkil. Muntasir was trying to win the hearts of the Turks. He had at his side Ultamish, the former page of Wathiq – and that is why Mutawakkil hated his son Muntasir, for Ultamish was working to bring the Turks over to the side of Muntasir.

On the other hand, the vizier Ubaid Allah ibn Khaqan and Fath ibn Khaqan had drawn away from Muntasir and inclined towards Mu'tazz, another of the Caliph's sons. They tried to sour Mutawakkil's heart against Muntasir. This last attracted to his side all the Turks who had left the service of Mutawakkil and thus gained the affection not only of the Turks, but of a large number of soldiers from Fergana and Ushrusana – until the day when that which we have described took place.

There are several other accounts of the murder of Mutawakkil. I have preferred the one which has just been given because it is the best written and most probable. As for the other versions of this event, I have not bothered to repeat them in the present work, since they are to be found in my *Intermediate History*.

MUTAWAKKIL'S LAST DAY

Never was Mutawakkil more gay than on the day that he was assassinated. He woke in good spirits, joyful, filled with happiness and said:

'I feel a certain movement in my blood,' and had himself bled.

Then he gathered his intimate companions and his musicians and gave himself over to pleasure and his excellent mood. But the gaiety turned to grief, and mourning succeeded joy.

And who can allow himself to be seduced by this world or put his trust in it, without fearing its betrayals and its calamities, except a man both deluded and ignorant? The world is a dwelling place where felicity is short-lived and joys are never perfect. Disaster is always to be feared, its pleasures are mixed with bitterness, its sweetness with violence, its happiness with misfortune. Everything is doomed to die. Sorrow is ever at enjoyment's side and mourning at the side of gaiety. That which one abhors follows close on that which one loves, as sickness health, death life, suffering pleasure, pain delight. Noble men are brought low, the powerful humbled, the rich despoiled and the great stripped of their grandeur. There is nothing eternal but the Living God, the Being Glorious and Wise, He Who will never die and Whose kingdom is without end.

VII:274-275
§ 2958

(Omitted: VII:275; § 2959. Two verses by Buhtari on Muntasir's betrayal of his father.)

THE REIGN OF MUTAWAKKIL

The reign of Mutawakkil, in its excellence, grace and luxury, the praise heaped upon it by noble and commoner alike, and their contentment with it, was undoubtedly a period of happiness unmixed with misfortune. As someone said:

'The reign of Mutawakkil was more excellent than the security of the roads, low prices, the hopes of love and the days of youth.'

A poet has expressed the same thought:

> Your presence was more delightful to us
> Than low prices or safe roads
> Or long successions of nights of love
> With wonderful days in the flush of youth.

They claim that in no century and at no period was so much spent as during the reign of Mutawakkil. His two palaces, the Haruni and the Jawsaq Ja'fari, cost him, they say, more than 100,000,000 dirhams. To this should be added the expense of his freedmen, his army, his special guard called the 'Shakiriya', on whom he heaped presents and who received every month enormous sums in extra pay and gifts. He had, they say, 4,000 concubines and slept with each one of them. At his death, there were in his treasury 4,000,000 dinars and 7,000,000 dirhams. Whosoever distinguished himself in his profession, whether serious or light, enjoyed his favours and grew rich under this reign, receiving considerable sums from the Caliph.

VII:275-277
§§ 2960-2961

(Omitted: VII:277-281; §§ 2962-2966. Two anecdotes and various poems.)

MAHBUBA

Ali ibn al-Jahm relates the following story:

'When Ja'far Mutawakkil became Caliph, he received gifts commensurate with the ranks of those who offered them. The present from Abd Allah ibn Tahir included 200 pages of both sexes and among them a young girl called Mahbuba – "The Beloved". Her first master, a man from Taif, had taken great care with her education, cultivated her mind and had enriched her with a wealth of knowledge on the most varied subjects. She composed poetry which she sang to her own accompaniment on the lute and, in a word, she excelled in all those things which distinguish people of talent. She was, therefore, well received by Mutawakkil and she held a place in his heart unrivalled by anyone else.

One day I entered the Caliph's presence,' added Ali, 'to attend a drinking party. When I had sat down, the Caliph rose and going into one of the private rooms came back laughing and said to me:

"My dear Ali, on going into the harem, I met a slave girl who had written on her cheek in letters of musk the name Ja'far. I have never seen anything so charming. Think up some lines on the subject."

"I, by myself," I asked him, "or with Mahbuba?"

"No, you and Mahbuba, of course."

Mahbuba called for an inkwell and paper and, stealing the march on me, composed some verses which she recited, then, seizing her lute, she sang in an undertone. After strumming her instrument until she had shaped her tune, she smiled for a moment and asked:

"Do I have the Caliph's permission to sing?"

The Caliph gave his assent and she sang:

> I swear by she who has written "Ja'far" on her cheek with musk
> That I would give my soul for the place that she has written on.
> Just as she has marked her cheeks with letters of musk,
> So she has written a line of passion on my heart.
> See how the master obeys the slave, in public and in private!
> See those eyes which have looked upon a man like Ja'far!
> May God shower blessings upon him!'

Ali went on with his story:

'Meanwhile my imagination drifted, unfocused, and it seemed to me that I would never be able to find even a few words of a verse.

"Well, Ali," enquired Mutawakkil, "how are you getting on with what I ordered you?"

"Pardon me, my lord," I replied, "but by God, my wits seem to have taken leave of me!"

From then on until his death Mutawakkil was always reminding me of this occasion and teasing me about it.

'One day I went in to him,' this same Ali relates, 'in order to take part in a drinking party, when he said to me:

"My dear Ali, you know that I am angry with Mahbuba? I have sent her to her rooms and have forbidden any of the servants to communicate with her; I don't want to speak with her."

"My lord," I replied, "if you are angry with her today, make peace tomorrow. May God prolong the happiness of the Commander of the Faithful and grant him many years!"

The Caliph sat meditating for some time and then said to his table-companions: "Be gone!" and had the wine removed. On the following day I appeared and he said to me:

"Well, Ali, last night I dreamed that I was reconciled with Mahbuba."

A young slave girl named Shatir, who was standing before the Caliph, then said to him:

"I have just heard, as I passed by her room, murmurings whose meaning I could not catch."

"Come," said the Caliph, "we will see what it is."

And he started off, his feet bare. I followed him. As we drew near her room, we heard Mahbuba turning her lute and humming in an undertone as if she were composing a tune. Then, raising her voice, she sang:

> I wander through the palace and see no one
> To listen to my laments or speak to me.
> It is almost as if I had committed some act of rebellion
> For which even repentance could never atone.
> Who will intercede for me with a king
> Who came to me in a dream and pardoned me?
> Until morning brought back our separation
> And the fact that he has abandoned me.

Mutawakkil clapped his hands with joy and so did I. He went straight in to his favourite. She kissed his feet and streaked her cheeks with dust, until the Caliph took her by the hand and raised her. Then we both went back the way we had come, with Mahbuba making a third.

After the murder of the Caliph,' added Ali ibn al-Jahm, 'Mahbuba, with the other pages, was made over to Bugha the Elder. One day as I was going into his house, being one of his table-companions, he had the curtains that separated us from the women drawn aside and on his orders his slave girls came forward, glittering with ornaments and decorations. Mahbuba alone appeared without jewels or splendid clothes, dressed in white – the colour of mourning. She was sitting, thoughtful, her head low. Wasif said to her: "Sing!" She excused herself. He insisted and had a lute brought, which was laid on the girl's lap. Seeing herself compelled to obey, she kept the lute on her knees and accompanied herself as she sang the following air, which she improvised:

> How could life please me, when I no longer see Ja'far?
> A king I last saw covered with blood and dust.
> All those who were mad and sick have found health,
> All save Mahbuba, who if she saw death for sale
> Would pay all she owns to die and be buried.

Wasif was furious and ordered her to be imprisoned. She was locked up and no one has heard her spoken of since.'

VII:281-286
§§ 2967-2972

(Omitted: VII:286-289; §§ 2973-2977. Necrology of scholars and learned men who died in the reign of Mutawakkil.)

THE CALIPHATE OF MUNTASIR

Muhammad ibn Ja'far al-Muntasir was proclaimed Caliph at the first hour of the day following the night in which Mutawakkil was assassinated – the night of Wednesday, the 3rd of the month of Shawwal 247 AH/861 AD.

He was known as Abu Ja'far. His mother, a Greek slave, was called Hubshiya. At the time he assumed the Caliphate he was twenty-five years old and the oath of allegiance was sworn at the Ja'fari Palace, built by Mutawakkil. Muntasir died in 248 AH/862 AD, after a reign of six months.

VII:290
§ 2978

THE CARPET OF ANNIHILATION

Mutawakkil was assassinated in the very place where Shirawaih killed his father Chosroe Parwiz, and it was known as Mahuza.*

Muntasir stayed on seven days in this place after the death of his father, then he went away and gave orders that it should be destroyed.,

Abu al-Abbas Muhammad ibn Sahl said:

'In the reign of Muntasir, I was secretary in the War Ministry of the Shakiriya, under the orders of Attab ibn Attab. I went up to one of the loggias on the upper storey and found it furnished with a floor carpet made at Susangird, a dais which served as a throne, a *musalla*, or small prayer rug, and red and blue cushions. The large carpet was edged with medallions enclosing pictures of men and an inscription in Persian – a language I read fluently. Now, to the right of the small prayer rug, I saw the portrait of a king with a crown on his head, shown in the posture of one who speaks. I read the inscription, which was as follows:

"This is the likeness of Shirawaih, murderer of his father, King Parwiz. He reigned six months."

I then noticed a number of other portraits of kings and to the left of the small prayer rug, in the last place, was a figure with above it the following words:

"Portrait of Yazid ibn al-Walid ibn Abd al-Malik, murderer of his cousin Walid ibn Yazid ibn Abd al-Malik. He reigned six months."

I was astonished by all this and also by the chance which had set these figures to the left and right of the place where Muntasir sat. I said to myself: "I do not think this reign will last more than six months."

And by God, my forebodings proved justified.

Leaving the loggia, I went to Wasif and Bugha, who were holding an audience on the second floor, and I said to Wasif:

"Couldn't the man in charge of furnishings find anything to put under the feet of the Commander of the Faithful other than a carpet showing Yazid ibn al-Walid, murderer of his cousin and Shirawaih, murderer of his father Parwiz – both of whom only survived their crimes by six months?"

Wasif was disturbed by my words and said:

"Bring me Ayyub ibn Sulaiman, the Christian!"

This man was the Keeper of the Carpets. When he entered, Wasif said to him:

"Could you not have found a carpet to spread under the feet of the Commander of the Faithful today other than that which was under the feet of Mutawakkil on the night when that which took place, took place? A carpet which depicts a

The Carpet of Annihilation

Persian king and certain other personages and which still bears traces of blood?"

The Keeper of the Carpets replied:

"It was Muntasir himself who mentioned this carpet to me and said: 'What became of the carpet?' I answered that it had dreadful stains and that it was my intention, after the night of the Event, never to use it again."

"Why don't you have it washed and scented?" inquired the Caliph.

"I was afraid that it would be a revelation to those who looked at it and saw the marks of the Accident."

"It is so well known that it hardly matters," the Caliph said – alluding to the murder of his father Mutawakkil at the hands of the Turks.

Consequently, we scented the carpet and placed it under his feet.

Wasif and Bugha then pressed the man, saying:

"As soon as the Commander of the Faithful leaves his audience, take the carpet and throw it on the fire."

And, indeed, immediately on the Caliph's departure, it was burned before the eyes of Wasif and Bugha.'

'A few days later, however,' adds Ayyub, 'Muntasir said:

"Spread out that carpet again!"

"Where indeed is the carpet to be found now?" I said to him.

"Well, what has happened to it?" the Caliph wanted to know.

I told him that I had been forced to burn it, on the orders of Wasif and Bugha. He remained silent and never mentioned it to me again as long as he lived.'

VII:290-294
§§ 2979-2982

(Omitted: VII:294-295; §§ 2983-2984. Miscellaneous verses.)

VICIOUS VIZIERS

Muntasir, having exiled Ubaid Allah, took as vizier Ahmad ibn al-Khasib – but he was not slow to regret it. One day, Ahmad was riding with his escort when a suppliant held out a petition to him, begging for justice. The vizier slipped his foot out of the stirrup and kicked the man in the chest with such violence that he knocked him down. The story of this piece of brutality spread among the people and a poet of the time said:

> Tell the Caliph: 'Cousin of the Prophet,
> Hobble your vizier, for he kicks.
> Hobble him so he'll stop kicking people –
> And incidently, if you need money
> Look in his house.'

If this poet had been a contemporary of the vizier Hamid ibn Abbas when he filled the position of vizier to Muqtadir, he would have been witness to acts of violence very like those of Ibn al-Khasib. For example, one day this vizier threw himself on a person who was talking to him, dragged his robes down over his shoulders and struck him viciously across the throat.

Another day, Umm Musa, of the House of Hashim, overseer of the palace – or another woman of the same rank – went to him over some matter of money, in response to a message from Muqtadir. The vizier, in replying to her, spoke in the following insulting manner:

'Fart and pick it up; count and don't make mistakes!'

The woman was dumbfounded. She cut short the business which had brought her there and ran straight to Muqtadir and his consort to tell them what had happened. But the Caliph – it just so happened it was a day on which a feast and concert were being held – ordered his musicians, the slave girls, to take this piece of invective as the theme for the song of the day.

Further details on Hamid and on others of the Abbasid viziers and on the Umayyad secretaries, up to the present year of 332 AH/944 AD, are to be found in my *Intermediate History*.

VII:296-297
§§ 2985-2986

ON THE DEATH OF MUNTASIR

I have the following story from Abu al-Abbas Ahmad ibn Muhammad ibn Musa ibn al-Furat:

'Ahmad ibn al-Khasib disliked my father, who was one of his agents. Someone attached to the staff of the inner council came and said:

"The vizier has sent someone into your jurisdiction with instructions to stir up trouble against your father and extort a considerable sum of money from him" – he told me the figure.

A secretary, one of our friends, was with me at the time. I sat down and hurriedly began to write the news to my father, without paying any attention to my friend. He propped himself up on the cushions and fell asleep. Soon, however, he awoke, profoundly disturbed, and said:

"I have just had a strange dream. I saw Ahmad ibn al-Khasib standing here in this room and saying: 'The Caliph Muntasir will die in three days.'" '

Ibn al-Furat continued his story:

'I pointed out to my friend that just then the Caliph was at the hippodrome playing polo, and that dreams of this kind were the result of phlegm and bile; besides, we had just finished eating. We were still discussing it when someone came in and said:

"I have just seen the vizier in the inner chambers. He was looking disturbed."

I wanted to know why and was told:

"The Caliph Muntasir left the hippodrome streaming with sweat and went to the baths. He then fell asleep in the *badhhanj* [a belvedere equipped with ventilators] and caught a cold, which has turned into a worrying fever."

Ahmad ibn al-Khasib hastened to him and said:

"How could you, my lord! You, so versed in philosophy, the wisest man of the age, how could you dismount, exhausted, and after bathing go to sleep still sweating, in a draught!"

"Well," answered Muntasir, "do you fear I will die of it then? Last night someone appeared to me in my sleep and told me that I shall live twenty-five years. I took these words as a promise of longevity and have concluded from them that that will be the duration of my reign."

'Three days later he was dead,' added Ibn al-Furat, 'and on calculating his age, it was found that he had just completed twenty-five years.'

Most historians relate that this Caliph was struck down with a chill on a Thursday,* five days before the end of the month of Rabi' I, and that he died at the hour of the afternoon prayer on the 5th of Rabi' II. The prayers at the funeral were recited by Ahmad ibn Muhammad al-Musta'in.

Muntasir is the first Abbasid Caliph whose burial place was not kept secret. Hubshiya, his mother, begged, and was granted, permission to raise a tomb for him in public view at Samarra.

According to another version of the story, he was bled with a poisoned lancet by the physician Taifuri. The Caliph was then considering disbanding the Turkish troops and had sent Wasif at the head of a considerable army on a summer campaign against the Byzantines at Tarsus. One day, seeing Bugha the Younger approaching the castle, surrounded by a numerous Turkish guard, he turned to Fadl ibn al-Ma'mun and said:

'May God slay me if I don't kill them and scatter their divisions in vengeance for their murder of Mutawakkil!'

It was then that the Turks, learning of his plans and the measures he intended to take against them, began to look for an opportunity to destroy him. One day he complained that his blood was over-heated and had himself cupped. After they had drawn off 300 drams of blood, he took a certain potion and at once felt his strength drain away. It is also said that the lancet used by the doctor was poisoned.

Ibn Abi al-Dunya has handed on the following account of a dream of Abd al-Malik ibn Sulaiman ibn Abi Ja'far:

'I saw in a dream Mutawakkil and Fath ibn Khaqan in the midst of the flames. Muntasir came and asked to be allowed to join them, but they would not let him in. Mutawakkil then turned to me and said:

"Abd al-Malik, repeat these words to Muntasir: 'You will drink of that same cup from which you made us drink.' "

On the following morning I went to Muntasir and found him stricken with fever. I visited him constantly and towards the end I heard him murmur these words:

"I cut short their lives and now mine is cut short."

And indeed, he died of that illness.'

VII:297-301
§§ 2987-2991

(Omitted: VII:302-309, §§ 2992-3000. Virtues of Muntasir and vices of his viziers; Desecration of the Alid tombs; Muntasir's sympathy for the Alids; Verses; Kharijite revolt; The succession.)

THE GENEROSITY OF MUNTASIR

Abu al-Hasan Ahmad ibn Ali ibn Yahya, known as Ibn Nadim, 'Son of the Courtier', told me the following story, which was handed on to him by his father Ali ibn Yahya al-Munajjim – 'The Astrologer':

'I have never seen,' Ali said, 'a man to equal Muntasir, nor one who knew so well how to be generous without pride or affectation. One day, he noticed that I was sad and thoughtful. Indeed, adjoining my estate there was a property I very much wished to buy and had very cleverly persuaded the owner to sell it to me – but just at that time I did not happen to have the necessary sum available. It was with all this on my mind that I went to see Muntasir, who, struck by my downcast and preoccupied air, said:

"You look very worried. What has happened?"

I would have preferred not to have told him the story and kept my plight hidden, but he pressed me and I was forced to tell him the whole unvarnished tale of the property.

"What's it worth?" asked Muntasir.

"Thirty thousand dirhams," I answered.

"And how much of that sum do you have put by?"

"Ten thousand."

He cut short the conversation without answering and seemed to pay no further attention to me. He had an inkwell and a sheet of paper brought and set his seal to some decree, the contents of which I did not know. Then, signing to a servant who stood behind him, he gave some order which I could not overhear. The page set off in haste and the Caliph tried to entertain me, making most of the conversational effort himself, until his messenger returned. When this last appeared before him, Muntasir rose and said:

"Ali, you can go home if you like."

I had reckoned, when the Caliph questioned me, that he would give me the whole sum, or at least half, and so I withdrew in consternation. When I reached home, my steward came out to meet me and said:

"A eunuch came just now from the Commander of the Faithful with a mule laden with two sacks each containing ten thousand dirhams. He delivered them to me and asked for a receipt."

I was almost out of my mind with joy,' continued Ali, 'and went into the house refusing to believe my steward's words until he actually showed me the two sacks. Then, having thanked God for the favour he had granted me, I had the owner of

273

The Meadows of Gold

the estate in question called without delay. I paid him in full and spent my day in the formalities involved in taking possession and obtaining the necessary witnesses to the sale.

The following day, I went to Muntasir, but he never said a word to me about the estate and never asked me a single question on the subject, until death parted us for ever.'

AN OLD LOVE REGAINED

Abu Fadl ibn Abi Tahir tells the following story in his book entitled *A History of Authors*, on the authority of Abu Uthman Sa'id ibn Muhammad al-Saghir, the Caliph's freedman:

'In the course of his reign, Muntasir was intimate with a certain number of courtiers, among them Salih ibn Muhammad, known as al-Hariri. One day the conversation fell on love and affairs of the heart. Muntasir asked one of those present:

"Tell me, what loss troubles the soul most painfully?"

"It is," came the reply, "the loss of a friend with whom one identifies, the death of a person with whom one is intimately linked."

Another courtier answered as follows:

"Nothing equals in violence the unquiet mind of one who loves and the agony of a soul torn from its beloved. The accusations of the censorious tear those hearts where love reigns and pierce the ears of lovers like earrings. The pains of love are like consuming fires in their hearts and their secret sufferings cause tears to flow from their eyes like water from a water wheel. Only those who have wept gazing at ruins or hearing a song will understand what I am saying."

"Poor lover," said a third, "everything is inimical to him. The sound of the wind moves him, the lightning flash breaks his slumber, reproaches wound him, absence gnaws at him, memory is pain and the approach of the beloved disturbs him. Night adds to his torments; sleep flees from his eyes, the sight of an abandoned dwelling place consumes his heart, while ruins produce a flow of tears. In vain do lovers seek relief from their suffering by meeting and parting – this remedy is useless and there is no abatement of their pain. This is what the following verses express so eloquently:

> They say a lover gets bored*
> When close to the object of his love
> And that absence heals his passion.
>
> We have tried all remedies
> And nothing has worked.
> But it is better to be close
> To one's love than far away."

The Meadows of Gold

Each gave his opinion and the conversation continued on this theme for a long time. Muntasir asked:

"Hariri, have you ever been in love?"

"Yes, O Commander of the Faithful, and by God, my heart still bears the imprint of that love."

"Who was its object?"

"O Commander of the Faithful, I was living at Rusafa in the reign of Mu'tasim. Qaina, one of the slave women who had borne a son to Harun al-Rashid, had a young slave girl who ran errands for her, looked after her affairs and received people with whom her mistress, who was then in charge of the domestic affairs of the palace, might have business. This girl often passed me and I always greeted her respectfully and looked at her admiringly. Later, I wrote to her, but she sent my messenger away with threats. I sat in her path, hoping to get a chance to talk to her, but when she saw me, she laughed at me and made a sign to her companions to mock and tease me. In the end, I gave up seeing her, but still in the depths of my heart there is a flame which does not go out, an unslaked thirst, a pain which constantly revives."

"Do you want me to summon your pretty one?" asked the Caliph. "If she is free, I will marry her to you; if she is a slave, I will buy her."

"O Commander of the Faithful, I have no more burning desire, no more pressing wish!"

Muntasir summoned Ahmad ibn al-Khasib and told him to send one of his pages to deal with this affair, carrying letters of confirmation for Ibrahim ibn Ishaq and for the eunuch Salih, the administrator of the royal harem at Baghdad. The messenger set out. The slave had been freed by her mistress Qaina and she had passed from the category of young slave girls to that of senior women. She was brought before Muntasir, who looked at her with some attention. He saw a woman already old, bowed and withered, yet preserving some traces of past beauty.

"Do you want me to arrange a marriage for you?" he asked her.

"I am only your freedwoman," she replied. "Do what seems good to you, O Commander of the Faithful."

Muntasir called Salih, married him to his old flame and provided a dowry. Then, wanting to amuse himself, he ordered nuts covered in sheet lead and almonds dyed with saffron, which he scattered over the married couple – in lieu of gold and silver coins.

This woman lived a long time with her husband, but in the end he got tired of her and they separated.

VII:311-315
§§ 3003-3006

(Omitted: VII:315-316; § 3007. Verses.)

LOVE AT FIRST SIGHT

Abu Uthman Sa'id ibn Muhammad al-Saghir tells the following tale:

'While Muntasir was in power, he sent me to Egypt with a mission to the Sultan. There I fell in love with a girl whom a slave dealer had put up for sale. She was beautifully made, charming to look at, and her qualities and perfections gave her great value. I offered a good price, but her master refused to sell her for less than a thousand dinars – a sum which I did not then possess.

I had to leave, but I carried the memory of her away with me in my heart. A real love took root and I ceaselessly regretted having let slip the opportunity to buy the girl.

On my return, having fulfilled my mission and reported on it to the Caliph – who approved of the way I had carried it out – he asked me how I was and whether there was anything I needed. I told him of the girl and revealed how I had fallen in love with her, but he turned away.

The more severely he treated me, the more my heart fell under her spell and the more my patience wore thin. I tried to forget her with other women, but they only served to fan my ardour, without providing any consolation. Meanwhile, every time I appeared before Muntasir or prepared to leave him, he took pleasure in talking to me about the girl and exciting my passion for her. In vain I begged his courtiers, his close friends, those of his slave girls who were in his good graces and those who had borne him children, and even his grandmother, to persuade him to buy me the girl I loved. But he would not agree to do what I wanted and made me ashamed of my lack of self-control.

In fact, however, he had ordered his vizier Ahmad ibn al-Khasib to write to the governor of Egypt and have him buy the girl and send her to him – all without my knowledge. His orders were obeyed. When she appeared before him and he saw and heard her, he found my love forgiveable and he turned her over to the superintendent of the slave girls to perfect her training.

One fine day, he bade me sit in his audience hall and ordered the slave girl brought as far as the curtain. As soon as I heard her sing, I knew it was she. I did not want to show that I had recognized her, but I was absolutely at the end of my tether and I betrayed my innermost feelings.

"Sa'id, what's the matter with you?" asked the Caliph.

"Nothing, O Commander of the Faithful," I answered.

He chose an air which I had told him I had heard this slave girl sing and which had given me the greatest pleasure, and she sang it.

The Meadows of Gold

"Do you know this piece?" he asked.

"By God, O Commander of the Faithful, I do, and I had hoped to become the possessor of she that sang it, but today my hopes are dashed and I am like a man who would kill himself with his own hand or willingly call down death upon his own head!"

"No, Sa'id," answered the Caliph, "it was for you and you alone that I bought this young girl, and as God is my witness, I have seen her face only once – when I went to visit her as she was recuperating from the fatigues of the journey and the tiresomeness of moving. Now she is yours."

I thanked the Caliph by every means in my power and those present joined their thanks to mine. He then gave orders and the slave girl was splendidly dressed and conducted to my house.

And thus I returned to life after nearly dying of despair. The girl became my favourite wife and the children she bore me became the best loved of all my children.'

MECCAN MORALS

Among those piquant anecdotes whose heroes are libertines and buffoons, there is one which has been handed down to Abu Fadl ibn Abi Tahir by Ahmad ibn al-Harith al-Khazzaz according to the account given by Mada'ini and Abu Ali al-Hirmazi, and here it is:

'In Mecca, there was a man of the most shameless character who gathered men and women at his house for very suspicious purposes. He was a *sharif*, of the family of Quraish, but his name is not given.

The inhabitants of Mecca complained and the governor exiled him to Arafat. The man took a house there and then slipped secretly back to the city, found his fellow debauchees of both sexes and asked them why they were avoiding him.

"How can we come and see you," they said, "now that you live out at Arafat?"

"It is only a two-dirham ride by donkey," he replied, "and at my house you will find safety, entertainment, privacy and pleasure."

"You are absolutely right," they said, and their visits became so frequent that a number of Meccan adolescents and servants fell victim to their practices. A new complaint was addressed to the governor, who had the offender brought to him.

"Enemy of God," he said, "I drove you out of the Holy City and you have reappeared at a sacred place to commit every sort of vicious and reprehensible act!"

"Amir favoured by God," answered the culprit, "they are jealous and so accuse me!"

To this the Meccans replied:

"Only one piece of evidence is required to settle the matter between us. Collect the donkeys which are hired out and loose them in the direction of Arafat. If they do not go straight to this man's house – having got into the habit of going there carrying libertines and debauchees – you can consider him to be in the right."

"Indeed, that would be a reasonable test," said the governor.

On his orders all the donkeys were gathered together and then set free. They stopped in front of the house in question. The governor was told of it by his agents. He exclaimed that he needed no further proof and ordered the guilty man to be stripped. The culprit, on seeing the officer of justice armed with a whip, said to the governor:

"Amir favoured by God, do I really have to be whipped?"

"You do indeed, enemy of God!"

"Well, strike then," said the man, "but by God the cuts of the whip will hurt

The Meadows of Gold

no more than the sarcasms the people of Iraq will make at your expense. 'The Meccans,' they will say, 'accept the testimony of donkeys in their lawcourts – the Meccans, who reproach us with being satisfied with a single witness and an oath from the plaintiff.' "

"You need not be whipped today," replied the governor, laughing, and set him free and ceased troubling him.'

The most interesting events in the life of Muntasir, his poems, witty remarks, private gatherings, letters and correspondence written before his accession to the throne are all – or at least all that I thought worth mentioning and have not set down here – related in my *Historical Annals, or History of the Peoples Whom Time Has Destroyed, Vanished Nations and Kingdoms Which Have Passsed Away*. This is also true of my *Intermediate History*, for what I put in one of my books, I do not put in another – otherwise they would all be the same and form a single work.

Once the present work is finished, I will write another, covering all sorts of topics, without confining myself to any regular plan or orderly system of compilation. Thus, I will gather together, just as I feel inclined, entertaining stories, literary anecdotes and miscellaneous information. This book will, God willing, provide a sequel to my earlier works and supplement my previous writings.

THE CALIPHATE OF MUSTA'IN

Ahmad ibn Muhammad ibn al-Mu'tasim was proclaimed Caliph the day Muntasir died, that is, Sunday, the 5th of Rabi' II 248 AH/862 AD. He was known as Abu al-Abbas. His mother was a slave of Slavic origin, named Mukhariq. Musta'in abdicated in favour of Mu'tazz. He reigned three years and eight months, or according to others, three years and nine months. He was killed on Wednesday, the 3rd of Shawwal 252 AH/866 AD at the age of thirty-five years.

THE AFTERMATH

Musta'in chose as his vizier Abu Musa Utamish, but the real work was performed by a secretary of Utamish named Shuja' ibn al-Qasim. After the murder of Utamish and his secretary Shuja', the post of vizier was occupied by Ahmad ibn Salih ibn Shirzad.

When Wasif and Bugha killed Baghir the Turk, the Turkish freedmen rose, and Wasif and Bugha fled to Baghdad, taking Musta'in with them. They kept him in the house of Muhammad ibn Abd Allah ibn Tahir. Musta'in had no power; power belonged to Bugha and Wasif, who reigned as absolute masters. Then Baghdad was beseiged, as I have related in my *Intermediate History*.

The following verses, composed at this time, refer to Musta'in.

> A Caliph in a cage,
> Between Wasif and Bugha.
> He repeats whatever they say,
> Just like a parrot.

VII:324-325
§ 3016

(Omitted: VII:325-347; §§ 3017-3041. Poems; The revolt of Yahya ibn Umar; Ja'fari's comments; An elegy; Yahya's character; More laments; The poet al-Himmani; His poetry; Revolts in Tabaristan, Rayy, Qazwin and Kufa; Musta'in makes over Mecca, Medina, Basra and Kufa to his son as fiefs and plans to name his heir presumptive.)

THINGS THAT GIVE PLEASURE

Abu al-Abbas al-Makki tells the following story:
'I was a familiar of Muhammad ibn Tahir when he was at Rayy, before his expedition against the House of Abu Talib, and I never saw him more gay and happy than in the days immediately before the Alid revolt in that city. It was in the year 250 AH/864 AD.

One night I was talking to him. His house was filled with gaiety and the curtain had just been lowered for the evening's entertainment.

"I think I would like to eat something," Muhammad said, "what shall I have?"

"The breast of a partridge, or a slice of cold lamb," I suggested.

Muhammad said: "O page, bring me a loaf of bread, vinegar and salt," and began to eat.

The following night he said to me:

"Abu al-Abbas, I think I feel hungry. What would you advise me to eat?"

"What you had yesterday," I replied.

"You don't understand the subtlety of my two questions," he went on. "Yesterday, I said: 'I think I would like to eat something,' but now I am saying: 'I think I am hungry,' which is quite different."

He had supper served and then said:

"Describe to me the pleasures of the table, of scents, of women and horses."

"In prose or verse?" I asked.

"In prose."

So I began as follows:

"The best meal is a dish seasoned by appetite."

"What is the best drink?" he enquired.

"A glass of wine to quench your thirst, which one hands on to a well loved friend."

"What is the most enjoyable music?"

"The four-stringed lute played by a girl sitting cross-legged, whose singing is wonderful and whose voice strikes the heart."

"What is the most delicious scent?"

"The breath of a lover and the presence of a son you have raised."

"Who is the most seductive of women?"

"She whom one leaves with regret and to whom one returns in rapture."

"And which is the most spirited of horses?"

The Meadows of Gold

"The horse which has a wide mouth, large eyes and escapes when pursued and catches up when he gives chase."

"Well spoken," said Muhammad ibn Tahir and, addressing a page: "Bishr, give him a hundred dinars!"

"What did I do to deserve two hundred dinars?" I asked.

"Ah!" said Muhammad, "so you are adding a hundred on your own initiative, are you? Page – first give him the hundred dinars as we ordered and then another hundred to reward him for the high opinion he has of our generosity."

And I took my leave of Muhammad ibn Tahir, carrying off this sum. Only a week passed between this meeting and his departure from Rayy.'

VII:347-349
§ 3042

AFRA AND URWA

The Caliph Musta'in had a profound knowledge of history and the famous battles of the Arabs before the coming of Islam, and everything connected with the past excited his curiosity. Here is an anecdote related by Ibn Duraid, as it was told to him by Abu al-Baida, the freedman of Ja'far Tayyar and a very agreeable story-teller:

'We had come from Medina as a deputation to the court of Musta'in at Samarra. Among our number were several descendants of Abu Talib and others descended from the Ansar. We waited for about a month to obtain an audience, but at last we were admitted and each of us had an opportunity to speak and express himself freely. Musta'in treated us in a pleasant and friendly way, and began to talk of Medina and Mecca and their histories. Now it so happened that no one knew as much as I did on this subject. I therefore asked:

"Does the Commander of the Faithful permit me to speak?"

"Yes," he said.

I told him much on the topic which so interested him. The currents of the conversations swept us from one historical question to another, and when at last we took our leave of him, the Caliph had us given money and presents.

As night was falling, one of his eunuchs, accompanied by a number of Turkish soldiers and horsemen, came to us. They had me mount a horse which they had brought on a leading rein for the purpose and thus I was brought before Musta'in. He was holding audience in the Jawsaq Palace. He received me kindly, signed me to draw near and, having spoken a few affectionate words, started a conversation on history, on the battles of the Arabs, and on those among them who died for love.

And thus it was that we came to talk of the Bani Udhra and the celebrated lovers of that tribe. He asked me what I knew of Urwa ibn Hizam and his adventures with Afra.

"Commander of the Faithful," I replied, "after leaving Afra bint Iqal, Urwa ibn Hizam fell prey to his regrets and died for love of her. A group of horsemen happened to pass and recognized him. When they reached the dwelling place of Afra, one of the riders sang out in a mournful voice:

O palace wherein dwell
Those who do not care,
We announce to you

The Meadows of Gold

The death of Urwa ibn Hizam.

She heard his voice and looking down from a high place, said:

O riders spurring on your mounts, woe to you!
Urwa ibn Hizam, dead? Can it be true?

One of the riders replied:

Yes! We left him in a far country
Lying among wasteland and hills.

She went on:

If what you say is true,
Know that you have proclaimed
The death of the moon in the dark.

May no youth after you taste pleasure,
May no one return safe from absence.
May no woman give birth to one so noble.
May no woman rejoice in her lover.
May you never reach your journey's end,
May your food lose all its savour.

She questioned him on the place where they had buried him. They told her where it was and she set out. Near the tomb she said:
'Let me dismount. I must satisfy a need.'
They helped her down and she ran to the tomb and flung herself full length upon it. Soon she gave a piercing cry which frightened her companions. They hastened to her and found her stretched out dead on the stone above the grave. And so they buried her there, beside his tomb."
Musta'in then said:
"Can you add any details to the story you have just told?"
"Certainly, O Commander of the Faithful," I answered. "Here is a tradition I have from Malik ibn al-Sabbah al-Adawi, to whom it was transmitted by Haitham ibn Adi ibn Hisham ibn Urwa, who had it from Urwa, his father:*
'Uthman ibn Affan ordered me to distribute alms among the Bani Udhra and the tribe of Baliyy, to one of their sub-tribes called the Bani Minbadha. I saw a new tent pitched a little way from the encampment. I went over to it. A young man was sleeping in the shade of the tent and an old woman was sitting in a corner. The young man looked up and saw me, and murmured in a weak voice:

I have paid the fee of the sorcerer of Yamama

Afra and Urwa

> And that of the one from Najran,
> So that they would restore me to health.
> They said "Of course you will recover,"
> And left with those who had come to visit me.
> They tried every spell they knew,
> And there is no potion they have not made me drink.
> They said: "May God heal you! Our hands
> Are not strong enough to lift the weight that bears you down."
> Yearning for Afra consumes me. It feels
> Like the point of a spear tearing my vitals.
> Afra is all I hold most dear,
> Afra stands me in stead of all other things.
> I am glad of the promise of resurrection,
> Since they say that on that day Afra and I will meet.
> May God curse the gossiping tongues that said
> "That woman is certainly very friendly with so-and-so!"

He gave a small groan. I looked carefully at his face. He was dead.

"Old woman," I said, "I think that he who slept in the shadow of your tent is dead."

"By God, I think so too!" she said. Then she looked in his face and cried: "By the Master of the Ka'ba, he is no more!"

I asked the name of that unhappy man.

"Urwa ibn Hizam of the Bani Udhra," she replied, "and I am his mother, and by God, for a whole year I have not heard him utter a single word of complaint; it was only this morning that I came upon him reciting these lines:

> If ever mothers should weep,
> Let them weep today,
> For today I will die.
>
> Let them sing the dirge for me now
> For when my friends carry me away
> On their shoulders I shall hear no more."

I did not want to leave before having taken part in the bathing of the corpse, the shrouding, the last prayers and the burial.

"Why did you not want to do that?" asked Uthman.

"In order to share in the merits of a martyr," I replied.

The Caliph,' added Abu al-Baida, 'offered a present to my companions, and gave me a gift superior to theirs.'

VII:349-355
§§ 3043-3047

(Omitted: VII:355-360; §§ 3048-3053. The loves of Majnun and Laila.)

BUGHA THE ELDER

In 248 AH/862 AD, the Turk, Bugha the Elder, died at the age of more than ninety years. No one had taken part in as many battles as he and yet he was never wounded. He invested his son Musa with all the honours that he himself had received and, after gathering all his supporters about him, conferred the command on his son.

Bugha was a very devout man among the Turks. At first, as a page of Mu'tasim, he witnessed the great battles of the age. He always exposed himself to every danger and emerged unscathed. He often said: 'Destiny is a coat of mail' and he never wore armour of any sort. When he was reproached for his carelessness, he would tell the following story:

'I dreamed that the Prophet, may prayers and peace be upon him, appeared to me, surrounded by a number of his companions and said:

"Bugha, you were good to a man of my people and the prayers he has offered for you have been granted."

"Messenger of God," I asked, "who was this man?"

"He whom you delivered from the wild beasts."

"Messenger of God," I went on, "pray to your Lord that He may lengthen my days."

The Prophet raised his hands to heaven and prayed thus:

"O God, lengthen his life and fulfil his destiny."

"Messenger of God," I continued, "I want ninety-five years."

Then someone who was standing in front of the Prophet added:

"And may he be preserved from all misfortune!"

I asked the man:

"Who are you?"

"I am Ali, the son of Abu Talib," he replied.

And I awoke murmuring the words:

"Ali, the son of Abu Talib." '

Bugha was always generous and benevolent to the Alids. When they asked: 'Who was the man you saved from the wild beasts?' this is what he replied:

'A man was brought before Mu'tasim accused of heresy. As a result of a secret deliberation held during the night, Mu'tasim ordered me: "Take him and throw him to the wild beasts." I led the prisoner away and, indignant at what he had done, was about to throw him into the pit when I heard him speak these words:

"You know, oh my God, I only spoke in Your name and that I wished to please

You by my obedience and by upholding the truth against those who had opposed You. Will You not deliver me?"

'At these words,' added Bugha, 'I began to tremble. I was deeply moved and fear possessed my heart. I snatched the man from the edge of the lions' pit into which I was going to hurl him and took him to my apartment, where I hid him. I then went back to Mu'tasim.

"Well?" the Caliph asked.

"It is done, I have thrown him in," I replied.

"What did he say?"

"I am a foreigner," I retorted. "He was speaking Arabic and I don't know what he said. Anyway he was a rough common fellow."

As day broke, I said to my protégé:

"The gates are open. I will have you go out with the guardsmen. You see that I am sacrificing myself for you and that I have saved you at the risk of my own life. Take care never to show yourself as long as Mu'tasim lives."

"I won't," he said.

"But what is your story?" I asked.

"One of the Caliph's agents descended on our country, committing all sorts of crimes and excesses and stifling the truth to make error triumph. His behaviour threatened to corrupt the purity of the Shari'a, and to overthrow the dogma of monotheism. Since I could find no one to help me against this man, I attacked him during the night and killed him, for his crime was one of those that the Shari'a punishes with death."''

MU'TAZZ ACCLAIMED CALIPH

When Musta'in had taken refuge at Baghdad with Bugha and Wasif, the Turks, Ferganians and *mawali* in revolt at Samarra agreed to send a delegation to the Caliph to entreat him to come back to his capital. In consequence, some of the most important of the *mawali* went to Baghdad, taking with them the staff and the striped mantle of the Prophet, several precious things from the royal treasury and 200,000 dinars. They begged Musta'in to return to the capital, recognized their guilt, admitted their faults and engaged on behalf of both themselves and their companions not to fall back into the wrong-doing with which he reproached them. But, despite their humble and submissive attitude, they received an unsatisfactory reply.

Returning to Samarra, they told their companions of the way they had been received and that they had nothing to hope from the return of the Caliph.

When Musta'in took refuge at Baghdad, he imprisoned Mu'tazz and Mu'ayyad instead of taking them with him, but, distrusting Muhammad ibn Wathiq, he took him along to Baghdad. This same Muhammad later succeeded in escaping under the cover of battle.

The *mawali* determined first to liberate Mu'tazz from his prison, swearing loyalty and obedience to him as Caliph and then agreeing to fight Musta'in and his allies, entrenched at Baghdad. They had Mu'tazz and his brother Mu'ayyad leave the place called 'Pearl of the Palace' – Lu'lu'at al-Jawsaq – where they were being held in captivity and swore allegiance to Mu'tazz on Wednesday, the 11th of Muharram 251 AH/865 AD.

On the following day, the new Caliph made his way in a great procession to the Audience Hall, where he received the people's oath of allegiance. He dressed his brother Mu'ayyad in a robe of honour and placed about his neck a necklace of black pearls and one of white, the first signifying that he was heir presumptive and the second that he was governor of the two holy cities, Mecca and Medina. After this ceremony, letters were sent out from Samarra to all the great cities of the empire, announcing the designation of Mu'tazz as Caliph. They were dated and signed by Ja'far ibn Mahmud, the secretary.

Next, Mu'tazz sent his brother Muwaffaq and some of his *mawali* to go and fight Musta'in in Baghdad. They set forth and war broke out in the city between the party of Mu'tazz and that of Musta'in. Muhammad ibn Wathiq succeeded in taking refuge with Mu'tazz. The fighting continued most bitterly between the two armies until the middle of the month of Safar and the cause of Mu'tazz

Mu'tazz Acclaimed Caliph

strengthened, while that of Musta'in grew weak and the revolt became general. It was then that Muhammad, the grandson of Tahir, entered into correspondence with Mu'tazz, became reconciled to him and inclined towards peace at the price of the dethronement of Musta'in. But the populace of Baghdad, when it learned of these plans, rose in indignation and gathered about the Caliph to protect him. The grandson of Tahir put Musta'in on view on the roof of his palace. The people, seeing him in the Prophet's striped mantle and holding the Prophet's staff, acclaimed him. Musta'in denied the rumours of his dethronement and expressed his gratitude to Tahir's grandson.

This last then met with Muwaffaq at Shammasiya – a suburb of Baghdad – and they agreed to depose Musta'in on the following conditions: he was to be granted an amnesty for his family and his children and for their private estates; he was to live at Mecca with those members of his family he wished to take with him, and that the town of Wasit in Iraq should be his place of residence until he set out for Mecca. Mu'tazz bound himself in writing and declared that if he broke any of his promises he should be accursed in the eyes of God and His Prophet and that his subjects' oath of allegiance to him should be abrogated. It would take too long to enumerate all the different clauses. Mu'tazz later tried to wriggle out of his oath when he broke his promises to Musta'in.

Musta'in announced his own deposition on Thursday, the 3rd of Muharram 252 AH/866 AD. A whole year had passed between that moment and his arrival in Baghdad. His reign, from the day that he was invested with the authority of Caliph, as we related above, until his downfall, lasted three years, eight months and twenty-eight days. But one must take into account the different opinions on this matter, which we have mentioned before.

He was first taken to the house of Hasan ibn Wahb at Baghdad, where he was reunited with his family and his children. Afterwards, he was moved to Wasit, guarded by Ahmad ibn Tulun, the Turk, who had not yet been appointed governor of Egypt. The public soon realized that Muhammad, the grandson of Tahir, had proved himself incapable of defending Musta'in when he asked for asylum, and that he had forsaken him in order to join the party of Mu'tazz. It was this which led a poet of the time who was living in Baghdad to say:

> For a whole year the Turks prowled around us,
> While that hyena, Tahir's grandson, kept to his lair.
> He hid, disgraced and despised
> And when he finally showed himself
> It was only to reveal his base treachery.
> You did not protect the rights of Musta'in!
> Instead you helped fate conspire against him.
> You have heaped up shame, cowardice and disgrace
> And will ever be a stain on the family of Tahir.

After the dethronement of Musta'in, which we have just related, Muwaffaq

The Meadows of Gold

went from Baghdad to Samarra. Mu'tazz gave him a robe of honour, crowned him and gave him two embroidered belts. He also distributed robes of honour to the generals of his suite. Ubaid Allah ibn Abd Allah ibn Tahir, the brother of Muhammad, brought Mu'tazz the striped cloak and staff of the Prophet, together with the royal sword and the crown jewels. The eunuch Shahak accompanied him and Muhammad wrote to Mu'tazz recommending this servant in the following terms:

'He who brings you the inheritance of the Messenger of God – may prayers and peace be upon him! – deserves that you should never violate the protection which is due him.'

At the time Musta'in was toppled from his throne, his vizier was Ahmad ibn Salih ibn Shirzad.

THE ASSASSINATION OF MUSTA'IN

In the month of Ramadan, in that same year 252 AH/866 AD, Mu'tazz sent his chamberlain Sa'id ibn Salih to intercept Musta'in, who had just left Wasit with an escort from that town. Sa'id met him on the outskirts of Samarra. He killed him and took his head to Mu'tazz. The corpse lay in the road until some of the common people thought to bury it.

Musta'in died on Wednesday, the 6th of Shawwal 252 AH/866 AD, at the age of thirty-five, as we said at the beginning of this chapter.

This is what the eunuch Shahak relates:

'I was Musta'in's travelling companion when Mu'tazz summoned him to Samarra, and we shared the same litter. When we reached Qatul, a considerable body of soldiers confronted us.

"Shahak," said Musta'in, "see who is commanding this division. If it is Sa'id the chamberlain, I am lost."

I recognized that officer and answered:

"It is he, by God!"

Musta'in cried out:

"We belong to God, and to Him do we return! My life is done!"

And he began to weep.

Sa'id, accosting him, struck him across the face with blows of his whip and then, forcing him to lie on the ground, sat on his chest and cut off his head, which he carried to the Caliph, as we have already said. From that moment, the power of Mu'tazz was established and his authority recognized by one and all.'

The events in the life of Musta'in which I have not given in this book, indeed in the present chapter, are to be found in the *Historical Annals* and the *Intermediate History*. I have only given such details as are to be read here so that no one will think that I have neglected them, or was in ignorance of them, for, thanks be to God, there are no historical events, biographical accounts, or important happenings which are not recorded in my various works.

'Above every learned man is One Who knows all.' (Koran 12:76).

THE CALIPHATE OF MU'TAZZ

Mu'tazz was proclaimed Caliph. His name was al-Zubair ibn Ja'far al-Mutawakkil and his mother was a slave named Qabiha. He was known as Abu Abd Allah. He was eighteen years old when he was proclaimed Caliph, following the abdication of Musta'in, on Thursday, the 2nd of Muharram 252 AH/866 AD as we have said before. After having received the oath of allegiance from the generals, the freedmen and the mercenary guards and people of Baghdad, the *khutba* was read in his name in the main mosques in both quarters of Baghdad. He abdicated on Monday, three days before the end of Rajab 255 AH/869 AD, and died six days later. He reigned four years and six months. He was buried at Samarra. The total length of his reign, from his election in Samarra, before the fall of Musta'in, till the day of his abdication, was four years, six months and some days, but if one calculates from the day of his election in Baghdad, he only reigned three years and seven months. He died at the age of twenty-four.

VII:372-373
§ 3065

(Omitted: VII:373-375; §§ 3066-3069. Poems on the deposition of Musta'in; Necrology for the years 248-50 AH/862-4 AD.)

A REMARKABLE RING

In 248 AH/862 AD the Caliph Musta'in drew out of his treasury a ring stone of red ruby, called '*al-Jabal*' – The Mountain. This jewel had been preserved most carefully by kings. Rashid bought it for 40,000 dinars; he had his first name, Ahmad, inscribed on it and wore it on his finger. This stone gave rise to all sorts of tales – that it had been handed down from one Chosroe to another in Persia and that it had been inscribed at a very early period. They also said that every king who had had his name inscribed upon this ring was murdered and that each murdered king's successor had the inscription of his predecessor obliterated and, finally, that most rulers, with rare exceptions, had therefore worn it without having their names incised on it.

This ruby shone in the night like a lamp. Set in a room where there was no light, it lit it with its fire. It was also observed that there were figures in the stone which glowed in the darkness.

I have, furthermore, given a long and interesting account of the jewel in question in my *Historical Annals*, while discussing the seals of the Persian kings. This ring was still to be seen during the reign of Muqtadir, but no one knows what has happened to it since.

VII:376-377
§ 3070

(Omitted: VII:377-383; §§ 3071-3080. Poems on the accession of Mu'tazz; The Caliph's viziers; Abu al-Hasan Ali ibn Muhammad ibn Ali ibn Musa ibn Ja'far ibn Muhammad dies, 254 AH/868 AD.)

THE DEATH OF MUHAMMAD, THE GRANDSON OF TAHIR

Under the Caliphate of Mu'tazz, Muhammad ibn Abd Allah ibn Tahir – Tahir's grandson – died, on the 15th of the month of Dhu al-Qa'da in the year 253 AH/ 867 AD, thirteen days after the death of Wasif and during an eclipse of the moon. His character was liberal and generous, his knowledge wide-ranging, his memory richly stored, while the distinction of his manners, his eloquence and his superiority in conversation set him above all his contemporaries.

Al-Husain ibn Ali ibn Tahir wrote an ode to him, from which these lines are taken:

> The moon and the amir are both eclipsed.
> The moon has vanished and the amir is gone.
> The moon's light will come back and shine.
> The light of the amir never will return.

VII:384
§ 3081

(Omitted: VII:385-393; §§ 3082-3089. Mani, the companion; His verses and witty exchanges.)

THE IMPRISONMENT OF MU'AYYAD

Mu'tazz was informed that Mu'ayyad was conspiring against him and that he had won a number of the Turkish *mawali* over to his side. As a result, he had him imprisoned, together with Muwaffaq, his full brother. Pressed to renounce his rights as heir apparent, Mu'ayyad relinquished them on oath, after having been given forty blows with a staff.

Shortly after, however, Mu'tazz learned that some Turks were scheming to break Mu'ayyad out of prison. On Thursday, the eighth day before the end of the month of Rajab 252 AH/866 AD, the body of Mu'ayyad was carried out of his cell. The qadis and doctors of law were called in to establish the cause of death, but they found no marks on the body. It is said that Mu'ayyad was wrapped in a sable cloak and that the ends were twisted until he died.

As for Muwaffaq, his imprisonment became increasingly harsh. Six months and three days passed from the time of his arrival in Samarra, where he had been received with so much honour, until the day that he was incarcerated. Next, he was exiled to Basra, thirteen days before the end of Ramadan and fifty days after the murder of Mu'ayyad. Ismail, the son of Qabiha and brother of Mu'tazz on both his father's and mother's side, was then named heir apparent in place of Mu'ayyad. The Turkish generals then gathered before the Caliph and asked that Wasif and Bugha should be spared. This was granted to them.

VII:393-394
§§ 3090-3091

(Omitted: VII:394-396; §§ 3092-3095. Revolts in Tabaristan and Mecca; 'In this year, 253 AH/867 AD, Safwan al-Uqaili, shaikh of the Diyar Mudar, died in the prisons of Samarra. In the same year the Fergana and Turkish troops living at Karkh-Samarra killed Wasif the Turk. Bugha managed to escape.')

THE MURDER OF BUGHA THE YOUNGER

In 254 AH/868 AD Bugha the Younger left Samarra to go to the Mosul region. The *mawali* pillaged his house and the troops under his command dispersed. Bugha boarded a boat in disguise, but some of the Maghribi soldiers attacked him at the bridge at Samarra and killed him. His head was exposed at Samarra, then it was sent to Baghdad and exhibited on the bridge.

Mu'tazz had never slept in peace while Bugha was alive and he was never parted from his weapons, by day or by night, so afraid was he of that man.

'I shall continue to act thus,' he would say, 'until Bugha has my head or I have his.'

He also used to say:

'I am always afraid that Bugha will suddenly drop from the sky or spring out of the ground in front of me.'

In fact, Bugha's plan had been to go down the Tigris secretly, to reach Samarra in the course of the night and to suborn the Turks of Mu'tazz's party by bribing them. But he ended as we have just described.

VII:396-397
§ 3096

(Omitted: VII:397-405; §§ 3097-3108. Abdication and assassination of Mu'tazz; Poems on the event; The luxury of Mu'tazz; Alid revolts; First hints of the Zanj rebellion.)

THE CALIPHATE OF MUHTADI

Muhtadi was proclaimed Caliph before midday on Wednesday, the last day of Rajab in the year 255 AH/869 AD. His mother, a slave of Byzantine origin, was called Qurb and he himself was known as Abu Abd Allah. He ascended the throne at the age of thirty-seven or thirty-nine and was killed before having completed his fortieth year in 256 AH/870 AD, after a reign of eleven months. He was buried at Samarra. Some historians give the year of his birth as 218 AH/833 AD.

Muhtadi, in spite of the brevity of his reign, had a number of viziers, all of whom escaped death and his wrath. One of these was Isa ibn Farrukhanshah.

The Caliph had built a great domed hall with four portals. He called it the Dome of Complaints, for it was there that he sat and heard the complaints of his subjects, both high-born and low. He 'commanded the good and forbade the bad'. He prohibited the use of wine and slave girl musicians and was remarkable for his justice. Every Friday he went to the congregational mosque and preached to the people and led them in prayer. But, tired of the burden which he imposed upon them in his efforts to lead them to the path of wisdom, his subjects, great and small, became impatient at his sway. They grew tired of his authority and began to hatch the plots which in the end cost him his life.

VIII:1-3
§§ 3109-3112

THE DEATH OF MU'TAZZ

Earlier in this book, in telling the story of Mu'tazz, I said a few words about the death of that Caliph, without going into the details of how it was brought about. Now, there is a great diversity of opinions concerning this matter and I have observed that there is a profound disagreement among the authors of biographies and chronicles and in general among all those who have concerned themselves with dynastic history. Thus, some have him die a natural death in prison under the Caliphate of Muhtadi at the date we have given, while others claim that he was deprived of food and drink during his imprisonment, so that he died of hunger and thirst. According to others, he was given an enema of boiling water, for it was noticed that when his corpse was exposed to view the belly was distended. Meanwhile, the most widespread version among historians of the Abbasids is that he was taken to a bath house, which he was forced to enter and prevented from leaving – but here again opinions vary. Some say he was left in this bath house until he breathed his last; according to others, he was dragged out at the very moment when the heat would have stifled him and made to drink iced water, which so disturbed his bowels and liver that he died on the spot.

This murder took place on the 2nd of the month of Shaban, 255 AH/869 AD. I have given the details, as well as the different theories to which this event gave rise, in my *Historical Annals*.

VIII:3-5
§§ 3113-3114

(Omitted: VIII:6-8; §§ 3115-3117. Alid and Dailamite revolts.)

THE DEATH OF MUHTADI

At this point, the revolt of the Kharijite Musawir al-Shari grew serious and he attacked Samarra at the head of his troops. The people suffered greatly, the lines of communication were cut and suddenly the Bedouin appeared everywhere.*

Muhtadi ordered Musa ibn Bugha and Baikbak to oppose this rebel. He even accompanied the two generals a certain way, but they came back, without, however, having met with the least resistance. The Caliph, told of their return, went to camp at Jisr Samarra – The Bridge of Samarra – with his regular troops from the Maghrib, Fergana and elsewhere, and prepared to fight Baikbak. It is thought that Baikbak had read a letter to Musa which Muhtadi had written him ordering that Musa be killed. It is also said that Musa had received an exactly similar message and that the two officers, realizing that the Caliph was trying to sow discord between them, gave up the expedition which they had undertaken.

Baikbak took up a position above Muhtadi's camp, while Musa skirted Samarra so as to avoid taking part in the fight against Muhtadi. A bloody battle with many casualties was then fought between Muhtadi and Baikbak. At first, the advantage lay with the Caliph, who forced his enemies to retreat, but he fell into an ambush which Baikbak had prepared for him and which was sprung by Yarjukh the Turk.

Muhtadi fled with his supporters and took refuge in Samarra, begging the common people to help and support him. But in vain he went up and down the markets of the city, with descendants of the Ansar before him, crying out for aid. At last, despairing of reinforcements, he went to the house of Ibn Khai'una and hid. Very soon, however, he was attacked, dragged from his place of refuge and taken to the house of Yarjukh.

'Do you want, then,' they said to him, 'to lead the people astray, along the road to disaster, along a path untrod before?'

'No,' replied the Caliph, 'I want to lead them along the way followed by the Messenger of God – may peace be upon him – by his family, and by the four Rightly Guided Caliphs.'

'But,' went on his adversaries, 'the Prophet had with him followers who had renounced this world and who longed only for the life to come, such as Abu Bakr, Umar, Uthman, Ali and many others, while your supporters and companions are Turks, Khazars, Ferganians, Maghribis, and other foreigners of all kinds, who know nothing of the duties required for their salvation and have no aim beyond the enjoyment of the good things of this world. How then can you lead them in the true path as you claim?'

A long debate with many passionate rejoinders then took place between Muhtadi and those who contradicted him on that point, and many other questions of the same kind were touched upon. They gave in, however, and appeared to yield.

The argument was almost over when the secretary, Sulaiman ibn Wahb, or perhaps someone else, said:

'You are being led astray and your agreement is a mistake. He gives you his tongue, but his intentions are something else again.'

And he added:

'Soon he will attack you all at once and throw you into confusion.'

At these words they turned and threw themselves on the Caliph with their *khanjars* in their hands. The first to wound him was a cousin of Baikbak. He cut his jugular with his *khanjar*, then threw himself upon his victim, set his mouth on the wound whence flowed great streams of blood, and sucked hungrily. This Turk was intoxicated. Having drunk great draughts of the Caliph's blood, he rose up over the body of his enemy, so newly dead, and cried:

'Comrades, I have just gorged myself on the blood of Muhtadi, as today I gorged myself with wine!'

The account you have just read of the death of this Caliph exists in different versions. The best known is that he was assassinated by being stabbed, as we have described. Others claim that he was killed by having his testicles crushed. Others maintain that he was squeezed between two great planks with cords until he died. According to some he was strangled, and to others again he was suffocated under carpets and cushions.

But, as soon as he was dead, his murderers bore him in procession, lamenting and weeping and showing their regret at having killed a Caliph whose piety and austere life was well known to them. It is said that this crime was committed on a Tuesday, the fourteenth day before the end of Rajab, 256 AH/870 AD.

Musa ibn Bugha and the Turk, Yarjukh, took no part in the Turkish outrage. The Turks hated the Caliph because he had killed Baikbak – in fact, when this leader fell into his hands, Muhtadi had his head cut off and threw it to his companions. Nevertheless, according to another version, Baikbak perished in the fighting mentioned above, which happened at the place known by the name of The Bridge at Samarra.

VIII:8-12
§§ 3118-3122

(Omitted: VIII:12-13; §§ 3123-3125. Muhtadi flogs his secretaries to death; Muhtadi leaves seventeen sons and six daughters; Other officials.)

THE ADVENTURE OF A GATE-CRASHER

Here is an amusing story which we owe to Ahmad ibn al-Mudabbir, and which is to be found in the collections known as 'The Histories of Spongers'. Ahmad ibn al-Mudabbir, who was not a man much given to the company of courtiers, had nevertheless gathered a select group of seven table companions, the only men he admitted to his home and with whom he relaxed. He had chosen them with care to keep him company and sit at his table, and each of them excelled in a particular art and had no rivals in it.

Now a certain gate-crasher named Ibn Darraj, a most exquisitely educated man, with a sharp and subtle mind, a master of every trick, manoeuvred so long and well that in the end he found out when Ahmad ibn al-Mudabbir and his friends met. He dressed like them and followed them into their host's house. The chamberlain, quite certain that the man was known to his master and the usual guests, let him in without the slightest difficulty. When Ahmad came out and saw the stranger, he said to the chamberlain:

'Go ask that man what he wants.'

The chamberlain was aghast. He understood that the trick played by the gate-crasher was about to be blamed on himself and it might well be that nothing but his own blood would satisfy Ibn al-Mudabbir's resentment. Dragging his feet, he made his way over to the stranger's side and said to him:

'The master wishes to know what business brings you here.'

'It is not a matter of business,' replied the gate-crasher.

His master having given him new orders, the chamberlain asked the intruder: 'How long have you been here?'

'We just arrived a moment ago, you tiresome man,' answered the gate-crasher.

'Go and ask him who he is,' demanded Ibn al-Mudabbir.

'Tell him I am a gate-crasher,' replied the other, 'and may God forgive you!'

'You are a gate-crasher?' Ibn al-Mudabbir said to him.

'Yes, truly,' he answered, 'may God give you strength!'

Ibn al-Mudabbir continued:

'Gate-crashers who push their way into people's homes, disturbing the pleasure of their privacy and searching out their secrets, are tolerated, but only on condition that they have certain talents – for example, that they play chess or backgammon, or that they can play the lute or the *tambur*.

303

The Meadows of Gold

'May God protect you!' answered the gate-crasher, 'I excel at all those.'

'What standard are you?'

'The highest.'

The master of the house asked one of his companions to play a game of chess with the stranger.

'May God favour you, my Lord!' said the gate-crasher. 'But what if I lose?'

'We will throw you out of the house.'

'If, on the other hand, I win?'

'A thousand dirhams shall be your reward.'

'May God protect you!' went on the intruder. 'But would you have someone bring the one thousand dirhams? Having them nearby will inspire me and be a sure pledge of victory.'

The sum in question was brought. The game began and the gate-crasher won. He was already stretching out his hand to seize the stake, when the chamberlain, who was trying to exonerate himself insofar as possible, said to Ibn al-Mudabbir:

'My lord, may God strengthen you! This man claims to be a first-class chess player, but your page, so-and-so, could beat him.'

The page in question was brought. He beat the gate-crasher. They were about to throw him out, but he said:

'Bring the backgammon!'

A set was brought, and he won. But the chamberlain intervened.

'My lord,' he said to the master of the house, 'this man is not a first-class backgammon player and so-and-so, our doorman, could certainly beat him.'

They brought the doorman, and indeed, he beat the gate-crasher.

'Get out!' everyone said.

But the gate-crasher turned to the master of the house:

'My lord, and the lute?'

They gave him a lute. He played it beautifully and everyone was charmed.

A new objection from the chamberlain:

'My lord,' he said to Ibn al-Mudabbir, 'we have in the neighbourhood an old man of the House of Hashim who teaches the slave girls music. He knows more about it than this man.'

The old man was brought in, and indeed, he was better than the gate-crasher. As they were about to throw him out, the gate-crasher demanded a *tambur*. The instrument was brought and he played it in a most superior manner and sang with such consummate skill that no one present had ever heard better.

'May God strengthen you, my lord!' cried the chamberlain yet again, 'our neighbour so-and-so, the fellow with the grain monopoly, is better than this man.'

The neighbour in question was called, and indeed, it was found that his playing was both more pleasant and more able. Ibn al-Mudabbir therefore addressed the gate-crasher:

'We have shown you all possible good will, but your gifts have only served to get you thrown out of this house.'

'O my lord,' answered the gate-crasher, 'I have one more remarkable talent.'

The Adventure of a Gate-Crasher

'What is it?'

'Will you have me brought an arbalest and fifty lead balls and have the chamberlain get down on his hands and knees. I will then aim all the balls at his backside and if even one misses you can cut my head off.'

The chamberlain shrieked with horror, but Ibn al-Mudabbir found it the perfect occasion to avenge his own discontent, feeling that such a punishment, inflicted on a careless servant who had allowed a gate-crasher into his palace, was perfectly just. He had two packsaddles brought and stacked one on top of the other, and then had the chamberlain tied on top. They then gave an arbalest to the gate-crasher, who set about shooting and never once missed his target. They then freed his victim, who was whining at the pain.

'Well now!' the gate-crasher asked him, 'and is there a better marksman than me about the place?'

'You cuckold!' shouted the chamberlain, 'no – not if they are going to use my ass as the target!'

VIII:13-18
§§ 3126-3128

(Omitted: VIII:18-19; § 3129. Comments on other stories of gate-crashers.)

THE AUSTERITY OF MUHTADI

Muhtadi had made austerity and religion the twin aims of his life. He liked to be surrounded with learned men and raised the status of jurists and overwhelmed them with favours.

'O descendants of Hashim,' he would say, 'let me follow the path of Umar ibn Abd al-Aziz,* that I may be among you as Umar ibn Abd al-Aziz was among the Umayyads.'

He cut down the luxury of clothes and carpets, of food and drink. He had the vessels of gold and silver brought out of the royal treasury and broken up in order to be converted into dinars and dirhams. On his orders the painted figures which decorated the rooms were obliterated. They slaughtered the rams and cocks which used to fight in the Caliph's presence, and the caged wild beasts suffered the same fate. He took up the brocade carpets and, generally, all carpets whose use is not authorized by Holy Law. While his predecessors had spent 10,000 dirhams each day at table, he made do for his food and general maintenance with a hundred dirhams daily and he used to fast.

They say that when he was murdered, they carried off his personal effects from the place where he had taken refuge. There was a locked basket which they thought was filled with gold and jewels, but when they opened it there was nothing inside but a woollen or horsehair robe and an iron collar, an instrument of self-mortification. One of his servants, questioned about this, replied as follows:

'As soon as night had fallen, Muhtadi would put on this hair shirt and fasten this collar about his neck and until morning broke he did not cease praying and prostrating himself. He would sleep a little after the evening prayer and then get up again.'

They add that one of his favourites was with him before his death, at the moment when, the sunset prayer being over, he was about to break his fast, and heard him utter the following prayer:

'O my God, it is said on the authority of Your Prophet Muhammad that there are three kinds of person whose prayers are never rejected: the prayer of the just Imam – now, I have tried to be just to my subjects; the prayer of the oppressed – now, I myself am oppressed; the prayer of he who fasts until the hour at which one breaks the fast – now, I am fasting.' After this prayer he invoked God's vengeance against his enemies and His protection against their violence.

The Austerity of Muhtadi

VIII:19-21
§§ 3130-3131

(Omitted: VIII:22-27; §§ 3132-3139. On the dogma of the creation of the Koran; A debate in the presence of Muhtadi; Some verses which pleased Muhtadi found on the back of one of the royal library catalogues.)

A TRADITION CONCERNING ALI

One of those who spent most time with Muhtadi was Muhammad ibn Ali al-Raba'i, a man who was good company and had a considerable knowledge of history and biography. He tells the following story:

'I often spent the night in Muhtadi's company. During one of these watches, the Caliph asked me if I knew the words gathered by Nawf from the lips of Ali ibn Abi Talib, one night that he spent sitting up with that Caliph.

"Yes, O Commander of the Faithful," I answered, "here is Nawf's own account:

'One night, I saw that Ali – may God be content with him – was wandering back and forth, his eyes fixed on the sky. Then he said to me:

"Nawf, are you asleep?"

"No, Commander of the Faithful," I replied. "I have been watching you since night fell."

"Nawf," continued Ali, "happy are they who have renounced the world and who aspire to nothing but the life to come!* For them, this earth, God's handiwork, is a rich carpet, the dust a couch, water a perfumed drink. The Koran is their cloak and prayer their covering. They consider this world as but a loan and follow in the path marked out by Jesus, son of Mary, on whom be peace! Know, O Nawf, that Almighty God revealed to his servant Jesus – may peace be upon him! – the following words:

'Say to the Children of Israel: Let no one enter into My houses unless their hearts be filled with submission, their looks modest and their hands pure, and tell them that I will not answer the prayers of him who has committed injustice towards any one of My creation."''

Raba'i adds:

'I confirm that Muhtadi wrote the preceding tradition with his own hand and that I saw him, more than once, in the middle of the night, in the room where he used to meditate, murmuring and weeping:

"Nawf, happy are they who have renounced this world and who aspire to nothing but the life to come!" and so on to the end of the tradition. And so it was, until the day on which he was murdered by the Turks.'

VIII:28-29
§§ 3140-3141

(Omitted: VIII:29-33; §§ 3142-3145. Muhtadi on the nature of man; The death of the twelfth Imam of the Shi'a; The leader of the Zanj; The Zanj rebellion.)

THE DEATH OF JAHIZ

In that same year 255 AH/869 AD, or others say, 256 AH/870 AD, Jahiz died at Basra, in the month of Muharram. Leaving aside his opinions on the legitimacy of the rule of the first three Caliphs,* there is no more prolific author among the Traditionists and scholars than Jahiz. It is true that Mada'ini has also written a large number of works, but he has limited himself to passing on material he has collected, while the writings of Jahiz, in spite of their well-known heretical tendencies,* polish the rust from the mind and seem to reveal the most incontrovertible proofs. These writings are very well organized and set down with consummate art; they are closely reasoned and embellished with all the allurements style can offer. When the author fears he is boring or is tiring his audience, he skilfully passes from the serious to the entertaining, and leaves the grave tomes of science for the lively ones of amusing stories.

Among many remarkable works, the *Book of Exposition and Demonstration* should be placed in the first rank. It is a work of mixed prose and verse, full of brilliant poems, interesting stories and choice rhetoric, and it is of a kind to satisfy even him who reads nothing but this one work. Let us also mention the *Book of Animals*, the *Book of Spongers*, the *Book of Misers* and other works no less perfect, in which the author neither tries to disparage nor to oppose. In a word, no Mu'tazilite, past or present, is more eloquent than Jahiz. This writer was in the service of Ibrahim ibn Sayyar as a page and there he had lessons and gathered his learning.

Yamut ibn al-Muzarra', of whom Jahiz was the maternal uncle, tells the following story:

'Some inhabitants of Basra, friends of my uncle, came to visit him during his last illness. They asked how he was and he answered them:

"I suffer from two things: pain and debt."

And he added:

"I am prey to ills which contend with one another; any one of them would be enough to put the fear of death into a man. But," he went on, referring to his age, "the worst is to have passed ninety years and more."

Indeed,' according to this same Yamut ibn Muzarra', 'Jahiz's right side was the seat of an inflamation so violent that it had to be constantly rubbed with a balm composed of sandalwood and camphor, while his left side was so numb and cold that it could have been slashed with scissors without his feeling a thing.

Here,' added Yamut, 'is something my uncle Jahiz told me:

"In Basra I knew a man who from morning to night did nothing but relieve other people's misfortunes."

'You are wearing yourself out,' I said to him. 'You are spoiling your clothes, overtaxing your mount and killing your page with work. You never grant yourself rest or pause. Why don't you slow down a little?'

This is what he replied:

'Neither the song of birds chirruping at dawn in the treetops nor the sweet voices of the singing girls accompanying themselves on the lute, give me such pleasure as the melodious sound of "thank you" spoken by those I have helped or to whom I have done some service.' "

Yamut refrained from visiting sick people for fear they should consider his name – which means 'He Will Die' – ill-omened.

He has left some interesting stories and fine poems. He lived at Tiberias, a town in the province of Jordan in Syria, where he died sometime after the year 300 AH/912 AD. He was an educated man, given to philosophical speculation, very skilled and talented in controversy.

His son, named Muhalhil, is one of the most distinguished poets of our age – 332 AH/944 AD. – and it is to him that the following verses, composed by his father, Yamut, are addressed:

> Muhalhil, I have drawn the milk
> Of good fortune and bad,
> But Fate has always opposed me
> And given me struggle and hardship.
> I have fought with men from every quarter
> And forced both strong and weak
> To yield to me.
> What pains my heart most
> Is the sight of a noble man
> Torn by the fangs of fate,
> The man of ancient lineage
> Brought low and the sons
> Of slaves on the throne.
> My eyes have forsworn sleep
> Although heavy from watching
> Lest you stray when I die.
> But by God's grace I have found
> My consolation in you,
> Whether I die or live.
> May you grow strong after my death,
> And may no disaster befall you!
> Say that your father shared his learning
> And when they ask his name,
> Say he was called Yamut.
> Far and near will pay tribute

The Death of Jahiz

> To your learning, which
> Calumny cannot bring low.

Other interesting details on the reign of Muhtadi will be found in my preceding works.

God is the giver of all help!

THE CALIPHATE OF MU'TAMID

Mu'tamid was hailed as Caliph on Tuesday,* the fourteenth day before the end of the month of Rajab, 256 AH/870 AD, at the age of twenty-five. He was known as Abu al-Abbas. His mother, a slave from Kufa, was named Fityan. Mu'tamid died in the month of Rajab 279 AH/892 AD. at the age of forty-eight, after a reign of twenty-three years.

VIII:38-39
§ 3153

(Omitted: VIII:39-46; §§ 3154-3162. War against the Zanj; Necrology; Muhtadi exiles Mu'tazz's mother, Qabiha, to Mecca; The revolt of Ya'qub ibn Laith al-Saffar, 'The Coppersmith'; His defeat.)

THE DISCIPLINE OF SAFFAR'S ARMY

Ya'qub ibn Laith al-Saffar died on Tuesday,* the seventh day before the end of Shawwal 265 AH/June 879 AD in the city of Gondeshapur, as we have said above, leaving in his treasury, 50,000,000 dirhams and 800,000 dinars. His brother, Amr ibn Laith, succeeded him.

The discipline which Ya'qub ibn Laith introduced into his armies leaves far behind everything we are told on this subject of the kings of antiquity, such as the Persians, and other rulers, ancient and modern. Nothing can be compared to the obedience of his soldiers and their unshakeable fidelity, and these were due both to the kindness and generosity which he showed towards them and to the respect which he succeeded in instilling into their hearts.

Here is a proof of this obedience. He was encamped in Persia and had allowed his men to put their mounts out to graze, when a change in circumstances compelled him to strike camp and leave the province he was occupying. He had his herald announce that the beasts should be brought in from the pastures. Then, a soldier was seen running to his mount and dragging the grass out of its mouth, for fear lest it should go on chewing after the proclamation. And he was heard to exhort the animal in Persian:

'*Amir al-Mu'minin davabra az tar buridand*,' which means: 'The Commander of the Faithful has forbidden the animals to graze.'

At the same time, one of his high-ranking officers was encountered wearing his breast-plate and armour with no clothing between the iron and his skin. He was asked to explain:

'At the very moment,' replied the man, 'that the Commander's herald cried "To arms!" I was naked and busy washing off the dirt. I had no time to dress before putting on my armour.'

When a man presented himself to enlist and expressed a wish to join up, Saffar studied his face and if the outward appearance of the stranger pleased him, he would question him and test his knowledge of handling the bow and lance and other skills. If this first examination satisfied him, he would then ask him who he was, what he had done, whence he came and in whose service he had been. If he approved of the replies to his questions, he would say to him:

'Tell me truly, what are your expenses, what do you own in the way of arms?'

Once he knew what the man had, he would have all the man's goods sold by special agents and the result of the sale, in gold and silver coin, would be made over to the Commander and set down in the register. From this moment on,

The Meadows of Gold

Saffar defrayed the soldier's expenses for clothes and weapons, food and drink, and provided him with horses, mules and asses from his own stables. In a word, he let him lack for nothing, in accordance with his rank and the requirements of his position. If, later, he was displeased with the man's behaviour and went back on his decision, he deprived him of the allowances he had granted him and the man left his service as he had entered it, but carrying with him the value of his personal possessions in gold and silver. If, on the other hand, the man had been recruited, he was granted extra pay, without his personal possessions being taken into account.

The army mounts were Saffar's property. He fed them at his own expense and had them cared for by stable boys and grooms. The only exception were certain special mounts, which belonged to Saffar, but were the responsibility of their riders. On all his expeditions, Saffar used a kind of wooden seat in the form of a throne. He was accustomed to sit on it, watching everything that went on in the camp, overseeing the animals' feed, observing any remissness on the part of his officers, so that the moment something troubled him he could set it right.

He had chosen from among his troops a thousand of the best men, celebrated for their wealth and courage, and had them formed into a company called 'The Golden Maces'. Each of these maces weighed one thousand *mithqals* of gold. A second company, also distinguished by their uniform and their wealth, followed them, and they were known as 'The Silver Maces'. On feast days and occasions when he wished to dazzle his enemies and display all his wealth, he would arm his men with the maces we have described, which had, in fact, also been made to serve as a cash reserve in case of need.

A most trustworthy man, who acted as Saffar's steward, was asked how the Commander lived in private life, who were his confidants and whether he received any one of them, alone, at night, to converse with intimately. The man replied that Saffar revealed his secrets to no one and that he took no one into his confidence as regarded his plans and decisions. He spent most of the day alone, meditating on his various enterprises, and he often appeared to support a plan quite different from that which he had secretly decided upon. He never asked either advice or counsel when making up his mind. His one relaxation and pastime was to summon the pages whom he was having trained and drilled. He would gather them together, hand out leather straps made specially for them and take pleasure in watching them fight in his presence. This was his favourite entertainment when he rested from the anxiety of his affairs.

In 260 AH/874 AD, or according to others, 259 AH/873 AD, Saffar gave battle to Hasan ibn Zaid al-Hasani in Tabaristan and, the latter having fled, pursued him most energetically. Saffar was accompanied by a delegation which had come to him with letters and a personal communication from Mu'tamid. On his return from this expedition against Hasan ibn Zaid, one of the Caliph's envoys, struck by the discipline and courage which Saffar's troops had displayed in the course of the campaign, said:

'I have never seen such a remarkable sight.'

The Discipline of Saffar's Army

'What I am about to show you is more remarkable still,' replied Saffar.

They soon reached the encampment of Hasan ibn Zaid. Piles of money, stores, arms, equipment, all was still just as the enemy had abandoned it at the moment of retreat. Not one of Saffar's soldiers had dared to touch it or even go near it, although they were camped nearby and from where their general had stationed them they could see all this wealth. At this the Caliph's envoy could not refrain from saying:

'What stern and severe discipline the Commander must have imposed on his troops to obtain such a result!'

Saffar had nothing to sit on but a piece of coarse cloth, which might have been seven spans long and two cubits wide, or a little more. Beside him he had his shield on which he leant and these comprised all the furnishings of his tent. When he wanted to sleep, by day or night, he stretched out against his shield, pulled down a banner and used it as a pillow. His clothing consisted of a caftan made of dyed stuff known as *fakhiti*.

He had established a custom whereby generals, chiefs and important men filed, according to their rank, past the threshold of his tent, so that he could see them as they appeared in the spaces between tent pegs and ropes. They entered a tent out of his line of vision, but placed so that he could see them entering and leaving. If he had something to say to one of them, an order to give, or an interdiction to enforce, he would summon him and give him his instructions. This march past took the place of the ceremony of ritual greeting. No one had the right to enter his presence except his brothers and an officer attached to his person, known as al-Aziz, 'The Powerful'. Behind his tent, another was pitched, near the pegs of his reception area. This was for the pages who served him. If he needed them, he raised his voice and called, and they came to him. Otherwise, he remained alone, day and night, with no servant at his bedside. Other tents were pitched in a circle around his; these were the quarters of 500 pages who watched by night, and over each of these was set a trustworthy man to prevent mistakes or negligence on their parts, for which he would be responsible.

Each day they slaughtered twenty sheep, which were then cooked in five great copper cauldrons. He also had stone vessels in which they served any other food he might want. Every day they prepared rice for him and *khabisa*, a pudding made of dates and cream, and *faludhaj*, a sweet made of honey and flour; this was in addition to the mutton stewed in the five cauldrons. After having eaten what he wanted of these fairly rough dishes, he distributed the remainder to the pages on duty at the entrance to his tent and to the men on guard round about in the different posts assigned to them, in accordance with their rank.

One of the envoys who had come to bring him a communication from the Caliph said to him:

'How is it, Commander, that given your power and your high rank, you have nothing in your tent but some arms and the coarse cloth on which you sit?'

Saffar replied:

'The actions and way of life of a leader of men are imitated by those around him. If I made use of rich furnishings, as you advise me, my army would hasten to follow my example and our beasts would be overloaded. Now, every day we cross vast empty spaces and valleys and plains which are very hard to traverse, so light baggage is the only kind we carry.'

Saffar only used a small number of mules for his army, but there were 5,000 of the kind of camels called *bukht* – a cross between the Bactrian and the dromedary – and an equal number of grey donkeys, the size of mules. These were known as 'Saffari' donkeys and were used instead of mules to carry the baggage. The reason for this preference is that camels and asses can, during halts, be left free to graze, which with mules is not possible.

The biographies of Ya'qub ibn Laith al-Saffar and his brother Amr, their admirable system of government, the tricks and stratagems which they employed in war, are to be found, together with a complete and systematic account of their campaigns, in my *Historical Annals* and in the *Intermediate History*. Here, I am only giving a glimpse of those aspects to which I have not given special treatment in my earlier works.

VIII:46-56
§§ 3163-3176

(Omitted: VIII:56-57; §§ 3177-3178. Necrology for the year 264 AH/878 AD.)

THE HORRORS OF THE ZANJ REBELLION

Muwaffaq set out on a campaign against the chief of the Zanj* in the month of Safar 267 AH/880 AD. In the month of Rabi' II, he detached his son Abu al-Abbas to march on Suq al-Khamis, where al-Sha'rani, one of the supporters of Ali ibn Muhammad, the leader of the Zanj, had entrenched himself with a large number of his followers. Abu al-Abbas seized this place with all its booty and conquered a number of other strongholds and slaughtered all the Zanj he found. Muwaffaq, for his part, entered the Ahwaz and repaired the damage caused by the Zanj. Then he returned to Basra and did not cease fighting the Zanj chieftain until he was killed. This rebel, whose ascendancy lasted fourteen years and four months, had massacred children and old people, men and women, and everywhere he sowed fire and destruction. In a single battle fought at Basra, he killed 300,000 men.

Muhallabi, one of the principal officers of the Zanj chieftain Ali ibn Muhammad, remained in Basra after this battle. He had a *minbar* set up in a quarter called the Cemetery of the Bani Yashkur. There he recited the communal prayers and preached the Friday sermon. He proclaimed first of all the name of his master Ali ibn Muhammad and then invoked God's mercy on Abu Bakr and Umar, but he omitted the names of Uthman and Ali from his address. Then he cursed the tyrants of the House of Abbas and likewise Abu Musa al-Ash'ari, Amr ibn al-As and Mu'awiya. We have spoken earlier of his doctrines and have mentioned that he belonged to the Kharijite sect known as the Azariqa.

As adherents of this sect who remained in Basra were firmly attached to the tenets of Muhallabi, and continued to assemble on Fridays, they were outlawed and put to the sword. Some managed to escape, others were drowned or massacred. A large number of them hid among the houses and in the wells. They appeared only at night and hunted dogs, rats and cats, which they killed for food; but soon this supply was exhausted and they found nothing left to eat.

Then they ate the corpses of their companions who had died, and they watched each other, waiting for someone to die. The stronger killed their comrades and devoured them. To these evils was added a shortage of fresh water. They tell of a woman watching over one of her friends who was about to breathe her last – the sister of the dying woman was also there – and all the women sat in a circle waiting for her death that they might feed on her flesh. Here are the actual words of the witness:

The Meadows of Gold

'She had not yet breathed out her last breath when we threw ourselves upon her, hacked off pieces of her flesh and devoured it. Her sister was with us. We were on the bank of the Isa ibn Abi Harb Canal, and the sister ran towards the river, her sister's head in her hands, and began to cry. Asked: "Why are you crying?" she replied:

"These women gathered about my sister and without letting her die a natural death, they cut her to pieces, and, what is more, they didn't give me any of the meat, only the head."

And she continued to lament on how she had been cheated in the division of the corpse.'

There were many such scenes, some yet more horrible than that we have just told.

The insolence of the army of the Zanj was such that they sold at auction the women of the Houses of Hasan, Husain and Abbas, and the descendants of Hashim, the Quraish and the noblest families of the Arabs. A young girl was sold for two or three dirhams and the auctioneer called out their genealogies as follows:

"So-and-so, daughter of so-and-so, of such and such a house!"

Each black had ten, twenty, even thirty of these women. They served the blacks as concubines and performed the tasks of the very humblest slaves for their wives. One of these captives, who was descended from Hasan ibn Ali ibn Abi Talib belonged to one of these blacks. She begged the chief of the Zanj, Ali ibn Muhammad, to give her another master, or free her from the one who owned her.

'No,' replied the chief. 'He is your master and more suitable for you than any other.'

The number of those who died during these years of war has been much disputed. Some place it very high, others are more moderate. According to the former, the number of those lost is beyond calculation, beyond estimate. Only God in His infinite knowledge can tell what it cost to take all those towns, cities and estates, with the accompanying massacres. The more moderate place the total casualties at about 500,000 souls; but both opinions rest only on empty conjecture – rigorous calculation is impossible.

VIII:57-61
§§ 3179-3184

(Omitted: VIII:62-73; §§ 3185-3200. Sa'id against Saffar; Necrology; The death of Ibn Tulun; An anecdote on Shafi'i; The wars of Ibn Tulun; Wars against the Byzantines.)

WILY MUSLIMS ADMIRED BY THE BYZANTINES

According to what a Greek, who had converted and become an excellent Muslim, told me, the Byzantines have placed in one of their churches portraits of ten men famous among the Christians for their energy, courage and resourcefulness, and also those of certain Muslims known for their ruses. Among them is to be seen the man whom Muʿawiya sent to steal away a patrician of Constantinople, who was then brought back to that city after he had been struck in fulfillment of the *lex talionis*. The other people represented were: Abd Allah al-Battal, Umar ibn Ubaid Allah al-Aqtaʿ, Ali ibn Yahya the Armenian, al-Ghuzayyil ibn Bakkar, Ahmad ibn Abi Qatifa, and Corbeas the Paulician, governor of the town of Ibriq,* which today belongs to the Greeks.

This Corbeas, patriarch of the Paulicians, died in 249 AH/863 AD.

In the same church there are also portraits of Chrysocheir,* sister of the above patriarch, Corbeas, the eunuch Yazman in procession, surrounded by his men, and finally, Abu al-Qasim ibn Abd al-Baqi. We have discussed elsewhere the dogma and doctrines of the Paulicians, a sect which partakes of the nature of both Christianity and Magianism. Today, in 332 AH/944 AD, they have become part of the Byzantine nation. I have mentioned this in my *Historical Annals*.

VIII:74-75
§ 3201

MU'AWIYA TAKES REVENGE ON A BYZANTINE

Here are the details of the story of Mu'awiya and the man who took captive the patrician of Constantinople.

In the course of an expedition against the Greeks during the reign of Mu'awiya, several Muslims were taken prisoner and led before the king of the Byzantines. On one of these prisoners uttering a few words, a certain patrician in the king's retinue came up to the Muslim and struck him full in the face. The prisoner, beside himself with pain and indignation – he belonged to the tribe of Quraish* – cried out:

'What a humiliation for Islam! Mu'awiya, where are you? You abandon us, our frontiers are undefended, the enemy lords it over our country and helps themselves to our lives and honour!'

Mu'awiya was told of this and felt the most profound indignation. He renounced the pleasures of food and drink, shut himself up, receiving nobody, and told his grief to no living creature. But he began to make all the preparations necessary for the success of the plan he was preparing.

An exchange of Greek and Muslim prisoners was negotiated, and the man who had been insulted was ransomed. When he was brought back to the lands of Islam, Mu'awiya summoned him to his presence and loaded him with marks of favour.

'We have not,' he said to him, 'either forgotten you or abandoned you, and we have delivered to the enemy neither your blood nor your honour.'

He used all the resources of his wit to ensure the success of the ruse he was planning. He sent to Tyre, on the Syrian coast, for a certain man, a sailor whom he knew had distinguished himself in innumerable naval expeditions against the Greeks. He was tempered and hardened by experience, and spoke the jargon of the Byzantines. Mu'awiya had him brought to court, and secretly told him of his plan, asking him to lend it all his skill and patience. In accordance with the plan they had hatched between them, this man was given a considerable sum of money which he used to purchase strange and exotic objects, precious materials, scents, jewels and so on, and they built a ship for him, most admirably made and so light that it outsailed every other ship.

The sailor set out. When he reached Cyprus, he saw the governor and told him that he was carrying a young slave girl destined for the king and that he wished to

Mu'awiya Takes Revenge on a Byzantine

trade in Constantinople and that for this purpose he wanted to see the king and his nobles. The Greek king was informed of this message, and, after making enquiries, gave him permission to come. The stranger entered the strait of Constantinople and so reached the capital. The length of this strait and its junctures with the Mediterranean and the Black Sea have already been mentioned in this book, in the chapter on the various seas.

As soon as he arrived in Constantinople, the Tyrian sailor offered presents to the king and the patricians and began to trade. He took great care, however, not to give the smallest present to the patrician who had hit the man of Quraish, although the author of this offence was the real aim of his mission, for Mu'awiya had warned him to act with the greatest circumspection. When the Tyrian left Constantinople for Syria, the king and the patricians commissioned him to buy all kinds of merchandise and different things, which they specifically requested.

Back in Syria, he visited Mu'awiya secretly and gave him an account of his journey. He was given the goods which he had been commissioned to buy and everything which he knew would appeal to the taste of the Greeks. Mu'awiya then gave him the following instructions:

'On your next voyage, the patrician will reproach you with having forgotten him in the distribution of presents and with showing disdain for him. Make your excuses to him, sweeten him with attentions and gifts, and behave in such a way that he becomes your advocate and the protector of your interests. Pay particular attention to what he asks you for at the time of your departure for Syria. In this you will obtain greater consideration and more influence among them. When you have faithfully carried out my orders and when you know what the patrician wants from you and have the commissions he will entrust to you, we will take action.'

The Tyrian then returned to Constantinople, carrying with him everything for which he had been asked and even more, which served to increase his prestige with the king, the patricians and the rest of the court. One day, as he was about to enter the king's presence, the patrician accosted him in the palace and said:

'How have I offended you? What have the others done that you visit them and accept their commissions, while you neglect me?'

The Tyrian replied:

'Almost all the people you are talking about took the initiative where I am concerned. I am a stranger. I only have access to your city and country disguised as a Muslim prisoner or one of their spies, for fear that my activities should be made known and denounced to the Muslims, which would be the end of me. But, since now I know that you are well disposed towards me, I don't want to entrust my interests to others and I don't want anyone but you to uphold them before the king – or indeed in any other circumstances. Give me your orders and tell me what you would like to have from the lands of the Muslims.'

He then offered the patrician magnificent presents – a chalice of cut glass, scents, jewels, all sorts of rare objects and splendid clothing.

Thus he continued to go back and forth between the Byzantines and

The Meadows of Gold

Mu'awiya, and from Mu'awiya to the Byzantines, fulfilling the commissions which the king, the patrician and the other dignitaries gave him. Several years passed without Mu'awiya finding an opportunity to carry out his stratagem. At last, on one of these voyages, the patrician said to the Tyrian, as he was preparing to return to the lands of Islam:

'Would you be so kind as so undertake a commission for me? Please be so good as to buy me a Susangird carpet with cushions and pillows. I would like it to be of various colours – red, blue and so on – and made in such-and-such a way. No matter how high the price, I will pay it.'

The Tyrian agreed to his request. Now, every time he went to Constantinople, he anchored near the patrician's palace. This dignitary had an estate consisting of a fortified palace and a magnificent park, some miles from the capital, on the shore of the strait. This pleasure park, where he spent most of his time, was between Constantinople and the mouth of the strait where it flowed into the Mediterranean.

The Tyrian went secretly to Mu'awiya and told him of all this. Mu'awiya procured a Susangird carpet, with cushions, pillows and couch. The Tyrian carried them off together with the other products of Muslim territory for which he had been asked, and provided also with Mu'awiya's instructions on the workings of his stratagem and how to carry it out. In the course of the numerous journeys which we have described, this man had insinuated himself into the good graces of the Greeks, who are greedy and rapacious in character, and had become so familiar with them that he was considered one of them.

When, leaving the Mediterranean, he entered the strait with a fair wind behind him, he approached the estate belonging to the patrician. He enquired of the sailors on the other boats and ships and they told him that the patrician was at his domain. The strait extends some 350 miles between the two seas, the Mediterranean and the Black Sea, as we have said earlier in this book. There are villas and estates lining both banks of the strait and innumerable ships and vessels go back and forth, carrying all sorts of merchandise and provisions from these estates to the capital. The number of these ships cannot be estimated.

When he was sure that the patrician was at home, the sailor from Tyre unrolled the carpet and arranged the couch with its cushions and pillows on the deck and poop of his ship. He placed his oarsmen below, with their oars shipped, but ready to row. No one would have suspected that they were there between decks and the only people to be seen were those whose duties called them on to the bridge. The ship, with the wind in its sails, entered the strait like an arrow from a bow. It would have been hard to examine it carefully from the shore, so swiftly did it speed and so straight was its course. It arrived in sight of the patrician's palace. The patrician was sitting in his belvedere in the midst of his harem and he had drunk much wine and abandoned himself to gaiety and joy. At the sight of the ship from Tyre, he began to sing a song and greeted its arrival with happy cries. Meanwhile, the ship had come in under the palace and the sails were struck.

Mu'awiya Takes Revenge on a Byzantine

The patrician looked down on the ship and the beauty of the carpets and the carefully arranged accessories, as brilliant as a bed of flowers; he could not keep still, and before the captain had even had time to disembark, he had come down to greet him. He ran to the ship, but scarcely had he set foot on board and drawn near the poop, when the Tyrian tapped on the carpet with his heel. Immediately below were his men and this was the signal he had arranged with them. As soon as the signal had been given, the oars sped the ship into the middle of the strait, making for open sea. A cry was raised, but no one knew what was happening, so nothing could be done. Night had not yet fallen when they left the strait and stood out to sea, carrying with them the patrician, in shackles. Winds and good luck favoured the ship; it swiftly crossed this stretch of water and on the seventh day was in sight of the Syrian coast. The prisoner was disembarked and on the thirteenth day was in the presence of Mu'awiya.

Mu'awiya was overjoyed at finding himself master of the situation and at the success of his ruse and its happy result. He said:

'Bring me the man of Quraish!'

He was brought. All the leading men were summoned. They took their places. A great crowd thronged the hall. Mu'awiya addressed the man of Quraish:

'Rise,' he said to him, 'take vengeance on this patrician who once struck you in the face on the carpet of the Greek ruler. We have neither abandoned you nor have we delivered up your honour or your blood.'

The Quraishi rose and approached the Greek. Mu'awiya added:

'Take care not to exceed the limits of what you received from him. Revenge yourself to the extent of the insult which he inflicted on you. Do not give way to anger and observe the *lex talionis* as God has ordained it.'

The Quraishi slapped his adversary several times and then struck him once in the throat. Then he prostrated himself before Mu'awiya and kissed his hands and feet and cried:

'May those who have made you their leader never lose you! May he who places his hopes in you never be disappointed! You are a king who cannot be offended with impunity. You are one who can protect your subjects and defend their rights.'

And he poured out thanks and praise.

After that, Mu'awiya treated the patrician kindly. He gave him a robe of honour, entertained him liberally, had him brought the carpets and to them added a number of other precious objects as well as gifts for the king.

'Go back to your king*,' he said, 'and say to him: "I have left the king of the Arabs on the carpet where you once sat dispensing justice and revenging the injuries done to his subjects in the palace that was once yours and the seat of your former authority." '

Then, turning to the Tyrian, he said:

'Take the prisoner back to the strait and leave him there with all those who had been captured at the same time – for several pages and intimates had run onto the boat with their master. They were taken back to Tyre with every sign of consider-

The Meadows of Gold

ation and embarked on the boat. The wind was fair, and on the eleventh day they touched Byzantine territory and approached the mouth of the strait which was closed by chains and defended by a garrison. The patrician was set on shore with his companions and the Tyrian at once returned.

The patrician immediately had himself conveyed before the king with the presents and merchandise he had brought. The Greeks celebrated his arrival and came out to meet him, congratulating him on his happy deliverance. The king was grateful to Mu'awiya for his humanity towards the patrician and for the gifts and henceforth during his reign no Muslim prisoner was subjected to ill-treatment.

'Mu'awiya,' the king said, 'is the subtlest of all kings and the most wily of the Arabs, which is why this people have placed him at their head and entrusted him with authority over them. By God, if he had wished to seize my own person, he would surely have succeeded.'

I have spoken earlier in this book of Mu'awiya. The details of his life, an account of the delegations of men and women who came to him from the principal cities of the empire are to be found in my earlier works, quite apart from the summary I have made of his reign in this book. The relations between the kings and patricians of Byzantium and the Umayyads and Abbasids, from ancient time to the present, together with their wars and expeditions, and those of the people of the frontiers of Syria and al-Jazira up until the present year 332 AH/944 AD form an interesting story, the details of which may be read in my previous works. In this book too, I have given a glimpse of their history, an assessment of their lives and reigns and a rapid account of their actions and deeds, as well as the histories of the kings of various other nations.

VIII:75-88
§§ 3202-3212

(Omitted: VIII:89-102; §§ 3213-3228. Ibn Khurradadhbih on musical instruments, singing, rhythm and dance.)

THE NIGHT CONVERSATIONS OF MU'TAMID

Mu'tamid's gatherings, his audiences, conferences and conversations have been recorded. They treated of literature and manners. There is, for example, a eulogy of the courtier, with an enumeration of his qualities, and a polemic against those addicted to *nabidh*, as well as passages of verse and prose dealing with these subjects. There are quotations on the manners of the courtier and descriptions of him – his moderation in taking pleasure and his lack of frivolity. The polite formulae for invitations are there as well, with examples of invitation and acceptance; the names of all the numerous different kinds of drinks, details of the various types of concerts; on the principles of singing and its origins among the Arabs and other peoples; the life stories of the most famous singers, ancient and modern; instructions on how to behave at gatherings; the place destined to master and subordinate, the rules of precedence to be observed and the arrangements to be made for seating guests. Lastly, the phrases used for greetings, as the poet al-Atawi says:

> Greet those guests who hasten to greet you
> And who know how to call out for a drink
> When you forget to pour. Drunk with pleasure
> At breakfast, by evening they are comatose,
> But not without life. In between, a carousel
> Of delights which even the feasts
> Of the Caliphs cannot equal.*

All this is to be found, with much fuller details, in my *Historical Annals*. There also you may read a whole mass of hitherto unpublished information on the kinds of wines, on different sorts of nuts and dried fruits and the ways of arranging them on trays and in bowls, either in pyramids or in symmetrical rows, with all kinds of explanations on this subject. There is also a glimpse of the culinary art, some knowledge of which is essential to the subordinate and, indeed, which no cultivated person should be without, and some indications of the new fashions in dishes and of the skilful combination of spices and aromatics in seasonings.

The different subjects of conversation are also mentioned; the way of washing one's hands in the presence of the host and of taking one's leave; the manner in

The Meadows of Gold

which the cup should be circulated, with several anecdotes from ancient authorities of kings and other important people on this subject; different points of view and some little stories on the intemperance or sobriety of the drinker; how to ask and obtain favours from important people during parties; a sketch of the courtier, his obligations and his master's obligations towards him; what distinguishes the subordinate from the master and the courtier from the host; the origins people have given to the word *nadim*, courtier.

Then, I deal with the rules of chess and explain in what way it differs from backgammon and on this subject I quote a number of stories and a whole series of historical proofs; I give the Arab traditions for the names of wine, the prohibition of which this drink has been the subject; the various opinions on the forbidding of different kinds of *nabidh*; the description of the cups and utensils used for banquets; by whom the use of wine was adopted in the era before Islam and by whom it was forbidden; finally, drunkenness and what people have said about it, whether it comes from God or man. In short, everything which deals with this subject or is related to this question. The résumé given here is meant to call the reader's attention to the subjects expounded in my earlier works.

VIII:102-105
§§ 3229-3231

(Omitted: VIII:106-109; §§ 3232-3236. The death of Muwaffaq; The evil vizier Isma'il.)

MU'TAMID DIES BY POISON

Mu'tamid sat down at table for his morning meal and drink on Monday, the eleventh day before the end of Rajab 279 AH/892 AD. In the afternoon, when food was again served, he said to his butler:

'Mushkir, what did you do with that stew of lambs' heads and neck?'

He had had a lamb stew made the evening before.

It was brought to him. He had at his side one of his intimates, known as Quff al-Mulaqqim, 'The Glutton', and another table companion who had been given the nickname of Khalaf al-Mudhik, 'The Buffoon'. The first to stretch out his hand towards the dish in question was Quff al-Mulaqqim. He tore off an ear, rolled it in a round of bread, dipped it in the sauce, stuffed it in his mouth and ate avidly. Khalaf al-Mudhik plucked a piece of cheek and the eyes off the skull and drew them over to his side and ate. Mu'tamid and his two companions ate with hearty appetites and did not leave a single bite. Quff al-Mulaqqim, who had eaten first, gave up the ghost during the night and Khalaf al-Mudhik before daybreak. As for Mu'tamid, he joined his two friends in the morning.

At once, Isma'il ibn Hammad the qadi appeared before Mu'tadid dressed in black, and was the first to greet him by the title of Caliph. Witnesses were summoned, among them Abu Awf, Husain ibn Salim and other notaries, and they examined the body of Mu'tamid. Badr, Mu'tadid's page, who accompanied them, said:

'Do you see any traces of violence on his body? He died suddenly, victim of his continual draughts of *nabidh*.'

The examination by the witnesses having established no sign of a violent death, the body was washed, wrapped in a shroud, placed in a coffin prepared for the purpose and carried to Samarra, where he was buried.

They also maintain – God knows the truth – that Mu'tamid died of a poison which was poured into the wine that was served to him and to his guests. This poison, called *bish* – a kind of aconite – comes from India, the mountains of the Turks and from Tibet. It is normally found in the stamen of the ranunculus. There are three kinds and they have some remarkable properties.

I have given both the broad outlines and the details of the fascinating history of Mu'tamid and a year by year account of the events which took place during his reign – the wars of Saffar and others in Khurasan; the story of the family of Abu Dulaf in the Jabal; that of the Arabs of the House of Tulun; the acts and deeds of Ahmad ibn Isa ibn Shaikh at Diyarbakr, in the lands of Asur, etc; and lastly, what occurred in Yemen – in my *Historical Annals* and *Intermediate History*, which saves me from going over it again here.

THE CALIPHATE OF MU'TADID

Mu'tadid was proclaimed Caliph on the very day of the death of Mu'tamid – a Tuesday, the twelfth day before the end of Rajab 279 AH/892 AD. His mother was a Greek slave named Dirar – 'Harm'. Mu'tadid died on Sunday, the ninth day before the end of Rabi II 289 AH/902 AD, after having reigned nine years, nine months and two days. He died at Baghdad, aged forty-seven years. But, according to another opinion, he was thirty-one when he succeeded to the Caliphate and hence forty and some odd months when he died. These are the different opinions of the chroniclers. God is He Who prospers.

When the Caliphate came to Mu'tadid, discord ceased, the provinces once again became obedient, war stopped, prices fell and turmoil simmered down. The rebels submitted to the new Caliph, his power was confirmed by victory, east and west recognized him, most of his adversaries and those who contested with him for power paid tribute to his authority. Harun-al Shari, the Kharijite, was overcome. But the real sovereign, the real holder of power, was Badr, the Caliph's freedman. He was recognized throughout the empire and exercised absolute power over the army and the generals.

Mu'tadid left in the state treasury 9,000,000 dinars and 40,000,000 dirhams. He also left 12,000 pack animals, such as horses, mules, dromedaries, donkeys and camels. This great fortune did not prevent him from being avaricious in the most sordid ways or from descending to check minute details which even commoners would despise.

Here, for example, is what Abd Allah ibn Hamdun, one of his courtiers, whom he admitted to his most private gatherings, has to tell:

'The Caliph diminished by one ounce the quantity of bread distributed to the members of his household and all those who had a right to rations, and he wanted to begin with the bread served at his own table. Now, every day his servants received a certain number of loaves – some three, others four or more. At first, I was surprised at this order,' added Ibn Hamdun, 'but I understood the implications when I saw that each month it yielded the Commander of the Faithful a considerable sum.'

He also enjoined the treasurer to set aside all the best cloth made at Sus and Dabiq and this he reserved for his personal use.

He was not a man much touched by pity and his character was both energetic and bloody. His greatest pleasure was to torture those whom he put to death . . . He also had vaulted cellars built and filled with instruments of torture, which he placed under the care of Najah al-Hurami, the public executioner.

Mu'tadid liked only two things – women and building. He spent 400,000 dinars on building his palace called Thurayya – 'The Pleiades' – which occupied an area of three leagues.

He confirmed Ubaid Allah ibn Sulaiman in the post of vizier; when this minister died, he replaced him with his son Qasim.

In this same year 279 AH/892 AD, that in which he became Caliph, on Monday, the day of the breaking of the fast of Ramadan, Mu'tadid went in a great procession to the place of prayer which he had built near his palace. He led the public prayers, pronouncing six *takbir* as he bowed for the first time, but only one as he bowed for the second. Then he mounted the *minbar*, but he was tongue-tied and not a word could be heard, which led a poet to say:

> The Imam is tongue-tied.
> He has not been able
> To explain clearly in his sermon
> What is allowed and what is proscribed.
> This is merely the result
> Of shyness; it is certainly
> Not because he stammers
> Or was nonplussed.

THE SPLENDID DOWRY OF QATR AL-NADA

In 279 AH/892 AD, Hasan ibn Abd Allah, known as Ibn al-Jassas – 'Son of the Plasterer' – arrived from Egypt as ambassador of Khumarawaih ibn Ahmad. He brought numerous presents, very valuable objects and materials embroidered with calligraphy in the royal workshops. On Monday, the 3rd of Shawwal, he was received by Mu'tadid, who gave robes of honour to him and to the seven men accompanying him. The envoy then tried to negotiate a marriage between the daughter of Khumarawaih and Muktafi, but Mu'tadid said to him:

'Your master wished to give us a mark of honour, but I wish to give him a yet more splendid one – I will marry his daughter.'

And indeed, he married her. It was Ibn al-Jassas who represented the father and offered the dowry. They say that in this dowry, which was brought from Egypt, there were precious stones the like of which no Caliph had ever possessed. Ibn al-Jassas took a certain number for himself, telling the daughter of Khumarawaih, who was called Qatr al-Nada – 'Dew of Generosity' – that he would only keep them, as it were, in safe-custody, until the day when she might need them. But the princess died and the jewels remained in the possession of Ibn al-Jassas – and this was the origin of his wealth and fortune. Later, under the reign of Muqtadir, he suffered reverses of fortune and was arrested and had all his goods confiscated on the grounds of obtaining restitution for these jewels and on other pretexts.

Mu'tadid was in the city of Balad when he had the bride-price for his daughter Qatr al-Nada carried to Khumarawaih. It consisted of a million dirhams and all kinds of precious things, scents and rarities from India, China and Iraq. Among the gifts which he sent to Khumarawaih, as a personal present, there was a bag of precious stones, which contained a pearl, a ruby, several other jewels, a belt, a tiara and a diadem. Others say there was a headdress and a little tiara. The envoys bearing these gifts arrived in Egypt in the month of Rajab 280 AH/893 AD. After their departure, the Caliph left the city of Balad and went down the Tigris to Baghdad, by way of Mosul.

VIII:117-119
§§ 3249-3251

THE WIT OF ABU AL-AYNA

Abu Sa'id Ahmad ibn al-Husain ibn Munqidh tells the following story:
'One day I went in to visit Ibn al-Jassas and I saw in front of him a silk-lined basket filled with precious stones which had been strung into chaplets. I admired their beauty and guessed that there were more than twenty of these strings.

"May God take my life for yours!" I said to my host, "but how many beads are there to each chaplet?"

"One hundred beads," he replied, "and each bead weighs the same, neither less nor more, so that the weight of each string is the same as that of the others."

I saw furthermore in this person's house ingots of gold which could only be weighed on a scale beam, like wood. On leaving his house, I met Abu al-Ayna, who asked me:

"Abu Sa'id, what was he doing when you left him?"

I told him what I had seen. Abu al-Ayna raised his face to heaven and cried out:

"Lord, since You have not allowed me to share his wealth, let him share my blindness!"

Then he dissolved into tears.

"Abu al-Ayna," I said to him, "what is the matter?"

"Do not blame me for these tears," he answered, 'if you had seen what I have seen, you would shed yet more."

He then went on:

"I bless God in my infirmity and, believe me, Abu Sa'id, never until this day have I praised God for having blinded me." '

The same narrator adds that he asked someone who knew all about Ibn al-Jassas's private affairs how each of these strings ended. The man replied that each chaplet was finished off with a great red ruby worth perhaps more than all the other stones below it.

Abu al-Ayna died in 282 AH/895 AD at Basra in the month of Jumada II. He was known as Abu Abd Allah. At about this time, he left Baghdad and went to Basra by river in a boat carrying eighty passengers. It capsized and all were drowned except Abu al-Ayna, who was blind. He clung to the side of the boat and was fished out alive, while all his companions died. It was after having escaped this danger that he came to Basra, where he died.

Abu al-Ayna had no rivals in wit, speed of repartee or liveliness of speech. He is the hero of some interesting tales and the author of a number of remarkable poems, in which he mentions people like Abu Ali al-Basir and others of note, as

The Wit of Abu al-Ayna

we have mentioned in our earlier works.

One day, he was with a vizier. The conversation turned to the Barmakids, their greatness of soul and generous natures. The vizier, tired of hearing Abu al-Ayna lavishing his praises on them, said to him;

'Most of these stories are the work of scribblers and are due only to the inventiveness of the panegyrists.'

Abu al-Ayna retorted:

'How is it, O vizier, that the scribblers have not lied in celebration of *your* munificence and open-handedness?'

The vizier fell silent and all present admired the boldness of his rejoinder.

Another day, he asked for an audience with the vizier Sa'id ibn Makhlad. The chamberlain replied that his master was busy. Abu al-Ayna waited. Tired of not being admitted, he asked the chamberlain what the vizier was doing.

'He is praying,' came the reply.

'You are right,' answered the blind man. 'Every novelty is delightful.'

By this sally he criticized Sa'id's recent conversion from Christianity.

Abu al-Ayna went to see the Caliph Mutawakkil in 246 AH/860 AD in the Ja'fari Palace.

'How do you find our place of abode?' enquired the Caliph.

'Other men,' he replied, 'set their dwelling place in the world – you have set the world in your dwelling place.'

The Caliph was charmed by his reply. He asked him next what his attitude was to *nabidh*.

'I would not be able to drink only a little,' replied Abu al-Ayna, 'and I make a fool of myself in public when I drink a lot.'

'Let your scruples alone,' went on Mutawakkil, 'and be our guest.'

Abu al-Ayna answered:

'I am blind. Now a man in my state makes sudden movements, he wanders out of his path and does not observe what others see in him. All those who are here lavish their attentions on you, but I need the care of another. Now it could be that you might look at me with a contented eye, yet be inwardly irritated; or you might appear irritated, hiding your inner satisfaction, and I, being unable to distinguish one state from the other, would be lost. I therefore prefer to hold tight to my safety rather than run the risk of danger.'

'A certain criticism has been made of you,' said the Caliph.

'O Commander of the Faithful,' replied the blind man, 'God alternately praises and blames. He said: "How excellent a servant! Ever did he turn to us!" (Koran 38:30) Yet elsewhere, 'He says: "Do not listen to the slanderer who spreads calumny.' (Koran 68:11) There is nothing reprehensible about criticism, as long as it is not like the scorpion, which stings, indifferent, the prophet and the Jew. It is as the poet said:

> If I did not recognize merit
> And if I did not find fault

The Meadows of Gold

> With the object of shame and contempt,
> How could I accept the concept
> Of good and evil? Why
> Would God have opened
> My ears and my mouth?'

'Where are you from?' asked Mutawakkil.

'From Basra.'

'How do you find your homeland?'

'Its water makes a bitter drink, its heat is torture and the city will provide an agreeable resting place when hell is a pleasure ground.'

The vizier Ubaid Allah ibn Yahya ibn Khaqan was standing near the Caliph.

'What do you think of Ubaid Allah?' Mutawakkil asked the blind man.

'An excellent servant, who divides himself between his obedience to God and his duty towards you.'

In the midst of all this, Maimun ibn Ibrahim, the director of the postal service, came in and the Caliph wanted to know what Abu al-Ayna thought of him.

'A hand that steals, an ass that farts,' replied Abu al-Ayna. 'You would think he was a Jew who had had half his treasure stolen. He takes one step forward and one step back. Doing good is a virtue he has borrowed, but ill-nature comes naturally.'

This reply made the Caliph laugh. He rewarded the blind man and sent him away.

AN IDOL COMES TO BAGHDAD

In 283 AH/896 AD the presents sent by Amr ibn al-Laith al-Saffar arrived in Baghdad. Noteworthy among them were a hundred Mehri camels from Khurasan, a great number of dromedaries, many chests of precious materials and 4,000,000 dirhams.

There was also a brass idol representing a woman. She had four arms and was wearing two silver belts embellished with red and white stones. In front of this idol there were other smaller ones, whose arms and faces were decorated with gold and jewels. The idol was placed in a wagon specially fitted out for them, drawn by dromedaries.

All the presents were first taken to Mu'tadid's palace. The brass statue was then sent to the police station in the eastern quarter to be exhibited in public for three days, after which it was taken back to Mu'tadid's palace – this happened on Thursday, 4 Rabi' II of the same year.

The people nicknamed the idol *Shughl* - 'A Hard Day's Work' – because everyone stopped what they were doing to go and see it during the days it was on view.

The idol in question was brought by Amr ibn al-Laith al-Saffar from one of the cities he conquered in India and the mountainous regions adjoining Bust, Ma'bar and Zamin-i Dawar. Now, in the year 332 AH/944 AD, these countries are the boundaries of Islam, surrounded by a number of different nations of infidel peoples, both sedentary and nomad. Kabul and Bamiyan, which border on Zabulistan and Rukhkhaj, are mentioned among the lands inhabited by a sedentary population. Elsewhere in this book, in the course of discussing ancient peoples and the kings of antiquity, I have mentioned that Zabulistan is known as 'the land of Firuz, son of Kabk' after the name of one of its kings. When Isa ibn Ali ibn Mahan was pursuing the Kharijites in the reign of Harun al-Rashid, he invaded Sind and its mountains, Qandahar, Rukhkhaj and Zabulistan. He devastated the country and won unparalleled victories.

The blind poet, known as Ibn al-Udhafir – 'Son of the Lion' – who was from Qumm, has said on this subject:

Isa has almost become a second Dhu al-Qarnain;
He has reached the boundaries the two wests and the two easts;
He did not omit Kabul or Zabulistan
Or the surrounding country as far as the two Rukhkhaj.

The Meadows of Gold

I have discussed the fortresses built by Firuz, the son of Kabk, king of Zabulistan, in various other works. According to certain persons who are widely travelled as well as reliable and conscientious witnesses, there are no fortresses more solidly built, better fortified, higher, or more remarkable than those of Zabulistan. I have described the particularities of this country, as far as the lands of the 'Two Tabas', and Khurasan and Sijistan, which lie on its borders. I have spoken of the marvels of Orient and Occident, their deserts and their inhabited places and have mentioned the peoples of different races and natures who live in the latter lands.

A DELEGATION FROM BASRA

A delegation of the inhabitants of Basra went to the Caliph Mu'tadid. It arrived on one of those boats whitened with quicklime and grease which are used in their waters. This delegation was made up of orators, theologians and men of standing in the community. Among them was Abu Khalifa al-Fadl ibn al-Hubab al-Jumahi, a freedman of the Jumah clan of Quraish. He later exercised the office of qadi.

These delegates came to complain to the Caliph of various misfortunes of the time – drought and famine were ravaging the country and everyone was victim of the abuses of power inflicted by the governors. From on board their boats on the Tigris, they wept and lamented ceaselessly, and at last the Caliph granted them an audience, hidden behind a curtain. He ordered his vizier Qasim ibn Ubaid Allah and the secretaries of the ministries to receive them in such a way that he could hear what was said and he instructed them to deal with their complaints in accordance with the policies of the different ministries.

The men from Basra were, therefore, admitted. Abu Khalifa walked among the first to enter. Wearing blue hoods, with their heads veiled, their appearance was so good and they looked so impressive that Mu'tadid was pleased with what he saw. Abu Khalifa spoke first, as follows:

'A fertile land has become untilled, its beauty obliterated; the constellation Boötes appears in the ascendant while Gemini is eclipsed. Every kind of calamity overwhelms us; in our land misfortune follows misfortune; everyone walks in darkness. Our estates are ravaged, our castles are crumbling. Look at us with the eyes of an Imam. May your days be long and may your will be obeyed! As for those of us from Basra, we never refrain from doing a good deed and we have no ambition other than glory.'

He spoke for a long time, always preserving the rhymed and balanced phrases of his discourse.

'Shaikh,' the vizier then said to him, 'I presume you are a teacher.'

'O vizier, replied the Basran, 'it was the teachers who put you in the position you now occupy.'

The vizier then asked him what tax was due on a herd of five camels.

'You have asked the right man,' replied Abu Khalifa. 'The tax due on five camels is one ewe, and on ten camels, two ewes.'

He then went on to explain the proportions of the tax, demonstrating what conformed to the law and what was disputable on this subject. He next passed to

The Meadows of Gold

taxes on cattle and sheep, using clear elegant language and ably wedding concision to lucidity. The Caliph, charmed by this speech, which had put him in an excellent humour, had a eunuch say to the vizier:

'Take note of their requests, accede to their demands and only send them away when they are fully satisfied. This man is a demon cast up by the Tigris, and it is from such men that opposition to kings is born.'

THE CLUCKING OF A GRAMMARIAN

There was nothing artificial for Abu Khalifa in using the flexional endings at the end of words in ordinary speech; it came to him naturally, having practised constantly since he was a boy. This scholar was an authority on the chains of transmission of Traditions, and interesting facts of his life have been collected in an anthology. Let us give a few examples.

One of the collectors of the land tax was relieved of his office at the same time that Abu Khalifa was dismissed from the position of qadi. This man sent to Abu Khalifa to say that he was expecting a visit from Mabraman, the grammarian, the student of Mubarrad, and there was to be a party that very day on the banks of one of the canals. Some friends chosen more or less at random came to ask him to join them very early in the morning. They all set out gaily by boat, having taken care to change anything about their clothing that might make them easily recognized. On reaching the nearby waterway, they saw a garden which looked very pretty and headed towards it, mooring alongside the bank and seating themselves under the palm trees which shadowed the banks of the canal. They then had served the meal which they had brought.

It was the season of the date harvest. At that time of year the dates begin to ripen and they are placed in great wicker baskets and pressed into solid blocks. The gardens were therefore full of country people, day labourers and so on, who were busy with the date palms. When the meal was over, one of the guests addressed Abu Khalifa, without, however, calling him by name, for fear lest the workmen busy with the harvest should recognize him, and said:

'May God grant you long life! In the following passage from the Koran: "O you who believe, save yourselves from the fires of Hell, both you and your families!" (Koran 66:6), how should the letter *waw* in the word "save", written *qw*, be vocalized, according to the rules of flexional endings?'

Abu Khalifa answered:

'It should be pronounced with a *damma*, a *u*, since the word *qū* is in the masculine plural of the imperative.'

'How would you say it in the masculine singular and in the dual?'

'The masculine singular,' went on Abu Khalifa, 'is *qi*, the dual *qiyā*, the plural *qū*.'

'How would you form the feminine singular, dual and plural?'

'The feminine singular is *qī*, the dual *qiyā*, the plural *qīnā*.'

The questioner added: `

The Meadows of Gold

'Could you conjugate, straight off, the masculine singular, dual and plural and the feminine singular, dual and plural?'

Abu Khalifa answered at high speed:

'*Qi,qiyā, qū,qī,qiyā,qīna.*'

Some peasants working nearby heard these words, and finding them quite extraordinary, upbraided the scholars who were talking thus:

'Atheists! Heretics! Reading the Koran and clucking like hens!'

Then they fell on them and beat them soundly, and it was only with great difficulty that Abu Khalifa and his friends managed to escape.

The remarkable events in the life of Abu Khalifa, what he said to his mule when she threw him to the ground, his conversation with a thief who had broken into his house, as well as other anecdotes are to be found in my *Intermediate History*. He died at Basra in 305 AH/917 AD.

VIII:131-134
§§ 3267-3270

UMM SHARIF, THE AUNT OF THE REBEL

In the month of Rabi' I 286 AH/899 AD, Mu'tadid encamped before Amid. Ahmad ibn Isa ibn al-Shaikh Abd al-Razzaq had died and his son Muhammad had taken refuge in that town. The Caliph had it invested by his army and set siege to it.

The following story has been handed down to Alqama ibn Abd al-Razzaq by Rawaha ibn Isa ibn Abd al-Malik, who had it from the lips of Shu'la ibn Shihab al-Yashkuri.

'Mu'tadid,' said Shu'la, 'sent me to Muhammad ibn Ahmad ibn Isa ibn al-Shaikh to prove to him that his rebellion was unjust. When I came to him, Umm Sharif, the aunt of the rebel, was told of my arrival. She sent to fetch me and said:

"Ibn Shihab, how was the Commander of the Faithful when you left him?"

"By God," I said to her, "I left a powerful king, a just judge, one who orders all things for the best and practises good works, proud before the disciples of error, humble before the truth and defying before God all the accusations brought against him."

"Yes," answered the woman, "it is indeed so. He is worthy of such praises and deserves them. How could it be otherwise? He is the shadow of God on the face of the earth, the vicar to whose care He has entrusted His servants. In him God glorifies His faith, revives His holy practices and consolidates His law."

Then she added:

"How did you find our friend?"

By this she meant her nephew, Muhammad ibn Ahmad.

"I found him a young man filled with the pride of youth, who allows himself to be ruled by fools, who relies on their counsel and listens to no words but theirs. By their artful speeches they are preparing him for most bitter regrets."

"Would you," she went on, "go back to him with a letter? Perhaps I can undo the knot these idiots have tied."

I agreed most willingly. She then wrote a charming and beautiful letter, full of excellent admonishments and sincere advice. The letter ended with the following lines:

> Listen to the advice of a mother
> Whose heart is moved for you

The Meadows of Gold

> By fear and tenderness: say
> 'This is good advice!'
> Think about my words
> And you will see as you reflect
> That they could lead you back
> Onto the right path.
> Don't trust those whose hearts
> Are filled with rancours
> Which engender nothing
> But envy and hatred.
> See how they hide in the back
> Rooms of their houses,
> Timid as sheep, but when
> The danger has passed,
> Lo! They are like lions.
> Heal the wounds while healing
> Is still possible – here
> Is a doctor who offers
> A helping hand. Give
> The Caliph the amends
> He asks – fortune, family,
> Children, refuse him nothing;
> Give Ibn Shihab a reply
> That will be a support
> Against evil and not an occasion
> For your enemies to gloat.

'I took the letter,' continued Ibn Shahib, 'and went to Muhammad ibn Ahmad. He read it and tossed it back, crying:

"Know, Ibn Shahib, that is not with a woman's advice that one governs empires and their minds are not fit to rule the state. You may go back to your master."

On my return, I gave the Commander of the Faithful an accurate and faithful account of my mission. He said:

"Where is Umm Sharif's letter?"

I showed it to him. He cast his eye over it and praised the poem and the wisdom it contained.

"In truth," he cried, "I would like, in order to favour this woman, to show mercy to several members of her family."

Indeed, after the taking of Amid, when Muhammad ibn Ahmad, terrified by the fighting, surrendered unconditionally, the Caliph had me summoned and asked:

"Ibn Shihab, do you have any news of Umm Sharif?"

"None, O Commander of the Faithful," I replied.

Umm Sharif, the Aunt of the Rebel

"Follow this eunuch," he went on, "and you will find her in the midst of her women."

I went to where she was. As soon as she saw me, she set aside her veil and spoke the following verses:

> Fortune's treachery and her whims
> And insolence force me to remove my veil.
> After so much glory our proud warriors,
> Our brave champions, are humbled.
> I gave advice; it was not followed.
> Yet my counsels have long been known.
> Destiny has demanded that we
> Should be divided up and sold as loot.
> How I long to know whether we,
> Who are separated today, will one day meet again!

Then she wept and beat her hands together.

"Ibn Shihab," she said to me, "by God, I saw ahead of time what would happen. 'We belong to God, and to God we return.'"

I consoled her by saying:

"It is the Commander of the Faithful himself who sent me to you and this action shows how well he is disposed towards you."

"Will you," she answered, "carry the Commander of the Faithful the message which I have written in this letter?"

"Willingly," I replied. And she set down the following lines:

> Say to the Caliph, the Imam chosen by God,
> Son of Caliphs born of the Quraish of the Valleys,
> Say from me: God has entrusted you
> With the task of bringing peace to the country
> And its inhabitants, after so many calamities
> Have banished it for so long.
> You have raised up the dome of glory
> Which without your help and God's
> Would not have been raised again.
> May your Lord grant your prayers,
> May you never know adversity!
> Now let mercy and pardon flow freely.
> Splendour of the World, bright moon of kings,
> Grant to those of us who are just
> The lives of the unjust and guilty.

I took this letter and gave it to the Commander of the Faithful. He read these verses and approved. Then he had coffers filled with rich materials and a considerable sum of money carried to the lady. He gave the same amount to her nephew, Muhammad ibn Ahmad, and in consideration of their protectress forgave many of her relatives who, by the gravity of their misdemeanours, rather deserved his punishment.'

VIII:134-139
§§ 3271-3276

(Omitted: VIII:140-146; §§ 3277-3287). Defeat of a follower of Saffar; An historian of the Zanj tortured to death; Defeat of the Bani Shaiban at the Wadi al-Di'ab; Campaigns in Oman and elsewhere; Events in Khurasan; Capture of a Khatun; Revolt of Wasif; A Greek defeat; An Alid revolt.)

ON EUNUCHS

In 282 AH/895 AD, Khumarawaih ibn Ahmad ibn Tulun had his throat cut at Damascus, in the month of Dhu al-Qa'da, in the palace which he had built at the base of a hill below Dair al-Murran, 'The Monastery of the Ash Tree'. He was murdered while drinking by night in the company of Tughj. The crime was committed by certain of his palace eunuchs. Arrested some miles away, they were killed and crucified, some being shot full of arrows, while the black slaves of Khumarawaih cut the flesh from the thighs and buttocks of others and ate it.

I have spoken in my *Historical Annals* of the eunuchs from the Sudan, the Slavic countries, Byzantium and China – for the Chinese, like the Byzantines, will castrate several of their children. I have discussed, in the same work, the contradictions in character of eunuchs which result from the removal of this member and what nature causes to occur in them when that happens, as has often been confirmed and described.

Mada'ini tells how Mu'awiya went in one day to his wife Fakhita, a woman gifted with considerable wisdom and tact, accompanied by a eunuch. Fakhita, whose head was bare, hastened to put on her veil when she saw the eunuch. Mu'awiya pointed out that the man was an eunuch, but she replied:

'Commander of the Faithful, do you imagine that the mutilation which he has suffered frees me from the prohibitions ordained by God?'

Mu'awiya repeated the prayer, 'We belong to God, and to God we return,' and, recognizing the justice of her words, henceforth allowed into his harem only elderly and broken-down eunuchs.

There has been a great deal of discussion on the subject of eunuchs and an effort has been made to establish the difference between those mutilated by cutting and those mutilated by dragging. It has been maintained that they are men with women and women with men. But these are false theories and bad arguments. The truth is that they remain men. Being deprived of one organ is not enough for them to be allotted this double role and the lack of a beard does not prevent them from belonging to the male sex. Claiming that they are closer to being women implies that the works of the Creator can be modified, since He created them men and not women, male and not female. The crime which has been perpetrated on their bodies does not alter the constituent elements any more than it destroys the work of the All-Powerful Creator who gave them life.

I have explained in another work why the armpits of a eunuch have no smell and have quoted the reasons for this set forth by the philosophers. It is in fact worth noting that the eunuch, slow in all his movements, has the peculiar advantage of giving off no odour from there.

THE FUNERAL OF KHUMARAWAIH

The body of Khumarawaih was placed in a coffin and brought back to Egypt. The news of what had happened arrived on Sunday, the 5th of Dhu al-Hijja, the murder itself having taken place in the last days of Dhu al-Qa'da. Allegiance was sworn to Jaish, the son of Khumarawaih – who was known as Abu Jaish – on the following day, which was Monday. When the corpse of Khumarawaih reached Old Cairo, it was removed from its coffin and placed on the bier in front of Bab Misr. The amir Jaish and the other amirs and men of note made their way there in procession with the judge Abu Abd Allah Muhammad ibn Abda, known as al-Abdani, at their head. He recited the funeral prayers. The ceremony took place at night.

Abu Bishr al-Dawlabi tells the following story, which he got from Abu Abd Allah al-Bukhari, a shaikh originally from Iraq who was a Koran reader in the houses and at the graves of the family of Tulun. On that night, Bukhari was one of those reciting at the cemetery when they brought the corpse of Khumarawaih to lower it into the tomb.

'We were,' he said, 'seven readers engaged in reading the chapter of Smoke, when the body was removed from the bier to be laid in the grave. We were in fact at the very verse of that same chapter where God says: "Seize him and hurl him into the midst of the blazing fire! Then pour boiling water on his head, saying: 'Drink this, you who were once mighty and honoured!' " (Koran 44:47)'

'Then,' continued the narrator, 'we lowered our voices and hurried on with our reading out of respect for those who were taking part in the ceremony.'

MU'TADID TAKES A THIEF

Among other anecdotes of the life of Mu'tadid, illustrating his shrewdness and judiciousness, the following is related.

He had assigned ten purses of money from the treasury to be used to pay the troops and this sum had been carried to the army paymaster for distribution. A hole, however, was made in the wall of this man's house that night and the purses removed. In the morning, as soon as he saw the hole, and didn't see the money, he called the chief of the military police, who at that time was Mu'nis al-Fahl.

'You know,' he said to him, 'that this money belongs to the government and to the army. If you don't find it, or at least find the man who broke in and committed this theft, the Commander of the Faithful will hold you responsible. Use all possible zeal to find it and capture the thief who dared such an audacious crime.'

So Mu'nis went to his audience hall and summoned the Tawwabin – The Repentants – and other police officers. The Repentants are old thieves, who, as they get on in years, give up their profession. When a crime is committed, they know who did it and can point out the culprit. It does, however, often happen that they share with the thieves the fruits of their thefts. Mu'nis ordered them to make enquiries and to spur them on he used in turn intimidation, threats and promises. The police spread out through all the streets and markets, entering rooms, taverns, eating houses and gambling dens. They soon brought before the chief of military police a poor devil, lean, weak, ill-dressed and wretched-looking.

'Sir,' they said, 'here is the man who committed the theft. He is a stranger in our town.'

Faced with their unanimity in pointing out this man as the author of the break-in and theft, Mu'nis al-Fahl, addressing the stranger, said:

'Wretch, who was with you? Who helped you? Where are your accomplices? I don't suppose that you alone could have carried off those ten purses during the night. There must have been ten of you, or at least five. Come, give back the money, if it is still intact, and denounce your companions, if you shared it among you.'

The man confined himself to denying everything.

Mu'nis used kindness. He promised him a reward, a pension, a splendid salary. He promised him anything if he would give the money back and confess. He then resorted to the most terrible threats. The man persisted in his denials and refusals.

Mu'nis, annoyed and irritated and no longer hoping to obtain a confession, submitted him to questioning and torture. Whip, knout, stick and lash all fell on the prisoner's back, belly, nape, head, foot-soles, joints and muscles. Soon there was no place left to strike and he had almost lost consciousness and the power of speech – but still he admitted nothing.

Mu'tadid was told of this. He had the chief of the military police brought before him and asked:

'What did you do about the money?'

The latter related the whole adventure.

'What!' said the Caliph. 'You seize a thief who has stolen ten purses from the treasury and put him in danger of death, reducing him to the last extremity, so that, if the culprit dies, our money will be lost? Where are the ruses of the masters?'

'O Commander of the Faithful,' replied Mu'nis, 'I am not clairvoyant and I know no other devices but those I have used on this man.'

'Have him brought!' said Mu'tadid.

The prisoner, who had regained consciousness, was carried in wrapped in a blanket and set before the Caliph. The Caliph questioned, the prisoner denied.

'My friend,' said the Commander of the Faithful, 'if you die, this money will be of no use to you; if you recover from the effects of this beating, I will not let you get back your treasure. However, I offer you pardon, the promise of a good position and a pleasant life.'

Always the same denials.

'Call the doctors!' cried Mu'tadid.

They came.

'Take this man home with you,' he said to them, 'and look after him with the greatest care. Anoint him with healing salves, and pay attention to his diet and well-being. Give him all possible aid and try to heal him as soon as possible.'

The doctors took the man away.

Meanwhile, Mu'tadid had taken from the treasury a sum to replace that which was missing and distributed it to the troops.

They say that the accused was healed and recovered in a few days. Assiduously attended as regards food and drink, lodging and scent, he soon regained health and strength. His colour revived, he came back to life. They told the Caliph of this and he had him brought in and asked after his health. The prisoner launched into blessings and thanks.

'I shall,' he said, 'always be well, so long as God preserves the Commander of the Faithful.'

But, interrogated yet again as to the stolen money, he repeated his first denials.

'Wretch!' said Mu'tadid, 'you cannot deny that either you and you alone stole this money, or else you received a part of it. If you took the whole sum to spend on feasts and pleasure, I doubt if you could get through it all during your lifetime, and you would die with this crime on your conscience. If you only took a part, we will give it to you, but you must confess and disclose your accomplices. If you refuse to admit these things, I shall have you executed and then it will do you no

The Meadows of Gold

good to leave this money behind you and your companions will not be much troubled by your fate. If, on the other hand, you confess, I will give you 10,000 dirhams and deduct a similar sum from the police. I will have you inscribed among the 'Repentants'; each month you will receive ten dinars, which will be amply sufficient for your food, clothes and scent. You will live honoured and you will have escaped death, as well as all responsibility for your crime.'

The accused still denied everything.

The Caliph ordered him to swear by the Holy Name of God. He swore. He showed him a copy of the Koran and told him to swear. He swore on The Book.

'In the end,' Mu'tadid said, 'I shall find the money and if I discover it after the oath you have just sworn, you are lost. Hope for no mercy.'

The accused continued his denials.

'Place your hand on my head and swear by my life,' said the Caliph.

The prisoner placed his hands on the Caliph's head and swore by his sovereign's life that he had not stolen the money, that he was being falsely accused, that he was the target for unjust suspicions and that the 'Repentants' simply wanted to get rid of him.

'If you have lied,' proceeded Mu'tadid, 'I shall have you put to death and I shall not be responsible for your blood.'

'All right,' said the prisoner.

Thirty black slaves were then summoned. The Caliph had them placed where they could see the prisoner and ordered them to watch over him in turns. For several days, he remained sitting without being allowed to lean back or rest on his elbow, or to stretch out on his back or side. If his head began to nod, a slap in the face, a blow on the head, woke him with a start. He was wasting away and in danger of death.

The Caliph had him brought in again and had the same conversation with him, ordering him to swear in the name of God and by other oaths. The accused swore everything they wanted and even produced oaths that had not been asked of him – that he had not stolen the money and did not know those who had stolen it. Mu'tadid turned towards those who had witnessed this scene and said to them:

'Yes, my heart tells me that this man is innocent, that what he says is true and that the "Repentants" know the real culprit. We have behaved criminally towards this man.'

There and then he begged the prisoner to pardon him, which he instantly did. The Caliph had a table laden with food and cool drinks brought in. The man sat down and, encouraged by the Caliph, began to eat with great appetite, washing down each mouthful with a brimming glass and going on until it was impossible for him to eat or drink another thing. Next, he was brought incense burners and scents. He fumigated his clothes with incense and perfumed himself. On the orders of the Caliph a feather bed was laid out and prepared for the man, who stretched out on it and rested.

But, at the very moment he was about to fall asleep, he was shaken roughly and forced to wake with a start. Then he was dragged out of bed and made to sit

Mu'tadid Takes a Thief

before the Caliph, his eyes heavy with sleep.

'Speak,' said Mu'tadid. 'How did you commit this theft? How did you break through the wall? Which way did you get out? Where did you take the money? Who was with you?'

The prisoner replied:

'I was alone and I got out through the gap I had made to get in. In front of the house, there is a bath with a heap of thorn-bushes for lighting the fire. When I had taken the money, I lifted up the brushwood, the heap of dry branches and canes, placed the money underneath and covered it up again in the same way. The money is there.'

The Caliph ordered them to take the prisoner back to his bed and this was done. Then he sent them to search for the money. The sum was brought back intact. Mu'nis al-Fahl, the vizier, the courtiers, were convened. The money was hidden under some carpets in the corner of the room. The thief was woken up. He had slept his fill and was now perfectly awake. Mu'tadid, before all these witnesses, addressed him as he had the first time. The thief denied everything absolutely. The Caliph had the carpets taken up and said:

'Wretch!' Isn't that the money? Didn't you steal it in such-and-such a way?'

And he repeated the man's revelations back to him.

The thief was thunderstruck.

VIII:151-160
§§ 3292-3298

(Omitted: VIII:160-161; § 3299. The thief is hideously tortured to death.)

THE MIMIC AND THE EUNUCH

There was in Baghdad a mimic who wandered about the streets entertaining the crowds with all kinds of tales and funny stories and jokes, and he was called Ibn al-Maghazili. He was immensely witty and literally no one could look at him or hear him without laughing. This Ibn al-Maghazili tells the following story himself:

'One day, in the reign of Muʻtadid, I was sitting in front of the Bab al-Khassa serving out my jokes and funny anecdotes. In the circle which had formed around me there was a eunuch belonging to Muʻtadid and it just so happened that I was mimicking a eunuch. He found my imitation wonderful and was delighted with my funny anecdotes. Then he went away. A little later he came back, took me by the hand and said:

"Just now, when I left the audience, I went back to the palace. I was standing before Muʻtadid when I remembered your imitation and funny stories and began to laugh. The Commander of the Faithful noticed this and finding my laughter ill-timed, said:

'Wretch! What's the matter with you?'

'O Commander of the Faithful,' I said, 'at the gate of the palace there is a certain Ibn al-Maghazili who tells funny stories and does imitations of a Bedouin, a Najdi, a Nabatean, a Gypsy, a Zanj, a Sindi, a Turk, a Meccan and a eunuch – and he peppers them with all kinds of jokes so that they would make a mother in mourning laugh and amuse a grave serious man as much as a child.'

The Caliph ordered me to bring you to him. I claim half your reward."

Scenting a lavish tip, I said to the eunuch:

"My lord, I am a poor man with a large family. Since God has favoured me by letting me meet you, couldn't you make do with just part of the sum – a sixth, for example, or a quarter?"

The eunuch held out for half and since even half tickled my fancy I decided to make do with it.

He took me by the hand and led me in. After having greeted the Caliph and made obeisance, I went and stood in the place pointed out to me. The Caliph returned my greeting. He was looking at a book and after having gone through most of it, he closed it and lifting his gaze, said to me:

"So you are Ibn al-Maghazili."

"Yes, O Commander of the Faithful."

"They tell me that you do imitations, tell funny stories and very entertaining

The Mimic and the Eunuch

jokes."

"Yes, O Commander of the Faithful," I replied. "Necessity makes a man ingenious. I draw crowds with my tales, I win their approval with my imitations, then I throw myself on their generosity and from what I receive I live."

"Let us see your imitations," said the Caliph. "Show us your talents. If you make me laugh, you shall have a reward of 500 dirhams. And if you don't bring a smile to my face, what can I demand from you?"

"Death and disappointment, O Commander of the Faithful!" I exclaimed. "I can only offer you the back of my neck and you shall hit it as much as you please with what you please."

"That's perfectly fair," said the Caliph. "So if I laugh you get the promised reward and if I don't laugh, I shall hit you ten times with this bag."

"Well," I said to myself, "a king who uses such a slight thing for his punishments! This will be quite all right!"

Turning round, I saw a bag made of supple leather in the corner of the audience hall and again said to myself:

"I wasn't wrong and my judgement wasn't faulty. What harm can a bag full of air do me? If I make the Commander of the Faithful laugh, it is pure profit; if I don't, being hit ten times with a bag of wind is a light punishment."

I therefore began my stories and imitations. I did my best to be entertaining and to speak well. I gave him all my imitations of Bedouin, grammarians, transvestites, judges, gypsies, Nabateans, Sindi, Zanj, eunuchs and Turks. I told him all my jokes, all the stories about thieves and all the naughty ones. I gave him every imitation I knew, and told every anecdote. At last I reached the end of my repertoire. My head was aching and felt as if it would burst. I fell silent. My spirits dropped and I felt chilled.

"Well, come on!" said the Caliph. "Serve up what you know!"

He was annoyed and I hadn't been able to make him laugh or even smile. On the other hand, all the eunuchs behind me and all the pages had been overcome with helpless laughter and, quite unable to control themselves, had had to leave the room.

"Commander of the Faithful," I said, "you've had the lot! My head aches and my store is exhausted. I have never seen gravity like yours. I have only one joke left."

"Well?" said Mu'tadid.

I went on.

"Commander of the Faithful, you promised me ten clouts on the head as a recompense. I am asking you to double the said reward and add ten more blows."

Mu'tadid was dying to laugh, but managed to keep a straight face. Then he said:

"I will do it. Page, hold his arms." The page obeyed and I stretched out my neck. At the first blow of the sack, I thought a castle had landed on my neck – indeed, the bag was stuffed with pebbles, as round and heavy as scale weights. I got my ten blows. My neck was out of joint, my back felt broken, my ears were ringing and I was seeing stars. The ten blows having been clearly counted, I cried out:

"My lord! A piece of advice!"

The Caliph interrupted my punishment, although he had decided to double it, as I had asked.

"Let's hear your advice," he said.

"My lord," I continued, "in religion, nothing is more beautiful than loyalty and nothing more odious than deceit. Now, I promised the eunuch who brought me here half my fee, whether it were great or small. The Commander of the Faithful – may God prolong his days! – has been willing, in his great generosity, to double the figure. I have had my half; now let the eunuch have his!"

At these words the Caliph fell back in peals of laughter. My first stories had also in fact amused him very much, but he had controlled himself and listened to them composedly. This time, he stamped and clapped his hands and clutched his sides. Finally the fit passed and when he had got his breath back he said:

"Bring so-and-so the eunuch!" and he was brought.

This man, who was tall and thin, was led before the Caliph, who gave the order that he should be beaten with the bag.

"Commander of the Faithful," cried the eunuch, "what have I done? What faults have I committed?"

I answered:

"This is my reward and you are my partner. I have had my half and it is your turn to have yours."

And as the blows fell on the nape of his neck, I added:

"I told you I was poor and had a large family. I complained to you of my needs and my penury. 'My lord,' I said to you, 'don't ask for half – make do with a sixth or a quarter,' but you insisted on having half. Ah! If I had known that the rewards of the Commander of the Faithful – may God prolong his life – consisted of blows, I would have given it all to you!"

These words, my reproaches to the eunuch, further increased the Caliph's mirth. When the punishment was over and his laughter had abated, he pulled out from under a cushion a purse, which had been prepared ahead of time and which contained 500 dirhams. Then he said to the eunuch, who was preparing to leave:

"Wait. I was going to give you this sum, but your meddling led you to get involved with a partner to whom I would probably not have given anything."

"O Commander of the Faithful," said I, "what about loyalty and the odiousness of cheating? I would have preferred you to have given everything to this man and for him to have had the ten extra blows to go with his 500 dirhams."

The Caliph divided the sum between us and we went away.'

VIII:161-168
§§ 3300-3304

(Omitted: VIII:168; § 3305. Necrology for the year 282 AH/895 AD.)

A MASTER THIEF

In 283 AH/896 AD, Mu'tadid went to Takrit while Husain ibn Hamdan, at the head of the crack troops, campaigned against the Kharijite Harun al-Shari. There was a great battle and the victory went to Husain ibn Hamdan. He brought Harun al-Shari and his brother to the Caliph as captives, with no question of amnesty.

Mu'tadid returned to Baghdad. Pavilions were erected in the capital and the streets were hung with banners. The Caliph drew up his army in perfect battle array before the Shammasiya Gate and then crossed the town to the Hasani Palace. To honour Husain ibn Hamdan, the Caliph gave him a splendid gala robe and clasped a gold chain about his neck. A number of knights of his entourage and important men of his family were also presented with robes of honour. As a reward for their courage and prowess, they rode in triumph before all the people and, on the orders of the Caliph, Harun al-Shari was mounted on an elephant. He was dressed in a sleeved robe of silk brocade and on his head was a tall headdress of raw silk. His brother followed, mounted on a Bactrian camel. They came immediately after Husain ibn Hamdan and his escort. Mu'tadid followed them, wearing a black robe and a tall pointed headdress; he was riding an ash-grey horse. To his left was his brother Abd Allah ibn al-Muwaffaq and behind him his page Badr, his vizier Ubaid Allah and the vizier's son, Qasim.

From every quarter a paean of thanksgiving arose. The crowd passing from the eastern quarter to the western became so dense, however, that part of the structure of the bridge gave way under the weight and collapsed onto a boat loaded with people. A thousand people died that day, without counting those who perished unrecorded. The bodies of the drowned were pulled out of the Tigris by means of grappling-irons and with the help of divers, while terrifying cries of distress and wailing rose from both banks.

In the midst of all this, one of the divers brought up a child decked with ornaments of gold and gems. An old thief who was in the crowd noticed the child and began to tear his face until blood came and to roll in the dust, making a great show of having just recognized his son. He began to lament, crying:

'You were not dead when they drew you from the river! The fish had not yet begun to eat you! You were not dead, my darling child! Why could I not see you once more before you breathed your last?'

Then he took the body, loaded it onto his donkey and vanished. Witnesses to this scene were still present when a man arrived, an eminent merchant, well

The Meadows of Gold

known for his wealth. He had just learned what had happened and hoped to find his son among the corpses. Indifferent to the precious jewels and rich clothes of the dead child, his only wish was to see him and shroud him and to have him laid in the earth and buried with the customary prayers. They told him what had just happened and both he and the merchants who were with him were deeply dismayed. All their questions and searches were useless and came to nothing. The ex-convicts on guard at the bridge*, who were very well acquainted with the old rascal, left the father of the drowned child no hope. They told him that this master thief wore them out with his tricks and had them absolutely at their wits' end. As proof of his sharp practices and guileful schemes, they told him the following story.

One day, very early in the morning, he went to the house of a wealthy and high-ranking man, a very important assistant to a qadi. He turned up carrying an empty jar on his shoulders, an axe and a palm-leaf basket. He was in rags. Without saying a word he began to swing the axe and wreck the shops standing in front of the lawyer's door, tearing out the bricks and throwing them down. The lawyer, his attention caught by the axe blows and sounds of falling debris, came out to see what was going on. He saw the old man busy demolishing his shops on the very threshold of his house. He said to him:

'Servant of God, what are you doing? Who ordered you to do this?'

The old man went on without paying any attention to the lawyer or answering him. During this scene, the neighbours gathered. They dragged off the thief, giving him a cuff here and a push there. He turned on them:

'Wretches! What do you want from me? Are you not ashamed of making fun of me, a venerable old man?'

'Fun, indeed!' they said. 'You old joker! Who told you to do this?'

'Jokers yourselves!' retorted the old man. 'It was the master of the house.'

'The master of the house!' exclaimed the neighbours. 'But he is right here – he was just talking to you!'

'No, by God, that's not him!' persisted the old man.

This reply and the whole misunderstanding in which the old man had become involved touched them and they said:

'Either this man is mad, or he is the cat's paw of some neighbours, who are jealous of the wealth God has granted the lawyer and who have led the old man into doing this.'

They made him stop his demolition. The old man went over to the big jar he had brought with him and reached his hand in, as if to pull out clothes hidden inside, then he gave a piercing cry and burst into tears. The lawyer, feeling sure the wretched man had been tricked by some thief who had stolen his clothes, asked him:

'What have they taken?'

'A new shirt which I bought yesterday, a cloak and my trousers,' answered the old man.

Everyone felt sorry for him. The lawyer comforted him with kind words, gave

A Master Thief

him clothes and a nice little sum in dirhams, as did the neighbours, then the old rogue went on his way, clutching his loot.

The old man in question was known by the nickname al-Uqab, 'The Eagle', or Abu al-Baz, 'Father of the Falcon'. He is the hero of all kinds of amazing adventures and ingenious tricks. One day the Caliph Mutawakkil made use of his talents. He had laid a bet with the doctor Bakhtishu' that if he could steal something recognizably his from the doctor's house within a three-day period fixed in that month, Bakhtishu' would pay 10,000 dinars into the Commander of the Faithful's treasury. If, on the other hand, the time limit elapsed without the practical joke coming off, the doctor would be given a particular estate named in the contract drawn up for the wager.

The famous thief – then in the flower of his youth – was called in by Mutawakkil. He undertook to filch something from Bakhtishu's own apartments that the doctor could not possibly deny belonged to him. During the agreed period, the doctor had his house very carefully guarded and barricaded himself inside, but al-Uqab contrived things so cleverly that he managed to carry off the doctor himself, whom he put in a chest and brought to Mutawakkil.

The story is really a very odd one. It seems that the thief passed himself off as an angel descended from heaven, a burning torch in his hand, sent to Bakhtishu' by Jesus, the son of Mary*. It also seems that he used some sort of drug of his own invention and that he poured *banj* into some food which he gave to the guards who were keeping watch that night at the doctor's house. I have related all this in the *Historical Annals*.

In a word, the above-mentioned old man surpassed in his thefts and ingenious ruses even the famous female confidence trickster Dallah* and all the other perpetrators of daring impostures and swindles, ancient and modern.

ALCHEMICAL TEXTS

Details of all those engaged in the transmutation of metals – gold, silver, precious stones, pearls and so on; the preparation of all kinds of elixirs such as that known as *farrar* – quicksilver – and others; the solidification of mercury and its conversion into silver; the various sorts of cheats and artifices they perpetrate with their *curcubita* retorts and alembics, by distillation, firing, the use of borax, wood, charcoal and bellows; in a word, an account of all the ingenious devices they employ in their investigations and the tricks and ruses to which they resort will be found in my *Historical Annals*. There I give a number of their poems on the subject and the traditions they have ascribed to Greek and Byzantine alchemists of old, such as Queen Cleopatra and Maria. Lastly, I cite the famous chemical formula of Khalid ibn Yazid, grandson of Mu'awiya, whom the adepts recognize as one of their masters. The formula is set out in a poem of which the following is an excerpt:

> Take talc and ammonia and what is found on roads,
> All in due measure, making no mistake;
> Then if you love your Lord,
> You will be master of creation.

There is an epistle in two parts by Yaqub ibn Ishaq ibn al-Sabah al-Kindi on this subject, in which he demonstrates the impossibility of man's rivalling the creative powers of nature and exposes the lies and artifices of the practitioners of this art. His treatise is entitled *A Refutation of Those who Falsely Claim that Gold and Silver Can be Artificially Produced*.

This work by al-Kindi was refuted by Abu Bakr Muhammad ibn Zakariya al-Razi, the philosopher and author of the *Book of Mansur*, a medical work in ten parts. In it, he demonstrates the falseness of al-Kindi's allegations and maintains the possibility of transmutation.

This same al-Razi has written a number of other books on the subject, each one devoted to a particular branch of this art – for example, one on metal ores, one on plants, and other subjects connected with the Great Task.

But there has been a great deal of argument about this subject and about the works of Qarun and other people. As far as I myself am concerned, I seek refuge in God from becoming obsessed by researches which weaken the brain, damage the sight and darken the complexion with clouds of vapours rising from sublimations, emanations from vitriol and other chemical substances!

VIII:175-177
§§ 3311-3312

(Omitted: VIII:177-180; §§ 3313-3318. Events of 283-4 AH/896-7 AD and necrology.)

MU'TADID'S GHOSTS

In this year, Mu'tadid was beset in his palace by an apparition, which appeared in different forms. Sometimes it was a monk with a white beard, wearing a habit, sometimes a handsome young man with a black beard, dressed in a completely different way, and sometimes an old man with a white beard, whose clothes were those of a merchant. One time the ghost appeared with a drawn sword in his hand and fatally wounded a eunuch. In vain the doors were chained and guarded. The apparition appeared wherever the Caliph was – in his apartments, in the courtyards, or elsewhere, as well as on the roof of the palace Mu'tadid had built. There was a great deal of talk about it. The news became known among both nobles and common people and spread everywhere, carried far and wide by the caravans. The stories multiplied, varying according to each man's private source of information. According to some, it was a rebel demon with a grudge against him who tormented him; according to others it was one of the believing jinn, who, seeing the wickedness and bloody behaviour of Mu'tadid, appeared to him in order to restrain him and keep him from crime. Others again maintained that it was one of the palace servants who, having fallen in love with a slave girl belonging to the Caliph, had resorted to magic spells, compounding very special drugs, which, placed in his mouth, rendered him invisible. But all this was guesswork.

The Caliph summoned sorcerers. Each day he became more troubled and gloomy. In his derangement, he had the throats of several of his eunuchs and slave girls cut, or else drowned them, and he caused many other people to be whipped and imprisoned. We have related all these events, together with the views on apparitions attributed to Plato, and also the story of Shaghab, the mother of Muqtadir and the reasons Mu'tadid had her thrown into prison and wanted to cut her nose off in order to disfigure her, in the *Historical Annals*, which should therefore be consulted.

VIII:181-182
§§ 3319-3320

(Omitted: VIII:183-184; §§ 3321-3322. Abu Laila al-Harith ibn Abd al-Aziz ibn Abi Dulaf inadvertently kills himself with his own sword; The tribe of Tayy attacks the pilgrims to Mecca in 285 AH/898 AD, winning booty worth 2,000,000 dinars.)

THE DEATH OF IBRAHIM AL-HARBI THE JURIST

In this same year, 285 AH/898 AD, Ibrahim al-Harbi, the jurisconsult and Traditionist, died in the western quarter of Baghdad, at the age of eighty-five, on a Monday, the seventh day before the end of the month of Dhu al-Hijja. He was buried near Bab al-Anbar and the Street of the Ram and the Lion.

He was a sincere man, learned, eloquent and generous, whose life was austere, pure and devout. In spite of his austerity and piety, however, he was cheerful, good-natured and easy-going, quite without arrogance and pride. He often made jokes at the expense of his friends, which were well received because they came from him, although they would have been held reprehensible in anyone else. He was the Shaikh of the Baghdad School at this period, on account of his merits, virtues and devoutness, just as he was its principal support through his authority as a Traditionist. He taught jurisprudence to the people of Iraq and held his course on Fridays in the main mosque of the western quarter.

TWO STUDENTS ENAMOURED

Abu Ishaq Ibrahim ibn Jahir tells the following story:

'Each Friday,' he said, 'I came to sit in the circle of those listening to Ibrahim al-Harbi. Two young men, exceptionally good-looking, charming in both face and general appearance, used to join us. They belonged to a family of merchants from Karkh. Dressed in the same way, they seemed like two souls in a single body. They rose together and sat down together.

On a particular Friday, only one of them came. His face was pale, his look downcast. I felt that the absence of his companion, who perhaps was ill, must be the cause of his sadness. On the following Friday, the absent one appeared, instead of him who had come the week before, but with the same pallor and dejection. I concluded that their separation and the intimacy which bound them was the cause. They continued to alternate in this way in joining the circle of listeners every Friday. If one of the two arrived first, his companion would not join us, which confirmed me in what I thought was the most probable theory.

One Friday, one of these young men had just arrived and taken his place among us when the other appeared. He examined the group from a distance and saw that he had been preceded by his friend. He looked at those present and sobs choked him. I read his grief in his eyes. He held some written notes in his left hand and, taking one of them in his right, he threw it into our circle and then, overcome with embarrassment, rushed away. I and several other people sitting in the group followed him with our eyes. Sitting beside me, on my right, was Husain ibn Hawthara, then in the flower of his youth.

The note fell in front of Ibrahim al-Harbi, who opened it and read it. This was his habit when he was thrown a note requesting his prayers and the prayers of those present on behalf of the author who was ill, or otherwise in need. He read the request with all the greater attention since he had seen who had thrown it. Then he prayed as follows:

"My God, reunite them, reconcile their hearts, let it so be that this union draws them closer to You and to each other before You!"

The audience answered this prayer with an amen, as was the custom. The Shaikh then rolled the note between his thumb and forefinger and tossed it before me. I had already tried to read it from a distance in order to understand the feelings of the man who had thrown it, so I now went over it with great attention and found the following:

> May God wipe away the sins of he
> Who helps with a prayer
> Two friends who were always in love
> Until the day an evil tongue,
> Jealous of their affection,
> Told one of some calumny
> He attributed to the other,
> So breaking their friendship's pact.

I kept the note in my possession. On the following Friday, the two young men reappeared together. All looks of pallor and dejection had vanished from their faces. I said to Husain ibn Hawthara:

"I see that God immediately granted their desire and that wishes expressed by the Shaikh will all be fulfilled, if God so wills."

During the same year, I made the pilgrimage and thought I saw, between Mina and Arafat, the two friends wearing the *ihram*. And I saw them always closely bound together from that time until they reached middle age. I believe that they belonged to the corporation of the brocade merchants of Karkh, or one of the other merchant guilds.'

THE QADI IBN JABIR

I had the story which you have just read from the qadi Ibrahim ibn Jabir, before he obtained his appointment. He was then living in Baghdad, struggling with poverty, which he accepted from God with great resignation, valuing it above wealth. Not long afterwards I met him in Aleppo, in the military district of Qinnasrin and al-Awasim in Syria, in the year 309 AH/921 AD. He was no longer the same man. Having now been made qadi, he took the side of wealth, which he valued above poverty.

'Qadi,' I said to him, 'do you remember what you told me of the governor of Rayy?:

"My thoughts," the governor said to you, "were floating undecided between the merits of poverty and those of wealth, when the Commander of the Faithful Ali ibn Abi Talib appeared to me in a dream and said: 'O so-and-so, the humility of the rich towards the poor is beautiful if it is inspired by a feeling of gratitude towards God.' Then I said to him: 'But far more beautiful is the pride of the poor in respect of the rich, for it is confidence in God which inspires them.'

The qadi Ibn Jabir replied:

'Men are subject to divine ordering and in none of their actions can they enfranchise themselves from its laws.'

How often, though, when he was poor, had not this same man condemned, in my presence, the thirst for riches and quoted the following words of Ali, may God ennoble his face:

'Son of Adam, do not add the troubles of the day which has not yet come to the troubles of the day which is already here, for if destiny grants you a tomorrow, God will provide for your survival. Know that everything you acquire over and above your needs is only stored up by you for the use of someone else.'

Nevertheless, it was this same man who afterwards gave himself up to the pleasures of life. I learned that with a single sweep of scissors he cut, for his wife, forty pieces of cloth from Tustar and other precious stuffs, and that he left behind him a considerable fortune.

VIII:188-190
§ 3326

(Omitted: VIII:191-199; §§ 3327-3337. Necrology; Events of the year 286 AH/899 AD; Basra fortified; A defeat of the Tayy; Various insurrections and campaigns against Qarmatians and Alids; The capture of Wasif.)

THE EUNUCH WASIF

Mu'tadid had intended to spare the eunuch Wasif, for he regretted having to put to death so energetic and courageous a man and one who had given such proofs of ability and daring. But then on reflection he considered that this eunuch had been born with a horror of submission and a taste for authority. When he had been arrested and clapped in irons, the Caliph had them ask whether he wanted anything.

'Yes,' answered Wasif, 'a bunch of basil flowers to breathe their perfume and books on the lives of ancient kings, to read what they have to say.'

When the Caliph's officer brought back the prisoner's reply, Mu'tadid procured what he had been asked and entrusted someone to see what passages the eunuch chose to read. When they reported that what interested him were the biographies of kings, their wars and their disasters, in preference to any of the other works he had been sent, Mu'tadid expressed his admiration and cried:

'This man is setting himself to despise even death!'

VIII:199-200
§ 3338

(Omitted: VIII:200-204; §§ 3339-3344. Necrology; The events of 288 AH/900 AD; The death of Wasif; Ibn Abi al-Qaws the Qarmatian executed; His claim that he would return in forty days; The effect of this on the masses.)

WHY MU'TADID PREFERRED THE ALIDS

A sum of money had been sent from Tabaristan by Muhammad ibn Zaid to be distributed secretly among the descendants of Abu Talib. This was denounced to Mu'tadid, who summoned the person in charge of the distribution and reprimanded him for having made a mystery of it and ordered him to act openly. On this occasion he showed his good will towards the members of the family of Abu Talib.

He was led to act thus towards the Alids, first of all because they were his close relatives, but also for another reason, which was revealed to me at Antioch by the jurisconsult Abu al-Hasan Muhammad ibn Ali al-Warraq, who came from that town and was known as Ibn al-Ghanawi. He had the story from Muhammad ibn Yahya ibn Abi Abbad, known as al-Jalis, 'The Table-Companion'.

Mu'tadid, when he was being held prisoner by his father, saw one day an apparition – an old man sitting on the banks of the Tigris. When this man stretched out his hand to the river, the water rose to meet it, leaving the river bed dry. Then, at another gesture, it resumed its normal course. Mu'tadid, telling of this, added:

'I asked who this old man was and they said Ali ibn Abi Talib. I rose at once and greeted him.

'Ahmad,' he said to me, 'one day the power will be yours. Beware of troubling my children and persecuting them.'

'Commander of the Faithful,' I replied, 'I hear and I obey!'

It was thus that Mu'tadid later came to extend to all his subjects the prorogation of the land tax, a measure which he had originally taken to favour the Alids. It was celebrated and sung enthusiastically by the poets, one of the finest pieces being that of Yahya ibn Ali, the astronomer.

VIII:205-206
§§ 3345-3347

(Omitted: VIII:207-210; §§ 3348-3353. The marriage of Qatr al-Nida; Amr ibn al-Laith, Saffar's brother captured; Necrology.)

THE DEATH OF MU'TADID

Mu'tadid died at the fourth hour of the night of Monday, the 22nd of the month of Rabi' II 289 AH/902 AD, at Baghdad, in the Hasani Palace.

His death is attributed to the poison which Isma'il ibn Bulbul administered to him before he was killed by the Caliph, a poison which slowly penetrated throughout his whole body. Others say he succumbed to the fatigues of his expedition against the eunuch Wasif, which we have discussed above. Yet others maintain that he was poisoned with a handkerchief which one of his slave girls offered him to wipe his face. There are still other versions, but we will pass over them in silence.

In his will, he enjoined them to bury him in the house of Muhammad ibn Abd Allah ibn Tahir in the western quarter of Baghdad. The house was known by the name Dar al-Rukham, 'House of Marble'.

In his last moments he fell into a swoon and as they did not know whether he was dead or not, the doctor came forward and felt one of his limbs. The Caliph, in his death-throes, was outraged by this examination. He pushed the doctor with his foot so hard that he rolled some yards away. They also say that the doctor died of the shock and that Mu'tadid expired at once.

While he was dying, Mu'tadid heard a clamour. He opened his eyes again and made a querying gesture with his hand. The eunuch Mu'nis said to him:

'My lord, it is the pages complaining with much shouting against the vizier Qasim ibn Ubaid Allah. We will have some money distributed to them.'

At these words, the Caliph knitted his brows and gasped out such terrible threats in his death agony that those present nearly died of fear. His body was carried to the house of Muhammad, the grandson of Tahir, and buried there.

The events connected with the history of Mu'tadid, his wars and expeditions, which are not to be read here are related, with the most important details, in the *Historical Annals* and *Intermediate History*.

VIII:211-213
§§ 3354-3356

THE CALIPHATE OF MUKTAFI

Muktafi was proclaimed Caliph at Baghdad on the very day of the death of his father Mu'tadid, that is, on a Monday, eight days before the end of the month of Rabi' II 289 AH/902 AD. The ceremony of swearing allegiance was presided over by the vizier Qasim ibn Ubaid Allah, the Caliph being then at Raqqa. Muktafi, who was known as Abu Muhammad, was at this time a little more than twenty years old. He arrived by river at Baghdad from Raqqa on Monday, the 7th of Jumada I 289 AH/902 AD and went to live to the Hasani Palace on the banks of the Tigris. He died on Sunday, the 13th of Dhu al-Qa'da 295 AH/908 AD at the age of thirty-one years and three months, after a reign which had lasted six years, seven months and twenty-two days, or, according to others, six years, six months and six days, following the different reckonings which are to be found in the chronicles. God knows best the truth.

The Caliphate has, up to the present year 332 AH/944 AD, been occupied by only two rulers bearing the name Ali – to wit, Ali ibn Abi Talib and Muktafi.

As soon as he entered the Hasani Palace, on the very day of his arrival in Baghdad, Muktafi bestowed a robe of honour on Qasim ibn Ubaid Allah. But he did not grant this favour to any of the generals. He ordered that the dungeons allotted by Mu'tadid for the inflicting of tortures should be destroyed. All those who were imprisoned there were freed and the buildings sequestered by the Caliph for the purpose of making dungeons were returned to their owners, who were also given indemnities. These measures caused Muktafi's subjects to bless him and wish him well.

But Muktafi allowed himself to be ruled by his vizier, Qasim ibn Ubaid Allah and by his freedman Fatik, and later, after the death of Qasim, by the vizier Abbas ibn al-Hasan and this same Fatik. It was the vizier Qasim ibn Ubaid Allah who had put to death Muhammad ibn Ghalib al-Isfahani, a man of learning and talent, who directed the state chancery. He also condemned to death Muhammad ibn Bashshar and Ibn Manara. Acting on a simple denunciation he had them put in chains and exiled to Basra. It is thought they were drowned on the way there – or at least no more has been heard of them until the present day. It was this which caused the poet Ali ibn Bassam to say:

> We can forgive you the death
> Of so many Muslims; we could say
> This was the result of sectarian quarrels.

But what was the crime of Ibn Manara?
You and he had always professed
The same religion.

QASIM'S HATRED OF BADR

Long before these events, Qasim ibn Ubaid Allah and Badr were at variance. Upon the accession of Muktafi, Qasim incited the new Caliph to hatred of his rival. Badr, seeing himself abandoned by a number of his supporting generals, who went over to the government, sought refuge in Wasit.

Qasim persuaded the Caliph to encamp on the banks of the Diyala River and there he made every effort to show his enemy's conduct in the most criminal light and to further envenom Muktafi's resentment. Then Qasim summoned the qadi Abu Hazim, a man distinguished for his learning and piety. He ordered him, in the name of the Commander of the Faithful, to go to Badr, offer him safe-conduct and bring him back to the court, promising him whatever he liked on behalf of the Caliph. But Abu Hazim refused, saying:

'I do not wish to transmit, as coming from the Commander of the Faithful, a message which I have not personally had from his mouth.'

Qasim entrusted the mission which Abu Hazim had refused to the qadi Abu Umar Muhammad ibn Yusuf. This last embarked on a boat and went to find Badr. He offered him a safe-conduct on behalf of the Caliph, guaranteed by the most solemn oaths and he pledged his word not to leave his side until he had actually brought him face to face with the Commander of the Faithful.

Badr left his camp and took the same boat as the messenger. They were making their way upstream and had reached the region of Mada'in and al-Sib, when a troup of eunuchs barred their way and surrounded the boat. Abu Umar abandoned his prisoner and fled in a light skiff. Badr, led to the bank, asked permission to make a prayer of two prostrations. This took place around noon on Friday, the 6th of the month of Ramadan 289 AH/901 AD. Permission was granted. As he bowed for the second prostration, they cut off his head. It was carried to Muktafi and set before him. Muktafi prostrated himself before it and cried:

'Now I shall taste the pleasures of living and ruling!'

He then returned to his capital, on Sunday, the 8th of the month of Ramadan.

The treachery of the qadi Muhammad ibn Yusuf and the promises and guarantees which he offered Badr on Muktafi's behalf, have inspired a poet to the following lines:

> Say to the qadi of the City of Mansur,
> 'By what right did you take the head of the Amir
> After having given your word and solemn

Promises, after a safe-conduct enshrined
In an official decree? What
Kind of oaths are these? God
Will bear witness that they
Were corrupt and perverted oaths.
Why did you swear by the triple divorce,
An oath that cannot be forsworn,
That your hand would not leave
That of Badr until you came
To the Master of the Throne?
Man of little shame, greatest
Liar of the Muslims, O bearer
Of false witness, it is not thus
That a qadi behaves. Such an action
Would dishonour even a toll-keeper
On a bridge. Now he is gone,
The man you murdered in Ramadan
As he bent in prayer and said
"God is Great!" And you committed
This crime on the holy day of Friday,
During the holiest action of the
Holiest of months! Prepare
To answer before the Judge of Judges,
After having endured
The interrogation of Munkir and Nakir,
The two angels of Death.
Sons of Yusuf ibn Ya'qub,
It is you who lead astray
The people of Baghdad.
May God disperse your family!
May he let me witness your shame
And the humiliation of the vizier!
You all deserve to be held ransom
To Abu Hazim – a man upright
In everything he has ever done.'

Badr ibn Khurr, the client of Mutawakkil, was free. He was first in the service of the page Nashi, Muwaffaq's equerry. Later, he attached himself to Mu'tadid and gained his affection. At first, in the time of Muwaffaq, he held only a lowly position, until the day when Fatik, one of Mu'tadid's highest-ranking pages, displeased his master and lost his position. This was the cause of his disgrace.

Mu'tadid, annoyed with one of his slave girls, gave orders that she should be sold. Fatik bought her back in secret. This intrigue, when revealed to Mu'tadid, was sufficient to alienate him from Fatik. From that moment, Badr's credit rose

The Meadows of Gold

and rose, until his influence became so powerful that all requests addressed to Mu'tadid invoked the favourite. Likewise the poets in their panegyrics associated the name of Badr with that of Mu'tadid and those who gave orations before the Caliph did the same.

VIII:216-220
§§ 3360-3363

(Omitted: VIII:221-223; §§ 3364-3368. More anecdotes concerning Badr; Various risings.)

THE RANSOMING OF TREACHERY

The exchange of prisoners known as the 'Ransoming of Treachery' took place in the month of Dhu al-Qa'da 292 AH/905 AD at Lamis. A certain number of Greeks and Muslims had already been brought back, when the Greeks violated the treaty. The final exchange took place between the Greeks and the Muslims in the same town of Lamis in the month of Shawwal 295 AH/908 AD under the direction of Rustam, the military governor of the Syrian frontiers, who presided over both transactions. The number of Muslims delivered up on the occasion presided over by Ibn Tughan in 283 AH/896 AD, which we have already mentioned, was as high as 2,495 prisoners of both sexes. In the 'Ransoming of Treachery', 1,154 Muslims were handed over and another 2,842 in the final exchange.

VIII:224
§ 3369

THE AVARICE OF MUKTAFI

On his death, Muktafi left 8,000,000 gold dinars in the state treasury and 25,000,000 dirhams. He left 9,000 head of horses, mules, camels and other mounts in his stables. In spite of this great fortune, he was miserly and mean. Here is an anecdote told by Abu al-Hasan Ahmad, the son of Yahya al-Munajjim, 'the Astronomer', known as Ibn Nadim. This same Ahmad was eminent in speculative research and in controversy. He was one of the exponents of the doctrine of Free Will and Unity*. It was to his brother, Ali ibn Yahya, that the poet Abu Haffan addressed these lines:

> Spring is a season in the turn of the years
> But Ibn Yahya's generosity is eternal spring.
> A man finds his house a veritable market of favours;
> He buys a whole age and it is we who sell.

Here then is Ahmad ibn Yahya's story:

'The daily menu at Muktafi's table was composed of ten dishes and, every Friday, a kid and three cups of sweets. Any of the sweet that was left over was served up again. One of the eunuchs dealing with the commissariat had orders to count the loaves left on the table. Any that were broken were set aside for the soup called *tharid*, while any that were whole reappeared at the next day's meal. The same was true of the hors d'oeuvres and sweetmeats.

When Muktafi wanted to build a palace in the Shammasiya quarter, opposite Qutrabbul, he expropriated for the purpose a number of estates and cultivated fields which were in the area, without compensating the proprietors, hence the chorus of complaints which was raised against him. But he died before having finished his palace. This grasping act is reminiscent of the behaviour of his father Mu'tadid, when he built his prisons.

VIII:225-226
§§ 3370-3372

(Omitted: VIII:227-237; §§ 3373-3386. The cruelty of the vizier Qasim; He puts to death Abd al-Wahid, Muktafi's pleasure-loving uncle, and the poet Ibn al-Rumi; Various poems and anecdotes.)

NOUGAT AND FRITTERS

I have the following story from Muhammad ibn Yayha al-Suli, nicknamed al-Shitranji, 'The Chess Player':

'One day,' he said, 'we were eating in the presence of Muktafi. They served us some *qata'if* [a kind of fritter] which had previously been served to him. They were exquisite, with a very light, perfectly prepared batter. The Caliph asked:

"Have any of the poets described this delicacy?"

My paternal uncle, Ahmad ibn Yahya, mentions them in the following lines:

> *Qata'if* stuffed tightly as bananas
> With almonds and powdered sugar,
> Swim on seas of walnut oil.
> My pleasure when I possess them
> May be compared with the joy
> Of Abbas when he became Caliph.'

Al-Suli adds:

'I then reminded the Caliph of this line by Ibn al-Rumi:

> Then in came delicious *qata'if*!

"Now there is a beginning which needs an ending!" cried Muktafi. "Recite the whole poem to me, right from the first verse!"

I continued as follows:

> A *samita* as yellow as a dinar –
> And it is just as shiny and valuable –
> Is served you by a young page.
> The fire has plumped it up
> Like a roast goose
> And as it is brought in,
> It seems as if its skin will burst.
> All around, the *judhaba*
> Begins to fall like scented rain,
> Soon followed by almond creams,
> All filled with sugar.

The Meadows of Gold

>What beneficent heaven
>Showers such a rain?
>What fortunate earth
>Is watered by its drops?
>How beautiful it looks
>On the table, swimming
>In molten butter!
>As we pull the skins
>From these almond meats,
>It is like removing silver
>From sheets of gold.
>First they served *tharid*
>Like a flowery garden,
>Worthy indeed to hold
>The highest place.
>And then mincemeat,
>Gilded with egg yolk,
>Clothing it like a robe –
>No, like a crown!
>Then in came delicious *qataʿif*
>Which enchant the palate
>And tickle the throat.
>A smile dawns on every face
>At the sight of the lovely
>Transparent sugar which covers them
>And which, with butter, forms
>A dew of tears.

Muktafi found these verses to his taste and signed to me to write them down, which I did.'

This same Muhammad ibn Yahya al-Suli also tells the following anecdote:

'A month after this occasion, we were again dining with the Caliph when *lawzinaj* – a kind of almond nougat – was served. The Caliph asked whether Ibn al-Rumi had mentioned this sweet in his verse.

"Yes, my Lord," I said.
"What did he say?"
"Here are the lines:

>Do not fail to bring me that *lawzinaj*
>The mere sight of which excites
>Admiration and delight
>In vain appetite closes its gates;
>The approach of such food
>Makes them re-open wide.

Nougat and Fritters

> Its aroma would make even a stone
> Open to let it in.
> The delicious scent rises
> From the plate in circles,
> The butter drips in spirals.
> Its outward appearance
> Matches its inner virtue;
> Its beauty makes its flavour
> Even more exquisite.
> The inside is heavy,
> But it is enfolded in something
> As light and airy
> As a spring breeze.
> You would say its dress were torn
> To let flow the crystal
> Sugar drops and that its delicate
> Outer skin had borrowed
> Its transparency
> From the cicada's wing.
> Teeth made of such material
> Would be white and shiny
> As the coins boys love
> To feel in their hands.
> Well-annointed with butter,
> Bluish without and grey within,
> It is like the *azraq* stone
> With its pale gleam.
> Every bitter almond is rejected
> By our connoisseur.
> Knowing gourmets have rivalled
> One another in the severity
> Of their criteria for choosing
> The kind of sugar used.
> Eyes will not tire of gazing
> Upon it and the teeth
> That sink into it shall never
> Be set on edge."

Muktafi learned these verses by heart and used to enjoy reciting them.'

VIII:238-242
§§ 3387-3389

(Omitted: VIII:242-243; § 3390. Verses by Muktafi.)

DUSHAB AND HARISA

I have the following story from the grammarian Abu Abd Allah Ibrahim ibn Muhammad ibn Arafa, known as Niftawaih, who was told it by Abu Muhammad Abd Allah ibn Hamdun:

'One day,' said the latter, 'we were discussing different kinds of drinks in the presence of Muktafi and had just got on to the kind of *nabidh* which is known as *dushab*, when it is improved by the addition of *dhadhi* and date honey. We had before us a great goblet or drinking cup. Ibn al-Rumi's lines on this drink came into my mind and I was about to recite them when the Caliph, anticipating me, asked whether any of us knew a poem on *dushab*. I hastened to quote this by Ibn al-Rumi:

> Take the best grain and the finest syrup;
> Press them and let them steep with care.
> Let them rest a long time at the bottom
> Of their jar and then you will drink
> The true old wine of Babel.

"Cursed poet!" cried Muktafi. "How greedy he was! He has really made me want to drink *dushab* today!"

When the meal was served, a large dish of *harisa* was set down before us and in the middle of it was a hollow like a bowl filled with fat from the chicken. The sight of this dish made me smile, because it reminded me of the story of the Caliph Rashid and Aban, the Koran reciter. Muktafi, noticing my smile, said:

"Abu Abd Allah, what is the joke?"

"Commander of the Faithful," I replied, "I was thinking of an anecdote of a dish of *harisa* and chicken fat in which your ancestor Rashid played a part."

"Let's hear this story."

"Here it is, O Commander of the Faithful. According to Utbi and Mada'ini, Aban the Koran reciter was eating with Rashid one day when a splendid *harisa* was served, in the middle of which – just as with ours – was a large hollow filled with chicken fat. I will let Aban speak for himself:

'I was very tempted by this fat, but out of respect for Rashid, I did not dare stretch out my hand and dip my bread in it. I did, however, make a little depression, so that the fat ran to my side.

'"Aban," the Caliph said to me, "Have you scuttled it in order to drown those

Dushab and Harisa

on board?"' (Koran 18:71)

"Indeed, no, O Commander of the Faithful," I replied, "We are pushing it towards a land parched by drought."' (Koran 7:57)

Harun al-Rashid laughed at this until he had to hold his sides."'

VIII:243-245
§§ 3391-3392

THE DEATH OF MUKTAFI

In the year 295 AH/908 AD, the gifts offered by Ziyadat Allah ibn Abd Allah, known as Abu Mudar, arrived in Baghdad. They consisted of 200 eunuchs, black as well as white, 150 slave girls, 100 Arab horses, and other precious things.

It was in the year 184 AH/800 AD that Rashid, who was then at Raqqa, invested Ibrahim ibn al-Aghlab with the government of Ifriqiya and it was there that the Aghlabid dynasty held sway until the expulsion of this same Ziyadat Allah in 296 AH/909 AD or, as others have it, 295 AH/908 AD. He was driven from the throne by Abu Abd Allah al-Muhtasib, known as the 'Missionary', who appeared among the Kutama Berber tribes and upheld the rights of Ubaid Allah, master of the Maghrib. I have already explained that this territory was given as a fief to Aghlab ibn Salim al-Sa'di by Mansur.

Muktafi was at Darb and felt his illness worsening. He had Muhammad ibn Yusuf the qadi and Abd Allah ibn Ali ibn Abi al-Shawarib summoned, and used them as witnesses to the will he was making in favour of his brother Ja'far, the heir apparent. Having already mentioned his death, there is no need for us to come back to it here.

The history of Muktafi and the main events of his time – such as the exploits of Ibn al-Balkhi in Egypt, the revolt of the Qarmatians in Syria, that of Zikrawaih and his expedition against the Meccan caravan – are all, together with yet other events of Muktafi's reign, set down in full in my *Historical Annals* and *Intermediate History*; I am thus absolved from having to go over them again in this book.

THE CALIPHATE OF MUQTADIR

Muqtadir was proclaimed Caliph on the very day his brother Muktafi died, which was Sunday 13 Dhu al-Qaʻda 295 AH/908 AD. He was known as Abu Fadl. His mother was a slave called Shaghab – 'Trouble'; the mother of Muktafi was also a slave, by name Zalum – 'Bad Tempered' – but there is no general agreement about this. Muqtadir was thirteen when he came to the throne and he was killed at Baghdad after the afternoon prayer, on Wednesday, 27 Shawwal 320 AH/932 AD. He had reigned for twenty-four years, eleven months and sixteen days and his age was thirty-eight years and fifteen days. But there are other estimates of his age; God knows the truth.

At the accession of Muqtadir, the post of vizier was occupied by Abbas ibn al-Hasan, who continued to officiate until the day he was attacked by Husain ibn Hamdan, Wasif ibn Sawartikin and other leading men and assassinated, together with Fatik. This was on a Saturday, eleven days before the end of the month of Rabiʻ II 296 AH/909 AD.

The facts about Abd Allah ibn al-Muʻtazz, Muhammad ibn Daʻud and others are common knowledge and can be found in my *Intermediate History* and other works. A number of authors have written histories of the reign of Muqtadir, some forming part of general histories of the Caliphate, while others are separate monographs. Among the first, I should mention the relevant part of the chronicle of Baghdad called *Dynastic Histories*. I am also indebted to Jahshiyari for a history of Muqtadir in several thousand folios. I have only had a small part of it in my own hands, but more than one learned man has told me that Jahshiyari's history of Muqtadir runs to this length. I am only giving here a historical summary of the reign of each Caliph; my aim in giving these summaries is to encourage the study of the history of the Caliphate and record memorable events by writing them down.

VIII:247-250
§§ 3396-3398

(Omitted: VIII:250-267; §§ 3399-3417. Poems of Ibn al-Muʻtazz quoted; On the jurisconsult Muhammad al–Isfahani; On the poet Ibn Bassam; His death in 303 AH/915 AD; His satires quoted, including some on his father.)

HOSPITALITY

Ibn Bassam's father, Muhammad ibn Nasr ibn Mansur, was a man of the greatest generosity and nobility. He was conspicuous for his luxury, the richness of his clothes, his affability and his passion for architecture. This is what Abu Abd Allah al-Qummi tells of him:

'I went to visit Muhammad at Baghdad one winter's day when the weather was bitingly cold and I found him in a large room with a domed roof plastered with red clay from Armenia of the most splendid lustre and vividness. In the middle of the room, which I estimate to have been twenty cubits square, there was a brazier with its two "giraffes"* which, when adjusted and set in place was not less than ten cubits in length and breadth. The brazier was filled right up with charcoal made of euphorbia wood. The master of the house was in the middle of the room, wearing a fine diaphanous cape made at Tustar. The area not covered by the brazier was carpeted in red brocade. My host had me sit down beside him and, as I was being roasted by the fire, he gave me a goblet containing a mixture of rose water and camphor to cool my face. He also called for water, which I found had ice in it. In a word, my only worry was that I would have to leave him. Then I left and went out into the clammy cold, and as I was going he said to me: "This house is not pleased with those who wish to leave it."

Another day,' the same narrator said, 'I went to visit him again. This time, he was at the far end of his house, in a room looking out on a pond. He was sitting on a ledge from the middle of which he could enjoy the view over his garden, his enclosure filled with gazelles and his aviary filled with turtle doves and other birds.

"Muhammad," I said, "truly you are sitting in Paradise!"

"Well then," he replied, "you must not leave Paradise before having had something to drink."

I sat down and scarcely had I taken my place than they brought us a table of onyx, the like of which I had never seen. In the middle of the table was a goblet also of onyx in variegated colours, the edges decorated with red gold. It was filled with rose water. There was also a dish of chicken breasts arranged in layers in the form of a tower and several onyx bowls containing sauces and different seasonings. After this came triangular mille-feuille pastries served hot and several goblets of nougat.

The table was removed and we went to where the curtain was hanging.* There they brought us a great platter of white porcelain on which Syrian apples – there

Hospitality

must have been a thousand of them – had been arranged symmetrically on a bed of violets, gillyflowers and others. I have never seen such an elegant meal nor such pretty flowers, but my host told me it was just their early refreshment. However, I have never forgotten the charm of that morning.'

I have quoted this anecdote about Muhammad ibn Nasr simply in order to show that his son Ibn Bassam painted him quite other than he really was and, again, to prove that no one escaped the poet's gibes.

I have already related several incidents in his life and given a large number of his satires in my different works, among others his verses against Qasim ibn Ubaid Allah. As I have already told, this vizier went in one day to Mu'tadid while the Caliph, who was playing chess, was humming this line from Ibn Bassam:

This man's life is like that man's death;
You cannot escape from misfortune.

Raising his head, the Caliph saw Qasim. He was somewhat embarrassed and said:
'Make it impossible for Ibn Bassam's tongue to harm you.'

The vizier got up and was going to give orders to have Ibn Bassam's tongue cut out when Mu'tadid added:
'By your kindness and by giving him a lucrative job – for I forbid you to do him any harm.'

As a result, Qasim gave Ibn Bassam the directorship of the ministry of posts and intelligence for the provinces of Jund Qinnasrin and al-Awasim in Syria.

VIII:267-271
§§ 3418-3420

(Omitted: VIII:272-274; §§ 3421-3424. The viziers of Muqtadir.)

THE DEATH OF MUQTADIR

As I said before, Muqtadir was killed at Baghdad at the hour of the afternoon prayer, on Wednesday, the third day before the end of Shawwal, 320 AH/932 AD. He died in the battle that took place between him and the eunuch Mu'nis near the Shammasiya Gate in the eastern quarter of the city. It was the common people who took the trouble to bury Muqtadir's body.

His vizier was then Abu al-Fath al-Fadl ibn Ja'far ibn Musa ibn al-Furat, as we have just said. It is related that this minister consulted the heavens when Muqtadir was about to mount his horse in order to ride into the battle which cost him his life. The Caliph asked:

'What time is it?'

'The sun is beginning to decline,' he was told.

The Caliph frowned and had just decided that he would not advance when he was attacked by Mu'nis' cavalry. This was the last time he was seen alive.

It is noteworthy that every sixth Caliph of the House of Abbas was deposed and put to death. The first was Amin, 'The Deposed'. The sixth succeeding Caliph was Musta'in and the last, counting thus, Muqtadir.

The interesting history of Muqtadir, the wars and battles of his reign, the story of Ibn Abi Saj, of Mu'nis, of what happened to Sulaiman ibn al-Hasan al-Jannabi at Mecca in 317 AH/929 AD, the history of the Muslim empire in both east and west, all these events, I repeat, are told in detail in the *Historical Annals* and are summarized in the *Intermediate History*. Here, I have only given the barest glimpse. But, if God grants me the time, if He gives me long life, if He adds some further days to my existence, I propose to follow the present work with another book which will include all kinds of accounts and recollections worthy of interest. Without tying myself down to a methodical scheme, nor to a regular order of composition, I shall set down all the important events and interesting stories that I can remember and I shall call it *The Reunion of the Assemblies – Collected Stories and Literary Anecdotes*; it will follow and complement our other writings.

VIII:274-276
§§ 3425-3428

(Omitted: VIII:276-282; §§ 3429-3435. Necrology for the year 297 AH/909 AD: 'During this same year the news reached Baghdad that the four pillars of the Ka'ba had been submerged and several pilgrims drowned in the flood, and also that the Well of Zamzam had overflowed, which had never been seen before'; Alid revolts up to 301 AH/913 AD; Necrology for the years 297-310 AH/909-22 AD; Death of Tabari; Natural disasters.)

CYPRUS SEIZED

At this same period, Damyana, the commander of the Muslim cruising fleet which was operating in the Mediterranean, seized the island of Cyprus, whose inhabitants had broken the treaty made at the very beginning of Islam, whereby they were to remain neutral between the Byzantines and the Muslims and to pay the land-tax, half to the Muslims and half to the Greeks.

For four months Damyana gave this island over to fire and pillage and captured a number of fortified points. As I have discussed Cyprus previously in this book, where I made our general remarks on the seas, the sources and mouths of rivers, I have not described it again at any length here.

VIII:282-283
§ 3436

(Omitted: VIII:283-286; §§ 3437-3440. Necrology continued; The rebel Ibn Abi Saj captured, 307 AH/919 AD; Other revolts.)

THE CALIPHATE OF QAHIR

Qahir – Muhammad ibn Ahmad al-Mu'tadid Billah – was proclaimed Caliph on Thursday, 28 Shawwal 320 AH/932 AD and was deposed after having his eyes torn out on Wednesday, 5 Jumada I 332 AH/934 AD. His reign thus lasted a year, six months, and six days. He was known as Abu Mansur, and his mother was a slave.

Qahir first appointed Ibn Muqla as his vizier in 321 AH/933 AD. After having removed him from office, he replaced him with Abu Ja'far Muhammad ibn Qasim ibn Ubaid Allah ibn Sulaiman. Later, he deposed Abu Ja'far and appointed as his successor Abu al-Abbas Ahmad ibn Ubaid Allah al-Khasibi.

It is difficult to give any very clear idea of the character of this Caliph, he was so unstable and changeable. Harsh and of an extreme severity towards his enemies, he put to death a number of high officials, among others Mu'nis the eunuch, Yalbaq and Ali, Yalbaq's son.

His fits of violence made him the fear and terror of his subjects. He was always armed with a long lance which he carried as he went about his palace and planted before him when he sat down. Those whom he wished to kill, he struck down with his own hand, using this weapon, and thus he kept in awe those who had shown so much disobedience and insolence to his predecessors. However, the inconstancy of his behaviour and the horror inspired by his rages – which we have described – gave rise to a conspiracy which was hatched against him within his very own palace. He was made prisoner and they gouged out his eyes.

Qahir is still alive today. He is living in the house of Ibn Tahir in the western quarter of Baghdad – if one can believe the stories and rumours which have reached me on this subject. His successor, the Caliph Radi, kept news of him hidden and let no information about him be divulged. When Muttaqi came to the throne, Qahir was found imprisoned in a secluded room. On the orders of the new Caliph he was taken to the house of Ibn Tahir, where, according to what I have been told, he is now being kept in close confinement.

VIII:286-289
§§ 3441-3443

QAHIR DEMANDS A TRUE HISTORY OF THE CALIPHATE

The following story originates from Muhammad ibn Ali al-Misri, the historian and native of Khurasan, who was an intimate of Qahir:

'One day the Caliph Qahir took me aside and said:

"Swear to tell me the truth, or beware of this!"

And he showed me his lance. And by God, I saw death rise up between him and me.

"I swear it, O Commander of the Faithful!" I cried.

"Pay heed," he went on – and he repeated the words three times.

"Yes, O Commander of the Faithful!"

"Pay heed to what I am about to ask you. Hide nothing from me. I want no embellishing touches, no rhymed prose in your story. But also, I will tolerate no omissions."

"Yes, O Commander of the Faithful!"

He continued:

"You have a thorough knowledge of the Abbasid Caliphs, their character and behaviour and are as well acquainted with Abu al-Abbas al-Saffah as with his successors?"

"Commander of the Faithful," I answered, "I set only one condition: that my life be spared."

"I promise it," said Qahir.

Then I began as follows:

"Abu al-Abbas al-Saffah was quick to spill blood. His agents in east and west followed his example and took him as their model. Such were Muhammad ibn al-Ashath in the Maghrib, Salih ibn Ali in Egypt, Khazim ibn Khuzaima and Humaid ibn Qahtaba. Saffah atoned for this defect by considerable nobility of mind and great generosity. He gave constantly and scattered gold with an open hand. Similarly, the governors whom we have just mentioned and, in general, all his contemporaries, followed in his footsteps and took him for a model."

"Tell me about Mansur," the Caliph said to me.

"The truth, O Commander of the Faithful?"

"The truth."

I continued as follows:

"Well, he was the first to sow discord between the children of Abbas ibn Abd al-Muttalib and the family of Abu Talib, who until then had made common cause.

The Meadows of Gold

He was the first of the Caliphs to bring astrologers to his court and make his decisions in accordance with the stars. The Magian astrologer Nawbakht lived with him and at his hands embraced Islam and became the head of the famous family of the Nawbakhti. I will also mention the astrologer Ibrahim al-Fazari, the author of the celebrated poem on the stars and other works on the study of the heavens, and another astrologer, Ali ibn Isa al-Asturlabi – 'The Maker of Astrolabes'.

Mansur was also the first Caliph to have foreign works of literature translated into Arabic, for example, *Kalila and Dimna*; the *Sindhind*; various of Aristotle's treatises on logic and other subjects; Ptolemy's *Almagest*; the *Book of Euclid*; the treatise on arithmetic and all the other ancient works – Greek, Byzantine, Pahlavi, Persian and Syriac. Once in possession of these books, the public read and studied them avidly.

Again, it was in the reign of Mansur that Muhammad ibn Ishaq published his books *On the Conquests and Expeditions* and his *Researches into Origins*, subjects which had never until then been studied or arranged systematically or gathered into a single work.

Mansur was the first ruler to distribute public offices among his freedmen and pages. He employed them in matters of importance and advanced them over the Arabs. This practice was followed after his time by the Caliphs who were his heirs and it was thus that the Arabs lost the high command, the supremacy and the honours which they had enjoyed until then.

From the time of his accession to the throne, Mansur devoted himself to learning. He applied himself to the study of religious and philosophical ideas and acquired a profound knowledge of the different sects as well as of the Muslim Tradition. During his reign, the schools of Traditionists increased in number and widened the scope of their studies."

"Good," said Qahir, "all that is very clear and unambiguous. Now go on to Mahdi and tell me what his character was like."

I went on:

"Mahdi was good and generous, and his character was noble and liberal. His subjects, following in his footsteps and inspired by his example, were also noteworthy for their open-handedness. This Caliph had the custom, when he appeared in public, of having purses filled with gold and silver carried before him. No one solicited his charity in vain and the steward who walked ahead had orders to give alms to those who did not dare to ask, anticipating their need.

Mahdi was merciless in exterminating heretics and all those who stepped aside from the path of Islam, for it was in his reign that religious heresies appeared and grew strong, especially after the promulgation of the works of Mani, Bardesanes (Ibn Daisan) and Marcion translated from Persian and Pahlavi by Ibn al-Muqaffa' and other learned men. The books of Ibn Abi al-Awja, Hammad Ajrad, Yahya ibn Ziyad and Muti' ibn Iyas, the continuators of the Manichean, Daisanite and Marcionite sects, were brought out at the same time. Dualist beliefs appeared and spread rapidly. Mahdi, then, was the first to order the

Qahir Demands a True History of the Caliphate

polemicists of the theological schools to compose books to refute the heterodox sects mentioned above, and other sectarians, in their works. They produced convincing proofs against their wrong-headed adversaries and overthrew the weak arguments of the heretics and made the truth shine forth to all who doubted.

It was Mahdi who rebuilt the mosque at Mecca and that of the Prophet at Medina in the form they stand today, and he rebuilt Jerusalem, which had been devastated by earthquakes."

Qahir said:

"Now tell me about Hadi, whose reign was so short. What was his character like and what were his customs?"

"Hadi was a proud and haughty ruler. He was the first Caliph to have guards precede him carrying naked swords, clubs over their shoulders and bows ready-strung. Since his officials followed his example, the use of arms became very prevalent during his reign."

Qahir interrupted me to compliment me on the clarity of my exposition and afterwards he asked me about the character of Harun al-Rashid.

"Harun al-Rashid," I replied, "was scrupulous in fulfilling his duties as a pilgrim and in waging Holy War. He undertook public works – wells, cisterns, strongholds on the road to Mecca and also in that city and at Mina, Arafat and Medina. He scattered both wealth and the treasure of his justice on all his subjects. He strengthened the frontiers, built cities, fortified several towns such as Tarsus and Adana, revived the prosperity of Missisa and Mar'ash and carried out innumerable works of military architecture, as well as building caravanserais and *ribats*. His officials followed his example. The people imitated his behaviour and followed in the direction he pointed out. Error was repressed, the truth reappeared and Islam, shining with new splendour, eclipsed all other nations.

The very type of generosity and charity in this reign was manifested in the form of Umm Ja'far Zubaida, the daughter of Ja'far and the granddaughter of Mansur. This princess had numerous caravanserais built at Mecca and she filled this city and the pilgrim road which bears her name with cisterns, wells and buildings which survive to this day. She also built several hospices for travellers along the Syrian frontier and at Tarsus and endowed them.

In discussing this period we should also mention the Barmakids, their generosity, their charity and the noble deeds which have made their name immortal.

Harun al-Rashid was the first Caliph to popularize the games of polo, shooting with the bow in the course of a tournament, ball games and racket games. He rewarded those who distinguished themselves in these various exercises and these games spread among the people. He was also the first among the Abbasid Caliphs to play chess and backgammon. He favoured the players who distinguished themselves and granted them pensions. Such was the splendour, wealth and prosperity of his reign that they called this period 'The Days of the Marriage Feast'. These qualities and yet others pass all description and are above all praise.

At this Qahir interrupted me:

"I think," he said, "you have shortened the account of the deeds of Umm

Ja'far. Why is that?"

"O Commander of the Faithful," I answered, "I want to be brief and am trying to be concise."

At these words the Caliph snatched up his lance and brandished it at me. I saw red death appear before me on the point of that weapon. The Caliph's eyes flashed like lightning. I resigned myself to my fate. I had no further doubts that the Angel of Death had come to tear out my soul. Indeed, the Caliph threw his weapon at me, but I ducked in time and the blow missed.

"You wretch!" cried Qahir, stepping back. "Why did you risk your head? Are you weary of life?"

"What is it, O Commander of the Faithful?"

"Come", went on the Caliph, "this story of Zubaida. I want to know more."

"Commander of the Faithful, I obey. The nobility and magnificence of this princess in serious matters as well as light have led her to be placed in the very first rank.

As regards her serious achievements, her charitable foundations, unprecedented in Islam and the drilling of the well called Ain al-Mushash in the Hijaz must be mentioned. It was Zubaida who dug out the spring and caused it to flow and with an acquaduct brought the water over hills and valleys, plains, mountains and stony wastes, a distance of twelve miles to Mecca itself. It is estimated that these works cost not less than 1,700,000 dinars.

I have already mentioned the public works, hospices, water-tanks and wells with which she endowed the Hijaz and the frontiers of the empire. She devoted thousands of dinars to it, without ever jeopardizing her other charities, the help and kindliness which she poured out on the needy.

As for the second category of expenses, those of which kings are most vain and on which they found their prosperity and the health of their states, those, in fact, which history records in its account of their deeds and achievements, Zubaida is equally remarkable.

She was the first to be served on vessels of gold and silver enriched with precious stones. For her the finest clothes were made of the varicoloured silk called *washi*, a single length of which, designed for her, cost 50,000 dinars. She was the first to organize as a bodyguard a troop of eunuchs and slave girls, who rode at her side, fulfilled her orders and carried her letters and messages. She was the first to make use of palanquins of silver, ebony and sandalwood, decorated with clasps of gold and silver, hung with *washi*, sable, brocade and red, yellow, green and blue silk. She was the first to introduce the fashion for slippers embroidered with precious stones and for candles made of ambergris – fashions which spread to the public.

Then, O Commander of the Faithful, when the Caliphate passed to her son, he gave precedence to his eunuchs, such as Kawthar and others, and showed his preference by bestowing upon them the highest honours. Zubaida, noticing her son's marked taste for these eunuchs and the ascendance they were gaining over him, chose young girls remarkable for the elegance of their figures and the charm of their faces. She had them wear turbans and gave them clothes woven and embroidered in the royal factories, and had them fix their hair with fringes and lovelocks and draw it back at the nape of the neck after the fashion of young men. She dressed them in close-fitting wide-sleeved robes called *qaba* and wide belts which showed off their waists and their curves. Then she sent them to her son. Amin, as they filed into his presence, was enchanted. He was captivated by their looks and appeared with them in public. It was then that the fashion for having young slave girls with short hair, wearing *qaba* and belts, became established at all levels of society. They were called 'page girls'."

This description moved Qahir. He showed a lively satisfaction and with a resounding voice cried out:

"Page, a cup of wine in honour of the page girls!"

Immediately, a swarm of young girls appeared, all the same height and all looking like young men. They were wearing tight-fitting jackets, *qaba* and all had fringes. They wore their hair in lovelocks and had belts of gold and silver. While the Caliph was raising his cup, I admired the purity of its jewels, the sparkle of the wine which gilded it with its rays and I went into raptures over the beauty of these young girls. But Qahir was still holding his formidable lance. He drank the cup straight off and said to me:

"Right! go on!"

"O Commander of the Faithful, I obey," I replied. "The Caliphate next passed to Ma'mun. At the beginning of his reign, this Caliph was under the influence of Fadl ibn Sahl and other courtiers. He devoted himself to the study of astrology and its rulings. He modelled his conduct on the Sasanid kings such as Ardashir ibn Babak and others. He had a passion for reading old books and studied them constantly, persevering in his researches until he succeeded in understanding them and getting to their very heart. We know what happened to Fadl ibn Sahl*, called Dhu al-Riyasatain – 'Minister with Two Portfolios'.

On his arrival in Iraq, Ma'mun gave up his favourite studies and professed the doctrine of Unity and of Rewards and Punishments – that is to say, the doctrines of the Mu'tazilites. He presided over conferences of theologians and attracted to his court polemicists famous in debate, such as Abu al-Hudhail, Abu Ishaq Ibrahim ibn Sayyer al-Nazzam and other doctors, partisans and adversaries of these two masters. He constantly had at his side learned jurists and literary men, whom he brought from many different cities and to whom he gave pensions. The populace acquired a taste for philosophical speculation, the study of dialectic became fashionable and each school wrote works in support of their arguments and the doctrines which they professed.

As to Ma'mun himself, he was the most clement and patient of men. No one has made better use of their power, been more liberal, more generous in their gifts or less inclined to regret them. Ministers and courtiers all imitated him sedulously, all followed his example and walked in his footsteps.

He was succeeded by Mu'tasim, O Commander of the Faithful. This Caliph adopted the beliefs of his brother Ma'mun. He was distinguished by his liking for

The Meadows of Gold

horses and by his wish to imitate Persian kings in his table services and in the fashion for wearing a turban over a soft cap. The people adopted this headgear in imitation of their sovereign and called it, for this reason, 'Mu'tasimi'.

Mu'tasim was good to his subjects. He ensured the safety of the roads and scattered largesse among his people.

The following Caliph, Wathiq, conformed to the religious beliefs of his father and his paternal uncle. He punished dissidents* and held inquisitions into the religious beliefs of the people. He forbade all the qadis of the empire to accept as witnesses before the law any who did not share his religious beliefs. He was a great gourmet, prodigal in giving, flexible and full of concern for his subjects.

Mutawakkil, O Commander of the Faithful, was his successor and rejected the beliefs professed by Ma'mun, Mu'tasim and Wathiq. He forbade, on the severest pains, the study of different religious opinions, and re-established belief in authority and the teaching of the Traditions. His reign was happy and his government stable and well founded. These facts, O Commander of the Faithful, and other details on the character of Mutawakkil are very well known."

Qahir then said to me:

"Listening to you speak, I seemed to see these sovereigns come alive as you depicted them. It seemed as if your portraits became real. I am delighted with what I have just heard. You have opened up the way to wise government and have shown me the road to sound administration."

Saying this, he granted me an honorarium and ordered that it should be paid immediately, in cash. Then he said:

"You may leave, if you wish."

I rose; he rose immediately after me, his lance in his hand. I thought at first that he was going to stab me in the back, but luckily he turned away and went towards the harem. A few days after this interview he was victim of the events which you all know.'

The person whose account I have just quoted is the author of several interesting stories. He is still alive today, in the year 333 AH/945 AD, exercising the profession of court panegyrist and as such he mixes with the highest ranking officers of the government. He is a man of extremely fine intelligence and good understanding.

During the Caliphate of Qahir, in 321 AH/933 AD, Ibn Duraid died at Baghdad. He was one of the best poets of our century and an accomplished master of lexicography, in which field he occupied the place left empty by Khalil ibn Ahmad. He enriched this discipline with a number of discoveries for which you would search in vain in the old books; and, as to poetry, he covered the whole field, now sublime, now subtle and delicate. He has composed so many pieces that it would be impossible to list or quote them here.

VIII:289-304
§§ 3444-3459

(Omitted: VIII:304-308; §§ 3460-3465. Poems by Ibn Duraid and others.)

THE CALIPHATE OF RADI

Radi, who was known as Abu al-Abbas, was proclaimed Caliph on Thursday, the 6th of the month of Jumada I 322 AH/934 AD. He held the throne until the 10th of the month of Rabi' I 329 AH/329 AD and died a natural death at Baghdad, after having reigned six years, eleven months and eight days. His mother was a slave named Zalum.

VIII:308-309
§§ 3466

(Omitted: VIII:309-310; §§ 3467-3468. Names of Radi's viziers; A poem by Radi.)

THE CALIPH RADI'S ACCOMPLISHMENTS

Abu Bakr al-Suli, who has preserved a large number of Radi's poems, praises the nobility of this Caliph's character, his fine discrimination, his solid grounding in science and literature, his learning and his deep immersion in the seas of religious controversy and philosophy.

They say that Radi, while walking about his pleasure palace Thurayya – 'The Pleiades' – noticed a charming garden bright with flowers. He asked his courtiers if they had ever seen anything so lovely. At once, each began to go into ecstasies over this garden, praising its beauty and setting it above all the beauties of the world.

'Well,' cried the Caliph, 'Abu Bakr al-Suli's skill at chess delights me more than these flowers and all that you describe!'

They also tell how when Abu Bakr al-Suli first appeared at Muktafi's court, whither he had been summoned on account of his skill at chess, he found a rival, Mawardi, who had conquered the good-will and affection of the Caliph, who admired his ability at the game. These two rivals played each other before Muktafi. This prince was predisposed in favour of Mawardi, whom he had respected and showed friendliness towards for a long time, lavishing good wishes and encouragement on him. This fact bothered Abu Bakr al-Suli at first, but as the game progressed he rallied his forces, headed straight for the goal and won an uncontested victory over his antagonist. The superiority of his game thus became obvious to Muktafi, who ceased to favour Mawardi and indeed, said to him:

'Your rosewater (*ma ward*) has become urine!'

CHESS AND BACKGAMMON

The general flow of the narrative and the logical sequel of this story lead me to talk of chess and to quote what has been said on this subject. I have already, in another part of this work, in the chapter on India, talked of the origins of chess and backgammon and the affinity between these games and the heavenly bodies. Here I will add a few new points. The authors, ancient and modern, say that all the different chess boards may be reduced to six types, the only ones used in this game:

(1) The ordinary square chess board, which is eight squares wide and eight squares deep – this is ascribed to the ancient peoples of India.

(2) The rectangular chess board, four squares wide and sixteen long. At the beginning of the game, the pieces are drawn up in four rows on each side, the knights in two rows and in front of them the pawns, also in two rows. The manner of moving the pieces is the same as with the first board.

(3) The square chess board, ten squares by ten. This one also has two pieces called *dabbaba* – 'war engines' – which move like the king, except that they can take and be taken.

(4) The round chess board attributed to the Byzantines.

(5) Another round chess board, connected with the stars, and called 'zodiacal'. It has twelve divisions, like the signs of the zodiac, which separate the board into two halves. On it move seven pieces of different colours. This number, seven, refers to the five planets and the two great luminaries, the sun and the moon. I have already mentioned, in the chapter on India, the theories of their learned men regarding the influence of the planets on the heavenly bodies and their attraction for the higher spheres. They believe the sphere moves as a result of a sympathetic attraction towards a higher sphere; that the soul descends from the world of intelligence to that of the senses; that it there loses all memory of its origins and becomes ignorant, though once it was wise. I have set down these confused theories, the knowledge of which is, according to them, connected to the game of chess.

(6) Another chess board, known as 'organic', has been invented in my own day. It has seven squares by eight and twelve pieces, arranged six against six on either side of the table. Each of these six pieces has the name of one of the organs or members which enables a man to sense, speak, hear, see, touch and move – that is to say, they represent the senses and the senses' common seat, the heart.

The Indians, Greeks, Persians, Byzantines and other peoples who play chess

The Meadows of Gold

have described its forms, moves, rules, the explanations that have been given to it, its peculiarities and the setting out of the pieces. Furthermore, players have collections of anecdotes and amusing stories, which, according to some of them, stimulate the player and serve to concentrate his mind. These perform for them the same function as do the mnemonic poems in the *rajaz* meter for the warrior on the field of battle, or the caravan leader when the caravan is worn out, or for the water-drawer hauling his bucket to give water to travellers. For the chess player, they are as valuable a stimulant as poems and *rajaz* verses are to those who fight. From among the many pieces of this kind, I will quote the following passages from a poem by a chess player:

> Chess anecdotes, aptly quoted,
> Burn like flaming coals.
> How many times have they given
> A weak player the edge
> Against his cleverer adversary!

Here is another passage in which the game is described with a rare felicity of expression:

> The square, red-leather chess board
> Is set down between two noble friends.
> They evoke memories of war,
> Producing its simulacrum
> But without shedding blood.
> One attacks, the other counters
> And the eye of war does not close in sleep.
> See how the knights of the two armies
> Manoeuvre without trumpets or standards!

Among the poems of this sort noteworthy for their elegance and the polish of their descriptions, is the following by Abu al-Hasan ibn Abi al-Baghl, the secretary. This man, who was distinguished both as secretary and as a leading governor, was also known for the skill and finesse of his game:

> An intelligent player moves the pieces
> In such a way as to discover
> Consequences which escape the ignorant eye.
> He foresees the future with the sure
> Eye of the sage, but under the guise
> Of frivolity. Thereby he serves
> The ruler's interest, showing in this game
> How disaster may be averted.
> The vicissitudes of the chess board,

Chess and Backgammon

If closely observed,
Equal those of squadrons and lances.

As to the game of backgammon, I have already explained, in the same chapter on India, how this game is played and who invented it, according to the various traditions. Connoisseurs say there are different ways of playing and various rules for arranging and setting out the pieces, but the number of points is always the same and can be neither increased nor decreased, according to the rules of the game. Thus, as I have said before, it is the two dice which are the law in this game. The player, although he has no freedom of action and cannot save himself from the decisions of the dice, must nevertheless show some discernment in moving the pieces, in scoring and in moving the counters. The game of backgammon and the thraldom of the players to the whims of the dice are the subjects of a large number of technical poems, often very detailed. I will quote a fragment:

Backgammon is no good, for during
A run of bad luck the practised player
Cannot count on his own wit!
You see how the dice rule and decide
The difference between good
And evil fortune on a single toss.
The more skilled player,
If luck abandons him can do nothing
To save himself from defeat.

The secretary Abu al-Fath Mahmud ibn al-Husain ibn al-Sindi ibn Shahak, known as 'Kushajim', an educated man, sagacious and well-read, told me he had sent the following verses to one of his friends. In them, the poet criticizes the game of backgammon, to which he was devoted:

Arrogant man, who tries to find
In the game of backgammon the means
To lord it over your friends,
Truly you would find me
A terrible adversary,
If the dice had not favoured you.
The hopes of the skilled player
Are dashed and he laments
The harshness of ill-fortune.
When the judges have passed sentence
The opponents cannot escape
Their decision. By my life,
I am not the first man
To be betrayed by destiny!

The Meadows of Gold

Kushajim also quoted to me the following passage from Abu Nuwas:

> She does the opposite of what she is bidden,
> She doesn't trouble herself as to what is just or unjust.
> Since she does not yield to my will
> And I submit to hers, it is I
> Who have become her slave.

At the beginning of this book, in the chapter on the kings of India, I cited the opinions of those who consider backgammon and dice as a sort of symbol of the possessions of this world, which are allotted neither on the grounds of cleverness nor cunning. The invention of the aforesaid game is, as I have said, attributed to Ardashir, the son of Babak. This king, struck with the spectacle of the mutability of fortune, divided the backgammon board into twelve points, in accordance with the number of the months and instituted thirty 'dogs', or pieces, according to the number of days in a month. The two dice represent fortune and its capricious effect on the inhabitants of this world. For all this information and more of a similar nature, I must ask you to refer back to the chapter mentioned and to my other works.

Lastly, a Muslim philosopher maintains that the inventor of chess was a Mu'tazilite, an upholder of the doctrine of Justice* – that is, Free Will – while the inventor of backgammon was a fatalist who wanted to show, by means of this game, that one can do nothing against fate and that true understanding is to mould one's behaviour to the decisions of destiny.

VIII:312-320
§§ 3472-3481

THE QUALITIES OF A GENERAL

Al-Arudi, who was one of the tutors of Radi and of several other Caliphs and their sons, tells the following story:

'One day I taught Radi the words the Qutaiba ibn Muslim al-Bahili on pride and, in general, the qualities to be found among rulers that are worthy of praise or blame. Radi, who was barely even adolescent, wrote down this tradition at my dictation and set himself to learn it by heart. I saw him studying it diligently and when he knew it perfectly he fell into transports of delight – a thing far from usual with him – and, coming up to me, said:

"The day will perhaps come when I shall be able to make use of the study of these qualities and when I may be in a position to be thankful for these precepts."

As to the tradition in question, here it is:

Somebody said to Qutaiba ibn Muslim, who had received the government of Khurasan and the supreme command in the war against the Turks from the hands of Hajjaj:

"Are you going to send so-and-so" – he pointed to someone in his entourage – "at the head of the army against the Turkish king?"

"No", replied Qutaiba. "That man has immense pride. Now vanity increases in direct proportion to pride. When one is full of confidence in one's self, one does not deign to consider a matter wisely nor yet to accept good advice. Inflamed by this feeling of vanity, proud of one's own superiority, one drives away success and prepares for oneself humiliating reverses. It is better to be wrong with the majority than to be right. Whoever thinks himself superior to his enemy despises him and underestimates him. Full of contempt for his opponent, convinced of the superiority of his own forces, the arrogant man neglects his defences and as a result of this neglect piles fault upon fault. Experience has taught me that the leader who despises his adversary ends by being beaten and shamefully defeated – even, by God, if this leader should have sharper hearing than the stallion, longer sight than the eagle, be more sure-footed than the sand-grouse, more prudent than the magpie, braver than the lion, more aggressive than the leopard, more vindictive than the camel, craftier than the fox, more generous than the cock, greedier than a young boy, more on his guard than the stork, more watchful than the dog, more patient than the lizard and thriftier than the ant – for truly, the mind only pays attention insofar as it is necessary, only guards itself insofar as there is fear and only covets insofar as it has needs. They say, with reason, that a

The Meadows of Gold

man never has enough wisdom and that the arrogant man has no friend, and that he who would be loved must begin by loving." '

THE BREECHES OF THE TALLEST MAN

'One day,' al-Arudi again relates, 'we were in conversation in the presence of Radi, who was still a child, and the company was made up of learned men, well informed on events of the past. The conversation turned to an episode in the life of Mu'awiya ibn Abi Sufyan. This Caliph had received a letter from the king of Byzantium asking him to send the breeches of the largest man in his country.

"I know no one larger than Qais ibn Sa'd," said Mu'awiya, and addressing Qais directly, he enjoined him to send his breeches as soon as he left the palace. Qais took them off without pausing an instant and tossed them down in front of Mu'awiya.

"Why didn't you wait to get home to send them to us?" asked Mu'awiya.

Qais replied:

> I want everyone to know
> In the presence of the embassy
> That these are in truth
> The breeches of Qais
> Lest it be said:
> 'Qais was not there;
> The breeches are those
> Of one of the giants
> Of the tribe of 'Ad,
> Given him by the tribe of Thamud.

A propos of this, one of those present remembered that a king of Ghassan, Jabala ibn al-Ayham, was twelve spans high and that when he was on horseback his legs trailed on the ground.

Radi himself added the following information:

"When this same Qais ibn Sa'd was in the saddle, his legs dragged on the ground too, and when he was on foot in a crowd one would have thought he was on horseback. My grandfather Ali ibn Abd Allah ibn Abbas was a big, handsome man, whose height amazed people, yet he nevertheless said:

'I only reached the shoulder of my father Abd Allah and Abd Allah only reached the shoulder of my grandfather Abbas. As for Abbas, when he made the ritual circumambulation of the Ka'ba, he looked like a great white tent.'"

The entire gathering was astonished that a child should be able to quote this tradition so well.'

THE MARVELS OF CREATION

The conversation then turned to the marvels of the earth and to the rare and curious things peculiar to each country, such as plants, animals, precious stones and so on.

'The most extraordinary thing in the world,' said one of those present, 'is to be found in Tabaristan. On the banks of the rivers in that country there lives a bird similar to the sparrow-hawk. The people there call it *kikam*, which is an imitation of its cry. This cry is to be heard only at one season of the year – the spring. Attracted by its voice, sparrows and little marsh birds gather round it and, at the first light of day, begin to feed it. At sundown, it seizes one of the birds within its reach and eats it. It does the same thing every day until the end of spring. Once this season is past, the other birds attack it in great crowds and chase it away by pecking it, forcing it to flee, so that its cry is not heard until the following spring. It is a beautiful bird, with many-coloured plummage and magnificent eyes.

Ali ibn Rabban al-Tabari, the author of the *Paradise of Wisdom (Firdaws al-Hikma)*, claims that this bird is very rarely sighted. It has been observed, he says, that it never puts both feet on the ground at once, but rests on first one and then the other, instead of standing on both together. Jahiz also lists this bird* among the curiosities of nature because of its habit of only perching on one leg as if it were afraid that the earth would give way beneath it.

The second marvel is a worm which weighs between one and three *mithqals*. This worm shines through the night like the flame of a candle; it flies by day, when its smooth green wings can be observed. It has no antennae. It eats earth, but never eats its fill, for fear this food should all be consumed and it should thus die of hunger. This insect has a large number of useful properties.

As to the third marvel, more astonishing yet than the bird or the worm, it is those men who sell themselves to death. In other words, mercenary soldiers.'

This recital having received the approbation of all those present, Radi replied as follows to the narrator of the first story:

'Jahiz lists the three most marvellous things of this world.

Firstly, there is the owl, which never appears by day for fear that his beauty should attract the evil eye, for he considers himself the most beautiful being in all creation; hence he only goes out at night.

The second marvel is the crane, which never rests on two legs at once, but stands first on one and then the other, and furthermore takes care not to press too hard and to walk softly lest the earth should give way under the weight of its body.

The third marvel is a bird like the crane, which is called Malik al-Hazin – 'Master of Sadness' – or heron. This bird stands on the edge of tidal flats, watching the water recede, since he is afraid water might disappear from the surface of the earth and he die of thirst.'

Al-Arudi ended his account by saying that all those present went away admiring the fact that a child the age of Radi could take part so easily in the conversation of serious and learned men.

In my other works I have spoken of the wonders of the earth and the seas, of the remarkable buildings, the animals, the solid and liquid metals – such as mercury – and so forth. I will therefore not return to this subject, but limit myself to telling the story of Radi, with some details of his youth, what his tutor tells us – in a word, all the kinds of information appropriate to this book.

ARABIC WORDS FOR LAVATORY*

Here is another anecdote which I got from al-Arudi:

'One cold misty winter night, I was talking to Radi. I noticed that he was very nervous and extremely restless.

"O Commander of the Faithful," I said, "you are in a very unusual state. I have never seen you so disturbed."

"Let's not talk about that," said the Caliph. "Instead, tell me a story. If you manage to free me from my cares, all that I have on me or under me shall be yours, but I set the condition that you must remove my cares by making me laugh."

So I told him the following story:

A man from the family of Hashim went to visit his cousin at Medina. While he was staying with his host, he did not once go to relieve himself. After a certain period of time, he wanted to return to Kufa, but his cousin begged him to stay a few more days and he agreed. The master of the house had in his service two slave girls, who were musicians. He said to them:

'Have you noticed my cousin's good manners? Since he has been here, he has not once gone to the lavatory.'

'We undertake to give him something that will make him go,' said the two slaves.

Their master gave them permission to do anything they liked, so they took *ushr* bark, which is a purgative and tipped it into the drink which was intended for their guest. When the time for drinks came, they offered it to him, taking care not to give any to their master. When the potion began to take effect, the host pretended to be asleep. The unhappy cousin, feeling his innards in a turmoil, said to the girl beside him:

'My lady, where can I find the privy?'

'What did he say?' asked the other girl.

The first replied:

'He wants you to sing these lines:

> The grazing lands are deprived
> Of the family of Fatima;
> The dwelling place of her folk
> Stands deserted.'

The Meadows of Gold

And the slave sang them.

'Undoubtedly, these are two girls from Kufa,' said the cousin to himself. 'They won't have understood.'

Turning to the second girl, he said:

'My lady, where is the closet?'

'What's he asking you?' enquired the other.

'He wants you to sing this tune:

> The gardens and the nunnery are enclosed,
> And there she frets, a captive in this lovely place.'

She sang.

The young man, controlling himself, said:

'These two girls are from Iraq. They have not been able to understand me.' And addressing the first, he said:

'For the love of God, tell me where the washroom is!'

'What does he want?' asked her companion.

'He would like you to sing:

> Wash and pray five times a day
> And call the prayer for the Prophet's sake.'

The other slave girl sang this song.

'I am dealing with women from the Hijaz,' thought the young man. 'O my lady,' he asked one of them, 'where is the cloakroom?'

'What does he want?' asked the other.

The first replied:

'He is anxious for you to sing:

> A troop of jealous lovers cloak
> Me on all sides, yet one
> Would be enough to keep
> Me from the one I love.'

When the song was over, the poor man said to himself: 'They must be from Yemen, and do not know what I am saying,' and turning to the other singer, he tried again:

'Look you, where is the chamber of ease?'

'What did he ask?' said the first.

'He is asking you to sing:

> Games and levity he flees,
> Love he hates, preferring
> To these, rest and ease.'

Arabic Words for Lavatory

The slave girl produced this tune.

The master of the house still pretended to be asleep, but in fact had not missed a word. His guest, no longer able to hold himself in, cried:

> I am dying to shit
> And they torture me with their eternal songs!
> But my patience is at an end and I
> Am going to spatter the faces of these whores!

So saying, he undid his breeches and let fly, spattering the girls from head to foot, thus teaching them a much needed lesson.

While this was going on, the master of the house pretended to wake up and, seeing his slaves in this wretched state, said to the guest:

'Friend, what ever gave you the idea of doing a thing like that?'

'Son of a whore,' replied the other, 'your slaves apparently consider the lavatory as the bridge over hell, for they refused to show me the way there. I could find no better revenge.'

This story threw Radi into an absolute paroxysm of laughter, and he rewarded me by giving me everything he had on him or around him in the way of clothes and carpets, and it came to about 1,000 dinars.'

BLACK AND GREEN

Al-Suli related the following anecdote:
'One day Radi asked me why the Caliph Ma'mun, having adopted green clothing and forbidden the use of black, afterwards reverted to the latter colour.
"This is the reason," I replied, "as it was told me by Muhammad ibn Zakariya al-Ghallabi, according to the account of Ya'qub ibn Ja'far ibn Sulaiman. When Ma'mun entered Baghdad, the members of the House of Hashim gathered at the palace of Zainab, the daughter of Sulaiman ibn Ali. Because of the authority which her age and her lineage gave her in the family of Abbas, they begged her to speak to the Caliph Ma'mun in order to have him stop wearing green. She gave her word and went to Ma'mun and addressed him thus:
'O Commander of the Faithful, you have behaved more dutifully towards your relatives, the descendants of Ali, than they have towards you; there is no need for you to abandon an old custom of your ancestors. Give up green clothes and do not encourage anyone's ambitious plans.'
'Beloved aunt,' replied Ma'mun, 'no one has ever spoken to me more persuasively on this subject or in a manner more consonant with my own feelings. As you know, however, when Abu Bakr was invested with the supreme authority, after the death of the Prophet – may the prayers and peace of God be upon him – he overwhelmed us, we, the members of the family of the Messenger of God, with honours. Umar, his successor, never, on this point, departed from the precedents laid down by Abu Bakr. It was Uthman who during his reign favoured the sons of Umayya to the prejudice of every other House. Power then passed to the hands of Ali ibn Abi Talib and times were no longer peaceful and calm as they had been under those who came before, but troubled and ominous. Nevertheless, Ali gave the government of Basra to Abd Allah ibn al-Abbas and that of Yemen to Ubaid Allah ibn al-Abbas and Bahrain to Qutham. In a word, he forgot none of the Abbasids when distributing the highest positions. These generous deeds created obligations which I wish to honour by treating his descendants as I have done. But from now on, your desires shall be satisfied.'
'As a result of this conversation, he went back to wearing black clothes.'*

VIII:333-335
§§ 3493-3494

(Omitted: VIII:335; § 3495. Verses by Ma'mun.)

THE GARDEN OF QAHIR

The Caliph Qahir, after having killed Mu'nis, Yalbaq and Yalbaq's son Ali, and other people, seized a considerable sum of money which he hid in a safe place. When he lost his throne and his eyes, and Radi succeeded to the Caliphate, this money was demanded of him. Qahir maintained that he had nothing left. He was maltreated and put to all sorts of tortures, but still he persisted in his denials.

Radi then changed his tactics. He pressed him to come to court, talked with him often and treated him with all possible courtesy, giving him his rightful due as uncle, and as his age and position as former Caliph demanded. He overwhelmed him with marks of friendship and favour.

Now Qahir, when he was on the throne, had possessed a little garden in one of the courtyards of the palace, planted with orange trees* which he had brought from India, by way of Basra and Oman. These trees intertwined their branches, laden with red and yellow fruit, shining like stars, above a bed of various aromatic plants and flowers. Turtle doves, pigeons, thrushes and parrots had been assembled there, as well as other birds from many different countries. It was in this magnificent garden that Qahir most liked to drink and gather together his courtiers. When the Caliphate came to Radi, this Caliph too showed a predilection for the place and, like Qahir before him, made it the scene of his meetings and feasts.

At the period in which he was showing kindness to Qahir, he told him of his attempts to levy money, his great need and the poverty in which he found himself. Since he was on the throne, he was obliged to ask his predecessor to help him with such funds as he still possessed and he promised to give him a place in his government and to reign guided by his advice. Radi finally swore by all he held most holy not to make any attempt on Qahir's life, nor to wrong him or his children.

Qahir welcomed these overtures and said:

'All the wealth I have in the world is hidden in the orange garden.'

Radi went to the garden with him and asked him to show him the place where he had buried it. Qahir replied:

'Now that I have lost my sight, I can no longer point it out with any certainty, but order excavations to be made and you will find the treasure. Your searches must inevitably discover it.'

They dug the garden in every direction. Trees, plants and flowers were all torn up, until nothing remained of the garden but a deep hole. The result was nil.

'They have found no trace of the treasure you mentioned,' said Radi to Qahir. 'What made you do it?'

'How should I have anything left in the world?' answered Qahir. 'But I regretted that you should sit in the garden and enjoy it. It was the thing I loved best in the world and it was with despair that I saw another master of it after me.'

It was with much grief that Radi recognized the success of the trick his predecessor had used to deprive him of the garden, and he regretted ever having followed his advice. He had Qahir removed and kept well away from him, for he feared for his own life in the presence of such a man.

THE GENEROSITY OF RADI

Radi used a great deal of scent. His appearance was pleasing and his nature open-handed and generous. He enjoyed talking of the men and things of the past and sought out scholars and men of letters and frequently summoned them to his presence and lavished marks of his liberality upon them. Never did any of his courtiers leave him without having received a sum of money, a gala robe, or some perfumes. Noteworthy among his courtiers were Muhammad ibn Yahya al-Suli and Ibn Hamdun, known as al-Nadim – 'The Courtier'. When Radi was reproached for his excessive generosity towards his entourage, he replied:

'I admire the behaviour of the Commander of the Faithful Abu al-Abbas al-Saffah. This Caliph had qualities found in no other man. None of his courtiers and no singer or entertainer ever left his presence without carying with him a greater or lesser gift of money or valuable robes. Abu al-Abbas al-Saffah never awaited the morrow to reward merit and on this subject he said:

"It would be odd if a man who entertains others should receive, as a reward for the pleasure which he offered so promptly, a return full of postponements and delays."

Every time Abu al-Abbas al-Saffah held an assembly, whether by day or by night, all those who had been present went on their way with well contented hearts. As for us, if our circumstances are less favourable than those of our predecessors, we should, nevertheless, reward our guests and, even more, our brothers, insofar as our resources will permit.'

Radi's generosity showed itself on every occasion. He never resented any of his courtiers for the gifts which he ceaselessly granted them, so that one of them, embarrassed by the frequency of this largesse, deliberately put off his visits to the palace.

Those who had most influence with him were, among the eunuchs, Raghib and Zirak, and among the pages, Dhaki and others.

BAJKAM THE TURK COINS HIS OWN MONEY

Radi's tutor, al-Arudi, tells the following story:

'One day, at the autumn equinox festival, I passed in front of the palace of Bajkam the Turk, on the banks of the Tigris. The noise of singing, the sound of musical instruments and games and the joyous hubbub emanating from that place surpassed anything I had ever come across.

I then went in to Radi. I found him alone and plunged in gloom. I stopped before him. He said:

"Draw near!"

I advanced. He was holding in his hand a dinar and a dirham, each weighing about ten *mithqals*. Both coins bore the portrait of Bajkam, armed head to foot and surrounded by the following inscription:

> Know that sole power
> Belongs to the great amir,
> Lord of men, Bajkam.

The obverse showed the Caliph himself, sitting with his head low, like a man plunged in thought.

"You see," the Caliph said to me, "the deeds of this man! You see how far he goes in his ambition and his pride!"

I avoided answering and began to talk of the Caliphs of the past and their relationships with their followers. I next passed to the history of the kings of Persia and the trials they underwent at the hands of their minions, and I reminded him with how much patience and politic wisdom they bore with them until the day when they re-established order and asserted their authority. My words calmed him.

"Commander of the Faithful," I added, "who prevents you from doing what Ma'mun in a similar situation recommended in these verses:

> On the festival of Khusrawani
> At the autumn equinox
> Offer the guests the ancient wine jugs.
> Give them a cup of the old

Bajkam the Turk Coins His Own Money

>   Royal vintage of the Chosroes,
>   For this is the feast of the Persian kings.
>   Let those who drink raisin liqueur
>   Keep away; their tastes are not mine.
>   I know the wine I drink is forbidden
>   But I ask God's pardon, for He
>   Is kind and indulgent.
>   Those who drink raisin liqueur
>   Claim it is licit and thus
>   The wretches commit a double sin.'

This quotation roused the Caliph and cheered him.

"You are right," he said to me. "Renouncing pleasure on a day like this would be an act of weakness."

He then had his courtiers summoned and went to sit in his throne room on the banks of the Tigris. Never did I attend such a splendid feast. All those who took part, courtiers, singers, entertainers, received gold and silver coins, robes of honour and scents. At this point, presents and greetings from Bajkam arrived from the land of Persia. In a word, the Caliph and his suite were very happy that day.'

All the facts and events of the reign of Radi have been set down summarily or in detail in my *Historical Annals*, the full title of which is: *History of the Peoples Whom Time Has Destroyed, Vanished Nations and Kingdoms Which Have Passed Away*.

I have told of this Caliph's expedition with Bajkam to the lands of Mosul and Diyar Rabi'a and also of the war which broke out between Bajkam and Abu Muhammad al-Hasan ibn Abd Allah ibn Hamdan, later known as Nasir al-Dawla. As for the stories in the present work, I have tried above all to be brief and to avoid explanation and long-windedness, for over-lengthy narrations weigh on the heart and tire the listener. A little knowledge gives much power.*

THE CALIPHATE OF MUTTAQI

Muttaqi, known as Abu Ishaq Ibrahim, the son of Muqtadir, was proclaimed Caliph on the 10th of the month of Rabi' I in the year 329 AH/940 AD and was deposed and blinded on Saturday, the 3rd of Safar 333 AH/944 AD after having reigned three years, eleven months and twenty-three days. He was the son of a slave.

When he became Caliph, he first appointed as his vizier Sulaiman ibn al-Hasan ibn Makhlad, then Abu al-Husain Ahmad ibn Muhammad ibn Maimun, who had been his secretary before he became Caliph. Then he appointed to this position Abu Ishaq Muhammad ibn Ahmad al-Qarariti, then Abu al-Abbas Ahmad ibn Abd Allah al-Isfahani, who was succeeded by Abu al-Husain Ali ibn Muhammad ibn Muqla. Tuzun the Turk was the man who controlled the state.

VIII:344-345
§§ 3506-3507

(Omitted: VIII:346-351; §§ 3508-3514. The Baridi revolt; Muttaqi stripped of his authority; The Turks and the Hamdanid dynasty dispute the power; Ikhshid, the Turkish ruler of Egypt, intervenes.)

THE BLINDING OF MUTTAQI

As soon as the general whom Ikhshid had left at the Caliph's side had gone with his men some distance on the road back to Egypt, Mustakfi was fetched and hailed as Caliph.

Muttaqi had his eyes gouged out. To drown his screams, which were echoed by the women and eunuchs, Tuzun had drums beaten around the tent.

Muttaqi, blind and stripped of the robe, sceptre and ring – these insignia of the Caliphate were made over to Mustakfi – was then taken back to Baghdad. Qahir was told of what had happened and he cried out:

'Now there are two of us – all we need is a third!'

Thus he alluded to the fate which threatened Mustakfi.

VIII:351-352
§ 3515

(Omitted: VIII:352-374; §§ 3516-3533. A poem of ill-omen; On horses – the different breeds, their characteristics; Poems on horses; On the poet al-Khubzawi, 'whom it seems the minister Baridi has had drowned in revenge for his epigrams, although some say he escaped from Basra and fled . . . to Bahrain'.)

SUMMING UP

I have related the story of Muttaqi and the events of his reign in detail in my *Intermediate History*, of which the present work is the complement. Here, I am giving nothing but a sketch of the history of the Caliphs, having made a rule for myself of concision and speed. Thus, I have given an account elsewhere of the death of Bajkam the Turk, in Rajab 329 AH/941 AD, his battles with the Kurds in the Wasit region; the story of Kurankij the Dailamite, how he made himself master of Bajkam's army, and the arrival of Muhammad ibn Ra'ik from Syria. I have mentioned the battle, which was fought at Ukbara, Ibn Ra'ik's betrayal, his arrival at Baghdad, the new battle waged in the capital, which ended in the flight of Kurankij, and the ascendancy of Ibn Ra'ik; the history of the Baridi family and how they installed themselves at Baghdad, and the flight of Muttaqi, together with Muhammad ibn Ra'ik al-Mawsili. As all this information is to be found in my *Historical Annals*, there is absolutely no need for me to go back to it here.

God favours all just enterprises!

THE CALIPHATE OF MUSTAKFI

Mustakfi, know as Abu al-Qasim Abd Allah, the son of the Caliph Muktafi, was proclaimed on Saturday, the 3rd of Safar, 333 AH/944 AD and was deposed on the seventh day before the end of the month of Shaban 334 AH/946 AD. He thus reigned for a year and a little less than four months. His mother was a slave.

I have said earlier, when speaking of the deposition of Muttaqi, that Mustakfi was hailed as Caliph at Bathq, a place on the banks of the Isa Canal, in the Baduraya district, facing the village called al-Sindiya. He was proclaimed at the very hour at which the eyes of his predecessor Muttaqi were being torn out. He first received the oath from Tuzan the Turk and from the generals, officials and judges who were then with him, among others, the qadi Muhammad ibn Abi al-Shawarib and a number of members of the House of Hashim.

After having recited the sunset and evening prayers with them, he set out and on the following Sunday reached Shammasiya. The next day, Monday, he set sail in one of those light boats called 'gazelles'. He was wearing a tall pointed cap, the same, it is said, as his father Muktafi had worn. With him were Tuzun the Turk, Muhammad ibn Shirzad and some pages. The ex-Caliph Muttaqi, blinded, and the qadi Ahmad ibn Abd Allah, who had just been arrested, were handed over to him. They then gathered together the rest of the qadis and members of the House of Hashim and they swore allegiance to the new Caliph.

At first, Mustakfi had for some time as vizier Abu al-Faraj Ahmad ibn Muhammad ibn Ali, originally from Samarra. Displeased with this minister, he rendered him destitute and placed all his confidence in Muhammad ibn Shirzad.

He held hearings and conducted an inquiry regarding the qadis and notary publics of the capital. Some were removed from office, others were sentenced to a public retraction of the lies they had told, while yet others were confirmed in their positions – all on the basis of things he had learned about them before he came to power. All the qadis had to submit to the Caliph's orders. Jurisdiction over the eastern quarter of Baghdad was given to Muhammad ibn Isa, known as Ibn Abi Musa, of the Hanafi school of law, and over the western quarter of the city, Muhammad ibn al-Hasan ibn Abi al-Shawarib, also of the Hanafi school, which caused people to say:

'The orders and prohibitions of the Caliphate reach this point and go no further.'

Before he came to the throne, Mustakfi had contacts of a neighbourly kind, in the house of Ibn Tahir, with the son of Muqtadir, Fadl, known as Muti'. They often argued over pigeon-racing or fighting rams, cocks and partridge, these last being known as *qabj* in Syria. When Mustakfi was led to the Isa Canal for his investiture, Muti', fearing the resentment of his rival, fled from his house. Indeed, once his authority was established, Mustakfi had him searched for everywhere. Unable to find any trace of him, he had the house where Muti' had lived demolished and confiscated as many of his gardens and other properties as he could.

THE UNWANTED PAGE BOY

Abu al-Hasan Ali ibn Ahmad al-Katib al-Baghdadi – the secretary from Baghdad – tells the following story:

'At the time of the accession of Mustakfi, Tuzun the Turk chose from his own entourage a Turkish page boy whom he assigned to the personal service of the Caliph. Now Mustakfi had a page who knew all about his habits, having grown up in his service, and as a consequence he showed an absolute preference for him. But, on Tuzun insisting that the new page should take precedence over the old, the Caliph resigned himself to entrusting his messages to the Turkish page, in order to make himself agreeable to Tuzun. Now, the new-comer was far from acquitting himself as well as his predecessor.

One day, Mustakfi, addressing the secretary Muhammad ibn Shirzad, asked him whether he knew of Hajjaj ibn Yusuf's adventure with the Syrians.

"Commander of the Faithful," answered Muhammad ibn Shirzad, "I don't know this story."

Mustakfi went on:

"They say that Hajjaj had chosen from among the inhabitants of Iraq certain officers in whom he found a zeal and aptitude which he would have sought in vain among the Syrian officers of his entourage. These last were deeply shocked at his preference and complained of it loudly. Their laments reached the ears of Hajjaj. Hajjaj mounted his horse and, accompanied by a certain number of officers from each of the two countries, went out with them a good way into the desert. A caravan of camels appeared in the distance. Hajjaj called one of the Syrians and ordered him to go and find out what the shapes in the distance were and to bring back an exact account. After a certain space of time, the officer returned and told Hajjaj that they were camels.

'Are they laden or unladen?' asked Hajjaj.

'I don't know, but I will go back and find out,' replied the officer.

Now, from the very first, Hajjaj had send after him an Iraqi officer, to whom he had given exactly the same mission. This officer, returning at this moment, Hajjaj turned to him and, in the presence of the Syrians, asked him for information:

'They are camels,' replied the Iraqi.

'How many?' proceeded Hajjaj.

'Thirty.'

'Their load?'

The Meadows of Gold

'Oil.'
'Where from?'
'Such-and-such a place.'
'Where are they heading?'
'To such-and-such a place.'
'Who is their owner?'
'So-and-so.'
Then Hajjaj turned to the Syrians and said:

> They reproach me for preferring Amr,
> But Amr, if you were absent or dead
> Few could replace you!

Muhammad ibn Shirzad spoke in his turn:
"Commander of the Faithful, a certain literary man has most eloquently expressed the same thought:

> The worst of envoys is he
> Who obliges his master
> To send him back again,
> Giving the same orders a second time.
> This is what wise men
> Meant by the proverb:
> 'The ignorant man
> Covers the same ground twice.' "

Mustakfi added:
"How skilfully Buhtari depicted the intelligent messenger in this line:

> It is as if his keen intelligence
> Casts light on the darkest affairs
> Like a burst of flame!"

Muhammad ibn Shirzad thus understood how much the Caliph loathed the Turkish page and told Tuzun of it. Tuzun agreed to deliver the Commander of the Faithful from him and withdrew the page from his service.

VIII: 379-382
§§ 3540-3542

(Omitted: VIII:382-406; §§ 3543-3565. In praise of wine; Poems of Abu Nuwas and others.)

THE BATTLE OF THE FLOWERS

Mustakfi turned next to a teacher from whom he had taken lessons as a child, a man who was extremely good company, whose wit the Caliph appreciated and with whom he enjoyed exchanging jokes.

'You heard,' he said, 'the verses which have just been recited – now it is your turn.'

'I understand,' replied the other, 'neither the remarks nor the quotations of your guests; but I must tell you how yesterday I went out walking as far as Baturunja. The sight of the lovely gardens of that village brought to my mind the lines which Abu Nuwas composed in their honour and, by God, I felt myself transported, deeply moved.'

'What did this poet say?' asked the Caliph. 'Let us hear his description in verse.'

The tutor then recited the following lines:

> That sleep which closes your eyelids, Ibn Wahb,
> Will last but little, for the fire which burns you
> Is the fire of love. Baturunja is my dwelling place.
> It is a place worthy of respect.
> As the drinking cup makes its rounds,
> I view it. Listen to my tale.
> One day I was walking there
> And love had stolen my heart.
> Suddenly Narcissus addressed my page:
> 'Stop!' said he, 'for a fine wine
> Has aged to maturity in our casks.'
> The quail sang, the waves of pleasure
> Broke and the flowers wantoned
> In their splendour. We wandered
> About the gardens whose eyes
> Were not the black eyes of houris
> But had lids fashioned of white petals
> And pupils of golden buds.
> At that moment the Rose called to us:
> 'Friends, drinkers,' said she,
> 'We have in our possession a delicious wine,

The Meadows of Gold

> By time forgotten, whose very existence is a mystery.'
> We ran to the Rose, not heeding the laments
> Of the double Narcissus, who, seeing
> What the Rose was about, cried out in a shrill
> Voice: 'Come to me, Camomile!'
> The Rose saw two bands of yellow
> Flowers advance. She called,
> And the Pomegranate ran to her aid.
> They summoned the army of the Apple
> Trees of Lebanon and soon
> The fighting grew fierce.
> Camomile drew up in battle lines
> Armies of Citron Trees, great and small.
> And then I saw Spring among
> The yellow ranks, but my heart
> Lay with the Reds, simply
> Because red is the colour of the cheeks
> Of those who treat us
> With such injustice and cruelty.

Never, since the day of his accession to the Caliphate, adds the narrator, had I seen Mustakfi filled with such lively enjoyment. He rewarded all the guests present, as well as the singers and entertainers, and despite the emptiness of his treasury, he had brought in all the gold and silver that he could. Alas, I never saw such a feast again, until Ahmad ibn Buwaih, the Dailamite, took him prisoner and put out his eyes.

THE BUWAIHIDS COME TO POWER

And here is the explanation of these last-mentioned events.

The war had lasted a long time. On one side was Abu Muhammad al-Hasan ibn Abd Allah al-Hamdan, who held the eastern quarter of the city with the Turks and his cousin al-Husain ibn Sa'id ibn Hamdan, and on the other Ahmad ibn Buwaih, the Dailamite, who occupied the western quarter and was with Mustakfi. The Dailamite came to suspect the Caliph of soliciting aid from the Hamdanids, of corresponding with them and of telling them of the secret plans of their enemy. These suspicions, added to other previous causes of resentment, made him decide to gouge out Mustakfi's eyes and replace him on the throne with Muti'. Using the strategy of night attack, he embarked the Dailamite soldiers in the dark of night and directed them, to the sound of trumpets and drums, against different points along the streets of the eastern quarter. This strategy disoriented the Hamdanids, who after various skirmishes between them and the Turks in the region of Tikrit, fled to Mosul.

So Ahmad ibn Buwaih, the Dailamite, came to power and he passed laws to restore the prosperity of the provinces and repair the ravages of war. Such at least is the information we have gleaned on his actions and deeds, despite the distances, cut roads, and cessation of news while we were in Egypt and Syria.

I do not have any more complete information on the very short reign of Mustakfi than that which I have given here.

May God favour all good undertakings!

THE CALIPHATE OF MUTI'

Muti' – his full name was Abu al-Qasim al-Fadl ibn Ja'far al-Muqtadir, Muti' li-Llah) was proclaimed on the 7th day before the end of the month of Sha'ban, 334 AH/946 AD or, according to another version, during the month of Jumada I of the same year.

The son of Buwaih the Dailamite had seized power. He held Muti' in thrall, deprived of all authority, and today neither the Caliphate nor the position of vizier are known or referred to. Abu Ja'far Muhammad ibn Yahya ibn Shirzad handled the affairs of the Dailamite, exercising the function of vizier but with the title of secretary. He sought refuge in the western quarter of Baghdad with Hasan ibn Abd Allah ibn Hamdan and then accompanied him to Mosul; in the end he was suspected of stirring up the Turks against his protector and his eyes were put out.

It is said that Abu al-Husain Ali ibn Muhammad ibn Ali ibn Muqla is now in charge of the official correspondence of the Dailamite and Muti', but with the title of secretary, not vizier; this is in Jumada I, 336 AH/947AD.

I will not dedicate a special chapter to the reign of Muti', although we have done so for his predecessors, since he is still on the throne.

IX:1-2
§§ 3571-3573

(Omitted: IX:3-4; §§ 3574-3576. The risings of Ahmad ibn Abd Allah and of Abu Abd al-Rahman al-Ajami and their deaths at the hands of Ibn Tulun; the insurrection of Ibn Rida.)

THE RISING OF UTRUSH

Next came the rising of Utrush – 'The Deaf' – in Tabaristan and Dailam. His full name was Hasan Ibn Ali ibn Muhammad ibn Ali ibn al-Hasan ibn Ali ibn Abi Talib – may God be contented with all of them. In the year 301 AH/913 AD he drove the Abbasids out of Tabaristan. Utrush had spent a number of years in Dailam and Jilan. The inhabitants of those countries were barbarous and some of them were Magians. Utrush summoned them to the worship of Almighty God. They responded and became Muslims, except for a small minority who lived in the midst of high mountains, in fortresses and valleys and retreats impossible of access. They have persevered in their polytheism down to the present day. Utrush built mosques in their country. The Muslims had already constructed a line of defenses, including Qazwin, Shalus and other places in Tabaristan. Shalus was protected by a massive fortress and high walls, which had been built by the Persian kings. It was there that the garrisons entrusted with the defence of the frontier with the Dailamites were stationed. This strong place survived the coming of Islam until it was destroyed by Utrush.

IX:4-5
§ 3577

(Omitted: IX: 5-34; §§ 3578-3605. War in Tabaristan between Utrush and Hasan ibn al-Qasim al-Hasani, 'The Missionary', who took Rayy in 317 AH/929 AD, then Qazwin, Qum, etc. The Caliph Muqtadir wrote to Nasr ibn Ahmad, governor of Khurasan, to reproach him for these disasters: 'I made you responsible for the goods and lives of my subjects. You have neglected their interests and let slip their defences and those of the country to the point of handing it over to the Alids!' Nasr appoints Asfar ibn Shirwayh to the army; His success; The death of the Missionary; The revolt of Asfar ibn Shirwayh; His battles against the Samanids; His death; The seige of Hamadan and the legendary lion; Death of Mardawij.)

MAS'UDI'S ADDRESS TO THE READER

I finished writing this book in the month of Jumada I of the present year 336 AH/ 947 AD, while staying at Fustat in Egypt. The actual masters of power at Baghdad are Abu al-Hasan Ahmad ibn Buwaih the Dailamite, who is known as Mu'izz al-Dawla; his brother Hasan ibn Buwaih, lord of Isfahan and the districts of the Ahwaz and other provinces and their elder brother, the real head of the family, Ali ibn Buwaih, known by the title Amid al-Dawla, 'Pillar of the State'. He resides in Fars. But of these princes, the one who presides over the government of the Caliph Muti' is Ahmad ibn Buwaih, Mu'izz al-Dawla – 'Strengthener of the State' – and it is he, accompanied by the Caliph, who is today waging war against the Baridi faction in the area around Basra, according to information that has reached me.

In this book, I have in very few words set down numerous happenings and have made brief mention of events of a considerable importance. In any case, each of my works contains information omitted in the book that preceded it, information which could not be ignored, knowledge of which is of the greatest importance and a genuine need. Thus I have reviewed every century, together with the events and deeds which have marked them, up until the present. Furthermore, there is to be found at the beginning of this book a description of the seas and continents, of lands inhabited and uninhabited, the lives of foreign kings, their histories and those of all the different peoples. If God gives me life, if He extends my days and grants me the favour of continuing in this world, I will follow this book with another, which will contain information and facts on all kinds of interesting subjects. Without limiting myself to any particular order or method in setting them down, I will include all sorts of useful information and curious tales, just as they spring to mind. This work will be called *The Reunion of the Assemblies* – a collection of facts and stories mixed together, to provide a sequel to my earlier writings and to complement my other works.

As to the events set down here, they are of the kind that a wise man cannot ignore and which it would be inexcusable to omit or to neglect. If one does no more than enumerate the chapters of this book, without reading each one carefully, the truth of what I am saying will not be appreciated, nor will its erudition be given its due. The knowledge I have gathered together here has cost me long years of painful effort and research and journeys and voyages across the

Mas'udi's Address to the Reader

lands of East and West and to a number of countries not under Muslim rule.

May the reader, therefore, be kindly in his perusal of this book and have the goodness to correct such copyist's errors and faults in transcription as may offend him; and, bearing in mind the deference and good relations which should exist among scholars and which the intellectual world demands, let him take my affairs into account! The author of this book compares himself to a man who, having found pearls of every kind and every shade scattered here and there, gathers them into a necklace and makes of them a precious piece of jewellery, an object of great worth which its purchaser will cherish with care.

Lastly, may the reader rest assured that I have not here taken up the defence of any sect, nor have I given preference to this doctrine or that. My aim has been to relate the most notable events in man's history, and I have pursued no other.

IX:34-37
§§ 3606-3609

(Omitted: IX:38-77; §§ 3610-3656. A chronological résumé; A list of leaders of the pilgrimage to Mecca down to the year 335 AH/946 AD.)

MAS'UDI'S FINAL WORDS

I, Abu al-Hasan Ali ibn al-Husain ibn Ali al-Mas'udi, add the following words:

In this work, I have set down all kinds of facts and information on the lives of prophets and kings, the histories of foreign peoples, a description of the continents and seas, together with a review of all the monuments and wonders of this world – in brief, everything connected with this subject. Similarly, I wished to indicate what my other works contain and provide a general introduction to all my books in their different fields of learning.

There is, indeed, not a single branch of the humanities, historical topic, or source of tradition, which is not mentioned here, either in detail, or abridged, or at the very least touched on in some quotation or mentioned briefly in passing; and this is as true for the accounts of foreign peoples as it is for the Arabs and for the general statements relating to nations in general.

And with regard to any man who should dare to alter the meaning of this book, overthrowing the foundations upon which it rests, tarnishing the clarity of the text, or throwing doubt upon certain passages, as a result of alterations or changes, extracts or abridgements and, lastly, as to any man who seeks to deprive us of the authorship of this book, by attributing it to another, or by effacing our name, may the wrath of God fall upon him and may swift punishment be his! May he be overwhelmed by calamities so dire that all his patience is exhausted and the very thought of them is enough to strike terror into his soul! May God make of this falsifier an example for those who know, a lesson for those who understand, a sign for those who reflect! (Koran 15:75) May God strip him of all he has! May God, the Creator of heaven and earth, take from him all his faculties and all the good things that He has granted him, no matter what his religious persuasion or opinions! God has power over all things! (Koran 2:19 et passim)

I placed this curse at the beginning of my book and now I repeat it at the end, as I have done with my other books and in my earlier works. May he who fears his Lord tremble at the catastrophe to come! Life is short, the journey swift and in the end 'it is to God we must return.' (Koran 3:28)

In a number of passages in this book, I have begged indulgence for any mistakes which may be found and for the errors and faults which the copyist is sure to introduce. I have also adduced to plead on my behalf my long journeys, my ceaseless wanderings from East to West and from South to North, and lastly the imperfections and carelessness inherent in human nature which impede men from reaching their goals and achieving success. If no one could write books but

Mas'udi's Final Words

he who possessed perfect knowledge, no books would be written. God, may He be exalted and glorified, has said: 'Above every learned man is One Who knows all.' (Koran 12:76)

May God place you in the number of those who walk in the paths of obedience, guided by His grace! We beseech Him to replace the evil in us with good and our frivolous works with things of weight. Lastly, may He extend to us His mercy and may His protection enfold us! For He is generous and merciful above all others. There is no God but He, Master of the Heavenly throne. (Koran 9:129)

May He grant His blessings and salvation to Muhammad, the foremost of men, and to all his holy posterity!

IX:77-81
§§ 3657-3661

GLOSSARY

abna   In Masudi this word refers to members of the House of Abbas and their supporters from Khurasan.

abu   Father – frequent element in names, e.g. Abu Hasan, father of Hasan.

AH   Anno hegirae = A.D. 622 – the year in which the Prophet left Mecca for Medina, where he established the first Islamic community; year one of the Islamic lunar calendar.

Allahu akhbar   God is greater – sc. than anything else; a pious interjection of frequent occurrence.

ansar   Literally 'helpers'; those inhabitants of Medina who aided and supported the Prophet after the *hijra* from Mecca.

arif   Literally 'expert'; commander of a group of ten men in the 'Vagabond' army.

badhhanj   Passive cooling system in Iranian architecture, essentially by means of air vents set in a tower, controlling draughts.

banj   Henbane (Hyoscyamus niger), used as a narcotic.

bint   Daughter – frequent element in names, see *ibn*.

bish   A poisonous plant of the aconite family.

bukht   An infertile cross between a dromedary and a Bactrian camel.

dabbaba   Literally 'crawler'; a siege machine; name of a chess piece.

damma   The mark indicating the vowel u in the Arabic script.

431

The Meadows of Gold

dhadhi   The meaning of this word escapes us – a kind of syrup perhaps.

dhikr   Here used for the first of the night prayers.

dinar   A gold coin of 4.233 grams of a remarkably high punity. The word itself derives from the Latin *denarius* and the weight was taken over from the Byzantine standard. S. D. Goitein, writing about a slightly later period in Egypt, gives 2 dinars 'as a monthly income sufficient for a lower middle class family'. (*A Mediterranean Society*, Vol. I Economic Foundations, University of California Press, 1968, p. 359).

dirham   A silver coin of very variable silver content. Theoretically, $14\frac{2}{7}$ dirhams = 1 dinar; but in practice the number ranged from 13 to 40, depending on their purity. The word derives from the Greek *drachme*.

diyar   Tribal grazing lands; common as an element in place names, e.g. Diyarbakr.

dushab   A Persian word for a drink consisting of a mixture of grain and sweet syrup.

fakhiti   A kind of cloth; perhaps named after the wife of one of the Ummayad caliphs.

faludhaj   A sweet made of honey and flour; now a fudge-type sweet.

farrar   Quicksilver.

hajj   The pilgrimage to Mecca.

harisa   At this date, generally a dish of flour or grain served with meat.

ibn   Son – frequent element in names, e.g. Hasan ibn Husain, Hasan son of Husain.

ihram   The seamless length of cloth donned by the pilgrims to Mecca at the boundary of the sacred precinct.

Imam   Leader of community prayers; spiritual leader.

istaghfar   Here used for the second of the three night prayers.

jinn   Unseen beings, who can be believers or unbelievers, good or evil.

Glossary

judhaba Meat grilled over a dish of breadcrumbs, pounded almonds and candied sugar, so that the bread absorbs the meat drippings.

Ka'ba The sacred square building in Mecca which pilgrims circumambulate during the *hajj*.

khabisa A pudding made of dates and cream.

khanjar Curved dagger.

Kharijite A group in constant rebellion against the Caliphate, which deemed them unorthodox because they believed, among other things, that the office of Caliph should be elective, not hereditary.

khud Helmet – a Persian word.

khutba The Friday sermon in which, as well as prayers for the well-being of the Faithful, it was customary to mention the name of the ruler. Failure to do so was of great political significance, as was pronouncing the *Khutba* in the name of some rival claimant in times of political unrest.

kikam A marsh bird, perhaps a crane.

lawzinaj A sweet made of almonds, rose-water and sugar of which there were numerous varieties; perhaps also horchata; the origin of our word lozenge.

mawali client of a tribe; a freedman.

ma ward Rose water.

mahri A particularly prized breed of riding and racing camel.

minbar The raised platform in a mosque from which the *khutba* (q.v.) is pronounced and sermons given.

mithqal A weight of about 4.68 grams (in Egypt), divided into 24 carats; it was often synonymous with *dinar* (q.v.) and in fact was the word generally used for this coin in North Africa and Spain.

mulhama A kind of cloth with a warp of silk and a woof of some other material.

mu'tazilite Adherent of a sect that believed in free will.

musalla An area marked off for prayer on special occasions, usually in the open air.

The Meadows of Gold

mutawakkiliya A variety of *mulhamma* cloth (q.v.) with a very beautiful weave. It was a favourite of the Caliph Mutawakkil.

nabidh Wine; semi-alcoholic drink made from a variety of fruit juices. Forbidden by Islamic law if fermented more than three days.

nadim Courtier; the root of this word (*nadam*) means to regret – hence the discussion on p. 188.

naqib Commander of 100 men in the 'Vagabond' army.

qaba A short robe, tightly-fitted and sleeved.

qabj A kind of partridge.

qadi One who interprets and applies Islamic law.

qa'id Literally 'leader'; commander of 1000 men in the 'Vagabond' army.

qalansuwa a tall, cone-shaped hat.

qarmatians An extremist equalitarian sect.

qata'if A kind of stuffed fritter.

rajaz A poetic metre, generally used for didactic verse.

ribat A fortified post, guarding a frontier or caravan route; later applied to centres manned by those fighting holy war (*jihad*), usually belonging to a particular religious order.

samita Parboiled and then roasted lamb, coated with saffron, which gave it a golden colour.

sawiq An infusion of water and grain; perhaps something like barley-water.

shaikh Literally 'elder'; often applied to a leader of an Arab tribe or of a school of theology or philosophy; an honorific term.

shakiriya A corps of body-guards; the word is from the Persian *chaker* – soldier.

shari'a The Holy law of Islam.

sharif A descendant of the Prophet or his immediate family.

shi'a Literally 'party'; used of the partisans of Ali and his descendants; after the *sunni*, the *shi'a* has the largest number of adherents in Islam.

shughl Literally 'work'.

shurah Plural of *shari*, as in Harun al-Shari; literally 'extremist'; used for the most fanatical wing of the Kharijite movement.

sunna The 'way' of the Prophet and the first four ('Rightly Guided') Caliphs; the *praxis* of majority Islam.

sikbaj A sort of stew.

tadruj The Persian word for pheasant, apparently sacred to the Manichaeans.

takbir The pronouncing of the formula *Allahu Akbar* – God is Greater.

tambur A mandolin-shaped instrument.

tarwiya The 8th of the month of Dhu al-Hijja; literally 'the Day of Moistening', because on this day pilgrims to Mecca provide themselves with water for the following days of the pilgrimage (*hajj*).

tharid A kind of soup with bread crumbled in it; said to have been the favourite dish of the Prophet.

umm Mother – frequent element in names, see *abu*.

ushr A purgative bark (Asclepius giganteus?).

washi Highly prized variegated or figured silk cloth.

BIBLIOGRAPHY

Works by Mas'udi

Mas'udi, *Les prairies d'or*. Texte et traduction par C. Barbier de Meynard et Pavet de Courteille. 9 vols. Société Asiatique. Collection d'ouvrages orientaux. (Paris, 1861–1877.)

Mas'udi, *Les prairies d'or*. Traduction Française de Barbier de Meynard et Pavet de Courteille. Revue et corrigée par Charles Pellat. Société Asiatique. Vol. I (Paris, 1962), Vol. II (Paris, 1965), Vol. III (Paris, 1971).

Mas'udi, *muruj al-dhahab wa ma'adin al-jawhar*. Publications de l'Université Libanaise. Section des Études Historiques. Vols. 1–5 (Beirut, 1965–1974), Vols. 6 & 7 (Index Volumes) (Beirut, 1979).

Mas'udi, *kitab al-tanbih wa-l-ishraf* (Leiden, 1894).

Mas'udi, *Le livre de l'avertissement et de la revision*. Traduction par B. Carra de Vaux. (Paris, 1896). (Translation of the above.)

Books on Mas'udi

Khalidi, Tarif. *Islamic Historiography: The Histories of Mas'udi*. (Albany, 1975.) (A good account of Mas'udi's methods and the tradition within which he worked.)

Shboul, Ahmad M. H., *Al-Mas'udi & His World. A Muslim Humanist and His Interest in non-Muslims*. (London, 1979). (An excellent account of this aspect of Mas'udi's work; contains much geographical information.)

Social Background

Mez, A. *The Renaissance of Islam*. English translation by K. Bakhsh and Margoliouth. (Patna, 1937.) (Still the best account of Abbasid society and daily life.)

The Meadows of Gold

Ahsan, M. M., *Social Life under the Abbasids*. (London, 1979.) (A detailed account of Abbasid literature, costume, food, housing, hunting, games and festivals.)

Historical Background

Muir, S. W., *The Caliphate: Its Rise, Decline and Fall*. (London, 1898; reprinted Beirut, 1963). (This is outdated and in many ways unsatisfactory, but still the most useful companion to this volume of Mas'udi.)

Bowen, H., *The Life and Times of 'Ali ibn 'Isa*. (Cambridge, 1928). (A fascinating and readable account of the life of this famous vizier of Muqtadir.)

Abbot, Nabia, *Two Queens of Baghdad*. (Chicago, 1946). (An excellent and entertaining account of Khaizuran and Zubaida.)

NOTES

Abu Ja'far Mansur

p. 21   *Sunday* – Actually Saturday.

p. 21   *a blind man* – This was the poet Abu al-Abbas al-Sa'ib ibn Farukh al-'A'ma; this story occurs in the *Kitab al-Aghani*.

In the Audience Hall

p. 28   *the battle of al-Hashimiya* – The Hashimiya were a Shi'a sect, followers of Hashim, the son of Ibn al-Hanafiyya.

The Caliphate of Mahdi

p. 34   *Jurjan* – Jurjan is not in the Sirawan district; Pellat suggests that a line may have been dropped from the text.

p. 34   *Arzan wa l-Ran* – This place name is unidentified; it is not Erzurum.

p. 34   *Raddain* – Tabari (3:523) locates the tomb of Mahdi in the village of al-Radhdh, of which this spelling may be a variant.

Mahdi and the Qadi

p. 35   *I have sold my faith* – Because he may be forced to give decisions in accordance with political expedience, rather than religious law.

Mahdi and the Bedouin

p. 38   *other preposterous claims* – That is, either to be a prophet or to be divine.

The Meadows of Gold

Unrequited Love

p. 43   *O camel, carry me swiftly* – Abu al-Atahiya's attempt to change the subject with these verses is singularly inept for a poet of his ability.

p. 44   *this penalty* – The punishment for slander was 80 lashes.

The Character of Hadi

p. 51   *Thursday* – Actually Friday.

p. 51   *A poet* – Salm ibn Amr, called Salm al-Khasir ('Salm Who Lost', because, asked by his father to choose between a copy of the Koran and some books of poetry, he chose the latter. He is mentioned in the *Kitab al-Aghani*.

Blood Feuds

p. 58   *Alas that our Shaikh* – This refers to the Imam Ibrahim ibn Muhammad ibn Ali ibn Abd Allah ibn Abbas, killed by the Umayyads at Harran. The battle of Abu Futrus took place on 15 Dhu al-Qadr, 132 A.H.

The Dream of Mahdi

p. 64   *his face shone with joy* – Although Harun disagrees with his brother Hadi on so many points, he concedes the essential: to recognize the claims of Hadi's children.

p. 64   *by the most illustrious shaikh* – That is, Mahdi, father of Harun and Hadi.

p. 65   *Ibn Ishaq al-Saimari* – This could not have been Ibn Ishaq al-Saimari (q.v.), who lived in the 3rd century A.H. In the parallel passage in Tabari, the name is al-Hakam ibn Musa al-Damari.

The Sword Samsama

p. 66   *a famous sword named Samsama* – The root of the word 'Samsama' means 'to persist'; cp. 'Durandel'.

p. 66   *50,000 dinars* – The text does not specify the coin, but merely reads '50,000'; we have supplied the word 'dinars'.

Notes

The Accession of Harun al-Rashid

p. 67 *on a Friday* – Actually Sunday.

p. 67 *on a Saturday* – Actually Sunday.

The Dream of Harun al-Rashid

p. 74 *Musa ibn Ja'far* – This was Musa al-Kazim, son of Ja'far al-Sadiq, the seventh Shi'a Imam.

Ma'n ibn Za'ida

p. 79 *Ma'n ibn Za'ida* – Ma'n ibn Za'ida died in 151 A.H., before Harun al-Rashid was born. The name is a mistake for Yazid ibn Mazyad.

Amin and Ma'mun as Children

p. 81 *any poems by heart* – The poem recited by Muhammad (Amin) is by Hatim al-Ta'i, the pre-Islamic poet famed for his generosity. The last lines of these poems recited by Amin and Ma'mun are presumably intended to reveal the difference in their characters.

Amin and Ma'mun

p. 83 *a fourth analogy* – presumably to the Prophet.

A Hard-Won Song

p. 91 *By Him who is in this tomb* – That is, the Prophet Muhammad.

The Death of Harun al-Rashid

p. 98 *the brother of Rafi' ibn al-Laith* – Marwan ibn al-Laith, whose brother Rafi' revolted against Abbasid rule in Transoxania and Khurasan in 189 A.H./A.D. 805.

The Meadows of Gold

The Barmakids

p. 102   *a descendant of Abu Talib* – That is, one of the Shi'a pretenders, who might be considered a threat to the Abbasids.

The Advice of Yahya

p. 103   *superintendent of the posts* – This official was also chief of intelligence, which explains why he is reporting on the behaviour of Fadl ibn Yahya.

The Avarice of Asma'i

p. 107   *Asma'i* – A famous grammarian.

The Fall of the Barmakids

p. 115   *But your privileges will end there* – Such an unconsummated marriage is contrary to Islamic law.

Elegies on the Barmakids

p. 121   *the following lines* – The fact that these verses were written the day after the death of Ja'far, in far away Khurasan, implies that the fall of the Barmakids had been planned long in advance.

p. 123   *Abu Nuwas* – The leading poet of the period. He figures in the *1001 Nights*, and became a by-word for libertinism.

The Mother of Ja'far

p. 126   *Day of Immolation* – The 10th of the month of Dhu al-Hijja. This is the day the pilgrims perform their sacrifice at Mina, near Mecca.

Trouble between Amin and Ma'mun

p. 135   *Ali ibn Isa ibn Mahan* – This is the same man whose death was foretold earlier by verses pinned to his castle in Khurasan; see *Elegies on the Barmakids*, p. 121.

Notes

p. 136   *We will fight like the Kharijites* – The force of this is lost on us; the battle described by Mas'udi seems quite conventional. The Kharijites were noted for their ferocity; perhaps it means that they will fight to the last man.

Ill-Omens for Amin

p. 138   *his mood grew darker still* – The singing girl is trying to shame the Caliph into fighting by her songs. The poems are all by well-known poets, and the audience's knowledge of the original context of the verses would have greatly added to their point here.

The Birth of Musa al-Hadi

p. 143   *the name Musa* – This passage refers to Musa, the son of Amin, who in turn was the son of Harun al-Rashid. It foretells the disastrous civil war which broke out during Amin's Caliphate.

Miscellaneous Anecdotes

p. 144   *the poet Abu al-Ghul* – In the *Kitab al-Aghani*, this poem is attributed to Ashja 'al-Sulami.

The Palace of Manbij

p. 145   *southernwood and artemesia* – These two plants were often used to indicate health and fertility. Southernwood is also a member of the artemesia family and was commonly used as a purgative.

Musa Declared Heir Apparent

p. 146   *Observe how a tyrant and a seducer* – That is, Amin and his vizier, Fadl ibn al-Rabi'.

p. 146   *Book of Light* – The Koran.

The Meadows of Gold

Rebellion

p. 147 *The Holy Law and the Psalms* – There do seem to be echoes of the Psalms in this poem.

p. 148 *Ram of the East* – There are suggestions of the legend of Alexander the Great – called by the Arabs 'Possessor of the Two Horns' – in this appellation for Tahir.

Amin at Bay

p. 165 *By the Amir* – The Amir is Ma'mun.

p. 167 *with all the power of 'Ad* – 'Ad was a legendary pre-Islamic tribe of giants in Southern Arabia.

The Death of Amin

p. 168 *Thursday* – Actually Saturday.

Amin's Head

p. 172 *the – of their mothers* – The Arabic is similarly coy, reading 'the such-and-such of their mothers'.

The Laments of the Women

p. 174 *as did A'isha for the blood of Uthman* – After the murder of the Caliph Uthman, A'isha, the favourite wife of the Prophet, actively sought vengeance against his murderers.

Sayings of Ma'mun

p. 176 *Anushirvan* – A pre-Islamic Persian vizier famous for his wisdom.

Ma'mun and the Sponger

p. 178 *Thumama ibn Ashras* – A famous mu'tazilite theologian.

Notes

p. 178   *tadruj* – This bird was apparently considered sacred to the Manicheans.

p. 180   *following air* – The poem is by Abu Nuwas.

The Caliph and the Poet

p. 185   *Mubarrad and Tha'lab* – Grammarians and 'belletrists' of the time.

The Caliph's Cooking

p. 191   *call to prayer* – The dawn call to prayer marked the end of curfew.

The Death of Shafi'i

p. 198   *Shafi'i* – Founder of one of the four schools of Islamic law. He lived 150–204 AH/AD 767–819.

The Marriage of Buran

p. 205   *Buran* – A dish named 'Buraniya', after this woman, is still eaten in the Middle East.

Ma'mun's Campaigns against the Byzantines

p. 220   *'Stretch out your feet'* – The Greek name for this place was Podandos (now Bozanti), hence the folk etymology (pod = foot in Greek).

Mutawakkil's Palace of the Two Wings

p. 240   *al-Hiri* – Pellat suggests that this is the palace of Balkuwara, built by Mutawakkil at Samarra. The description recalls the pre-Islamic palace depicted in the mosaics of the Umayyad mosque in Damascus.

Saved from Rape

p. 243   *He governed the city* – He was actually chief of police.

445

The Meadows of Gold

Love's Despair – Jahiz

p. 249 *Juhaina* – A large town near Mosul.

p. 249 *Jahiz* – The most important stylist of the 9th century, considered the founder of Arabic artistic prose. He died in 255 AH/AD 868.

The Death of Ahmad ibn Hanbal

p. 254 *Ahmad ibn Hanbal* – Founder of the school of law named after him.

p. 254 *Thursday* – Actually Tuesday. Despite the date, this was *not* Halley's comet, which was not visible from Baghdad.

The Carpet of Annihilation

p. 268 *Mahuza* – This represents the Aramaic word Mahōzē, the old name for Ctesiphon, known to the Arabs as Mada'in. But here it seems to refer to a place near Samarra.

On the Death of Muntasir

p. 271 *Thursday* – Actually Friday.

An Old Love Regained

p. 275 *They say a lover . . .* This poem is by Ibn Dumaina and occurs in the *Kitab al-Aghani*.

Afra and Urwa

p. 276 *Urwa, his father* – This is Urwa ibn al-Zubair.

The Death of Muhtadi

p. 301 *the Bedouin appeared everywhere* – A sign of the breakdown of central authority.

Notes

The Austerity of Muhtadi

p. 306 *Umar ibn Abd al-Aziz* – This was the Umayyad Caliph Umar II, noted for his piety.

A Tradition Concerning Ali

p. 308 '*Happy are they . . .*' – This tradition exists in other sources with a number of variants.

The Death of Jahiz

p. 309 *the legitimacy of the rule of the first three Caliphs* – Jahiz supported the legitimacy of the first three Caliphs in his *Kitab al-Uthmaniyya*, which Mas'udi rejected because of his Shi'a sympathies. This is one of the few places where Mas'udi's own beliefs are made explicit.

p. 309 *well-known heretical tendencies* – Jahiz was a Mu'tazilite.

The Caliphate of Mu'tamid

p. 312 *Tuesday* – It was really a Monday.

The Discipline of Saffar's Army

p. 313 *Tuesday* – It was actually a Thursday.

The Horrors of the Zanj Rebellion

p. 317 *The zanj* – The *zanj* were black slaves from East Africa and Zanzibar who were brought to Iraq to work in the salt pans of the Shatt al-Arab. Inflamed by Kharijite egalitarian doctrines, they revolted and plunged Iraq into chaos.

Wily Muslims Admired by Byzantines   p. 337

p. 319 *Ibriq* – Classical Tephrikè, the modern Turkish town of Devriğe.

The Meadows of Gold

p. 319 *Chrysocheir* – Chrysocheir was not the sister of Corbeas, but the brother. Chrysocheir was a leader of the Paulicians, a Christian heresy influenced by Manicheanism. In 871 the Byzantine emperor sent an army against Ibriq; the town was taken the following year and razed. Chrysocheir's head was sent to Constantinople. There is an excellent account of these events in Runciman's *The Medieval Manichee*.

Mu'awiya Takes Revenge

p. 320 *tribe of Quraish* – This was the tribe of the Prophet, so the insult was even greater than it might otherwise have been.

p. 323 *'Go back to your king'* – This passage literally reads: 'Go back to your king', he said, 'and say to him: "I have left the king of the Arabs on your carpet, dispensing justice and revenging the injuries done to his subjects in your palace and at the seat of your authority." ' This refers to Mu'awiya's position as ruler over the former Byzantine province, hence our emendations.

The Night Conversations of Mu'tamid

p. 325 *'Greet those guests . . .'* – As so often in Mas'udi, the poem is not only very bad, but seems to be in direct contrast with what has just been said.

A Master Thief

p. 356 *The ex-convicts on guard at the bridge* – The phrase is *tawwabū al-jisr* 'the repentants of the bridge' – hence our translation. It is possible that the phrase simply means 'police informers'.

p. 357 *sent to Bakhtishu' by Jesus* – Bakhtishu' was a Christian.

p. 357 *Dallah* – This famous trickster appears in the *1001 Nights*.

The Avarice of Muktafi

p. 374 *doctrine of Free Will and Unity* – That is, Mu'tazilites.

Notes

Hospitality

p. 382   *a brazier with its two 'giraffes'* – The text clearly reads *zirāfain*, 'two giraffes', which may be a technical term for the supports of a brazier or indeed refer to the fact that this brazier was supported on the backs of bronze giraffes.

p. 382   *where the curtain was hanging* – This was presumably the curtain which separated musicians from guests.

Qahir Demands a True History

p. 391   *we know what happened to Fadl ibn Sahl* – He was assassinated in his bath.

p. 392   *He punished dissidents* – Wathiq was a Mu'tazilite, and demanded adherence to the tenets of that sect.

Chess and Backgammon

p. 398   *an upholder of the doctrine of Justice* – The Mu'tazilites believed a just God could not condemn men to be ruled by fate, hence their belief in free will.

The Marvels of Creation

p. 403   *Jahiz also lists this bird* – The stories ascribed to Jahiz here do not occur in his *Book of Animals* as we know it today.

Arabic Words for Lavatory

p. 405   *Arabic Words for Lavatory* – This story clearly shows that Arabic dialects were already quite divergent at this date.

Black and Green

p. 408   *he went back to wearing black clothes* – Black was the colour of the House of Abbas, while green was the colour of the Shi'a. Green is still the colour reserved in the Islamic world for descendants of the Prophet.

The Meadows of Gold

The Garden of Qahir

p. 409   *planted with orange trees* – This is one of the earliest mentions of orange trees in Arabic.

Bajkam the Turk

p. 413   *A little knowledge gives much power* – This sentence could also mean: 'a few good stories are worth more than a lot of specialized knowledge'.

INDEX

This index is topical rather than anomastic and the names of some minor characters and places have been omitted. Most identifiable place names are located on the map, the plan of Baghdad, or in the notes.

ABBADA, mother of Ja'far al-Barmaki: connives at his seduction, 116; her poverty relieved, 126

ABBAS AL-ALAWI: dissuades Ma'mun from shedding blood, 214–15

ABBASA, sister of Rashid: married to Ja'far al-Barmaki, 115; tricks Ja'far into consumating their marriage, 116; sends their son to Mecca, 116–17; and to Yemen, 117

ABD ALLAH IBN MALIK AL-KHUZA'I: Rashid's chief of police, 74

ABD AL-MALIK: criticized by Mansur, 23

ABU AL-ATAHIYA: his love for Utba, 43–5; one of his poems moves Harun al-Rashid, 99; cheers Ma'mun, 190; becomes a Sufi, 216; his death, 216; poems, 216; on the death of Alexander, 236

ABU AL-AYNA: and Ibn al-Jassas, 332; saved from drowning, 332; his wit, 332; praises the Barmakids, 333; reasons for not drinking, 333

ABU AL-BAIDA: a good story-teller, 286–7

ABU BAKR IBN AYYASH: prophecies death of Harun al-Rashid, 71

ABU FADL IBN ABI TAHIR: his book *A History of Authors*, 275; tells a love story, 275–6; anecdote of debauches at Mecca, 279–80

ABU FUTRUS, battle of, 58

ABU ISHAQ, see IBRAHIM AL-HARBI

ABU KHALIFA AL-JUMAHI, grammarian: delegate to Mu'tadid, 339; an amusing anecdote, 339–40

ABU NUWAS, poet: poem on flowers, 421–2

ABU ZAKKAR, singer, 118

ABYSSINIANS, 74

ACONITE: used to poison Mu'tamid, 327

ADANA: fortified by Harun al-Rashid, 389

AFRA: love for Urwa, 285–6; dies at his tomb, 286

AGHLABIDS, 380

AGRICULTURE: Mu'tasim's love of, 223; excellent at Samarra, 229

AHMAD IBN AL-KHASIB: viciousness as vizier, 270; reproves Muntasir's imprudence, 271

AHMAD IBN SALLAM: describes Amin's last hours, 170–71

AHMAR, the grammarian: instructed on education of Amin, 83

AHNAF IBN QAIS: his ugliness and wit, compares Basra to Kufa, 61

A'ISHA, wife of the Prophet, 113, 174

ALCHEMY, 358–9

ALEMBICS, 358

ALEXANDER THE GREAT: aphorisms on his death, 236

ALI IBN ABI TALIB: his place of death in Kufa, 71; dream of, 365; appears to Mu'tadid, 366

ALI IBN ABI TALIB, *see* BLIND POET

ALI IBN ISA IBN MAHAN: verses on the gate of his castle, 121; appointed by Amin to lead army into Khurasan, 135; contempt for Tahir, 135; killed in battle against Tahir, his body thrown down a well, 136; educated Amin's son Musa, 146

ALIDS: reasons why favoured by Mu'tadid, 366

ALOE, 138

AMBERGRIS, 105; 205; candles of, 390

AMIN: as a child recites a poem for Kisa'i, 81; educated by Ahmar, the grammarian, 82; dispraised by Umani, 83; favoured by the House of Hashim and placed first in the succession, 84–5; Zubaida pleads for him, 86; agreement concerning his succession hung in the Ka'ba, 87; mentioned by

451

The Meadows of Gold

Rashid on his death bed, 99;
proclaimed Caliph, 132; outline of his
reign, 132; Zubaida dreams of his fate,
133; decides to attack Ma'mun, 135–6;
his army defeated at Rayy, 136–7; ill-
omens, 138–9; his love for Nazm, grief
at her death, 140; loses fish with earrings,
141; kills lion with dagger, 142;
dismisses Zubaida, 144; spoken ill of by
the Blind Poet, 148; defeated by Tahir,
148; besieged at Baghdad, 149; pleads
unsuccessfully with Tahir, 149–50;
civil war against Ma'mun, 150–67;
melts down his gold and silver to pay
army, 156–7; supporters hungry and
defeated, 162–3; extorts money, 164;
his despair, 165; refuses to plead with
Tahir, 166; arranges safe-conduct with
Harthama, 167; escape plan fails; boat
capsizes, 168; his last words, 169; his
throat cut, 169; another version of his
death, 170–71; his head offered to
Tahir, 171; his head embalmed;
insulted; buried, 172; laments for him,
173; only recognized in Baghdad, 175
AMORIUM: patriach of, 230;
Mu'tasim's conquest of, 231
AMR AL-RUMI: relates a dream of
Mahdi's, 64–5
AMR IBN MA'DIKARIB: his sword
Samsama ransomed for 50,000 dinars,
66
ANBAR: Ja'far the Barmakid murdered
there, 118–20
ANGEL: thief pretends to be, 357
ANUSHIRVAN, 176
APPARITION: of Ali to Mu'tadid, 366
APPLE, 422; inscribed with musk and
ambergris, 105–6; Syrian, 382
ARABS: lose supremacy under Mansur,
388
ARAFAT, 279
ARDASHIR, 391; invented chess, 398
ARISTOTLE, 388
ARITHMETIC: treatises on, 388
ARMENIA: red clay from, 382
ARMENIAN CARPETS, 40
ARMENIAN CUSHIONS, 40, 142
ARMOUR, 154
ARMY, NAKED, 154–5
ARTEMISIA, 145
ARUDI, AL-: tutor to Radi, 399, 401,
404, 405, 412

ASMA'I: relates Rashid's preoccupation
with the succession, 84; recites poem
for Rashid, 94; describes Rashid
reading a poem, 99; tries to make Ja'far
the Barmakid laugh, 107; his avarice,
107; elegies on the Barmakids, 121–5
ASSASSIN: testing of, 255–7
ASTROLABES, 388
ASTROLOGERS: introduced by
Mansur, 388; Ma'mun follows advice
of, 391
ASWAN, 60; Masudi hears story of
Shafi'i's death there, 198
ATIKA, 55
AUSTERITY: of Muhtadi, 306; of
Saffar, 315–16
AVARICE, 107; of Muktafi, 374
AVIARY, 382

BACKGAMMON, 304, 326; inventor of
a fatalist, 398
BADGHIS, Afghanistan: Ma'mun's
mother from, 175
BADHHANJ, 271
BADR, Mu'tadid's freedman, 327, 355;
real holder of power, 329; treacherously
killed by Qasim, 370; his career, 371–2
BAGHDAD, passim: its various
historical calamities, 157; siege of, 141,
144; besieged again, 282
BAGHIR, the Turk; tested as an assassin,
255–7; given Indian sword to protect
Mutawakkil, 258–9; uses Indian sword
to kill Mutawakkil, 260; killed by Wasit
and Bugha, 282
BAGHL, ABU AL-HASAN IBN ABI
AL-, 396
BAHRAIN, 408
BAIKBAK, the Turk, 301–2
BAJKAM, the Turk: coins his own
money, 412–13; his death, 416
BAKHTISHU', the doctor. (*see also*
JABRA'IL): at Ma'mun's death bed,
219–20; attends Wathiq's debate on
medicine, 233–5; cleverly tricked, 357
BALKH: fire temple at, 131
BALL GAMES: introduced by Rashid,
389
BAMBOO: word avoided out of respect
for Khaizuran, 97
BAMIYAN, 335
BANANAS, 375
BANJ, 357

452

Index

BARBER: shelters al-Mahdi, 207–9
BARDESANES (*see* IBN DAISAN)
BARIDI, family of, 416,426
BARMAK THE ELDER, 131
BARMAKI, FADL IBN YAHYA AL-, 122; in prison, 124, 128–30; cruelly lashed, 128; healed by a man who refuses payment, 128–30; his death, 130
BARMAKI, JA'FAR AL-, 55; forces Amin to swear his oath three times and earns Zubaida's resentment, 87; reproved for his frivolity, 103; reforms, 104; disapproves of Asma'i's avarice, 107; poem on him and Rashid, 108; Rashid marries him to Abbasa, 115; silliness of his mother, 115–16; tricked into consumating marriage, 116; feasts with Rashid, 118; pleads with Yasir, 119; is executed by Yasir, 119; elegies on, 121–5
BARMAKI, YAHYA IBN KHALID AL-, 55; persuades Hadi not to bar Harun from the succession, 62; given absolute power by Harun, 67; advises Harun on the succession, 84–5; reproves his son, 103; introduces a singing girl, 105; symposium on love, 109–13; offends Zubaida, 117; in chains, 122; his wife destitute, 126; advised to sacrifice his wealth, 127; in prison, 128; his death at Raqqa, 130
BARMAKIDS, 99, 102, 391; the family praised, 101; drinking with Rashid, 105; reasons for their fall, 115–17; Rashid swears revenge on, 117; elegies on, 121–5; before Islam, 131; praised by Abu al-Ayna, 333
BARRENNESS: of Zubaida cured, 137
BASIL FLOWERS, 365
BASRA, passim: its wealth, 61; compared to an old woman, 61; Wadi al-Qasr Palace, 68–9; Jahiz dies at, 309; delegation complains of governor of, 337–8
BATHS, 271
BATTLE OF SUNDAY, 163
BEDOUIN, 83; feeds Mahdi, 36–7; prophecies civil war between Amin and Ma'mun, 87; appear at times of unrest, 301; mimicked, 352
BERBERS, 380
BILQIS, Queen of Sheba, 218

BIRRA: nurse of Abbasa's child, 116–17
BISH, (aconite): used to poison Mu'tamid, 327
BLACK, colour of Abbasid dynasty: 408; exchanged for green by Ma'mun, 202–3
BLACK SEA, 321–3
BLACK WOMEN: black woman teaches Miskin a song, 91–3
BLIND POET OF BAGHDAD, 'ALI IBN ABI TALIB': verses on Amin's son Musa, 146; on nobility of Ma'mun, 147; on siege of Baghdad, 151–3; on destruction of Baghdad, 156–8; lament for Dar al-Raqiq, 158–9; on the Vagabond Warriors, 160–1; on the desolation of the city, 162; the Battle of Sunday, 163–4; just revenge, 164–5
BLOOD: of Muhtadi drunk by Turk, 302
BOAT: Rashid travels to Mosul by, 96; tithe levied on, 150; Amin moved by, 167; Tahir's boats intercept Amin, 168; overturned, 169; suicide from, 249–50; used to abduct Byzantine, 320–4; blind man saved, 332–3; of Basra described, 337; party in, 339; sunk by collapsing bridge, 355; called gazelles, 417
BONE-MARROW, 35
BONE SETTER: sets Amin's hand, 142
BOOKS (*see also* KORAN, HISTORICAL ANNALS, and INTERMEDIATE HISTORY): *The Book of Ibrahim al-Mahdi*, 175, 207; *Tales of Doctors and Kings*, 207; of Waqidi, 210; *Diwan* of Abu al-Atahiya, 216; *Ways of Merit*, by al-Kindi, 231; *Book of the Orchard* by Fath ibn Khaqan, 239; *Treatise on Unusual Questions*, by Muhammad ibn Sama'a, 242; *A History of Authors*, by Abu Fadl ibn Abi Tahir, 275; *Book of Exposition and Demonstration*, by Jahiz, 309; *Book of Spongers*, by Jahiz, 309; *Book of Misers*, by Jahiz, 309; *Book of Animals*, by Jahiz, 309; *A Refutation of Those Who Falsely Claim That Gold and Silver Can Be Artificially Produced*, by al-Kindi, 358; *Book of Mansur*, by al-Razi, 358; *Biographies of Kings*, 365; *Chronicle of Baghdad called Dynastic Histories*, 381; *History of Muqtadir*, by Jahshiyari, 381; *Reunion of the Assemblies*, projected work by Mas'udi, 384; *Kalila and Dimna*,

453

The Meadows of Gold

translation of commissioned by Mansur, 388; *Sindhind* translation of commissioned by Mansur, 388; *Almagest*, translation of commissioned by Mansur, 388; *Book of Euclid*, translation of commissioned by Mansur, 388; translations from Greek, Pahlavi, Persian, Syriac, 388; Ma'mun's love of, 391; of Ibn Duraid, the lexicographer, 392; *Paradise of Wisdom*, by al-Tabari, 403; Mas'udi expatiates on scope and intention of his, 426–9
BORAX, 358
BREAD, 378; barley, 36; cooked in ashes, 37; eaten with cold meat by Mahdi, 50; its price in besieged Baghdad, 162; eaten with stew by Mutawakkil, 248; eaten with salt and vinegar, 283; Mu'tadid reduces rations, 329; left-overs used for soup by Muktafi, 374
BREECHES, 401
BRIDE PRICE: of Qatr al-Nada, 331
BRIDGE AT SAMARRA: fighting at, 301–2
BROCADE, 24, 355; Basra rich in, 61; green woven with red and gold in Amin's kiosk, 138; worn by Mu'tasim's Turkish guard, 228; Brocade carpets banned by Muhtadi, 306; merchants of Karkh, 363; red carpet of, 382
BUDANDUN: Ma'mun dies at, 175, 219–25; meaning of, 220
BUGHA THE ELDER: given Mahbuba, 266; his devoutness; death of, 288–9
BUGHA THE YOUNGER 268–9, 272, 290; plans death of Mutawakkil, 255–7; kills Baghir, imprisons Musta'in, 282; spared, 297; killed, 298
BUHTARI, 262; on Mutawakkil, 256–60
BUKHARI, AL-: reader at Khumarawaih's funeral, 347
BURAN: marries Ma'mun, 205
BURIAL: of Mansur, with face uncovered, 21; of Musta'in, by common people, 293; of Muqtadir, by common people, 384
BUTHAINA, 113
BUST, 335
BUWAIHIDS, 423, 424, 426
BYZANTINES, 319; patrician abducted by Mu'awiya, 320–4; taste for luxuries from Islamic dominions, 320–2; play chess, 395; emperor asks for breeches of tallest man, 401
BYZANTIUM, *see also* RUM, 131; Ma'mun's campaigns against, 218–19; Muntasir campaigns against, 272; Byzantines castrate their children, 345; the 'Ransoming of Treachery', 373

CAFTAN: worn by Saffar, 315
CALIPHATE, *passim*; analyzed by Ma'mun, 196; history of, 387–92
CALLIGRAPHY, 99, 121, 268; cloth embroidered with, 331
CAMELS, BACTRIAN, 142, 355; crossed with dromedaries and called *bukht*, 316; anecdote concerning, 419–20
CAMEL PATROLS, 77
CAMOMILE, 422
CAMPHOR: used for ointment, 309
CANALS: dug at Samarra, 229
CANNIBALISM: during Zanj rebellion, 317–18; black slaves of Khumarawaih eat his murderers, 345
CARAVANSERAIS: built by Zubaida, 389–90
CARAWAY, 224
CARPET, 24, 308; Harun al-Rashid's mount led up to edge of, 64; Mutawakkil's body wrapped in, 260; ill-omened carpet described, 268–9; used to smother Muhtadi, 302; banned by Muhtadi, 306; red and blue Susangird ordered by a Byzantine, 322; King of the Arabs sits on one which belonged to King of Rum, 323; of red brocade, 382
CASTRATION, 345; as revenge, 54
CELERY, 224
CENSUS: of descendants of Abbas, 202
CHAPLET: of gems, 332
CHARITABLE FOUNDATIONS: of Zubaida, 389–90
CHESS, 304, 326, 383, 395–8; Mahdi plays with Rashid, 96; Rashid first Abbasid to play, 389; symbolism of; inventor of a Mu'tazilite, 398
CHINA: rarities from, 331; Chinese castrate their children, 345
CHOSROE, 138, 268, 295, 412–13
CHRISTIANITY, 218, 319; a convert from, 333

CHRISTIANS, 268
CITRON, 422
CITY OF ABU JA'FAR: Old Baghdad, 166
CITY OF PEACE (*see* BAGHDAD)
CITY PLANNING: of Samarra, 229
CIVIL WAR: between Amin and Ma'mun, 150–67
CLEOPATRA: as alchemist, 358
CLIMATE: of Egypt, 59
CLOTH (*See also* BROCADE, SILK): scented with musk, 44; coarse white worn by Sufis, 195; *mulhama* favoured by Mutawakkil, 239; *fakhiti* worn by Saffar, 315; embroidered with calligraphy, 331; precious cloth from Khurasan, 335; of Tustar, 364, 382; *washi* made for Zubaida, costing 50,000 dinars a length, 390
CLOTHES, 207; scented over brazier, 195; 207; new clothes for children at Ramadan, 210; Muhtadi's austerity, 306; worn in a triumph, 355; of Zubaida, 390; of Zubaida's page girls, 391; 'Mu'tasimi' headgear, 392; black versus green, 408
CONCUBINES: Mutawakkil has 4000, 263; noble Arab woman taken by black as, 318
CONFIDENCE TRICKSTERS, 355–7
CONSTANTINOPLE 319, 320–4; from Constantinople to Syria in 13 days by boat, 323
COOKERY CONTEST, 191–2, 243–7
COOKING: the Caliph cooks, 191–2; al-Mahdi cooks a stew, 208; for Saffar's army, 316
CORBEAS, Patriach of the Paulicans, 319
COTTON: Amin's head packed in, 172
CROCODILES: in the Nile, 59–60
CRUCIFIXION: of Khumarawaih's murderers, 345
CRYSTAL: goblet set with gems, 138–9
CUMIN, 224
CUPPING, 272
CURFEW: imposed on Zubaida by Yahya the Barmakid, 117
CURSES: Mas'udi curses those who abridge his text, 428
CUSHIONS: Armenian, 40; filthy cushions in Asma'i's house, 107; elegant leather cushions in Barber's house, 208; ordered by a Byzantine, 322–33
CYPRUS, 320; seized, 385

DABIQ, town in Egypt famous for weaving, 329
DA'F, 'Weakness': ill-omened slave-girl of Amin, 138
DAILAMITES, 423, 424, 425
DALLAH: female confidence trickster, 357
DAMASCUS, 29
DAR AL-RAQIQ: on west bank of Tigris; slaughter there, 158–9
DATES: pudding of, 315; harvest, 339
DAY OF IMMOLATION, 126
'DAYS OF THE ARABS': taught to Mahdi (q.v.) by Sharqi (q.v.), 46; Musta'in's knowledge of, 285
DEBAUCHERY: at Mecca, 279–80
DEMONS, 337, 360; present at childbirth, 133
DENTISTRY, 235
DIOGENES, 236
DISCIPLINE: superb in Saffar's army, 313–14
DISTILLATION, 358
DHU AL-QARNAIN (*see also* ALEXANDER), 335
DHU AL-YAMINAIN (*see* TAHIR)
DOCTORS: Mahdi's doctor Ibn Ishaq al-Saimari, 65; Harun al-Rashid's doctor Jabra'il ibn Bakhtishu, anecdote of a fish, 72–3; a Persian doctor examines Harun al-Rashid's urine, 98; physiology of love, 112; an unnamed man heals Fadl al-Barmaki, 128–30; at Ma'mun's deathbed, 219–20; discuss Mu'tasim's health, 223–4; poison Mu'tasim, 273; al-Razi on medicine, 358; at Mu'tadid's death, 367
DOME, GREEN: in Baghdad, 29; in Wasit, 29
DOME OF COMPLAINTS: built by Muhtadi, 299
DONGOLA, 60
DONKEY, 70; ridden by Hadi, 51–2; Harun al-Rashid too weak to mount, 98; Mu'tasim pulls donkey out of ditch, 227; in love, 241; as witnesses, 279–80
DOVE, 382; poem on, 78
DOWRY: of 20,000 dirhams, 184;

455

The Meadows of Gold

fabulous dowry of Qatr al-Nada, 331
DREAMS: of Mansur's mother, 21;
  Mahdi dreams of giving branches to
  Hadi and Harun al-Rashid, 64–5;
  Harun al-Rashid dreams he must free
  Musa ibn Ja'far, 74–5; Musa ibn Ja'far
  dreams of the Prophet, 74–5; Zubaida
  dreams of her son's fate, 133–4; The
  Prophet appears in a dream to
  governor of Baghdad, 243–4; dreams
  on the death of Muntasir, 271; dream of
  Mutawakkil and Fath ibn Khaqan in
  the flames, 272; Bugha the Elder
  dreams of Muhammad and Ali, 288;
  Mu'tadid haunted, 360; of Ali, 365;
  Mu'tadid sees vision of Ali, 366
DROWNING: suicide by, 249–52; saved
  from, 332; major accident at Baghdad,
  353; child drowned, 356
DUNGEONS: man from Hamadan
  unjustly held in, 80
DUSHAB (See NABIDH)

EARTHQUAKE: at Jerusalem, 389
EGYPT, 331; climate of, 59–60; Ma'mun
  visits, 218; mission to sultan of, 276
EARRINGS, 275; worn by Amin's fish,
  141
ELEGIES (see also LAMENTS): on the
  Barmakids, 121–5
ELEPHANT: at Baghdad, 355
ELIXIRS, 358
EMBALMING, 59
EMBROIDERY: on belts, 292; of
  calligraphy, from Egypt, 331; on
  slippers, 390
ETIQUETTE: at Mu'tamid's court,
  325–6
EUCLID, 388
EUNUCHS, *passim*, but especially: on the
  making and characteristics of, 345–6;
  amusing anecdote concerning, 352–4;
  Amin's preference for, 390
EUPHRATES, 59
EXILE: from Mecca to Arafat, 279;
  Muwaffaq exiled to Basra, 297

FADL IBN AL-RABI', 145; relates
  anecdote on Mansur, 23–4; describes
  Mansur's death, 32; tells anecdote of
  Mahdi and a qadi, 35; tells anecdote of
  Mahdi and a peasant, 36; offers to cut
  off Sufyan al-Thawri's head, 49–50;
  racing at Raqqa with Harun al-Rashid,
  94; presides over oath of allegiance to
  Amin, 132; Amin's vizier, 146;
  defeated, 147
FADL IBN SAHL, DHU AL-
  RIYASATAIN, 136, 391; his mother's
  words on his death, 193; murdered in
  his bath, 202
FAKHITA: Mu'awiya's wife veils before
  eunuchs, 345
FAKHKH: battle of, 55–6
FAMINE: in Baghdad, 162; during Zanj
  rebellion, 317–18; at Basra, 337
'FATES': Zubaida dreams of three
  'fates', 133–4
FATH IBN KHAQAN, 248;
  Mutawakkil's freedman, 239; killed
  defending Mutawakkil, 260
FATIMA, DAUGHTER OF HARUN
  AL-RASHID: marries Ismail ibn
  Hadi, 65
FIGHTING ANIMALS: slaughtered by
  Muhtadi, 306; rams, cocks, partridges,
  417–18
FIGS: best kinds of, 229
FIRUZ IBN KABK, 335
FISH, 69; analyzed by Harun al-Rashid's
  doctor, 72–3; Harun al-Rashid
  considers fish tongues extravagant, 95;
  Amin loses fish wearing earrings, 143;
  causes Ma'mun's death, 210; eaten
  with sauce by Mu'tasim, 224
FLEET: Muslim fleet takes Cyprus, 385
FLOWERS: battle of, 421–2
FOOD, 179–80, 207; marrow cooked
  with sugar, 35; peasant food, 36;
  wholesomeness analyzed, 72–3; fish
  tongues, 95; Harun al-Rashid eats hot
  before cold, 95; gift of nuts and fruit to
  Harun al-Rashid, 97; cooked by
  Ma'mun and his friends, 191–2; sauce
  for fish, 224; at Mu'tasim's table,
  245–7; stew, 248; pleasures of, 283;
  austerity instituted by Muhtadi, 306; in
  Saffar's army, 315; presentation of,
  325–6; menu at Muktafi's table, 374;
  extremely elegant, 382–3
FOOD PRODUCTION: Egypt exporter
  not importer, 60
FORTRESSES: in Zabulistan, 336
FRITTERS, 375–6
FULLER: hits king of Hira with his
  mallet, 46–8

Index

FUNERAL PROCESSIONS, 68; of Khaizuran, 67; of Khumarawaih, 347

GALEN, 235; on attraction, 113
GARDENS, 421–2; of Tahir, 150; Amin's body buried in, 172; of Qahir, 409–10
GATES (OF BAGHDAD): Bab al-Anbar, 151, 156, 361; Bab al-Hadid, 172; Bab'al-Harb, 156; Bab al-Kunasa, 150, 163; Bab al-Muhawwal, 149; Bab Qutrabbul, 156; Basra Gate, 29; Khurasan Gate, 29, 149, 167 (also called Dynasty Gate)
GATE-CRASHER: adventures of, 203–5
GAZELLES, 69, 152, 382; boats called, 417
GENERALS: Qutaiba ibn Muslim on qualities needed by, 399
GHOSTS: ghost appears to Mahdi before his death, 50; haunt Mu'tadid, 360
GILLYFLOWERS, 383
'GIRAFFES', 382
GLASS: chalice of cut glass, 321
GONDESHAPUR: Saffar dies at, 313
GRAVE, 133; Harun al-Rashid orders his grave dug, 98
GREAT BEAR, 165
GREEKS (*see also* BYZANTINES): character of, 322; alchemists, 358; prisoners exchanged for Muslims, 373; at Cyprus, 385; philosophy and literature of, 388; chess players, 395
GREEK SCHOOL OF MEDICINE, 234
GREEN: adopted as dynastic colour by Ma'mun, 202–3; and later abandoned, 408
GUILD OF MERCHANTS, 363
GYPSY: mimicked, 352

HADI, 51–66, *passim*; his character, 51–2; courage when attacked by Kharijite, 51–2; laments death of descendant of the Prophet, 55; put off visiting Egypt, 59–60; hears Basra and Kufa compared, 61; dissuaded by Yahya ibn Barmak from removing Harun al-Rashid from the succession, 62; dies holding Khaizuran's hand, 63; Hadi, Harun al-Rashid and the succession, 64–5; given the sword Samsama by Mahdi, 66; his arrogance, 389
HAGAR, 137

HAIR SHIRT: worn by Zubaida, 174; worn by Muhtadi, 306
HAIR STYLES, 391
HAJJAJ: builds green dome, 29; died 95 A.H./713 A.D., 29; compares Iraqis and Syrians, 419–20
HAMADAN: a man from freed by Mansur, 29–31
HAMDANIDS: 414, 423, 424
HAMDUNA, DAUGHTER OF HARUN AL-RASHID: married to Ja'far ibn Hadi, 69
HANBAL, AHMAD IBN: whipped by Mu'tasim, 227; death of, 254
HAND: Ibrahim ibn al-Mahdi seduced by sight of, 179, 183–4
HANDKERCHIEF: Mu'tadid believed poisoned with, 367
HAREM, 152, 276; Yahya the Barmakid superintendant of Harun al-Rashid's harem, 117
HARISA, 378
HARRAN, 40
HARTHAMA IBN A'YAN: Tahir's general, 149–50; occupies Baghdad, 166; agrees to take Amin to Tahir, 167
HARUN AL-RASHID, 174; receives oath of allegiance for Hadi, 51; Hadi attempts to bar him from the succession, 62; defers to Hadi over the succession, 64; length of reign dreamed by Mahdi, 65; marries his daughters to Hadi's sons, 65; length of his reign; death at Sanabadh, 67; invests Yahya ibn Khalid al-Barmaki with absolute power, 67; his last pilgrimage, 71; shows off his sons to Kisa'i, 80; foretells war between them, 81; instructs Ahmar on educations of Amin, 82; praises Ma'mun, 83; preoccupied by the succession, 84–5; fears Amin's intentions towards Ma'mun, 86; performs pilgrimage with his sons, 87–8; rewards al-Mawsili for a song, 89–90; rewards Miskin with 4000 dinars for a song, 93; his horse wins race at Raqqa, 94; shocked at price of fish tongues, 95; travels by boat to Mosul, 96; sent gift of fruit and nuts, 97; his last illness and death, 98–100; warned of Ja'far the Barmakid's frivolity, 103–4; and a singing girl, 105–6; poem on him and Ja'far, 108; marries

457

The Meadows of Gold

Ja'far to his sister, 115; makes Ja'far swear not to consumate the marriage, 115; gives Yahya authority over Zubaida's household, 117; Zubaida tells him of Abbasa's child, 117; plans revenge, 117; feasts with Ja'far, 118; orders Yasir to kill Ja'far, 118–19; orders Yasir's death, 120; tells Asma'i of Ja'far's death, 121; love of wealth, 127; acquires slave girl, 137; envies Abd al-Malik palace, 145
HASANA; laments Mahdi, 34
HASHIM, HOUSE OF, 40, 82, 143, 153 *passim*; favours succession of Amin, 84–5; summoned by Rashid to his death bed, 99; Hashimite Caliphs, 144; colours of, 408
HASHIMIYA INSURRECTION, 28
HAZEL NUTS, 97
HEADS: Amin's head embalmed, insulted, buried, 172; head of Musta'in brought to Mu'tazz, 293; head of Bugha exposed on bridge at Samarra, sister's head eaten, 318
HELMETS: of palm-leaf, 154
HERESY: man accused of condemned to death by Musta'in, 288–9; heretical tendencies of Jahiz, 309; Mahdi extirpates, 388–9
HIPPOCRATES, 235; on love, 112
HIRA, 46–8, 72
HISHAM: only Umayyad approved by Mansur, 23; old soldier's loyalty to, 26
HISTORICAL ANNALS, by MASUDI, 66, 99, 131, 174, 231, 243, 293, 295, 300, 316, 318, 319, 326, 328, 345, 357, 358, 367, 380, 384, 413, 416
HONEY, 35, 248; pudding of, 315
HORSES: race, 94; men act as, 154; Amin's, 168; in lottery, 205; the best, 283
HOSPICES: founded by Zubaida, 390
HOURIS, 421
HUBSHIYA: Greek slave mother of Muntasir, 267; raises tomb for Muntasir at Samarra, 272
HUNAIN IBN ISHAQ: at Wathiq's debate on medicine, 233
HUNTING: Mahdi hunts, 36, 37; Harun al-Rashid hunts to avoid Hadi, 62; over indulgence in by Ja'far al-Barmaki, 103; Amin's lion hunters, 142; Mu'tasim hunts, 229

HUSAIN IBN ALI: descent from the Prophet, his revolt and death, 55

IBN ABI DU'AD : discusses food, asks favours for the needy, 245–7
IBN A'ISHA: executed by Ma'mun, 214–15
IBN AL-JASSAS: and Qatr al-Nadr's jewels, 331; his chaplets of gems and ingots of gold, 332
IBN AL-MAGHAZILI, mimic: performs for Mu'tadid, 352–4
IBN AYYASH, 46
IBN BASSAM: his poems, his sharp tongue, 382–3
IBN BUWAIH, AHMAD: blinds Mustakfi, 422; takes power, 423
IBN DA'B, 46; favoured by Hadi, his character, 53; relates tale of vengeful Indian, 54; comforts Hadi for cruelty of the Umayyads, 58; describes defects of Egyptian climate, 59–60; tells story comparing Basra and Kufa, 61
IBN DAISAN (BARDESANES), 388
IBN DURAID, lexicographer, 392; on Afra and Urwa, 285
IBN ISHAQ AL-SAIMARI: interprets a dream, 65
IBN JABIR, qadi: corrupted by wealth, 364
IBN KHURRADADHBIH, geographer, 324
IBN MASAWAIH, doctor: at Ma'mun's deathbed, 219–20; on Mu'tasim's health, 224–5; debates with his son Mikha'il before Wathiq, 233–5
IBN MUNQIDH: on Abu al-Ayna, 332-4
IBN MUQLA. vizier and calligrapher, 386
IBN NADIM, 273–4, 374
IBN SAMA'A, scholar, 242
IBN TULUN, AHMAD: Musta'in guarded by, 291; his descendants, 331, 345, 347
IBRAHIM, Imam: Muzna refuses Zainab his corpse, 40
IBRAHIM AL-HARBI: his death, praised as scholar and traditionalist, 361; his teaching, two of his students enamoured, 362–3
IBRAHIM AL-MAWSILI, musician:

relates anecdote about the king of Hira, 46–8; verses on Harun al-Rashid and Yahya, 67; on pilgrimage with Harun al-Rashid, 76; charms a black with his songs, 76–7; learns a song from Satan, 89–90; tells the story of learning a song, 91–3; tells story of a singing-girl, 105–6

IBRAHIM IBN AL-MAHDI, 72; tells story of a dish of fish tongues, 95; plays chess with Harun al-Rashid, Ibrahim an unlucky name, 96; tells how Khaizuran's name was tactfully avoided, 97; story of Amin's fish with earrings, 141; book of, 175; tells story of himself as uninvited guest, 179–84; proclaimed caliph, 202; captured, 204; sheltered by black barber, sings for him, 207–9

ICE, 382; iced water, 72–3

IDOL, 335

IHRAM, 363; worn by Mansur at his death, 21

IKHSHID, 415

IMAMITES: views on love, 109–11

INCENSE: for scenting clothing, 195

INDIA, 327, 331; sword from, 258–9; Saffar's conquests in, 335; chess in, 395, 397, 398; oranges from, 409

INFIDEL: in Zabulistan, 335

INK: scented, 105

INTERMEDIATE HISTORY, by MASUDI, 29, 33, 34, 50, 66, 131, 174, 231, 261, 270, 282, 293, 318, 328, 367, 380, 381, 416

IRRIGATION WORKS: of Harun al-Rashid, 389; of Zubaida, 389–90

ISA IBN ALI IBN MAHAN, 335

ISA IBN JA'FAR: alleged architect of palace at Basra, 68–9

ISAAC, 137

ISABADH (near Baghdad): Hadi dies there, 51

ISHAQ IBN IBRAHIM AL-MAWSILI: teases a poet, 185–6; his ex-servant shelters Mahdi, 208–9

ISHAQ IBN IBRAHIM IBN MUS'AB, governor of Baghdad: a curious story, 243–4

ISHMAEL, 137

ISMA'IL, brother of Mu'tazz: named heir apparent, 297

ISMA'IL IBN BULBUL: possible poisoner of Mu'tadid, 367

IVORY: Basra rich in, 61

JABRA'IL IBN BAKHTISHU': Harun al-Rashid's doctor, anecdote concerning a fish, 72–3

JAHIZ: relates story of Asma'i, 107; dismissed by Mutawakkil for his ugliness, 249; tales of unhappy love, 249–52; his death, last illness, on his works and character, 309–11; on marvels, 403–4

JAHSHIYARI: his history of Muqtadir, 381

JAIHAN, 59

JAISH: succeeds Khumarawaih, 347

JAWHARI, 189

JEALOUSY: of Zubaida, 137

JERUSALEM: mosque in rebuilt by Mahdi, 389

JESUS, 308, 357

JEWS, 333, 334

JEWELS: of Qatr al-Nada, 331; strung into chaplets, 332

JINN: believed responsible for Mu'tadid being haunted, 360

JURJAN: Hadi fights there, 51

KA'BA, 144; agreement between Amin and Ma'mun hung in Ka'ba falls down, 87

KABUL, 335

KARKH: in flames, 156–7

KATIB AL-BAGHDADI, ABU AL-HASAN ALI IBN AHMAD AL-, 419

KEEPER OF CARPETS: a Christian, 268

KHAIZURAN, MOTHER OF HADI AND RASHID, 51; charitable to a political opponent, 39–41; excluded from power by Hadi, 57; at Hadi's death bed, 62–3; Harun al-Rashid walks in her funeral procession, 67; her name tactfully avoided, 97

KHALID IBN YAZID, grandson of Mu'awiya: alchemical formula of, 358

KHALIL IBN AHMAD, lexicographer, 392

KHANJAR: used to kill Muhtadi, 302

KHANS, 161

KHANSA', poetess: quoted by Asma'i, 94

KHARIJITES, 136; Kharijite attacks Hadi, 51–2; views on love, 109; revolt

459

The Meadows of Gold

of, 301; links with Zanj, 317; in Sind, Zabulistan, etc, 335; leader Harun al-Shari captured, 355
KHUMARAWAIH IBN AHMAD IBN TULUN: his daughter marries Mu'tadid, 331; his throat cut, 345; his funeral at Cairo, 347
KHURASAN, *passim*, 121, 335–6; sides with Ma'mun, 147
KHUSHAJIM, 397–8
KHUSRAWANI: autumn equinox festival, 412–13
KINDI, YAQUB IBN ISHAQ AL-: his work on alchemy, 358
KIOSK, domed: favourite place of Amin, 138
KISA'I, the grammarian: meets Amin and Ma'mun as children, they recite poems for him, 80–1
KORAN, 57, 81, 82, 227, 307, 308, 340; king of Nubia discusses its prohibitions, 24; oath on, 350
KORAN, citations of (**Sura: verse**, Page) **2:19**, 428; **2:238**, 204; **3:26**, 172; **3:28**, 428; **3:49**, 201; **7:57**, 59, 379; **9:58**, 68; **9:120**, 214; **9:129**, 429; **10:88**, 200; **12:41**, 139; **12:76**, 293, 429; **15:75**, 428; **16:112**, 41; **18:71**, 379; **20:20**, 201; **21:69**, 201; **24:32**, 177; **26:33**, 201; **26:63**, 201; **26:227**, 30; **27:35–6**, 218; **38:3**, 167; **38:30**, 333; **44:47**, 347; **57:21**, 70; **66:6**, 339; **68:11**, 333; **69:28–9**, 98; **79:34**, 201; **89:27–9**, 113
KORAN, reciters of: dispensation to fight, 161; Kulthum al-Attabi excelled as, 186; anecdote of, 378–9
KUFA: Sufyan al-Thawri appointed qadi of, 49–50; its productivity, compared to young girl, 61; place of Ali's death, 71
KULTHUM AL-ATTABI: teased, 185–6; his qualities, sayings, 187–8
KURANKIJ, the Dailamite, 416

LAMENT: for Baghdad, 151–3; over Amin, 173
LAMIS: prisoners exchanged at, 373
LASHING: Fadl al-Barmaki lashed, 128–30; Musta'in before his assassination, 293; of a thief, 348–9; eunuchs and slave girls by Mu'tadid, 360
LAVATORY: Arabic words for, 405–7
LAWS: enforced at Hira, 46–7; cleverly circumvented at Hira, 48; Holy Law, 70
LAWZINAJ, 376–7
LEEKS, 36
LIBRARY CATALOGUES, 307
LIONS: dreamed of by Mansur's mother, 21; black lion killed by Amin, 142
LOTTERY, 205
LOVE: debate on its nature, 109–13; tales of hopeless love, 249–52; pains of love, 275; an old love regained, 276; at first sight, 277–8; of two students, 362–3
LUBBADA: wife of Amin, her lament, 173
LUTE, 89, 138, 180–3, 208, 249–51, 264–66; 303–4; four-stringed, 283
LUXURY GOODS: Muslim luxury goods in great demand among Byzantines, 320–22; of Zubaida, 390

MABRAMAN, grammarian, 339
MACES: Saffar's crack troops provided with, 314
MADA'INI, historian: quoted, 21; on Meccan morals, 279–80; compared to Jahiz, 309; an anecdote on Mu'awiya, 345; anecdote on Rashid, 378–9
MADINAT AL-MANSUR (*see* BAGHDAD)
MADMEN, 240; 'Sheep's Head', 68
MAGHRIBIS: kill Bugha, 298
MAGIANS, 319; views on love, 111; astrologer converts to Islam, 388; converted by Utrush, 425
MAHDI: *passim*, 34–50; caliphate of, 34; and a qadi, 35; fed by a peasant, 36; fed by a bedouin, 37–8; and the treasurer, 39; his generosity praised, 39; approves Khaizuran's kindness to Muzna, 40–2; adjudicates between Abu al-Atahiya and his love Utba, 43–5; taught the 'Days of the Arabs' by Sharqi, 46; Sharqi tells him a story about the king of Hira, 46–8; refuses to condemn Sufyan al-Thawri, 49–50; sees an apparition, 50; dies, 50; dreams of Hadi and Harun's reigns, 65; gives Hadi the sword Samsama, 66; the birth of his son Musa al-Hadi, 143; his generosity, appeases heresy, 388–9
MAIL: coat of, 288
MA'MUN: born night of Hadi's death

Index

and Harun's accession, 63; as a child recites poem for Kisa'i, 81; praised by Umani and Harun al-Rashid, 83; favoured by Harun al-Rashid but placed second in line of succession, 84–5; governs a country at war, 86; agreement concerning the succession hung in Ka'ba, 87; his horse comes second, 94; mentioned by Harun al-Rashid on his death bed, 99; learns of Harun al-Rashid's death at Marv, 132; addressed as caliph after Amin's defeat at Rayy, 135–6; praised by Blind Poet, 147; civil war against Amin, 150–67; believed dead by Amin, 170; sent Amin's head in Khurasan, 172; addressed by Zubaida, 174; his caliphate, 175; birth, death, recognition in Khurasan, 175; sayings, 176; wedding speech by, 177; told stories of guests and spongers, 178–84; teases a poet, 185–6; generosity, 189; cheered by Abu al-Atahiya, 190; has cooking contest with his friends, 191–2; embarrassed, 193–4; Tuesday discussions on jurisprudence, 195; questioned by a Sufi, 195–7; gives his view of the caliphate, 196; takes census, favours Rida, excludes Abbasids, 202–3; captures, forgives, Mahdi, 204; marries Buran, 205; with Mahdi, 207; relieves Waqidi's poverty, 210–11; and a sponger, 212–13; puts Ibn A'isha to death, 214–15; campaigns in Egypt and against Byzantines, 218; camps at Budandun, last illness and death, 219–21; his passion for learning, becomes a Mu'tazilite, his clemency, 391; on black and green clothes, 408; and wine, 412–13
MANBIJ: palace of, 145
MANGONELS, 154–5
MA'N IBN ZA'IDA: generosity to a poet, 28; amnestied by Mansur, 28–9; pardoned by Rashid, 79
MANI, 220, 388; followers of denounced and executed, 178–9
MANSUR: *passim* 21–33; his death, 32; his character, 33; on the name Musa, 143; his caliphate, 387–8
MANTLE, OF THE PROPHET, 290–1
MARCION, 388
MARIA, the alchemist, 358

MARIDA BINT SHABIB: mother of Mu'tasim, 222
MARISIYA: poisonous wind called, 59
MARV, 202; reached in 12 days from Baghdad, 132
MARVELS OF CREATION, 403–4
MARWAN, 21–2, 58; his wife Muzna destitute, 40–2
MARY, 308, 357
MASABADHAN (in Jurjan), 34
MASRUR, the eunuch, 84; brings lash to punish Ja'far al-Barmaki, 128
MAS'UDI (see also *HISTORICAL ANNALS* and *INTERMEDIATE HISTORY*), 29, 66, 99, 131, 188, 207, 215, 216–7, 220, 231, 261, 293, 300, 302, 325–8, 336, 381, 413, 416; at Aswan, 198; on Mu'awiya, 324; on eunuchs, 345–6; his disapproval of alchemy, 358–9; plans another book, 384, 426; addresses the reader, 426–7; his final words, 428–9
MAWALI: in rebellion at Samarra, 290–91
MECCA, *passim*, but see below and PILGRIMAGE: Abbasa's child sent there for safety, 116–17; anecdote of immorality in, 279–80; Musta'in learned in history of Medina and Mecca, 285; mosque rebuilt by Mahdi, 389
MECCAN: a Meccan mimicked, 352
MEDICINE (*see also* DOCTORS): debate on, 233–5
MEHRIS (*see also* CAMELS), 335
MERCURY, 358
MIHRIJAN (festival of the autumn equinox), 44
MILK, sour, 37
MILLE-FEUILLES, 382
MIMIC: story of, 352–4; his repertoire, 352
MISKIN, singer from Medina: tells story of learning a song, 91–3
MISRI, MUHAMMAD IBN ALI AL-: gives Qahir a history of the caliphate, 387–92
MONASTERY, 240; land of bought to build Samarra, 229; of the Ash Tree at Damascus, 345
MONKS, 229
MOSQUES: deserted during siege of Baghdad, 157; at Mecca, Medina and

461

The Meadows of Gold

Jerusalem rebuilt by Mahdi, 389
MOSUL, 96
MOTHERS, of the caliphs: Mansur; Sallama, a Berber slave, 21; Mahdi; Umm Musa, descendant of kings of Himyar, 34; Hadi; Khaizuran bint Ata' of tribe of Jurash, 51; Harun al-Rashid; Khai'uran bint Ata' of tribe of Jurash, 67; Amin; Zubaida bint Ja'far ibn al-Mansur, 132; Ma'mun; Murajil, an Afghan, 175; Mu'tasim; Marida bint Shabib, 222; Mutawakkil; Shuja, a slave from Khwarizm, 236; Muntasir; Hubshiya, a Greek slave, 267; Musta'in; Mukhariq, a slave of Slavic origin, 281; Mu'tazz; Qabiha, a slave, 294; Muhtadi; Qurb, a Byzantine slave, 299; Mu'tamid; Fityan, a slave from Kufa, 312; Mu'tadid; Dirar, a Greek slave, 329; Muktafi; Zalum, 'Bad Tempered', a slave, 381; Muqtadir; Shaghab, 'Trouble', a slave, 381; Qahir, a slave; 386; Radi: Zalum, a slave, 393; Muttaqi; a slave, 415; Mustakfi; a slave, 417

MOURNING: worn by Zubaida, 174; (white), worn by Mahbuba, 266

MU'AWIYA, 319; takes revenge on a Byzantine, 320–4; delegations come to him, campaigns, etc., 324; his wife and a eunuch, 345; and the Byzantine king, 401

MU'AYYAD, full brother of Mu'tazz: heir presumptive, 290; imprisoned, lashed, smothered, 297

MUBARRAD, grammarian, 185, 339; anecdote on Abu al-Atahiya, 44–5; anecdote on Asma'i, 107

MUHALHIL, poet: great-nephew of Jahiz, 310–11

MUHAMMAD IBN ABD ALLAH IBN TAHIR: Musta'in takes refuge with, 282; on the nature of pleasure, 283–4; his character, his death, 296; 'House of Marble', Mu'tadid buried there, 36

MUHAMMAD IBN AHMAD: in rebellion, 341; despises advice of his aunt Umm Sharif, 342; forgiven by Mu'tadid for her sake, 343–4

MUHAMMAD IBN RA'IK, 416
MUHAMMAD IBN SHIRZAD, 419, 420
MUHAMMAD IBN SULAIMAN: dies, goods sequestered by Harun al-Rashid, 68; anecdote of his meeting with a madman, 68; his palace, 68–9

MUHTADI: his caliphate, 299; the people bored by his virtue, 299; theories regarding his death, 301–2; his austerity, 306–7; a tradition concerning Ali, 308

MUKTAFI: does not marry Qatr al-Nada, 331; his caliphate, destroys Mu'tadid's prisons, his vizier Qasim, 368–9; pleased at murder of Badr, 370; his avarice, 374; anecdotes on food, 378–9; his death at Darb, 380; his mother, 381

MULE, 70
MUNAJJIM, AL-, the astrologer: on Muntasir's generosity, 273–4
MU'NIS, vizier to Qahir: 386, 409
MUNTASIR: hated by Mutawakkil, Turks side with, 261; caliphate of, 267; uses carpet on which his father was murdered, 268–9; his vicious vizier, 270; theories regarding his death, his burial, 272; his generosity, 273–4; marries Hariri to his old love, 275–6; tracks down a slave girl for al-Saghir, 277–8

MUQTADIR: viciousness of his vizier, 270; his mother imprisoned, 360; his caliphate, 381; death of, common people bury him, 384

MURAJIL: Ma'mun's mother, 175
MURJITES: views on love, 111
MURAQIB, the eunuch: Harun al-Rashid reproves his extravagance, 95
MUSA: Amin's son by Nazm, attempts to disinherit Ma'mun in favour of, 140; named heir apparent, education, verses on, 146

MUSA AL-HADI (*see* Hadi): name considered inauspicious, 143
MUSA IBN JA'FAR: freed by Harun al-Rashid after a dream, 74–5
MUSK: cloth scented with, 44; Amin betrayed by, 169; flavoured food, 191; balls of, 205; for writing on slave girl's cheek, 264

MUSTA'IN: caliphate of, 281; imprisoned by Bugha and Wasif, 282; profound knowledge of history, 285; listens to story of Afra and Urwa, 285–6; condemns man to death for

heresy, 288–9; deposed, 290–2; assassinated, 293
MUSTAKFI: raised to the caliphate, 415; his caliphate, 417; and the unwanted page boy, 419–20; enjoys poems, 421–2; blinded, 422; deposed, 423
MU'TADID: acclaimed as caliph, 326; his caliphate, his avarice, love of torture, women, and building, 329–30; tongue-tied when leading the prayers, 330; idol on show at his palace, 335; receives a delegation from Basra, 336–7; on Abu Khalifa, 338; forgives the rebel Muhammad ibn Ahmad for the sake of his aunt, 343–4; deals with a thief, 348–51; listens to a mimic, 352–4; at triumph over Kharijite rebel a bridge collapses, 355; haunted by ghosts, cuts throats of his eunuchs and slave girls, 360; admiration of the eunuch Wasif, 365; preference for the Alids, vision of Ali, 306; death, theories of, 367
MU'TAMID: his caliphate, 312; his conversations, 325–6; his death by poison, 327
MU'TASIM: cookery contest with Ma'mun, 191–2; advises execution of Mahdi, 207; encourages Ma'mun to execute Abbas al-Alawi, 214; at Ma'mun's deathbed, 217; his caliphate, 222; his love of agriculture, 223; his health, 224–5
MUTAWAKKIL: his caliphate, 238; his orthodoxy, his character, 239; his palace of the Two Wings, 240; anecdote of a donkey, 241; entertains his friends, 243–7; dismisses Jahiz for his ugliness, 249; has his secretary slapped, 253; buys Indian sword, 258–9; assassinated with Fath, 260; his corpse rolled in a carpet, 260; hated by Bugha, hatred of his son Muntasir, 261; his last day, 262; his reign, his extravagance, 263; loved by Mahbuba, 264–5; carpet on which he was killed, 268–9; and Abu al-Ayna, 333–4; tricks Bakhtishu', 357; his orthodoxy, 392
MU'TAZILITES: views on love, 109–10; Jahiz a most eloquent Mu'tazilite, 309; Ma'mun becomes one, 391; and chess, 398

MU'TAZZ: made Caliph by the Mawali, 290; has Musta'in assassinated, 293; caliphate of, 294; and a remarkable ring, 295; murders Mu'ayyad and imprisons Muwaffaq, 297; terror of Bugha, 298; abdication and assassination, 298; various theories on his murder, 300
MUTI'; raised to caliphate, 423; still in power at time of writing, 424
MUTTAQI, 416; his caliphate, 414; blinded, 415
MUWAFFAQ, brother of Mu'tazz: 290–2; imprisoned and exiled, 297; campaign against the Zanj, 317
MUZNA, wife of Marwan: destitute and relieved by Khaizuran, 40–2

NABATEAN: language, 227; people, 228; mimicked, 352
NABIDH, 91, 119, 129, 180, 208, 326, 333, 378
NAJDI, mimicked, 352
NARCISSUS, 421–2
NATURAL HISTORY, 403–4; birds and plants collected by Qahir, 409–10
NAWBAHAR: fire temple at, 131; Tahir at, 138
NAWBAKHT, the astrologer: converts to Islam, 388
NAZM: beloved of Amin, mother of Musa, 140
NAZZAM, IBRAHIM IBN SAYYAR AL-, 391
NICEPHORUS, 131
NIMROD, 96
NOAH, 229
NOTEBOOK, 58
NILE: only river full of crocodiles, 59–60
NOUGAT, 376–7; 382
NUBIA, 24; poisonous wind emanates from, 59

ONYX: table, goblet, bowls, 382
ORANGES: in Qahir's garden, 409
OVERSEER, of the palace: 270
OXUS, 59

PAHLAVI, 111; book in, translations of, 388
PAINTINGS: obliterated by Muhtadi, 306
PALACES: of Ashnas, 40; Wadi al-Qasr, 68–9; Khuld, 139; of Manbij, 145;

The Meadows of Gold

Salih, 157; Jawsaq (at Samarra), 222, 245; built by Mu'tasim at Qatul, 228; built by Mu'tasim at Samarra, 229; Mu'tasim born at Khuld, 231; Khaqani (on the Tigris), 231; at Hira, described, 240; Ja'fari, 267, 333; Haruni and Jawsaq Ja'fari cost 100,000,000 dirhams, 263; Musta'in at Jawsaq, 285; Lu'lu'at al-Jawsaq, 290; Muhtadi's Dome of Complaints, 299; of a Byzantine, 322; Thurayya cost 400,000 dinars, 330; of Khumarawaih at Damascus, 345; Muktafi's opposite Qutrabbul, 374; magnificent house of Ibn Bassam's father described, 382–3; garden of Thurayya admired by Radi, 394; of Bajkam the Turk, 412
PALM LEAF: helmets of, 154, 160, 161, 163
PAPER: 99, 273
PARROT: Musta'in compared to, 282; in Qahir's garden, 409
PARTRIDGE, 283
PAVILLION: over spring at Budandun, 219
PARADISE, 382
PALANQUINS, 390
PAGE GIRLS: invented by Zubaida, 390–1; Qasim's, 391
PEARLS: black and white, symbolism of, 290
PEASANT: feeds Mahdi, 36; offended by scholars, 340
PERFUME (*see also* SCENT), 227; Amin betrayed by, 169; a carpet perfumed, 269
PERSIANS, 228, 268–9, 295, 313, 412–13; kill Amin, 171; soldier insults Amin's head, 172; Persian books and literature, 388; imitated by Mu'tasim, 392; chess players, 395
PHEASANT: sacred to Mani, 178
PHILOSOPHY: Ma'mun's passion for, 391; Radi's passion for, 394
PIGEON RACING, 417
PILGRIM ROAD: endowed by Zubaida, 389–90
PILGRIMAGE: performed in fulfillment of a vow by Mansur, 22; Mansur dies on pilgrimage, 32; Harun al-Rashid's last, 71; al-Mawsili loses his way, 76–7; Harun al-Rashid and Abu al-Atahiya on, 216

PISTACHIOS, 97
PLATO, 114; views on apparitions, 360
PLEASURE: discussed, 283–4
POETS: a blind poet praises Marwan to Mansur, 21–2; a poet makes disobliging verses on a peasant, 36; Ibn Yamin wins 50,000 dinars praising the sword Samsama, 66; poem on Rashid and Ja'far, 108; Muhalhil, nephew of Jahiz, 310–11; *see also* ABU-ATAHIYA; BLIND POET; IBRAHIM IBN AL-MAHDI
POISON: Mu'tadid poisoned, 367
POLICE, 204, 356; al-Khuza'i, Rashid's chief of police, 74; Mu'nis al-Fahl, chief of military, police informers, 348–51
POLO, 271; popularized by Harun al-Rashid, 389
POLYTHEISM, 425
POMEGRANATE, 422
PORCELAIN: white platter of, 382
PORTICOES, 69
PORTRAITS: on a carpet, 268–9; of men known for their cunning, 319
POSTAL SERVICE, superintendant of, 103, 334, 383
POVERTY: tradition on, 364
PRAYERS, 308; Amin's last prayers, 170–1; Muhtadi assiduous in leading Friday prayers, 299; of Muhtadi, 306; Mu'tadid tongue-tied at, 330; of al-Harbi requested, 362; Badr killed while praying, 370
PRAYER RUG, 268
PRICE: on the head of al-Mahdi, 208
PRISON, 214; prisoner freed, 29–31; Fadl and Yahya, the Barmakids, in prison, 128–30; prisoner freed by Bugha the Elder, 288–9; exchange of prisoners with the Byzantines, 320; Mu'tadid's destroyed by Muktafi, 368
PROPERTY: bought for 30,000 dirhams, 273
PROPHETS, FALSE: amuse Ma'mun, 200–1
POEMS (*see also* POETS): recited by Amin and Ma'mun as children to Kisa'i, 81; by Umm Sharif, 341–3; on sweetmeats, 375–7; on chess, 396–8; on wine, 412–13; on flowers, 421–2
PSALMS, 147
PTOLEMY, 114, 388
PULSE: of the dying Ma'mun, 219–20

Index

PUNS: on the word lavatory, 405–7

QABIHA: slave girl mother of Mu'tazz, 294; mother of Ismail, 297; exiled to Mecca, 312

QADI: seduced by fine food, 35; rewarded for obliging decision, 70; Ibn Jabir altered by wealth, 364

QAHIR, 237: caliphate of, his violence, blinded and hidden, 386; demands true history of the caliphate, 387–92; his garden, 409–10; on the blinding of Muttaqi, 415

QAINA: slave mother of son of Harun al-Rashid, 274

QANDAHAR, 335

QARATIS: mother of Wathiq, 232

QARMATIANS: in revolt, 380

QASIM IBN RASHID, 87–8

QASIM IBN UBAID ALLAH: gains excessive influence over Muktafi, 368; his hatred of Badr, kills him treacherously, 370–1; and Ibn Bassam, 383

QATA'IF, 375–6

QATR AL-NADA: marries Mu'tadid, 331

QATUL, Mu'tasim's city there, 228; canal, 228–9

QURAISH AL-DANDANI: Tahir's page, kills, Amin, 169

QURAISH, tribe of: a member of Quraish takes revenge on a Byzantine, 320–4

QURB: Byzantine slave, mother of Muhtadi, 299

QUTAIBA IBN MUSLIM: on generalship, 399–400

RACING: at Raqqa, 94; pigeons, 417

RADDAIN: Mahdi dies there, 34

RADI: keeps Qahir sequestered, 386; his caliphate, 393; his learning, love of philosophy, passion for chess, 394; taught a tradition, 399; on marvels, 403–4; amused by al-Arudi, 405–7; on black and green clothes, 408; and Qahir's garden, 409–10; his generosity, 411

RAMADAN: new clothes for, 210

RANUNCULUS: used to poison Mu'tamid, 327

RAPE: girl saved from, 243–4

RAQQA: horse racing at, 94; Harun al-Rashid at, 95; Yahya al-Barmaki dies at, 130

RAYY, 283–4; Mahdi appointed governor by Mansur, 46; Hadi born at, 62; Harun born at, 63; Amin's forces defeated at, 136

RAZI, AL-: refutes al-Kindi on alchemy, works, 358

RECRUITING: Saffar's policies of, 313–14

REED MATS: for breastplates, 154, 160, 161, 163

'REPENTANTS', i.e. police informers, 348, 350, 356

REVENUES: of Fars and Ahwaz allotted by Ma'mun to his father-in-law, 205

RICE, 315

RIDA: his rise under Ma'mun, marriage, death, 202–3

RING: remarkable ring described, 295

RIYASH, the eunuch: Abbasa's son entrusted to, 116–17

ROBE OF HONOUR, 292, 355; given by Mu'awiya to a Byzantine, 323

ROSE, 421–2

ROSE-FLAVOURED CANDY, 35

ROSE WATER, 382, 394

RUBY, 295

RUM, *see also* BYZANTIUM, 131

RUSAFA: city founded by Hisham, 26

SABLE, 390; cloak used to smother Mu'ayyad, 297

SAFFAH: his character and caliphate, 387

SAFFAR, AMR IBN AL-LAITH, 312–16; brings spoils and an idol to Baghdad, 335; conquests in India, etc., 335–6

SAFFAR, YA'QUB IBN LAITH AL-: his revolt, 312; superb discipline of his army, 312–13; recruitment policy, 312; 'gold and silver maces', 314; drills his pages, 314; his austerity, 315; food, 315; pack animals, 316

SAGES: Greek, 236; Indian, 236

SAGHIR, ABU UTHMAN SA'ID AL-: his love for a slave girl, 277–8

SA'ID, (Upper Egypt): poisonous wind from, 59

SAIHAN, 59

465

SAILOR: Mutawakkil eats a sailor's stew, 248
SALAMAWAIH: at Wathiq's debate on medicine, 233–5
SALIH, the eunuch: administrator of the harem, 276
SALIH IBN RASHID: sends news of Rashid's death to Ma'mun, 132
SALLAMA, mother of Mansur, 21
SAMARRA: Mu'tasim buried at, 222; site chosen, 227–8; Muntasir buried at, 272; Mu'tamid buried at, 327
SAMSAMA, (*see* SWORDS)
SANDALWOOD, 138, 309
SARAH, 137
SARAKHS: Fahl ibn Sahl dies there, 202
SARDINES, 36
SASANIDS: imitated by Ma'mun, 391
SATAN, 90
SAUCE: eaten with fish by Mu'tasim, 224
SAWAD, (Iraq), 226
SAWIQ: water infused with grain, 76
SCENT, (*see also* PERFUME), 70, 105, 253, 321, 331, 413; distributed to Amin's army, 150; that gives most pleasure, 283; Radi fond of, 411
SELF-MORTIFICATION: of Muhtadi, 306
SHAFI'I: death of, 198–9
SHAGHAB, mother of Muqtadir: imprisoned by Mu'tadid, 360
SHAKIRIYA: Mutawakkil's guard, 263
SHALUS (in Daylam, Iran): massive defences of, 425
SHEARS: pawned for two dirhams, 92
SHIELDS: Tibetan, 154; of reed mat, 154, 160
SHIRAWAIH: portrait on a carpet, 268
SHROUD, 133; Harun al-Rashid chooses his shroud, 98
SHUJA': mother of Mutawakkil, 238; death of, 258
SIEGE, of Baghdad, 150–67
SIKBAJ, 248
SILK, 24, 355; painted robe of silk, 89; in Amin's kiosk, 138; silk-lined basket, 332
SILVER DISH: 'ransomed' for 200 dinars, 95
SIND: tale of revenge in Mansura, 54; Kharijites in, 335; Sindi mimicked. 352
SINGING GIRLS (*see also* SLAVES): sing for Harun al-Rashid, 105–6; sings ill-omened song to Amin, 138–9; exchanges songs with Ibrahim ibn al-Mahdi, 180–3; suicides of, 249–52; loved by Mutawakkil, 264–5; loved at first sight, 277–8; the best music played by, 283; forbidden by Muhtadi, 299; tease a guest, 405–6
SLAVES (*see also* SINGING GIRLS *and* MOTHERS OF THE CALIPHS), 117, 118, 264–6; an Indian slave takes his revenge, 54; black slave charmed by a song and rewarded by Harun al-Rashid, 76–7; slave girls consulted by Amin, 84; Abbasa poses as a slave, 116; Abbada, Umm Ja'far, escorted by, 236; in lottery, 205; unhappy loves of, 249–52; sing insulting song, 270; slave girl loved by Hariri, 276; bought by Muntasir for a friend, 277–8; throats cut by Mu'tadid, 360; poison Mu'tadid, 367; cause disgrace of Fatik, 371–2
SLAVS: slave girl, 281; eunuchs, 345
SLINGS: used by naked warriors, 160
SOCRATES, 236
SONGS: al-Mawsili charms a black slave, 76–7; al-Mawsili taught a song by satan, 89–90; Miskin taught a song by a black woman, 91–2; Harun al-Rashid rewards Miskin with 4000 dinars for a song, 93; on an apple, 105–6; of Mahdi, 180–3
SORCERERS: summoned by Mu'tadid, 360
SOUTHERNWOOD, 145
SPELLS, 360
SPINDLE, 57
SPONGERS: stories of, 178–9, 212-13, 303–5
STEW: sweet and sour, 248; lamb, used to poison Mu'tamid, 327
STRAW MATS, 208
STROKE: suffered by Jahiz, 309
STUDENTS: in love, 362–3
SUDAN: eunuchs from, 345
SUFIS, 114; interrogates Ma'mun, 195–7; Abu al-Atahiya becomes a Sufi, 216
SUFYAN AL-THAWRI: spared by Mahdi and appointed qadi of Kufa, 49–50
SUICIDE, 112; love suicides, 249–52

SULAIMAN, the eunuch: tells story of a fish, 72–3
SULI, ABU BAKR AL-, 394, 408
SUNNA, 82, 113
SUS, town near Gondeshapur, famous for textiles, 329
SUSANGIRD: carpet and cushions from, 322–3
SWEETMEATS, 374, 382; described in poems, 375–7
SWORDS: Amr ibn Ma'dikarib's sword Samsama given to Hadi by Mahdi, 66; Indian sword costs 10,000 dirhams, 258–9; used to kill Mutawakkil, 260
SYRIAC, 388

TABARI, 403
TAHIR IBN HUSAIN: defeats Amin's army at Rayy, 135–6; known as Dhu al-Yamanain, 136; considers Amin led astray, 144; triumphant, 147; refuses to grant Amin safe conduct, 149; incites Amin's disaffected officers, 150; various sectors of Baghdad go over to him, 156–8; gains control of Baghdad, 160–1; intercepts Amin, 168; his page kills Amin, 169
TAIF: singing girl educated at, 264
TAIFURI, the physician: bleeds Muntasir with a poisoned lancet, 272
TAILOR: Miskin the singer a slave and tailor, 91–3
TAMBUR (musical instrument): 118, 249, 303–4
TAR, 154
TARSUS, 218, 272; Ma'mun buried at, 175; fortified by Harun al-Rashid, 389
TAWWABIN, (*see* 'REPENTANTS')
TAXES, 39; of a Hamadani remitted, 30; Hadi gives half to Harun al-Rashid, 64; of two dirhams per day paid by slave to master, 91–2; land-tax, 223; discussion on, 337–8; in Cyprus, 385
TEAK: Basra rich in, 61
TENT: description of Saffar's, 315
TENT-DIVIDER, 50
THA'LAB, grammarian, 185
THIEF: treatment of, 348–51; famous thieves, *see* UQAB and DALLAH
TIBERIAS, 310
TIBET: Tibetan shields, 154; poison from, 327
TIGRIS, *passim*, 29, 59; lovers drown themselves in, 249–52
TIRAZ, *see* CLOTH
TITHE: on boats, 154
TIZANABADH (between Kufa and Qadisiya): known for its agriculture and wine, 72
TOMB: at Hira, called 'The Two Fair Effigies', 46; love stronger than, 113; of Shafi'i described, 198; of Mu'tasim at Samarra, 222; Muntasir first Abbasid Caliph with public tomb, 272; Afra dies at Urwa's, 286; of the House of Tulun, 347
TORTURE, 54, 351; Harun al-Rashid on his death bed has Rafi' ibn al-Laith's brother tortured, 98–9; Mu'tadid's taste for, 329–30; Muktafi destroys Mu'tadid's dungeons, 368
TRADITIONS (*Hadith*), 70, 81, 82, 242; on love, transmitted through A'isha, 113; Waqidi poor transmitter of, 210; collected by Ma'mun, 212; on Ali, 308; Abu Khalifa authority on chains of transmission (*isnad*), 339; Abu Ishaq respected as Traditionist, 361; of Ali on wealth and poverty, 364; Mansur's interest in and knowledge of, 388; taught Radi by his tutor, 399
TRANSMUTATION, of metals, 358
TREASURER: reproves Mahdi's improvidence, 39
TREASURY: sum left by Mansur, 33; Mahdi's inheritance, 39; Saffar leaves 50 million dirhams and 800,000 dinars, 313; Mu'tadid left nine million dinars and 40 million dirhams, 329; Muktafi left eight million dinars and 25 million dirhams, 374
TURKS: cause trouble in Baghdad, 228; plot against Muntasir, 272; rise, 282, 290–1; side with Mu'ayyad, 297; drink Muhtadi's blood, 302
TUS: Harun al-Rashid's last illness on the way there, 98; Imam Rida dies there, 202
TUZUN, the Turk: holds real power, 414; with Mustakfi, 417; forces page boy on Mustakfi, 419–20
TYANA, 218
TYRE: wily seaman from, 320–4

UMANI, the poet: praises Ma'mun to Harun al-Rashid, 83

The Meadows of Gold

UMAR IBN ABD AL-AZIZ: criticised by Mansur, 23
UMAYYADS: Hadi laments their cruelty, 58
UMM JA'FAR, wife of Hadi: richly rewards an obliging qadi, 70
UMM MUSA, mother of Mahdi, 34
UMM MUSA: overseer of the palace, 270
UMM SHARIF: 341-4
UQAB, AL-: a very famous thief; his tricks, 355-6; Mutawakkil makes use of him, 357
URINE: Harun al-Rashid's urine examined, 98
URWA: love for Afra, 285-6; death, 287
UTAMISH, vizier of Musta'in, 282
UTBA (Khaizuran's slave girl): rejects the love of Abu al-Atahiya, 43-5
UTBI, 189
UTRUSH: converts Dailam and Jilan, 425

'VAGABONDS' (*see also* WARRIORS), 150, 154-5, 156-7, 160-1; 'vagabond' poet on Mu'tasim, 228
VARNISH: used to preserve Amin's head, 172
VEIL, 152; Amin veiled, 170; woman's veil worn by Ibrahim ibn al-Mahdi, 204; Umm Sharif sets hers aside to write, 343; Fakhita veils before a eunuch, 345
VIOLETS, 383
VIZIERS, *passim*; of Mansur, 26; vicious, 270-1; Abbasid, 270

WAGER: between Bakhtishu' and Mutawakkil, 357
WALNUTS, 224
WAQIDI, historian: his death, his poverty, his generosity, 210-11
WARRIORS, 156-7; naked, 150; their armour described, 154-5; their savage fighting, 160-1; suggest desperate plan to Amin, 168-9
WASIF, 267-9; campaigns against the Byzantines, 272; kills Baghir, imprisons Musta'in, 282; killed by Turkish troops, 297; his courage, in prison asks for basil and books, 365
WASIT, 29
WATER, 76-7, 308
WATHIQ: his caliphate, 232; debate on medicine, 233-5; on death of Alexander, 236; death, 237; orthodox, a gourmet, 392
WEAPONS: allotment in Saffar's army, 313-14
WEDDING: speech by Ma'mun, 177; of Ibrahim ibn al-Mahdi, 184; of Ma'mun to Buran, 205
WELL OF MAIMUN: death of Mansur there, on the pilgrimage, 21, 32
WINE (*See also* NABIDH): 24, 89, 180-2, 421-2; offered to Mahdi by a bedouin, 37; king of Hira commits murder while drunk, 46; of Tizanabadh and Qutrabbul considered good, 72; used in experiment with a fish, 72-3; Ja'far al-Barmaki seduced by Abbasa while drunk, 116; Mutawakkil assassinated while drunk, 260; pleasure of, 283; prohibited by Muhtadi, 297; Byzantine abducted while drunk, 322; how to serve, 325-6; Khumarawaih killed while drinking, 345; thief confesses while drunk, 350-1; Radi and wine, 412-13
WOOL, donning the, i.e. becoming a Sufi, 216

YAHYA IBN AKTHAM, qadi, 185, 191
YALBAQ, 386, 409
YAMUT IBN MUZARRA', nephew of Jahiz, 309-10; his son Muhalhil, the poet, 310-11
YASIR, servant of Harun al-Rashid: ordered to execute Ja'far al-Barmaki, 119; conversation with Ja'far, 120; executed, 121
YAZID IBN ABD AL-MALIK, 250-1
YEMEN, 117
YUSUF IBN IBRAHIM, secretary: friend of Ibrahim ibn al-Mahdi, tells story of Jabra'il and a fish, 72-3; his books, 207

ZABULISTAN: conquest of, infidel nations in, 335-6
ZAINAB BINT SULAIMAN: her lack of charity, 40-2; on black and green clothes, 408
ZANJ: mimicked, 352
ZANJ REBELLION, 308, 312; first signs of, 298
ZOROASTRIAN, 253

Index

ZUBAIDA: demands better treatment for Amin, 86; grudge against Ja'far ibn Yahya al-Barmaki, 87; offended by Yahya al-Barmaki's behaviour, 117; reveals Abbasa's seduction of Ja'far, 117; mother of Amin, 132; dreams of Amin's fate, 133–4; conceives Amin out of jealousy, 137; verses to console Amin on death of Nazm, 140; in tears, 144; her lament for Amin, 173
ZUHAIR IBN MUSAYYAB, 154–5
ZUHAIRI: Amin's horse, 168

Printed in Great Britain
by Amazon